American Education
and the Dynamics of Choice

American Education and the Dynamics of Choice

*James R. Rinehart
and
Jackson F. Lee, Jr.*

PRAEGER

New York
Westport, Connecticut
London

Copyright Acknowledgments

The authors and publisher gratefully acknowledge permission to reprint from the following:

James R. Rinehart and Jackson F. Lee, Jr. "The Optimum level of Ignorance: Marginal Analysis in Education." *The Educational Forum*, Winter, 1988. Reprinted with permission.

"First Class Fiasco." *Florence Morning News*. 21 March 1990. p. A4. Material originally published in *Detroit News Sunday Magazine*, 15 March 1981. Reprinted with permission.

Library of Congress Cataloging-in-Publication Data

Rinehart, James R.
    American education and the dynamics of choice / James R. Rinehart and Jackson F. Lee, Jr.
        p.   cm.
    Includes bibliographical references and index.
    ISBN 0–275–93823–9 (alk. paper)
    1. Public schools—United States. 2. School, Choice of—United States. 3. Privatization—United States. 4. Education—United States—Aims and objectives. I. Lee, Jackson F., Jr. II. Title.
LA217.2.R56   1991
370′.973—dc20   90–21312

British Library Cataloguing in Publication Data is available.

Library of Congress Catalog Card Number: 90–21312
ISBN: 0–275–93823–9

First published in 1991

Praeger Publishers, One Madison Avenue, New York, NY 10010
An imprint of Greenwood Publishing Group, Inc.

Printed in the United States of America

The paper used in this book complies with the
Permanent Paper Standard issued by the National
Information Standards Organization (Z39.48–1984).

10 9 8 7 6 5 4 3 2 1

To my father, Charles Ray Rinehart,
and my beloved mother, Corine,
who sacrificed so much to see that I had access
to educational opportunities they never had;
and
To my much loved parents, Jack and Virginia Lee,
who had the love and strength of character
to educate four children,
often in spite of the system.

Contents

Preface

Public education in the United States is definitely on the firing line. Criticism is ubiquitous and intense. Falling test scores, rising dropout rates, and decreasing literacy levels combine to keep public attention focused on the system. The reform movement of the 1980s has spawned endless debates and numerous prescriptions for change, but the schools continue to operate with little, if any, significant improvement.

American Education and the Dynamics of Choice grew out of a series of discussions with friends and colleagues over what could be done to improve education. Each of the authors confronted the problem from a different perspective: one as an economist accustomed to exploring the ramifications of human decision making, and one as an educator involved in trying to improve public schools. Comparing what was really going on in the schools with professional and popular literature led the authors to conclude that any meaningful gain in educational standards is virtually impossible under the present organization. Public schools are a government monopoly, and predictably operate contrary to the best interests of their customers. The lack of competition and parental control is the root cause of the poor performance of our schools.

This book develops the notion that the only realistic solution to our current difficulties is through increased parental and student choice, deregulation and ultimately privatization of schools. By permitting choice of schools and unencumbered competition among schools, incentives for excellence would emerge leading to dramatic improvements in education. Limited opportunities for choice are currently being tried in several states and districts, and where they are being tried, literacy rates rise, dropout rates decline, and overall parental and student satisfaction increases.

In preparing this presentation, the authors sought to achieve three main goals. First, we wanted to demonstrate that public school systems consistently fail because they ignore certain fundamental laws of human behavior. Second, we wanted to make the case that the current reform movement in education will fail or fall far short of expected benefits for the same reasons. Third, we wanted to propose challenging yet realistic solutions to our educational dilemmas. These solutions focus on educational choice and the privatization of public schools. Providing parents and students with choices, especially among private alternatives, represents a bold experiment that holds a wealth of promise for improving the quality of life and learning for our young and thus for strengthening our nation.

Acknowledgments

The development of ideas, the linking of those ideas into logical arguments, and finally attempting to present such thoughts with clarity and fluidity make the process of writing both a joy and an effort. The writing of this book was no exception. Our enjoyment, however, was enhanced and our effort was lightened by generous assistance from our spouses, friends, and colleagues. Our wives, Elaine and Sandy, offered copious and continuous support. How many times did they patiently listen and respond to questions such as "What do you think about this?" or, "How does this sound?" We also sought input from our colleagues. Dr. Barry O'Brien, Associate Professor of Economics at Francis Marion College; Dr. Wayne Pruitt, Professor Education at Francis Marion College; and Dr. Tom Sills and Dr. Jerry Kinard, Deans of the Schools of Education and Business respectively, offered invaluable help and constructive criticism. Our efforts were further aided by the Francis Marion College Faculty Research Committee, which provided financial assistance in the early stages of this work. We extend our deepest gratitude to Dr. David Kendall, Associate Professor of Economics, Clinch Valley College of The University of Virginia, Wise, Virgina, for his insightful, challenging, and provocative critique of an earlier draft. His comments were indispensable and most appreciated. Finally, we wish to express a special appreciation to Ms. Mary Greene, Administrative Assistant to the Dean of the School of Business at Francis Marion College. She unfailingly and good-naturedly sat at her word processor, deciphered illegible handwriting, and met seemingly impossible deadlines in preparing numerous drafts of this manuscript.

Although we owe debts to these and other friends and colleagues, the authors are solely responsible for the final arguments set forth in this work.

Part 1

What Is Happening to America's Schools?

Chapter 1

The Growing Interest in Educational Choice

In one form or another, education has always been important to Americans. We realized almost from the beginning that some level of learning was absolutely necessary to allow us to practice our religion, maintain our freedom, conduct our civic affairs, and get more out of life. Education is significantly more important today than it was in the past.

Even though we agree about the importance of education, we have not always agreed as to how it should be provided. Most schools were privately owned and operated until the 1800s, when Massachusetts initiated the first large scale effort to make elementary and secondary schools public. Reformers such as Horace Mann pushed for free public education and succeeded far beyond their wildest dreams. State after state went public. Today, almost 90 percent of American children attend public schools. The fact that all children are given the opportunity to receive a basic education is something of which we should be proud. The fact that they are not receiving a much better education is something that should concern and challenge us.

It is safe to say that Americans are generally unhappy with the results they are getting from their schools. In a recent speech, Lauro Cavazos (1988), former U.S. secretary of education, gave just a hint of the extent of our educational problems.

The top 5 percent of our high school students know less about math than the average high school student in Japan. In science, our best high school students ... rank near the bottom of a list of 13 countries in chemistry and physics. In biology, our students finished dead last.

He went on to point out that only half of our high school juniors can do junior high school math. Fewer than half of them know enough science to perform jobs requiring technical skills or participate effectively in civic affairs. Only half of minority high school juniors can perform well enough to match the standards of their majority counterparts.

The essence of the problem with education is the way it is currently being provided. We have turned to government to supply us with education and to make almost all of our educational decisions. Public schools are a governmental monopoly that is owned, financed, and operated by governments at various levels. With the exception of being able to select a neighborhood with outstanding schools, or being able to choose among a few high school course electives, parents have very little to say about where and how their children are educated. While the average American would scream loud and long were some government board to tell him or her which model and color of automobile to purchase, parents willingly renounce their freedom to choose something as significant as education.

Regardless of good intentions, governments and those whom they employ have the annoying habit of eventually serving their own best interests. The public school monopoly provides so much comfort and security for the educator that the real needs of the "educatee" often take a back seat. At its most fundamental level, then, the educational problem reduces itself to a mismatch between the way people act and the way the system expects them to act.

How do human beings actually think and act? For starters, we are on safe ground if we assert that, in general, all human beings can be expected to

- see and experience life from their own unique point of view;
- seek to increase their personal welfare whenever they can;
- desire to obtain the most satisfaction possible for the least possible expenditure of effort.

Unfortunately, society expects teachers, administrators, parents, and students to behave in ways that are in direct conflict with these human traits. Our public school systems operate in a manner that consistently discourages the individual initiative of our teachers and suppresses the infusion of high levels of creative energy. By providing automatic salary increases regardless of student achievement and parent satisfaction, we make mediocrity acceptable. By limiting the rewards available to educators for increased levels of student performance to purely personal satisfaction, we encourage teachers to seek more meaningful compensation outside of their profession. By requiring the same educational programs and standards in all schools, we insure that most parents and students will never be satisfied with the results. By failing to insist on accountability on the part of schools and students, we invite educational failure.

The problem is not necessarily a lack of good people in education. Many of our teachers perform excellently in the classroom. Yet, most of our nation's teachers are capable of performing at levels far above those currently exhibited. Some of our schools provide students with an outstanding education, yet far too many fall short of this mark and need to be radically improved or eliminated altogether.

The problem is not a lack of good ideas for improving education. Professional journals and conferences constantly bombard practitioners with different ways of teaching and managing education. Education-oriented entrepreneurs, researchers, and theorists continue to generate excellent ideas. Unfortunately, the opportunities and incentives to try new arrangements or approaches are sorely lacking. The drive to do things better and to do better things just is not strong enough.

Contrary to what many have alleged, the woes of our public schools cannot be blamed on poorly trained teachers and staff, inadequate numbers of teachers, or insufficient financial commitment. American teachers and administrators are better educated and trained today than at any time in our history. As recently as 1966, only 7 percent of public school teachers had less than a bachelor's degree. Today that figure is less than one-half of one percent. In 1966 only 23 percent of our teachers had a master's degree or at least six years of college. Today that figure is over 50 percent. The number of teachers holding earned doctorates has tripled during the same period (National Center for Education Statistics, 1989(a), p. 72).

Nor can we argue that the cause of our problems lies with too many students for each teacher. The number of students per teacher in public schools at the elementary level has fallen from 29 pupils in 1959-60 to 20 pupils in 1985-86. This is a reduction of students per teacher of almost one-third. At the secondary level, the reduction has been slightly less than one-third. In 1959-60 there were 22 students per secondary teacher and in 1985-86 only 16. Significantly, these figures are not exaggerated by including noninstructional staff, which has grown markedly over this same period (U.S. Department of Education, 1987, p. 24).

It is equally unlikely that we can drag out that old scapegoat of lack of funds as the source of our problems. Our nation has made significant increases in both the dollar amount of spending (adjusted for inflation) and as a share of the average taxpayer's income. Between the 1949-50 and 1986-87 school years, the amount of spending per pupil (adjusted for inflation) increased more than threefold. In constant dollars, the increase in total expenditures per pupil for elementary and secondary schools rose from $963 to a whopping $3,555 (National Center for Education Statistics, 1989(a), pp. 45-46).

To gain a better perspective on the real burden education places on the average taxpayer, we can look at the proportion of personal income spent for this purpose. In 1950 approximately 2.5 percent of the nation's personal income went toward education. In 1987 this figure was 4.6 percent in spite of a declining student population. These figures represent an 84 percent increase in the share of personal income going for education.

In an article in the *Wall Street Journal*, John Hood (1990) compared spending levels in the United States with other countries. When comparing per pupil instructional expenditures, the United States outspends most of the advanced countries in the world. In 1985 the United States spent $3,310 per pupil; Sweden spent $3,214, Canada $3,192, Denmark $3,089, West Germany $2,253, France $1,996, Britain $1,897, and Japan $1,805 (p. A10). Clearly, our schools are not suffering from a lack of financial commitment (National Center for Education Statistics, 1989(b), p. 20). While one might debate the question of just how much money should be spent on education, the case for increased spending is clearly weakened by the fact that more money has been accompanied by poorer student performance. The financial burden on the taxpayer has been increasing. More funds are being shifted to the educational sector, yet satisfaction with the output from the public schools remains at low levels.

If we want to make anything more than marginal improvements in our schools, it will take nothing short of a major upheaval in the governing and operational structure. America is ready for such a precipitous change. More and more states and communities are breaking the limits of tradition and attempting new and exciting approaches to education. Some new ideas that have the potential to galvanize us into action have begun to emerge. If there is one word that surfaces more than any other in this movement, it is "choice." Citizens and educators alike are realizing that the element of personal choice that has made us strong economically holds the promise of making us strong educationally as well.

Unfortunately the term "choice" has been used rather inconsistently in both the educational and the popular press. In a general sense choice can represent any situation in which parents or children have an opportunity to select an educational option that they feel is best for them. Typically, current options involve choice among public schools. But the real potential of choice lies beyond such narrow restrictions.

Although currently limited, opportunities for choice are appearing in a wide variety of settings. Most allow parents to select from among existing public schools. Magnet schools, for example, permit some parents to select a public school that caters to the special interests and talents of their children. Performing arts and science magnet schools are typical examples. In some districts parents may choose any public school they consider most appropriate for their children. Other programs allow teachers and schools to have a greater say in determining the direction of learning within their schools. Terms such as "empowerment," "school-based management," and "restructuring" are now frequently used to describe efforts to provide a break from the uniformity of district-wide or statewide mandates. School-based management plans, for example, attempt to place more of the decision making and accountability at the school building level.

With all of the diversity of experiments with choice, it is encouraging to note that results thus far have been generally positive. Such positive outcomes from choice portend even more benefits if the choice system were based on a deregulated and privatized school system.

Joe Nathan (1987), who recently coordinated the National Governors' Association report, *Time for Results: The Governors' 1991 Report on Education*, found that 15 states have some form of choice built into their public school system. In general, educators in these states have realized that providing some choice among schools has helped to

reduce dropouts,

increase student achievement and appreciation for learning,

improve parental involvement and satisfaction,

encourage racial and economic integration,

provide extra challenge for students dissatisfied with the conventional program, and

raise the morale of educators who were allowed to create distinctive programs from which families can choose (p. 751).

The success of choice systems is not limited to relatively affluent families and communities. Given the opportunity to choose, disadvantaged parents have demonstrated their ability to make effective educational decisions. In the low-income Community District 4 in Harlem (New York City), junior high schools specialize by centering their curriculum around some central academic theme. Since the schools are "open-zoned," students are allowed to select the one whose program is best suited to their needs. In the open-zoned district, any school's existence is totally dependent on its ability to attract and retain students. Thus far, two schools have been closed for failure to attract adequate numbers of students. The most significant outcome of choice in District 4, however, has been an improvement in student learning.

Before the principle of choice was embraced, reading scores here were the lowest among New York City's 32 local school districts.

By 1982, they had moved to 15th. In 1988, nearly two-thirds of the students in District 4 were reading at or above their grade level ("Real Choice," 1989, pp. 12-13).

Choice is also a viable option for reducing segregation. The initial fear of resegregation of schools under choice appears to have been a chimera. In the Kansas City, Missouri, Metropolitan School District, the courts have ordered new desegregation efforts. One group of minority parents has boldly asserted that they could move 10 percent closer to the mandated standards by forming an alliance with existing parochial and private schools, and they could do so for between $3,000 and $4,000 less per pupil than could the public schools alone (Nadler and Donelson, 1989, pp. 28-29).

The issue of choice in public schools is gaining support daily in many quarters. The most recent Gallup/Phi Delta Kappa Education Poll (and Gallup Elam, 1989) has pointed to the high acceptability of choice at least among public alternatives. Nationally, the approval of choice was better than 2-to-1 with 60 percent of the respondents favoring some form of public school choice while only 31 percent opposed. Interestingly enough, choice was more strongly favored by nonwhites (67 percent) than by whites (59 percent) (p. 43).

Overwhelmingly, respondents felt that choice would not hurt student achievement (82 percent)—40 percent felt that achievement would improve while 42 percent felt that it would not make much difference. Those polled felt even more positively about the rise in parental satisfaction if choice were provided—49 percent felt that satisfaction would be higher while 37 percent felt that it would not make much difference (p. 43).

Showcased by the success of existing programs, choice promises to grow even more. Joe Nathan (1987) anticipates three trends for the coming decade:

1. policy makers will show more interest in expanding choice among public schools;
2. regardless of what legislatures do, educational options will increase for affluent families; and
3. part of the pressure for expanding options will come from parents, business people, and others outside education. (p. 751)

Many other educators are predicting an expansion of choice in some form. Van D. Mueller (1987), professor and director of graduate studies in the Department of Educational Policy and Administration at the University of Minnesota, provides six reasons why he thinks parents will be provided with more choice in the future:

1. The primary responsibility for the education of children lies with the family.
2. Research findings confirm that students learn more when their parents are involved in their education.
3. Choice for parents means empowerment and voice.
4. Parents' satisfaction with schools increases as their influence on their children's school environment grows.
5. Parental choice makes for more accountability—both for parents and for teachers and administrators.
6. Choice allows public schools to become more diverse (p. 761).

Charles Glenn (1986), director of the Bureau of Equal Educational Opportunity of the Massachusetts Department of Education, is also a firm supporter of choice and has presented strong arguments for choice.

The extension of school choice can help to realize the promise of the Common School of the Republic, can permit us to respond to the diversity of beliefs about how children should be educated, and can place us in a competitive posture which is essential to our long-term prosperity. Choice can help us to break out of what is fast becoming a dead end for public schools (p. 11).

Choice is also becoming a hot topic in many political circles. Minnesota, through the leadership efforts of the governor, has implemented a statewide choice plan. Other governors have expressed support and pushed through their own plans. Both the Reagan and Bush administrations have strongly supported choice for parents and students.

If publicity furor is any indication, the new Brookings Institute report by John E. Chubb and Terry M. Moe, *Politics, Markets, and America's Schools,* is adding a significant dimension to the debate over choice. These authors have assembled massive data to support their contention that successful schools are more autonomous and parents must have the right to choose.

Although the current experiments with choice are promising, many limits are clearly evident. At the least, choice must be expanded to include private schools. But to realize its full potential, choice should be coupled with the privatization of public schools. The current public school monopoly must disappear in the wake of intense competition and change. In its place will emerge a more healthy, dynamic, and effective educational system.

If we have learned one thing in recent decades, it is that government activity is a poor substitute for the market process. Throughout the world, government-run enterprises are a drag on their individual economies. What they are able to produce is produced at a very high cost. Governments can never really know what people want; and if they could know, they cannot respond effectively because of the ponderous weight of bureaucracy and the self-interest pursuit of government employees. Governments cannot know the most efficient ways to produce goods or services, and even if they could, the incentives for bureaucrats are not conducive to efficient operation. In light of the government's dismal track record in the many activities in which it is involved, why should it seem like heresy to question the efficacy of government-run schools?

In other sectors of the economy, privatization and deregulation efforts have been bipartisan and steady. Recently we have either totally or partially deregulated airlines, rails, trucks, and buses—all with very positive results. We have benefited to the tune of between $39 and $63 billion annually from the deregulation of trucking alone. Airline deregulation produced another $15 billion per year and the deregulation of railroads gave us efficiency gains of $9 to $15 billion annually. Current moves are under way to deregulate cable television. Further benefits are accruing to consumers from the deregulation of financial markets and overnight mail service. Savers get higher interest rates and senders get better and cheaper service.

Similar results are possible from a deregulated and privatized educational system. Will choice and privatized schools solve all of our educational problems? Emphatically not. Such a system will, however, bring even more time, talent, and effort into the educational process. It will free the innovators and entrepreneurs to try new and exciting options. It will reward those who succeed in educating our children and penalize those who do not. The abused child, the child who starts out a lap back because of an impoverished background, or the child who determines that he or she will not learn may still be with us, but each will have a better chance. Increased efficiency in the use of resources and more highly motivated educators will raise the level of education for all children.

It is high time we begin to deregulate schools. We have a great opportunity in the 1990s to channel the reform movement of the 1980s along these lines. The challenges presented by a deregulated school system will not be accepted amicably. Our species has never been very comfortable with change, and the more radical the change, the more uncomfortable it makes us. Those who have the most stake in the present system will be the least accepting of new directions. Radical change will be frightening to teachers and administrators, but the best of them will most certainly rise to the challenge and even prosper.

America stands at a crossroads in the development of its educational system. We can make real and meaningful changes in schools if we have the courage to depart from the self-limiting practices of the past.

Chapter 2

Do We Really Need a Change?

Anyone who was fortunate enough to see the Academy Award-winning film *Amadeus* had to be struck by the final scene in which Antonio Salieri, the half-insane court musician and rival of Mozart, is wheeled through the asylum absolving the inmates (and us) from the sin of mediocrity. To whom shall we turn in the next generations for forgiveness if this nation continues to fall into the doldrums of mediocrity? On whom can we place the blame if this nation fails to solve its pressing national problems of the homeless, the poor, public safety, environmental quality, medical treatment, and national security?

Certainly the educational system cannot be blamed for society's failure to solve these problems. Yet just as certainly, the schools and those who control them have done far less than they are capable of doing in providing progress toward their solutions. "The 21st Annual Gallup Poll of the Public's Attitudes Toward the Public Schools" (Gallup and Elam,

1989) indicated that 66 percent of those polled gave the nation's schools a grade of C, D, or F. These are mediocre grades
at best. Although the respondents were slightly happier with
their local schools (only 48 percent gave them grades of C,
D, or F), these data indicate that a significant number of
Americans feel that our schools could be doing better (p. 50).

Criticism of the public schools is common and widespread.
Displeasure over the results we get from our schools has been
voiced from the right, left, and middle and from both laymen
and professionals. Dr. W. James Popham (1987) of the UCLA
Graduate School of Education, for example, has commented
on the poor quality of American schooling:

> Although there are pockets of pedagogical brilliance, far too many
> classrooms can be found in which teaching is intolerably weak—
> classrooms choked with irrelevant, time-filling activities that leave
> hordes of students bored, unmotivated, and lacking mastery of even
> the most basic skills.
>
> Whatever the causes of such ineffectiveness, its consequences are
> visible whenever a high-stakes test [usually a professionally pub-
> lished test which is used to evaluate student progress] is initially
> installed. Far too many students know far too little (p. 681).

WHAT DO WE WANT FROM OUR SCHOOLS?

Declaring that Johnny or Suzie cannot read, write, or cal-
culate is no longer front-page news—everybody has known
that for years. But when E. D. Hirsch, Jr., claimed in his best-
selling *Cultural Literacy* (1987, pp.1-10) that students are
essentially ignorant of basic knowledge, that was news.
Claiming that even our most successful students have not
really learned the essential information and ideas that lie at
the core of our culture, he proposed a list (Hirsch, pp. 152–
215) of some 4,500 names, dates, events, and expressions
that he feels are "essential." The list includes such items as

absolute zero	parvenu
ampersand	*reductio ad absurdum*
basta	Slough of Despond
bilateralism	teenybopper
Casey at the Bat	*vox populi vox Dei*
chutzpah	Virginia Woolf

Visions of future classes being reduced to yearlong training sessions for "Trivial Pursuit" notwithstanding, it would be difficult to disagree in principle with the assertion that all students should know some basic information about American and world culture. The difficulty arises, however, when we are forced to decide which information should be presented, how often it should be presented, how it is to be measured, and what must be eliminated to make room for it. Are all of the sample terms given above really essential? Is knowing them proof of a good education and not knowing them proof of a poor one? Are we interested in having students master certain information and skills or do we simply wish to expose them to large quantities of information and pray for intellectual osmosis? Time, money, motivation, and developmental readiness, along with other factors, place strict limits on how many and which experiences can be provided to students.

In attempting to meet all of the diverse goals set for them, schools have become less and less able to accomplish any goal well. Although seven hours a day, 180 days a year for 12 years seems more than an adequate amount of time to educate our young, it is amazing how rapidly that time allocated for learning is consumed. Every special interest group tries to secure as much time as possible within the school day. The most difficult task for educational planners is deciding what to exclude. Interestingly enough, the final decisions as to what stays and what goes in the curriculum are more often based on political and economic concerns than on educational ones.

The de facto curriculum in most schools, for example, is determined by the content of the textbooks, which are ultimately dictated by the educational demands of Texas and California due to the sheer size of their purchasing power.

Confronting the myriad of demands placed upon them, schools have generally chosen to provide all students with more or less identical experiences at more or less the same pace. A uniform approach to dealing with students is adopted and all students receive the same treatment for as long as possible. Society's egalitarian goal represents both a noble accomplishment and a monstrous headache for education. Noble because all students are provided with more or less equal opportunities while at school; a headache because no two people are exactly the same and thus will not take equal advantage of those opportunities. Almost no one is really satisfied with what is provided. Regardless of what the school offers, the curriculum will either ignore, avoid, or understress something that someone sees as essential or it will overstress something that others deem unimportant, if not downright harmful. Disagreements resulting from differing priorities result in heated school board elections, debates, lawsuits, and private educational alternatives.

SCHOOL REFORM MOVEMENT OF THE 1980s: IDEAS FOR CHANGE

When the history of the 1980s is written, a major section will have to be devoted to the expansive educational reform efforts during the decade. About 30 national reports on educational reform were written, most of which concluded that the nation's public schools were poorly educating students and that the nation must take drastic measures to improve its educational system. In addition, the 50 states appointed nearly 300 task forces and have sent them forth in search of excellence (Cross, 1984, p. 168). Although A. Graham Down of the Council for Basic Education has called the suggestions offered by the various reform groups a "litany of the obvious (1983)," the rash of highly publicized reports written by prestigious national committees led by distinguished educators and scholars has focused public attention squarely on the schools. The extent to which they have had any permanent or meaningful impact on education is another issue altogether.

The reform movement of the 1980s is actually the second major reform movement to affect the schools in the last 30 years. The first occurred during the late 1950s and early 1960s. The orbiting of Sputnik by the Soviets in 1957 made education a hot topic. The nation became painfully aware of some of the shortcomings in education, especially in the areas of mathematics and science.

Some of the ideas of the first reform movement were quickly put in place and made definite contributions to American education. Others came and went on the whims and priorities of politicians and educators. The funding and effort devoted to improvement of science instruction during the late 1960s, for example, were redirected during the 1970s into human rights programs while science programs were generally put on hold before they were fully implemented. Today science is once again receiving attention from reformers. The significant point is that national priorities can change without notice, often before previous innovations and reforms have been brought to fruition.

MASTERING THE BASICS

Many of the reform reports of the 1980s were especially concerned with the current low achievement of American students in the three R's. A Nation at Risk (National Commission on Excellence in Education, 1983), for example, reported many problems with our schools, including the following disturbing facts:

—About 13 percent of all 17-year-olds in the United States can be considered functionally illiterate. Functional illiteracy among minority youth may run as high as 40 percent.

—Average achievement of high school students on most standardized tests is now lower than 26 years ago when Sputnik was launched.

—The College Board's Scholastic Aptitude Tests (SAT) demonstrate a virtually unbroken decline from 1963 to 1980. Average verbal scores fell over 50 points and average mathematics scores dropped nearly 40 points.

—Many 17-year-olds do not possess the "higher order" intellectual skills we should expect of them. Nearly 40 percent cannot draw inferences from written material; only one-fifth can write a persuasive essay; and only one-third can solve a mathematics problem requiring several steps.

—Business and military leaders complain that they are required to spend millions of dollars on costly remedial education and training programs in such basic skills as reading, writing, spelling, and computation. (pp. 8-9)

Responding to such criticism, some states have passed new legislation, raised taxes, and plunged into reform efforts with a variety of programs and activities. Using standardized test scores as their guide, states and communities have pursued a costly and dubious strategy of trying to match or exceed the illusive national average.

Our experiences with averages may lead us to assume that half of the states must be below the national average. Using this interpretation, it becomes virtually impossible for schools, systems, or states that are behind to make a significant gain in rank if everyone else is progressing at the same pace. Most standardized tests, however, report their results by comparing the current scores with some previous reference group. The comparison, then, is today's scores versus yesterday's scores. Using this criterion, all states can theoretically exceed the national average by improving their scores above the average of the reference group. Not unlike the children in Garrison Keillor's whimsical Lake Wobegon, every state can be above average. Whether this really means anything, however, is open to serious question.

Regardless of the instrument used in setting and measuring educational achievement, many state and local efforts spawned by the reform movement of the 1980s are probably going nowhere. This is not to say that there are no bright spots on the horizon. But many of the reform efforts to date involve little more than putting more money into an inherently flawed system.

ECONOMIC CONCERNS

The recent reform movement also reflects the concerns of many political and business leaders about the international standing of the economy. Business competition in recent years has been very keen with the Japanese, West Germans, and Koreans. "Made in Japan" has changed from a derogatory slogan for inexpensive, often shoddy goods to fighting words in many sectors of the American economy. Calls have been heard for such countermeasures as tariffs, quotas, and "Made in the USA" labels. Many see education as a critical factor in the United States' ability to remain competitive in world markets. Such a view provides strong impetus toward change.

Students in countries such as Japan, Russia, and Germany are academically far more advanced than American students of the same age. Whether or not the frequent comparison with the Japanese is fair remains to be seen. Although Japanese culture has much that is worth emulating, the tremendous cultural diversity of America makes matching their efforts difficult and probably undesirable. The immediate concern in some quarters, however, remains whether or not America can even hope to maintain its place as a world leader without developing the level of intellectual learning and sophistication necessary to allow us to compete successfully in world markets (Howe, 1983, p. 168).

It is not at all certain that America's economic position in the world is threatened. Although this view is widely held and helps to drive the reform forces, former Chairman of the President's Council of Economic Advisors Herbert Stein (1990) makes the point that America has not lost its economic standing in the world. But even if we had, he maintains that the relevant comparison as to our economic prosperity is not in terms of other countries but in terms of our own production and productivity. Concern for being number one

is a distraction from our real problem, which is not to get richer than someone else or to get richer faster than someone else but to be as good as we can be, and better than we have been, in the areas of our serious deficiencies, such as homelessness, poverty, ignorance and crime (p. A16).

In 1988, yet another reform report described new concerns for educators. Produced by the William T. Grant Foundation Commission on Work, Family and Citizenship, *The Forgotten Half: Non-College Youth in America* focused on the increasing plight of noncollege youth. According to the report, the economic opportunities for this substantial group of young people have been steadily declining. Examples cited by the committee include such disturbing facts as these:

—In 1986 males between the ages of 20 and 24 who had high school diplomas and were employed earned 28% less in constant dollars than a comparable group in 1973. The income decline was 24% for white males and 44% for black males.

—High school dropouts have suffered an even larger income decline. In 1986 dropouts between the ages of 20 and 24 earned 42% less in constant dollars than a comparable group in 1973.

—In 1973, 60% of all employed young males earned incomes high enough to support a three-person family above the poverty level, but by 1985 only 43.7% earned incomes that high (pp. 22-23).

Here then is another dilemma facing education. What will be the response of the education community to these non-college-bound students? The committee has recommended a federal expenditure on this priority alone of at least $5 billion each year for the next ten years (pp. 75-76).

DECIDING WHERE TO GO

Each of the reform reports looked at schools from a slightly different perspective and each generated related but somewhat different conclusions and recommendations. Although they have alerted the public to what many educators already knew, few of the changes emerging on the horizon will greatly improve the nation's schools. The most promising reform by far is the growing interest in parental and student choice. In this movement is the very real potential for significant change. Chester Finn, Jr. (1990), professor of Education and Public Policy at Vanderbilt University, made this point in a powerful and hopeful article in the *Wall Street Journal*. He concluded that "education reform may have only just begun. Perhaps the '90s will turn out to be the decade in which we actually make the changes that yield results" (p. A14).

One of our difficulties in education is that new issues and concerns are constantly arising, diverting our attention from the main course and keeping the nation's schools in a constant state of turmoil. A partial list of issues and concerns that have affected the nation's schools over the last few decades and continue to influence them today would include such familiar fads, trends, and issues as:

Prayer in schools   Women's issues/rights
AIDS awareness   Environmental education

Integration/human relations	School drug and alcohol abuse
Violence in schools	Cultural literacy
Computerized instruction	Scientific literacy
Teacher competency	Back-to-the-basics
Merit pay/career ladders	Bilingual education
Vouchers/tuition grants	Values education

Each of these issues represents hundreds of thousands of dollars spent in presenting and attending conferences, conducting research, and paying consulting fees. All of these issues have been debated exhaustively. Conflicting solutions, each with its own cadre of zealous supporters, have been tried and tested. Some efforts have had a significant impact on educational practice; some have been pushed aside after a brief moment in the sun; some are currently being debated as "hot topics"; and still others have died only to await resurrection like the phoenix in some future generation. But out of all this comes one thing for sure: few communities, parents, or students are truly satisfied with the type, amount, and quality of education being delivered. This general dissatisfaction, coupled with current concerns about our deteriorating social fabric and threatened international position, is fueling the continued soul-searching concerning our schools. With courage, concerted effort, and some luck, perhaps the educational reforms of the 1990s will be able to transform the schools into something more powerful and creative than they are currently.

Part 2

Critical Questions: Deciding What We Want from Our Schools

The difficulties we are having with our schools have two root causes. The first we shall characterize as *natural*. This cause stems from limits and restrictions that are present in all societies. They arise from the existence of scarcity and the varied and complex array of human motives and differences. All individuals and institutions face these restraints and can never achieve or acquire all they would like. We shall examine this natural cause in chapters 3-7.

The second cause we shall call *artificial*. It arises from government monopolization of education. Schools are burdened by this limit in many serious ways. Chapter 8 focuses on this constraint.

The bottom line is that with publically owned and controlled schools, we achieve far less than we desire. The natural limits handicap us, but the artificial constraints cripple us. As we shall see, many of the proposals for educational improvement deal only with symptoms rather than root causes. Only by confronting and coming to terms with both the natural limitations and the artificial constraints will we ever achieve meaningful reform.

Chapter 3

The Question of Limited Means

At the risk of being labeled masters of the obvious, we will begin by asserting that education, like all other aspects of human life, is limited by scarce resources. There will never be enough facilities, personnel, time, or funds to provide everyone with all the education that he or she wants or needs. Thus, any system with a chance of success must deal effectively with the issue of scarcity and the severe limits it imposes. The best way to provide education is by making the most efficient and effective use of available resources.

THE LIMITATION IMPOSED BY SCARCITY

Our world is a finite place. We can fly around it in a space shuttle in a matter of hours. What the earth contains in the way of land area, water, and raw materials is strictly limited—often severely so. This point is frequently brought home when our use of such basic items as water and gasoline is restricted by government through rationing or conservation efforts. In fact, whether or not we realize it, almost all of the natural resources in our world must be rationed.

Our personal lives are restricted by such limitations. We all want an unlimited variety of goods and services—big homes, thick steaks, designer suits, European vacations, frequent movies, and degrees from prestigious colleges for our children. The production of all these things requires the application and commitment of time and resources such as labor, capital, and raw materials. But our time and resources on this earth are strictly limited—each day has only 24 hours, a year has only 365 days, a lifetime has only so many years, and the world contains only so much in the way of resources.

Since virtually all resources are scarce, the goods and services that emerge from their use are also scarce. With insatiable human demands for such things as housing, transportation, clothing, medical care, food, vacations, and education, the result is perennial scarcity—there simply is not enough of everything to go around.

A numerical limit of resources does not by itself make goods and services scarce. The desire and willingness to obtain something also contributes to scarcity. If no demand for a particular item exists, there would be no scarcity even if the resource were available in limited amounts. Few people, for example, become depressed over the lack of crabgrass in their yards. What makes scarcity a reality for us is the fact that we want more of something than is available. All of us fantasize from time to time about having unrestricted supplies of something, anything from designer clothing to vintage wines. Unfortunately, everyone cannot have all he or she wants. We live in a finite world with insatiable wants and must accept the scarcity that such a condition imposes.

On a day-to-day basis, we tend to look at scarcity as being applicable only to some impoverished third world country, in crisis situations such as the infamous oil shortages of the 1970s or the plight of some special group such as the homeless. In point of fact, the condition of scarcity prevails for every society in the world at all times.

Every society must decide how it intends to allocate its limited resources among the unlimited demands for them. This process of allocation always entails some form of rationing. In this general sense, rationing is how choices are made among the many options available. Somehow, someone or some system will decide who gets what and how much. On an international level, it is the type of rationing system used that constitutes the primary difference between the free market system used by the United States and one that is centrally planned and controlled. The rationing system selected has a powerful influence on almost every aspect of our lives.

In any type of choice making, a decision to choose one option automatically precludes picking another. Every decision requires a trade-off. Every hour spent in one effort, say repairing your lawn mower, denies you the benefit of what you could have gained by using that time in other ways, such as painting your house, catching up on office work, watching a ball game, or taking a siesta. Your pleasure of seeing a freshly cut front lawn is obtained only at a cost. Part of that cost is in the displeasure of seeing a house fading from the want of fresh paint, feeling pressured at the office on Monday morning, missing an important ball game, or feeling generally "out of it" at the Saturday night cocktail party. Limited time prevents us from avoiding the necessity of choosing.

Choice may also be viewed from a national perspective. A nation that gains by devoting more steel to the production of another million automobiles will suffer from a decline in the production of tractors or bridges that otherwise might have been made with the same steel. It is the necessity of choice that makes for such acrimony in political debates focusing on defense spending versus domestic spending, public housing versus highway construction, and so on.

It is largely the recognition of the principle of scarcity that

has forced the Soviet Union to negotiate arms reduction with
the United States and to reduce their presence in neighboring
countries. They understand that all of those tanks and guns
require resources that could have been used to make automobiles, apartments, clothing, and food. Such costs are especially heavy for a relatively poor country such as the Soviet
Union. The United States is also mindful of the possibility of
a "peace dividend" (the availability of more nonmilitary
goods) resulting from reduced military spending and such
prospects give us added incentive to negotiate weapons
reduction.

SCARCITY AND EDUCATION

The concepts of scarcity and the trade-offs that must ensue
are vitally important in understanding some of the problems
faced by our public school system (Rinehart and Cummings,
1965). Education requires the use of scarce resources as does
every other good or service and consequently necessitates the
making of painful choices. Acrimonious debates over proposed local school bond issues or millage increases bring this
point home for many citizens year in and year out. More
taxes for schools simply means less money available for personal use.

To hear most educators talk, it is easy to infer that education is the only institution in our society with inadequate
funding. On the positive side, this constant desire for more
funds grows out of the creative energies of educators who
can always envision better ways of providing for the needs
of students. On the negative side, this desire reflects an un-
willingness and inability to make the most out of the scarce
resources available. While many would view scarcity as a
curse, the point is irrelevant since we still must live with it.
Scarcity should be seen as one of the forces that drive all our
choices, including those in education.

The limits that restrict individuals also restrict governments. Each million dollars allocated to public education programs is a million dollars unavailable for other public efforts such as roads, hospitals, police protection, or shelter for the homeless. Additionally, the more money government collects via taxes, the less money individuals have available for their private use such as purchasing clothing, housing, food, insurance, recreation, transportation, and making charitable contributions. We cannot escape the fact that we will never satisfy all of our wants. Benefits gained from a beautiful new school gymnasium will be at least partially offset by the reduced satisfaction of taxpayers who have less spending money. To leave this essential scarcity factor out of educational choices or even to downplay its importance is to severely limit any meaningful debate about public schools, often leading to unwise decisions regarding investments in educational programs.

All too often in the discussions concerning educational choices and expenditures, there is an implied notion that education is so important that scarcity of funding should not be allowed to restrict expenditures. If we lack sufficient money to fund a worthy program, the solution is simple and more or less automatic: we raise taxes. Yet as important as education is, spending decisions can always be reduced to the fact that spending more on education is of necessity spending less on something else. Many citizens would undoubtedly prefer a newer car, a bigger home, more clothing, or a longer vacation to more buildings, equipment, and staff in schools. Others feel that education is cheap ⁀. any price.

The William T. Grant Foundation Commission on Work, Family and Citizenship's report (1988) focused on the increasing plight of noncollege youth. The commission recommended an additional federal expenditure of at least $5 billion in each of the next ten years. They expected that this expenditure would be covered through some combination of a general increase in tax rates, the elimination of existing tax preferences, the realignment of priorities related to military and domestic spending, or a new dedicated tax (i.e., a surcharge on the personal income tax) for children and youth (pp. 75-76). The difficult choices evident here explain in large measure why moving ahead on any new idea or program is frustratingly slow.

The resources or income in our society will never be sufficient to buy all of the education we want without painful sacrifices of other goods and services we also want. This puts us in the position of having to make some tough and agonizing choices among several highly desirable alternatives. All societies have faced this problem since Adam and Eve first made that rather unwise decision to choose apples over oranges.

Once we recognize that choices must be made, we must decide who should have the power to make such choices. Should the school boards, teachers, principals, superintendents, county councils, taxpayers, parents, state legislatures, or Congress make the difficult choices of how much education to produce and concomitantly how much of other things not to produce?

We must recognize the fact that to spend more money on education is to spend less on something else. We cannot assume automatically that more educational expenditure is always preferable to less. To arrive at the correct choice, we must weigh the benefit of a dollar spent on one against the benefit of a dollar spent on the other. This is no easy task. The amount we spend on education, how it is financed, and who decides represent crucial choices that must be made. How these choices are made is critical in shaping the organization and direction of our schools. Those school reforms which will eventually prove most successful will be the ones that come to terms with the problem of scarcity.

Chapter 4

The Question of Individual Differences

If you ever need to remind yourself of just how different we all are as individuals, a quick trip to the local Wal-Mart or K-Mart will serve nicely. Miles of shelves packed with goods and for only a few of these items can we imagine any useful value to us. Yet at some time, every item shelved there will sell out, attesting to the wide variety of consumer tastes and needs.

All of us come into this world desiring many of the same things, such as food, drink, shelter, love, and security. As we get older the specific nature of our wants grows in number, diversity, and sophistication.

As with our problem of limitations due to scarcity, any successful reform attempt in education must accept and deal successfully with human differences. Ours is a rich and diverse nation having been molded by cultures from around the world. Before we can make lasting reforms in our schools, we must meet this issue of individual differences head on.

Abraham Maslow (1970) developed a list of needs that

must be met by everyone if they are to live the fullest possible lives. He ordered them in the general sequence in which they must be satisfied. Beginning with the most essential, these needs are survival, safety, belonging, self-esteem, intellectual achievement, aesthetic appreciation, and self-actualization. From those seven needs, and our efforts to meet them, arise a bewildering diversity in human behavior. Our different tastes, interests, and values translate into varied desires, goals, aspirations, and behaviors. In short, everyone does not want the same things, nor are we all going in the same direction.

Even those who seem to be most like us place vastly dissimilar amounts of energy, time and money into a wide array of interests and goals. Consider the multitude of variations that usually exists within a single family. Even under the same roof, different children approach life in very disparate ways. These differences are noticeable almost from birth. One may deeply desire an *A* in mathematics while another is perfectly content with a solid *C*. One may want to spend the evening talking on the telephone, while another prefers drawing, reading a book, or solving algebra problems.

Each of us gains satisfaction from fulfilling our needs and desires. The more we can satisfy, the more pleasure, happiness and general sense of well-being we experience. Surely this is the key motivator driving most of us day after day.

In a free society, citizens have the prerogative of making personal choices in ways compatible with their own desires. There are no right or wrong choices for everyone. Individuals more or less go their own ways, choosing those goods and services that, in their opinions, are right for them. If freedom is to have any meaning, it is to be found in society's toleration of highly divergent lifestyles and consumption behavior.

All of us from time to time have raised an eyebrow at someone wearing unorthodox or out-of-style clothing or someone who just seems different. We sometimes frown on those with unrefined tastes or unhealthy appetites for products such as unlawful drugs, cigarettes, and alcohol. But this is the plight of a society that values human freedom over coerced regimentation. In a free society, diversities in human characteristics and tastes will surely engender differences in terms of what people buy and consume.

In the United States, people are able to use the majority of their time and money as they see fit, their choices reflecting their own values and beliefs. As a consequence, human welfare is higher than it would be under any other arrangement, yet decisions are often restricted, sometimes painfully so. Through laws and regulations, the government at local, state and national levels frequently interferes with private decisions of individuals and groups.

All of us are restricted by legislative decisions. Examples that come readily to mind are laws prohibiting drugs, gambling, prostitution, owning machine guns, and other laws requiring that we use seat belts, purchase clothes impregnated with flame-resistant chemicals, and attend school for a certain number of years. Why is it that most states have laws against gambling? The answer is that in our republic we allow laws to be passed by majority vote. A majority of the citizens in some states (or at least the majority that votes) does not think it is a good idea to gamble. Not only do they believe that it is a bad idea for the gamblers, they also think it is a bad idea for nongamblers as well. The same thing holds for prostitution and drugs. This type of thinking also explains why some states limit our right to purchase certain items on Sunday by passing or maintaining so-called "blue laws." The majority voting system also explains why we are often forced to buy products and services some of us may not want, such as smoke alarms for our homes, life jackets on boats, seat belts in cars, and safety caps on medicine bottles. We are not arguing for or against gambling, smoke alarms, life jackets, seat belts, drugs, or safety caps. Instead, we wish to emphasize the point that when laws are passed, someone's freedoms are usually being limited, and there is often a fine line between public good and public tyranny.

Lest we lose our perspective, we must remember that in comparison to the rest of the world, the United States offers its citizens one of the freest arenas of choice-making available anywhere. The past and present influx of people from the rest of the world speaks loudly for the freedom we have. Hordes of people, of their own volition, continue to risk their lives to flee from societies where a few leaders make most of the decisions for the masses.

What does all of this have to do with education? The answer is simple. Individuals define education differently and place differing degrees of emphasis on it. Educators may think they know what education should be and how much of it students should have. But what students and parents actually want is often something else. One person may want a classical education based on the great books, while another might prefer education with a more practical emphasis. One person may have a flair for languages while someone else is more interested in the sciences. One student may be a highly motivated achiever anxious to push on to higher levels of learning, while another may be content with only modest educational attainments.

Is it any wonder that attempts at designing a single curriculum, one single set of standards or approach to schooling, always fall short of success? This is one of the reasons for the high level of dissatisfaction with public schools. It also explains some of the difficulties faced when attempts have been made to standardize the curriculum and course requirements on a national basis. Where is the room for individual expression of personal desires and wants? What should be the role of parents and students in the educational process? Is it not important for parents and students to get some significant measure of what they want from their schools regardless of the opinions of the educators who run them?

The current choice movement in education is a move toward providing for individual differences. It represents modest experimentation with a market-oriented approach to education. Markets are renowned for tolerating a myriad of variations in human behavior. Nobel prize-winning economist Milton Friedman (1962) made such an observation many years ago when he observed that

the great argument for the market is its tolerance of diversity; its ability to utilize a wide range of special knowledge and capacity. It renders special groups impotent to prevent experimentations and permits the customers [students and parents] and not the producers [public schools] to decide what will serve the consumers best (p. 160).

Debates over the future of America's public schools must center on student and parental wants. No one knows what and how much education anyone else should have. The concern of the educational establishment must be in satisfying the interests of its clients. If not, the prospects for making any meaningful changes in the world of education are slim indeed.

Chapter 5

The Question of Individual Decision Making

It is fascinating to speculate as to what the world might be like if every child were somehow naturally predisposed to learn as much as he or she could. Think of how much more satisfying life could be. No doubt the quality of our lives would improve since many of our serious problems would be solved, or at least greatly reduced in severity. Pollution, AIDS, cancer, mental illness, and poverty are just a few of our current problems that might be solved through the expansion of brain power and changes in behavior. Unfortunately, not every child enters school with an overwhelming hunger for knowledge. Many who do lose it well before they are ready to complete their formal education.

Ultimately each person must choose for him- or herself what to learn, how much to learn, and how to learn.

The lesson we have to learn ... is that we cannot pressure any student to work if he does not believe the work is satisfying. We can force many students to stay in school, which we do to some extent by closing off full-time job opportunities, but we can no more make those students work than we can make the proverbial horse drink even though we tether him to the water trough (Glasser, 1986, pp. 11-12).

Given our national commitment to individual freedom, we can be sure that any educational reform which does not take into account personal differences will ultimately be doomed to failure. We are a diverse people seeking diverse goals in diverse ways. We constantly seek ways to make our lives as successful and rewarding as possible.

ALL OF US PURSUE OUR OWN SELF-INTEREST AS WE PERCEIVE IT

Whether in or out of school, every behavior we exhibit is a balancing act. Every voluntary action has some conscious or subconscious anticipated benefit. Every such action also imposes a cost, determined by the alternatives we must sacrifice. We are constantly attempting to weigh the expected benefits against expected costs. Suppose, for instance, Mr. M. purchases his dream car for $30,000. The benefit to him is obvious, but the cost goes beyond the sticker price of the car. The real cost must include all those other opportunities that would have been possible with that $30,000.

No matter what decisions we make, they will always be aimed toward improving our welfare. At times we feel that others seem to be breaking this rule, but that is because we do not understand the situation from their point of view. Even masochists expect psychological benefits from self-inflicted pain. Sometimes decisions are based on too little or inaccurate information, and other times the quality of our decisions is affected by the difficulty of accurately measuring benefits and costs. But nonetheless, all of us go through life making thousands of choices in an attempt to get the most satisfaction from the resources available to us.

The fact that each of us seeks his or her own self-interest does not mean that individuals are necessarily selfish in the negative sense of the term. It *does* mean that individuals weigh alternatives in light of how they personally expect to gain or lose. The benefits we derive and costs we pay need not be monetary; often they are simply feelings, good or bad. We may benefit personally merely by gaining a sense of satisfaction, as we do when giving to a worthy charity. The satisfaction we gain from giving will always be greater in some way than the satisfaction we feel we might have received from keeping the gift, otherwise we would not give. It is in this sense that we act in our own self-interest. We may be preached to, bribed, or influenced in a variety of powerful ways. In the final analysis, we all make our choices by weighing benefits and costs consistent with our preferences and values in an attempt to maximize our own individual welfare.

What anyone chooses to do with his or her money is clearly subjective. One person simply cannot know what particular choice is in the best interest of someone else—we can only guess. Two individuals, each with the same amount of money, may make very different choices about that money's use. One person may save his; the other may spend it. One may spend his on a movie and a hamburger; the other on a new book. Can any third party sit in judgment and conclude who made the wiser choice? Many of us are led to believe that saving is better than spending or, if the money is to be spent, that it would be better to spend it on something tangible like a book instead of a movie. The "right" choice, the one producing the most pleasure and least pain, can only be determined by the person receiving the benefit and paying the cost.

Society is, of course, loaded with people who enthusiastically attempt, and often succeed, in forcing us to make choices in line with their values and interests. Is this not precisely what is involved when a majority of a community's citizens support laws that prevent the minority of citizens from gambling or buying alcoholic beverages on Sunday? The majority already had the right to abstain from these activities, but they wanted more. Barring some unusual condition such as coma, the best decision for any individual can never be made by someone else, no matter how fervently he or she believes in the value of a particular course of action.

You might argue that 20 years from now, anyone who chooses not to save some of his money will be sorry. Perhaps so, but if such were the case, it would only attest to the uncertainty and risks in living and making decisions. All our decisions are made based on what we anticipate to be the relative gains and losses. We often admire those who saved and later in life have more material things than those who did not save. But does that always make savers better off than spenders? We cannot tell. What about that person who saved for the future only to develop poor health and thus was unable to enjoy the fruits of his saving? What if the investment in which the saving was placed became worthless? What if the sacrifice associated with the saving caused such family strife that the saver and his or her spouse were separated or divorced? The point should be clear. Since each individual has a unique set of values and preferences that produce satisfaction for him or her, the best option is to leave the choice up to each individual.

We should never confuse how people ought to behave with how they do behave. The bad press given to self-interest notwithstanding, we can reasonably expect even the most caring people to look out for their own interests. Whether people *ought* to behave this way is irrelevant. They *do* behave in their own interest, and the failure to recognize this fact will lead us to make many unwise government policies. Efforts to improve health care through Medicare and Medicaid, for example, have served to increase the demand for medical services. Since the government pays the bill, self-interest leads more people to seek and consume more health care. Similarly, efforts to provide for the needy with welfare programs have led to generations of government dependency. Increase the rewards for being poor and more people will be poor.

Unless we recognize that individuals pursue their own self-interest, we may never make significant improvements in public education. Interestingly enough, pursuing our own self-interest will often involve doing something for someone else. Yet, we must avoid the flawed notion that people are sufficiently altruistic to consistently take the "higher road" toward satisfying the interest of others. We often mistakenly attribute these higher standards of behavior to professional types such as medical doctors, lawyers—and yes—teachers. Until we come to understand, though, that professionals and public servants are motivated by the same self-interest that motivates everyone else, we will never really understand why we get such poor results from our schools.

SELF-INTEREST AND PUBLIC SCHOOLS

One of the classical gambits in negotiating an agreement is called "good guy, bad guy." It has probably been used on each of us at one time or another. An automobile salesman, for example, may try to sell you a new car at a higher price than you really want to pay. To keep from giving too much away in the negotiations, he keeps referring to that tough-as-nails sales manager who is so hard to convince. But your salesman will give it his best shot—just for you. He talks to that tough manager and comes back with a counteroffer that is still a bit too high, but you feel obligated to buy at that price since your "selfless" salesman was good enough to fight it out with his sales manager "just for you." What we forget is that they are both on the same team. When one wins, they both win. In spite of how it seems, your salesman is operating in his own best interest, as you, in one of your less emotional moments, would expect him to do.

The same phenomenon happens in education. For some reason we have assumed that, like the good-guy salesman, educators are selfless people who only have our best interest at heart: nothing is in it for them except hard work, frustration, and poor pay. We have to remember that these people are just like the rest of us. They pursue those directions in life that give them the most benefit for their time and effort.

An English teacher might agree that helping Mike after class would significantly improve his writing skills. He or she will, however, measure his or her personal cost of doing so (time away from family, hobbies, friends, or a second job), and compare that to the negligible benefit he or she would receive from Mike's improvement. It is easy enough to understand why the teacher might opt to let Mike continue to struggle without any additional assistance. Fortunately, every school has at least a few highly dedicated teachers who consistently go the extra mile for their students, and they should be admired and recognized for their devotion. Nothing in the educational system itself, however, consistently and systematically rewards or reinforces this unusual behavior. Under our present school system, teachers and administrators are generally neither rewarded nor penalized based on how well a student learns. Salaries are, by and large, based on the number of degrees held and years of experience. Supplements, when they are available, are typically provided for those who assume other extracurricular duties, such as coaches, bus supervisors, and student newspaper advisors.

The present system does not provide for compatibility between the educators' self-interest and that of their students. Exhorting teachers and administrators to go above and beyond the call of duty to improve education will produce meager results at best. Indeed, since little or no penalty is associated with poor to mediocre student performance, the incentive system actually encourages educators to limit their efforts to the minimum amount required. The absence of innovation and creativity is one of the prices we pay for maintaining a system that encourages support of the status quo, and educators, bureaucrats, and politicians have virtually no incentive to change it.

Understanding incentives can help us understand why we often get less than many of us want and expect from our public schools, and how we might produce some truly meaningful changes. The present incentive structure within the public school system also reveals why current attempts to improve education are probably going to be far less than satisfactory.

When you and I make decisions, the benefits and costs we personally expect to incur weigh very heavily in the choices. The impact a decision may have on others is not ignored, but it normally is a secondary consideration. We tend to rationalize this "selfishness" in one of two ways. We may simply claim that it is necessary for us to look out for ourselves, because after all, if we do not, who will? Sometimes we may turn the logic around by claiming that the way we behave is actually in the best interest of others. This latter argument is perhaps best captured by the expression, "But, dear, I'm only doing it for your own good." As presumptuous as this position may be, it is used frequently. In order to have a realistic picture of the world, we must shed our mistaken belief that self-interest is evil. All of us are currently reaping the benefits produced by the self-interest of businessmen, inventors, philanthropists, and artists, among others. The pursuit of self-interest is as much a part of all of us as is eating and sleeping.

In order to be fair, we must stress the fact that any person can be expected to behave the way educators do if given similar circumstances. A teacher in a private school, for instance, would want to go home at quitting time just as much as a teacher in a public school. This is the way all of us are, and it is for this reason that we must tie performance to reward in order to get the best results. Perhaps teachers would be better teachers if they read certain professional books, attended particular seminars and prepared better lessons, but each of these activities imposes personal costs. Maybe administrators could improve student performance if they hired better teachers, were more creative in program development, and monitored school activities more diligently, but each of these activities imposes personal costs.

Public schools rarely, if ever, compensate teachers and administrators based on their performance or how well the students perform. The benefits of improved student achievement to the educators are small, compared to the costs. Is there any wonder that they would be strongly tempted to substitute other activities, such as going to the beach for the weekend or watching television, for lesson preparation or paper grading? In a similar vein, unusually effective teachers often create problems for their superiors and conflicts with their peers. To avoid such hassles and the risks associated with them, good teachers are tempted to reduce their level of effort and commitment.

Are teachers, administrators, school board members, and politicians any different from the rest of us? Does being classified as a public servant somehow make them behave any differently when it comes to making personal decisions? Once we accept the notion that these people place their own interests ahead of others' just like everyone else, some of the mystery as to why our educational problems persist disappears.

A conflict naturally occurs between the self-interests of the providers and the recipients of services. This conflict is frequently exacerbated by the entry of a regulatory agency. The reason the government finally eliminated the Civil Aeronautics Board (CAB) was that regulated airlines had gained enough influence over the members of the regulatory board that the agency no longer protected the interests of the public. In short, it protected the airlines from the threat of competition. The CAB routinely blocked the entry of new airlines, thus ensuring high profits for the old established airlines and high wages for airline employees at the expense of the passengers. As with the late CAB, state education boards and local school boards consciously and unconsciously promote the interest of the educators in power at the expense of students, parents, and taxpayers. This is an inevitable consequence of the way government bodies function.

The incentives are simply not adequate in the current public school system to offer much hope for improvement. Unless there is a drastic change in the governing structure of the school system, most reform efforts will fail. School decision makers pay little of the cost associated with their decisions and receive little of the direct educational benefit; consequently, it is impossible for them to measure the true costs and benefits for students and parents. Educators can always be expected to push for more emphasis on education and funding for their programs. From such efforts they expect to receive personal benefits in the form of higher salaries, improved facilities, increased job satisfaction, employment security, and increased prestige. It is in the self-interest of those who control and operate public schools to advocate more funding while concomitantly expending less and less personal energy on its production. Is there any wonder that students and parents are so often dissatisfied and frustrated with the schools?

ESTABLISHING PRIORITIES

People generally agree on the broad goals for our schools, such as literacy, appreciation for democratic institutions, and development of community responsibility. The efforts toward achieving these worthwhile goals often falter at the individual decision-making level. A student choosing how long and what he will study will view his choices in terms of how he thinks he will benefit and how much cost will be imposed on him personally. If he is lucky, he will have a parent or some other responsible adult who will help him get his priorities straight. Nonetheless, he will always consider what opportunities he will have to forgo to achieve any worthwhile goal. He may have to give up watching television, playing video games, sleeping late, or talking with friends on the telephone.

Parents and administrators make their school decisions on a similarly personal basis. They might desire a new or remodeled football stadium despite the fact that the money needed to construct it will be pulled away from other uses, such as adding books to the library, providing more in-service training for teachers, or upgrading the quality of science laboratory equipment. Parents whose children play football will naturally see the football stadium as an excellent use of limited funds. They are not against books for the library or enriching the academic side of the school's education program, but they are voting their own individual interest, and the consequence is less money for books.

Taxpayers are generally in favor of better schools, but they too are strongly influenced by their own self-interest. The higher millage rates on their property required to improve education will reduce the amount of money available for other uses. Although typical tax increases may be small, they add up. These increases make it necessary for some taxpayers to delay the purchase of a car, furniture, or a new television set. Thus, in an effort to maintain their purchasing power, they may vote against a tax increase and consequently the educational program that it would have funded. These taxpayers are probably still in favor of a strong educational program; the car, furniture, or television set, however, is more important to them personally than any gains they might expect to derive from the proposed increase in educational expenditure. This is why we typically find strong support (financial and otherwise) for schools in communities with large numbers of children per household and less support in retirement communities. It is also why some people favor federal support for the schools. They assume that individuals from other states will pick up the tab for their school improvement.

In light of the fact that individuals consider how they are
affected personally by any decisions they make, how can we
organize our schools so that educators will make decisions
that are more in line with the interests of students and parents? The only solution is to provide tangible personal rewards for promoting the student's welfare and impose
penalties for doing otherwise.

Some might argue that the current hierarchy of principals,
over teachers, superintendents over principals and school
boards over superintendents was established to provide just
such penalties and rewards. It is true that the heightened levels
of concern engendered by this top-down management arrangement may have some positive effect on a teacher's or
administrator's level of performance. Unfortunately, the
checks and balances do not work very well. Firing or de-
moting ineffective teachers is as uncommon in education as
it is with many other government-provided services. Moreover, formally and informally, educators at all levels band
together to promote their own interests through teachers'
associations and unions. The National Teachers Association
and the American Federation of Teachers are two such organizations lobbying for educators' interests. From the president and Congress, down to state and local legislatures and
school boards, educators are a force to reckon with. The
interests of parents and students always seem to suffer when
they come into conflict with the interests of educators.

The only way we can have any confidence that teachers
and administrators will consistently act in students' and parents' best interests is to provide for a system of dependable
rewards for good results and certain penalties for bad results.
Such a system can be accomplished only through competition.
The reason your favorite restaurant cares about the quality
of its service is that you are not forced to eat there. You hold
the power, through your freedom and willingness to visit a
competitor, to go somewhere else if the quantity and quality

of the food or service are inadequate. The restaurateur has power only to the extent that he can serve your welfare. Public schools have nothing analogous to this type of competitive pressure, and this fact is the critical factor in explaining the limited responsiveness of school officials to student and parental concerns.

To make this point more emphatically, consider your last trip to a government agency. With luck this agency will have one or more people who are effective and pleasant, but the mechanism to insure the presence of this type of person does not exist. If the clerk behind the desk was friendly and helpful, you no doubt considered yourself fortunate or in the "twilight zone." You are forced to deal with this agency, and the people working there are well aware of your lack of alternatives. The service suffers accordingly, unless the governor, mayor, senator, or congressman walks in. Here the clerk will sense the potential danger associated with poor service and the service level will rise markedly, but only for the VIP, not for the typical person.

Where is parental and student leverage in public schools? For the average student and parent, there is little or none. A privileged few, such as children of school board members or other local VIPs, have influence and are capable of changing some things in their interest, but for most of us this option does not exist.

CONCLUSION

If we want to isolate at least one of the causes of our dissatisfaction with public education, we need look no further than our basic human trait of operating in our own self-interest. There is little we can do about it. Self-interest is neither good nor bad, it just is. Yet springing from this trait we see many educational problems that result from the frequently conflicting self-interests of the educators and their clients. Unless we are somehow able to better align the interests of educators and students, we will continue to pursue expensive and ineffective remedies. Part 3 of this book will explore possible solutions in greater depth.

Chapter 6

The Question of Deciding How Much: Seeking the Optimum Level of Ignorance

Before we can seriously begin to create the kind of educational system most appropriate for this country, we must examine several additional critical questions. What kinds of education should we produce? How much education should we produce? And how should we produce the kinds and quantities of education we select? All three questions are essential since scarcity insures that the resources and time necessary to produce all the education we want are limited. The first two of these questions will be dealt with in this chapter. The third question will be examined in Chapter 7.

Many of our difficulties with public education stem from the fact that parents, students, educators, and politicians rarely see eye-to-eye on what and how much students should learn. These differences between how much and what kinds of education we wish to provide form the basis for much of our educational controversy.

Educators and noneducators alike believe that children

should learn to the fullest extent of their capabilities, but for many parents and students, this standard imposes prohibitively high costs. This must have been what Linus meant when he said, "There is no heavier burden than a great potential." Such a standard simply does not square with how most individuals approach decisions about education, or anything else for that matter. Attempting to prescribe what all children need inevitably produces too much or too little overall education, and too much or too little of some kinds of education. The result is often wasted time for the students and wasted money for the taxpayers.

WHAT SHOULD STUDENTS LEARN?

Experts and laymen alike have been struggling with the "what" question in education as long as there have been schools. Elementary schools generally have answered this question in about the same way. If we could randomly visit several hundred elementary schools in several different states, we would find that they are remarkably uniform in their curricula. What should be taught? On a weekly basis, almost all students receive about the same blend of reading, language arts, mathematics, science, social studies, physical education, health, art, and music. Although variations in schools certainly exist, they are most often merely variations in emphasis.

Middle schools and high schools show more differences than do elementary schools, but aside from a few bright spots here and there, the courses and programs are still amazingly similar. The relatively recent middle school movement has demonstrated some exciting variations for early adolescents. Modern middle schools have developed special programs to help students deal with the difficulties of becoming an adolescent in today's society. Students are allowed to explore a wide variety of interests. These schools place a special emphasis on developing a positive relationship between each student and at least one advisor from the faculty. As effective as these and other efforts have been in helping early adolescents, many communities still operate as if no such alternatives to the traditional junior high school existed. By choice or default, they deny their students the opportunities that might be available in a more flexible and student-oriented middle school.

Even more unfortunately, the gap between the needs of the students and the structure of the program is even greater at the high school level. Since the advent of Carnegie units at the beginning of the century, most high schools provide more or less the same offerings in their programs for college preparatory, general education, and vocational education. Recent experiments with specialized magnet schools have shown that variation and specialization in high schools can be a tremendous source of academic and cultural richness. In some communities students with gifts or interests in the arts, sciences, or mathematics are able to select a school that allows them to expand their talents in ways that would have been impossible in most traditional comprehensive high schools.

When we focus on some of the more innovative high schools, the power of variety becomes even more apparent. Opportunities for specialization allow both students and faculty to become caught up in areas of intense interest. Since many of these schools are selective, they gain strength from the increased level of student commitment. Unencumbered with having to be all things to all people, innovative high schools are able to make even greater strides toward meeting the needs of their students.

What should students learn? The short answer is "no one can know for sure which set of skills or content will be appropriate for all students." Experiments with innovative schools and programs have proven that many different combinations can be suitable if provided effectively.

CHANGING OUR PERSPECTIVE ON LEARNING

How we perceive a situation depends in large part on our personal perspective. We can view an egg as a chicken's way of making another chicken, or we can view a chicken as an egg's way of making another egg. As our perspective changes, that seemingly insignificant change often makes a significant difference in how we behave. Certainly a farmer who accepts the egg as producing chickens will probably treat the lowly egg with a great deal more respect than one who sees the chicken as the focus of the whole cycle.

Our perspective can definitely limit the way we envision any problem and thus place unnecessary restraints on our search for a solution. Educators, for instance, have sought for years to identify some ideal level or body of knowledge that, once obtained, would define an educated person. Call it the basics, the common core, or the essentials, it represents a search for the essence of what all people should know to be considered properly educated. In an effort to break free from what may well be a serious constraint on our pursuit of educational improvement, we might look at the problem from a different perspective—a reversal similar to the chicken-egg one. What if, instead of deciding how much we need to learn, we tried to decide how much we did *not* need to know?

None of us would even attempt to learn everything there is to learn. As a result, our personal welfare is greater because we have more time to devote to those experiences we value most. Instead of seeking a maximum level of learning, we really choose one that is optimum for us. Once we understand this seemingly contradictory idea (i.e., that maximum learning is an unreasonable goal), we will be able to make better decisions with regard to education. The assumption that more education is always preferred to less is simply incorrect.

No single ideal level of learning will ever exist for all students, nor would the optimum mix of courses of study be the same for everyone. Some students may reach their ideal level of learning after the tenth grade, while for others it may not occur until after high school, college, or even graduate school. For some the ideal level may include courses in philosophy and foreign language; for others heavier course emphasis in the social or natural sciences would be more appropriate.

How many times have we heard the expression, "Anything worth doing is worth doing well"? This statement is so readily accepted as truth that few take time to consider its merits. To begin to explore why this expression may hold less wisdom than at first appears, let us examine part of the process involved in learning the game of tennis, a learning situation that at least initially involves a relatively simple task of skill development. If you are a tennis player, you know that the more you practice each day the better your game becomes (if you are not a tennis player, substitute here any other activity you prefer that involves the development of some degree of skill). We could assume for the sake of argument that three or four hours of practice each day is what it would take to play tennis well. But what if your involvement is limited to a few hours of social tennis on weekends? Would all that required practice be worth it? Do you really want to "do" tennis that well? Certainly the time spent on practice would have to be taken from some other activity—something you might consider more worthwhile than improving your tennis skills. You might, for instance, choose to spend the extra time on your job, working around the house, playing with your children, or taking naps. Choosing to *not* do tennis up to your full potential may in fact be the best course of action for you.

MAKING DECISIONS

Would it not be great if we could be fantastic at everything (just us, mind you, not everyone else). Unfortunately, the acquisition of anything of value, such as playing the piano, hitting a golf ball, or being a super salesman, simultaneously entails both benefits and costs. Whether any particular thing is worth obtaining or doing depends on how we perceive the additional cost relative to the additional benefit. We have to judge whether the satisfaction of becoming a better tennis player is really worth all that we must give up to gain and maintain this skill. All of us routinely go through such benefit-cost comparisons when we make decisions.

A trip to the supermarket requires many such benefit-cost comparisons. To buy a carton of ice cream is to have less money available for a six pack of soft drinks. The enjoyment from eating the ice cream must be weighed against the refreshment of the soft drinks we gave up to buy the ice cream. If we choose to buy both a carton of ice cream and a six pack of cola, we must forgo something else of value to us. And so on it goes. Limited budgets insure that we all are required to make choices.

For some people, the monetary cost of the ice cream would not be the critical factor when making a decision. They might place greater emphasis on other cost factors such as the number of calories, level of saturated fats, or presence of artificial ingredients.

Benefit-cost decisions are just as necessary in education as in the supermarket. Students constantly weigh the costs of their behavior against the benefits they hope to receive. Is the benefit I get from passing a note to my girlfriend worth the pain associated with the scolding I'll receive if I get caught? Is the higher grade I might earn by studying an additional hour worth the sleep I lose or the televised basketball game I miss?

Such decisions are further complicated by the fact that additional amounts of something we obtain give us diminishing returns. One more unit makes us better off but better off by an amount less than the previous unit. For example, the more ice cream we buy (say a second or third carton), the less each additional carton will add to our satisfaction.

We just do not enjoy the fourth carton of Heavenly Hash as much as we did the first. At some point, one more carton of ice cream will not be worth as much to us as the brownies we could purchase with the same money. While it is true that the more of an item we purchase, the higher our satisfaction level (we still enjoy Heavenly Hash), we must keep in mind that each additional unit raises our satisfaction level by smaller and smaller amounts.

At some point the added benefit we gain from one more unit is simply not worth the cost. The satisfaction from the skill we gain from one more hour of tennis practice may not be worth the cost of the business opportunities sacrificed for that hour. Diminishing returns applies to everything we acquire, including education. Even though each additional hour of study will theoretically improve both a student's level of knowledge and his or her grades, the amount of learning or improvement in grades he or she gains each hour will typically mean less and less to the student.

As increments in satisfaction or benefit decline, there is a simultaneous incremental rise in the cost. The first improvement in tennis skill takes a relatively small outlay of time and effort: we learn a lot quickly. Additional improvements demand increasingly higher levels of effort and more lost opportunities to produce smaller and smaller rises in skill. Similarly, in most cases, increments in educational improvement can only be obtained by larger and larger additional costs. To raise a history grade from an 80 to an 85, for example, might cost a student an additional hour of study time each week and the sacrifice of other opportunities that were not taken. Assuming that the student is working near capacity and not coasting, a second five-point gain would cost a student even more time and even more loss of other alternatives. If a student had only four hours per day of free time, each additional hour devoted to studying becomes more precious in terms of lost opportunities to watch TV, talk with friends, or practice the trumpet. Once the cost of an additional gain in learning exceeds the benefit expected, we generally back off on our drive to continue learning. The tennis analogy also fits here. Additional gains in skill will decline as we put in more hours on the court, while at the same time we pay higher and higher costs in forgone alternatives as leisure hours become more precious. At some point we would stop taking lessons and use our money and time for something else like a new racket, shoes, or even membership in a health club. Our tennis skill is not maximized, but it is optimized.

Admittedly tennis involves primarily the development of a limited set of skills, whereas education is extremely complicated. Education is certainly more than just skill enhancement, yet there are diminishing returns in its acquisition and students do compare any additional cost associated with a learning activity with what they think they will get out of it. Whether we are deciding how hard to study or which courses to take, we make our decisions by weighing falling additional benefits against rising additional costs.

DECIDING HOW MUCH TO LEARN

Just how much and what kinds of schooling are enough? In choosing how much learning we want to acquire, we could conceive of a point at which the benefit we hope to gain from additional learning is less than the benefit we might expect to gain from doing something else. Choosing to spend more time studying means giving up other things, such as earning money, socializing with friends, or developing some other skills. For everyone there is a level of learning beyond which it is just not worth the effort to gain more. Such a condition might be termed an *optimum level of ignorance* (Rinehart and Lee, 1988). Just as it is not worth adding a third or fourth hour of practice once we reach our optimum level of tennis ability, it will no longer be worth attending school for an additional year or even taking one additional course once the optimum level of ignorance has been reached. We will have learned all we want to know at that time. If our circumstances in life change, such as getting married or desiring a higher paying job, so will our optimum level of ignorance.

Understanding the concept of optimum level of ignorance helps to clarify several problems that we see in the schools. One of the current major issues in public schools is knowing exactly how to deal with students whose optimum level of ignorance does not match the expectations set by the school. These "at-risk" students are currently the focus of numerous conferences, summits, and seminars all around the country. In the absence of being able to get these students to desire higher levels of learning, schools are forced to devote considerable time, energy, and funds to incarcerate them until they can leave legally.

On a less severe level, this concept helps to explain why some students, to the dismay of their parents and teachers, are satisfied with achieving less than their maximum potential. Given the tremendous complexity of factors that can influence human learning, one can observe students who give far less than their best or who do not try at all. Many students are satisfied with a C when a B is possible or settle for a B when an A is achievable. The lack of effort demonstrated by many American-born students stands in stark contrast to the recent outstanding achievements of immigrant Asian students.

The real cost of higher grades is inevitably judged by each student in terms of sacrifices such as money not earned from a part-time job, or an afternoon not spent enjoying friends. At some point the extra sacrifices necessary for improved achievement are greater than any perceived gain. At that point no additional academic efforts will be forthcoming.

No matter how much we might prefer it to be otherwise, in the end it is the student who compares the costs and benefits associated with one more year of school or earning a higher grade. It is the student who acts according to this personal assessment. As we shall see, ways can be developed to help a student desire more schooling, but the present structure of the public school system lacks the incentive, flexibility, and sensitivity necessary to deal with the problem effectively.

HELPING STUDENTS MAKE BETTER CHOICES

We must continue to keep in mind that we are still exploring how *individuals* perceive a situation. Unfortunately, children and adolescents may not always see things the way parents, teachers, and friends want them to. Conflicts often arise as to what really constitutes a young person's optimum level of ignorance. Decision-making, combining as it does a wide range of logical and emotional elements, is difficult for anyone of any age. A young student, lacking experience in the real world, is probably especially incapable of weighing all of the costs and benefits and hence is in a poor position to choose his or her optimum level of ignorance. This is perhaps the primary reason we have mandatory school attendance to age 16.

The decision-making process of balancing costs against benefits is unbelievably complex. Many of the costs and benefits can only be measured subjectively, and often reliable information is scarce. Such complications, however, do not mean that students should not, cannot or do not go through the process of weighing costs and benefits in search of their own optimum level of ignorance.

Parents, teachers, and community advisors should most definitely play a key role in helping students identify the relevant costs and benefits of education so that the most beneficial decisions can be reached. Students need help in choosing courses of study and levels of effort to expend. Ultimately, however, the individual student makes the final choice as to how much effort he or she will expend toward education. Concerned adults must recognize that the best they can do is to attempt to influence that decision in a positive

way through providing information, superior learning opportunities, moral support, encouragement, and incentives.

The National Commission on Excellence in Education report, *A Nation at Risk* (1983), called for longer and more
school days and years. What confidence can we have that
these measures will solve our problems? More to the point,
will parents and students perceive the gain to be worth the
higher cost? Commission members and educators cannot
measure for individual students and parents the magnitudes
of any possible gains and losses. Until a greater range of
choices is available, we cannot expect to get a better mix of
courses, programs and levels of education.

Decisions regarding the kinds and amounts of education
produced in this country are made by legislators and educators. Neither can possibly weigh and measure all of the
costs and benefits that ensue from their choices. Decision
makers bear little of the costs of their actions but receive
many of the benefits. This is especially true regarding expenditures on big-ticket items such as buildings or personnel.
More money for education means enhanced welfare levels for
politicians and educators. Moreover, the addiction to feelings
of magnanimity that come from spending other people's
money also encourages educational leaders to push for ever-
increasing educational budgets.

A brief historical survey of the percentage of per capita
income spent on education is all that is needed to document
this push for higher budgets. In 1950 the nation spent 15.7
percent of per capita personal income for each public school
student. By 1960 this figure had risen to 18.9 percent; in
1980 it stood at 24.8 percent; and by 1987 it was 27.6 percent
(National Center for Education Statistics, 1988, p. 95). Based
on the system's inability to determine the real needs of parents
and students, we can have no sure way of knowing if this
increase is either desirable or undesirable. Each person can
measure benefits and costs only as they affect him or her.
Students and parents may not necessarily assign the same

value to an expanded program as do state and federal legislators, superintendents of education, or members of a school
board.

Most of us would agree that education is very important
for children and young people. Just how important it is, one
person cannot determine for another. Yet all students certainly need at least some functional level of literacy to have
a fair chance at succeeding in our society. Some level of literacy is also necessary for social and political stability within
the nation, although exactly which level is best is debatable.
Many see some role for the government to play in defining
and financing this minimum level of literacy. But there is wide
latitude for disagreement over the exact extent of that involvement. A small but rapidly growing number of educators
and laymen believe that government has had far too much
control of the schools. Increasing parental and student choice
would be more compatible with individual pursuit of self-
interest. Ultimately each person must choose what and how
to learn.

Chapter 7

The Question of How Education Should Be Produced: The Problem of Cost

Because of society's limited resources, we want our businesses to produce efficiently. We want them to make goods and services at their lowest possible cost and pass that saving on to us as consumers in the form of low prices. The same wish holds true for the production of education. The evidence is overwhelming that public education in the United States is not cost-effective. Every day the cost of running our public schools and the taxes required to finance them go up. Getting the best return for the taxpayers' dollars in terms of both learning and satisfaction apparently is not a high priority item. Perhaps this condition stems from our almost sacred reverence for education, a reverence that stands in the way of raising the tough critical questions about the structure and operation of the public school system.

COSTS IN THE REAL WORLD

In the real world beyond the schools, goods and services

are produced by those who are willing to accept the cost of acquiring resources necessary to get them to their finished state and to market. If you wanted to manufacture shirts, for instance, you would have to accumulate the resources, necessary for that endeavor. The resources, or "inputs," such as a building, sewing machines, workers, electric power, and raw materials (including cloth, thread, and buttons), are necessary to produce your "output," which would be shirts. The money you spend in acquiring the necessary inputs would constitute your costs, while the money taken in when selling the shirts would be revenue. With a lot of hard work and some luck, your revenue will exceed costs and you will make a profit. That profit would compensate you for risking your economic neck and putting in the long hours, sleepless nights, and lost weekends to start and operate the business.

Unfortunately, the already complex enterprise of producing shirts and selling them for a profit is further complicated by other energetic people who would also like to make and sell shirts. The fact that others can go into shirt manufacturing, just as you did, serves to keep the pressure on you to operate efficiently and in the best interest of your customers. If you make a large profit, others will be enticed to enter the business. Competition will rise, prices will fall, and everyone's profits will shrink. What will ultimately emerge from this competitive process is a product that is most suitable to the buyer and at a price barely high enough to cover all costs.

In many ways the production of shirts and the production of education are similar. The producer of education uses a wide variety of resources such as buildings, land, workers (teachers, administrators, secretaries, etc.), equipment, and materials (books, paper, chalk, etc.). The output, while more difficult to determine, may be measured by the higher levels of knowledge and skills that students reach. But here the similarity between the two types of production ends. In many other respects the two are very different.

Almost none of the advantages the shirt customers receive

from shirtmakers are apparent in public education. Since public education is a government monopoly, competition is minimal. Contrary to most business owners, producers of education are influenced very little by the demands of their individual customers. Furthermore, since the government finances education, it does not have to depend on revenue from the sales of learning to cover costs the way a shirt producer does. Although schools pay for most of the inputs they use, the money to cover their expenses comes from compulsory taxes, not from revenue generated by sales. Public schools give their product away. In an alarming number of cases, schools can only try to give education away. Some students choose to reject "free" education by dropping out altogether.

The shirt producer constantly receives clear messages as to whether or not he is meeting the needs of his customers. Educators in a public school system, on the other hand, do not have and probably cannot have an accurate picture of how well they are meeting the needs of the community, parents, and students. To understand why educators have trouble getting an accurate picture, it is helpful to focus on the nature of cost and several of the factors that normally determine cost, factors that are typically not accounted for by decision makers in public education.

NO COST: FREE GOODS AND SERVICES

A first step in understanding cost might be to explore just what really determines the cost of anything, from shirts to education. Goods and services may be classified in terms of those that are free and those that are not. Free goods and services are unfortunately not very common. Aside from air, desert sand, and perhaps ocean water, virtually everything has a cost. In fact, in some places such as in outer space, deep in a coal mine, or in certain cities, breathable air is indeed limited and actually carries a cost. Even the ocean is not as free and unlimited as we once thought. We are reminded of its limitation when we read of floating garbage and oil slicks spotted hundreds of miles out to sea. The recent massive oil spill in Valdez, Alaska, reminds us once again of the very real costs related to using the "free" ocean for transporting goods. What makes something a free good, then, is not its lack of intrinsic value. Nor is it free because there are large amounts of it. Something is free if more of it is available than people want, even when the price is zero. Thus, in many places, air is available in larger quantities than desired by consumers, so, for them, it is a free good. It is not free at 30,000 feet in a jet airplane or in the Los Angeles community where the demand for clean air exceeds its availability.

The fact that virtually all goods carry a price stems from the nature of scarcity itself. As we saw earlier, to put any scarce resource to one use is to forgo the use of that same resource in some other situation. We can measure the cost of using any resource by determining the value of what was given up to purchase or obtain it. Price is thus a measure of this forgone opportunity. Unless a seller expects to receive a price at least high enough to compensate him for his lost opportunity, he would not be interested in going into that particular business or service.

As an illustration of the relationship between cost and scarcity, let us compare the leisure-time activity of a jogger and a book reader. The jogger will use more oxygen than the reader. This increased use, however, imposes no cost on the reader since an ample supply of oxygen is available for both of them. In fact, the number of joggers could be doubled, tripled, or even quadrupled without causing any appreciable effect on the reader's oxygen supply. The air a jogger breathes, therefore, has no cost because it imposes no burden on anyone else. A cost occurs only when someone's use of a thing denies a benefit to someone else.

Compare the case above with that of several individuals trapped in a coal mine without a source of oxygen. It becomes clear that, in such a case, oxygen does indeed have a cost.

The more oxygen consumed by any one individual or activity (such as burning a lantern), the less will be available for other individuals or activities. In this situation, then, oxygen does have a cost, a cost that is determined by what is being denied for other uses.

OPPORTUNITY COST AND EDUCATION

With the rare exception of free goods, all things are scarce; and since they are scarce, it is in society's best interest to pay close attention to how they are used. When anyone uses something that is scarce, someone else is automatically denied its alternative use.

As a rule, when we think of the cost of an item, we normally think only in terms of its monetary price. The monetary cost of attending a college football game might be $16 for a ticket plus $5 for parking. An obvious cost is the forgone items that could have been purchased with the $21. The total cost, however, should also include the value of what else could have been done with that same time. To the dollar cost of an enjoyable day spent in cheering on our alma mater, we must factor in the cost stemming from what we did not do. We gave up an opportunity to work overtime, spend time with the children, or just rest up for next week's grind. Our estimate of the actual cost of the game would have to take into consideration what we spent on tickets and parking in addition to what we gave up to go.

In *The Moon Is a Harsh Mistress*, award-winning science fiction writer Robert A. Heinlein portrays a rebellion of colonists on the moon against the government back on earth. The lunar colonists had to learn from the beginning that, other than rock, everything in their environment had a cost. The national flag of the lunar colonists was thus TAN-STAAFL—There Ain't No Such Thing As A Free Lunch. Unfortunately, here on earth we tend to forget that wisdom. Even though the lunch may appear to be given away, it is not. The food itself, the resources that went into the food's production, and the money spent in purchasing it could have been otherwise employed. What is sacrificed may be called the opportunity cost of the lunch. The person giving out the lunch could eat it himself, sell it to someone else, or even spend the time required to prepare the lunch some other way such as playing racquetball. That is the way it is for all scarce resources. When owners of resources use them in a particular way (for instance, choosing to donate money to a college or putting junior through that expensive prepschool), they must be rewarded. They must feel that the reward is in some way at least equal to the benefit they could have received by putting those resources into something else, such as purchasing a new runabout, a sports car, or just watching their investments grow.

The concept of opportunity cost all too rarely finds its way into debates over educational funding. While administrators often struggle with decisions over how best to use their allotted public funds, they do not consider alternative uses of money on the part of taxpayers. They do not consider the cost because they do not bear the cost. The educator (along with the school board) makes the educational decisions that establish how much you will spend (via taxes) and on what. A shirt producer, on the other hand, attempting to get you as a customer, must be extremely sensitive to the cost you will incur.

Suppose, for example, a friend takes you out to lunch and suggests in advance that he will place the tab on his business expense card. Lunch is free to both of you, and you will have little incentive to order conservatively. The real cost falls squarely on his boss's wallet. School administrators are in a situation similar to your lunch offer. Although they do not deliberately intend to waste money, the result is waste nonetheless. To them, zero or little cost is associated with spending taxpayers' money. The cost burden does not fall on the administrators doing the spending, but on the taxpayers. Happiness is spending someone else's money.

MAKING SPENDING DECISIONS—PUBLIC AND PRIVATE

Remember our venture into shirt production? As a shirt manufacturer, you were forced to weigh every cost very carefully. Failure to do so gives an edge to competitors who might be operating more efficiently. School boards and superintendents are not under the same pressure. Their business will not close regardless of the level of their inefficiency.

Since it costs educators nothing to spend other people's money, new school programs are constantly being initiated in spite of often small, dubious, zero, or even negative net benefits to their communities. Almost any program or initiative showing the slightest hint of beneficial results finds supporters and often funding. A standing joke in research circles is what is called the "superintendent's fallacy." If students with very low achievement scores in, say, math or reading are selected for a special remedial program, we can predict statistically that the average of the group will automatically improve due to a phenomenon called "regression to the mean." Improvement will occur whether or not the students are given any help. After all, they can only stay the same or get better—they cannot score much lower. Thus many so-called "successful programs" represent more of a statistical phenomenon than real progress.

As an illustration of how schools can often avoid making tough financial decisions, let us suppose that two programs are under consideration—one to improve reading comprehension of slow learners, and the other to provide enriched courses for gifted and talented learners. Let us further suppose that each program will cost $100,000 per year and produce positive benefits, but only $100,000 is available. The promoters of both programs will most likely push hard to insure that each program is funded despite the budget limitation. There is a strong possibility that such pressure will lead to higher taxes and $200,000 to fund both programs.

An individual person spending his or her own personal funds would painstakingly weigh the relative benefits of any two competing alternatives and would quickly realize that he or she cannot have both—to spend on one is to forgo the benefit from the other. The wise choice would automatically be to select the use yielding the higher benefit for the same expenditure of money. To increase the income necessary to pay for both would require working overtime or at another job, both actions imposing more cost. The school system is not nearly so constrained. The administrator is inclined to urge support for both programs on the grounds that they both produce positive benefits, and are vitally necessary for their respective students. Most importantly, the members of the administration will not personally pay the costs. The funds come from taxpayers. A typical administrator would pressure legislators or the school board for additional funding to support both programs. No private institution or individual would have that option. In those situations where budget pressures are felt, a typical result would be to keep everyone happy and half-fund both programs. Neither may actually help anyone when funded at this reduced level, but those concerned will be grateful nonetheless.

Although the above description of the budgeting process is admittedly oversimplified, the essential difference in incentive to economize remains. The budget decision-making process used by public schools is virtually devoid of the intense pressure individuals feel to economize or minimize cost. After all, only a few dollars will come out of the pockets of the school board members or the superintendent. On the other hand, our shirt manufacturer has a powerful incentive to economize. He must sell his product at a competitive price that he hopes will allow a profit. All of the revenues come from shirt sales, and if revenue is insufficient to cover costs, expenses must be reduced or the venture into shirt making will fail. How often does a school district meet that end? The inability of government decision-makers to make the most effective use of available resources is not due to negligence, stupidity, or malice on anyone's part; it is just the way individuals typically act when they are spending other people's money. A school principal, to take a second example, who would spend many hours agonizing over a decision to buy the best computer for the lowest price for his own child, might commit thousands of taxpayers' dollars to buy school computers with far less worry over price and quality. Also, he would rarely spend less than the budgeted amount, even if it were possible to do so.

It is important to note at this point that when we say that educators have no strong pressure to economize, we are not implying that they are totally without restraints. School boards and administrators examine budgets and provide some critical direction. If waste can be eliminated, more money can be made available for other programs in much the same way it is for private individuals. But since educators and school boards are always spending someone else's money, and not their own, the pressures toward economy are weak indeed.

COST AND EDUCATIONAL DECISIONS

The decisions each of us makes are strongly affected by how we perceive costs involved. Administrators, teachers, students, and taxpayers do not all bear the same cost burden.

Let us suppose that we ask a typical 17-year-old high school student to compile a list of all of the costs of her education for the year. She might begin by putting down expenditures for clothes (most 17-year-olds would place a big emphasis on this one), school supplies, club dues, special fees for band and labs, automobile costs (if she is lucky).

First Estimate of Costs for One School Year

Clothing	$500
Supplies, dues, and fees	$100
Automobile gas and maintenance	$200
Total cost	$800

If she stopped with only this list of expenses, the cost of her year in school would be grossly inaccurate. Apply the opportunity-cost concept and you will see why. First, most of the clothing and automobile expenses should not be specifically attributed to education. The truth is that our typical student would have incurred these expenses even if she had not attended school. Therefore, they should not be counted as educational costs. Second, she failed to list a major cost factor—the loss of income that could have been earned if she were employed full time rather than going to school.

If she did not have to spend seven hours each day in school and one or more hours devoted each day to homework and studying, then that time could be spent doing something else, such as working. If she worked 40 hours per week for 42 weeks at $4.25 per hour, she could earn $7,140 per year. We will not count the summer since school does not interfere with work during this time. Going to school means that this income is sacrificed, thus making it the largest single educational cost for the individual.

Revised Estimate of Costs for One School Year

Books, supplies and fees	$ 100
Not taking a job	$7140
Total cost	$7240

When we delete the cost of clothing and automobile expense and add in the lost wages, we get a much more accurate estimate of the cost to the student. The actual cost to the student of a year of education, then, would not be $800, but rather $7,240, a significantly different value. Of course elementary and middle school students would not incur the $7,140 wage cost since they cannot legally be employed.

At a conscious or subconscious level, individual students and parents do take into account these costs in their educational decisions, and rightly so. They personally bear the cost. It is the parent who is out $100 when supplies are purchased. And it is the student who forgoes the $7,140 in lost wages.

We need to emphasize that, for all but a very few students, the benefits of remaining in school and completing the requirements for a diploma far outweigh the value of a minimum wage salary. In fact, it is not unreasonable for communities to try to provide strong incentives to encourage young people to finish high school. Unfortunately, not everyone places the same value on completing school. Whether in high school, technical school, college, or graduate school, every student will eventually arrive at a time when the expected benefits of further formal education (such as prospects for a better job, greater pleasure in understanding the world, or better adjustment to society) are of less value than the costs of the opportunities they are giving up for the education. At this point, the student will choose to quit school.

It is interesting to speculate on the wisdom of using 16 as the magic age at which a student can legally leave school. Many students below that age are clearly being held in school against their will. Is a school as we traditionally envision it the best place for these students? Do we really need college-trained professional teachers to merely supervise these students? Would we be better off hiring psychologists and advisors to deal with these students instead of expecting certified teachers to supervise them? Would an alternative approach combining work and school be even more effective?

While parents and students do take into account the costs examined above in their decision making, other costs are usually ignored. Since education is "given away," students and parents do not take into account such costs as teachers' salaries, construction and maintenance of school buildings, utilities, transportation, special programs, and supplies. These are ignored because they are "free." Since parents would pay school taxes whether they have children in school or not, they realistically make no association of such costs with the decision to go or not to go to school. They are spending someone else's money. Students, therefore, often remain in school longer than they would otherwise. Students also undervalue their own education. They frequently avoid studying, fail to complete assigned homework, and refuse to pay attention in class. Another example of this can be seen in how most students take care of their school buildings, equipment, and supplies. Students who would never write on a wall or deface a book at home will often do so at school without a second thought. More education expense is generated than would be the case if all costs were personally paid by students and parents. By not having to bear these costs directly, many students often waste significant amounts of educational resources by just hanging on.

As an extended example of the impact of students who are forced to remain in school by law, consider the problems and costs that surround those at the middle and high school levels. These students often exert a strong negative influence on a school. They discourage teachers, cause a reduction in the personal freedom of regular students, use excessive amounts of teacher and administration time, and retard the educational progress of other students who would like to learn. The school uses already limited funds to provide special programs and special consideration. Most schools are forced to employ one or more administrative assistants whose duty it is to handle the discipline problems caused primarily by these students. The costs of this negative influence are not charged to the individuals themselves and are consequently ignored in their decisions regarding learning and personal deportment.

The limitations of free public education are much greater than most people wish to admit. These limitations were well expressed in an untitled article in the *Detroit News Sunday Magazine* (1981):

The truth is that the public school system can guarantee quality education only to certain types of children. These are the children who are obedient or creative and have a respect for the educational process and a desire to learn.

Not only must they be physically and mentally capable of learning on their own, but they must come from a family that cares for the child, respects the educational process and is willing to cooperate with the school system.

There are other qualifications, but these are the basic ones. True, some children who do not fit this game plan will succeed, but the exceptions are few and the failures are many.

It would be much more honest if educators would tell the public: We cannot educate the child who changes schools several times during the semester. We cannot educate the teenage alcoholic, the teenage junkie or the teenage prostitute. We cannot educate children who are hostile, violent or indifferent. We cannot educate the child whose parents are abusive, neglectful or apathetic toward the child and belligerent toward the school system.

That's saying it briefly, precisely, correctly. Education begins with the quality of the child and the quality of parents before it begins to take root in the classroom. It's best to get that priority in place before trying to evaluate the worth of a superintendent or the quality of a school system. Yet states and school boards feel compelled to spend significant amounts on programs which in essence are de-signed to keep those students off the streets and out of the job market (p. A4).

Certainly education is for all students, not just the brightest and most gifted. Schools ought to provide excellent oppor-tunities for all students whether gifted, normal, handicapped, or slow learners. Normal students constitute a significant mis-sion for the schools, one which is often forgotten in many secondary schools as they push for high-powered programs for students at the lower and upper ends of the achievement spectrum. Society, however, needs to seriously reconsider the costs involved in attempting to educate students who refuse to be educated. Savannah, Georgia, is spending $3 million a year on a program for at-risk students, and spokespersons for the project complain that it is not nearly enough. If this example is indicative, it leads us to ask just how much is enough?

Knowing that individuals compare costs with benefits and that many of the costs of public education are hidden because of the way it is financed opens up new possibilities for better decision-making. Society, for instance, is in a position to influence the level of education a student seeks by manipulating costs and benefits. Our current national concern about at-risk students reflects a strong belief that too many students exhibit too little interest in learning and subsequently drop out of school before earning a high school diploma. Putting more money into courses, buildings, and teacher salaries will have little impact on student incentive and consequently may generate only marginal improvements in educational achievement. The data collected by Chubb and Moe (1990) led them to conclude that more money will likely produce only insignificant gains in educational improvement. But requiring, for example, a certain score on a nationally standardized basic skills or subject matter test as a basis for eligibility for a driver's license would undoubtedly have a positive impact on educational outcomes for many students. It would raise the student's cost of not learning or, looking at the other side of the equation, it would raise the benefit for his or her staying in school and learning. The net effect is that one would expect educational levels to rise. Failure to pay attention in class or prepare homework assignments might result in failure and the subsequent postponement of the right to drive.

Cash awards for remaining in school and meeting designated academic standards might be another way to accomplish the same goal. Such a plan might, in fact, represent a far more efficient use of taxpayers' money for improving academic performance than investing in school buildings, teacher salaries, more media equipment, or outside experts.

Schools could charge tuition, thus raising the cost for the student, thus forcing each student to include more of the actual cost of education in their decision making. For students who cannot afford the tuition, work-study programs could be established. Again, the cost to the student would rise, forcing him to take it into account.

We need a new structure for our school system that can break free from the rules of the past and experiment with new methods and approaches. Such a structure must also have the capacity to jettison ineffective programs.

THE SPECIAL PROBLEM OF VESTED INTERESTS

Any move toward a more realistic weighing of the costs and benefits of education is highly desirable. As long as public schools remain a monopoly, however, our ability to do so will be severely limited. Enter the vested-interest phenomenon. People have a vested interest in any enterprise in which they expect to benefit or be harmed. Their benefit might be monetary or nonmonetary. A contractor might push for a new school building hoping for an opportunity to submit a winning bid. A school board member might promote a new building in the hope of having his or her name in big letters on the front.

Having people with vested interests is not necessarily negative, but it ought to remind us to be cautious. We must be particularly skeptical whenever people personally benefit from making decisions and running programs but do not personally pay the cost. In public education, vested-interest groups push for their pet projects as a way of life. The bigger the project or program, the better.

The power of vested interests is so strong that the solutions to our education problems will never spring from the initiatives of public school teachers, school administrators, or professional educators. Although they may have much to offer in the way of expertise, they have a powerful interest in maintaining the status quo. It is simply not possible for them to be completely objective and willing to make radical changes that might be potentially threatening.

People with vested interests always confuse the issue by making us feel that what they want is best for everyone. "Few responses are more natural than the sincere belief that those things which threaten our private interests also threaten the public interest" (Lee, 1986, p. 32). This is no less true for educators than it is when U.S. postal employees decry any plan allowing private firms to carry first-class mail. The consequence of adopting such a plan would undoubtedly produce radical changes, one of which would be unemployment and displacement among the ranks of U.S. postal workers.

If a person's job or income is threatened or disrupted, we can expect that person to oppose the cause of this ordeal of change. Do we really think medical doctors would vote in favor of expanding the number of medical schools and training more doctors with the effect of reducing their power and income? Could we expect lawyers to adopt reforms that would make entry into the profession easier or, more radical yet, require them to talk and write in language that normal, educated humans could understand? Could we expect accountants to favor a truly simple way to compute tax rates, say a blanket 15 percent? It should, therefore, come as no shock that society cannot rely on the education establishment to propose and carry out many of the necessary reforms in our school systems.

Suppose the school board decides to build a new high school. To be idealistic, let us further suppose that everyone with an interest is consulted about what should or should not go into it. What will the art teacher want? The music teacher? The physical education teacher? The football coach?

The principal? The guidance counselor? Each will push for all he or she can get with little regard for overall budget limitations. Why not? The building cost is going to be paid for by taxpayers even though the educators will derive many of the benefits from the new facility. None of these educators has anything to lose and all have much to gain by requesting as much money as possible. The bigger the budget the more amenities and power.

No one is really rewarded for efficiency. How many football coaches would earn a bonus for squeezing one more year's use out of the old uniforms? How many mathematics teachers would receive a salary increase for getting an extra year or two out of the old textbooks?

The tendency of educators with vested interests is to formulate grand designs for building and equipment, designs that are "absolutely essential" for the school system and the community. Anyone who opposes the resulting bloated budget will inevitably be seen as an enemy of education. The strongest supporters of tax increases for public schools are educators themselves. Much of their ardent support is based on the fact that they benefit personally from the tax increases and subsequent expenditures. Is there any wonder that schools never seem to have enough? Here again, educational decision-makers are not villains. They are acting exactly as one might expect them to act as rational human beings. The problem lies with incentives which are all wrong, and nothing we do will change that fact short of changing the system itself.

The following case illustrates the argument we are making. In a small town in South Carolina, voters recently turned down, by a margin of 3 to 2, a school-proposed 18-mill tax increase to build a gym, an athletic complex, and a fine arts facility. Responding to the defeat the school superintendent expressed his disappointment by saying, "We gave our citizens an opportunity to vote for the students, and, obviously, they don't think that education is important for our high school students." He went on to say that "voters used a tax excuse to ignore the needs of the students." He finished his statement with "I'm not giving up. Some kind of way, we will find a way to fund it because they need it" (O'Quinn, March 7, 1990, p. A1.). It is doubtful that citizens of that town are unconcerned about the education of their children. For them it is a matter of weighing the benefits of the new facilities against the lost benefits of what the 18-mill tax could have been used for. Such analysis explains the behavior of both parties.

The system must be refashioned and reformed from outside by citizens who have no conflict of interest with the proposals that are put forth. As Paul Berman (1985) said in commenting on Minnesota's critical examination of its educational system, "Tinkering with the status quo is not enough; the structure and incentives of public education must change" (p. 193). All possibilities must be on the table, and we should view them with open minds. We must stop assuming that schools must always remain more or less as they are now. But only when a consensus emerges can we pressure legislators into passing laws and adopting policies that will bring about meaningful reform.

Lasting and significant improvements in public schools can never come unless educators begin to incur more of the risk and cost when they make decisions. They must also be able to gain personally from any successful efforts to help students achieve important learning objectives. This is what free markets do so well, and it is to this concept we must look to seek lasting, positive change in our school system. It is clearly in the best interest of the taxpayer and the nation to deliver the highest possible quality of education at the lowest possible cost.

SUMMARY

Understanding the nature of cost and the production of education is complicated but essential in making better educational choices. Present decision makers do not factor in all of the relevant costs. We know that people do not treat free goods in the same way they do those that are not free, yet we continue by and large to treat education as a free good. This practice accounts for some of the poor results we get from our public schools.

Schools produce education in much the same way private firms produce the many items sold in the marketplace. Both use labor, capital, and raw materials to produce their products. Public schools, however, are a monopoly, owned and operated by government, and this greatly distorts the way they produce education. Students and parents do not take into account all of the costs when making decisions, often leading to unwise choices. Educators likewise do not consider all costs in their choices since they do not bear these costs—taxpayers do. Since education is given away, we tend to overspend and make grossly inefficient use of taxpayers' money.

Better decisions could be made if a better alignment of costs and benefits was developed. What is needed is to make certain that parents, students, and educators weigh more completely the real costs and benefits of education. Our current educational structure all but guarantees that the necessary information and incentives will never be available.

Chapter 8

The Question of Educational Quality: Can Government Provide It?

Education has been a hot topic in America for decades. Every generation seems to convene its share of blue ribbon committees to study why the schools are not up to snuff. Certainly society has undergone incredible changes over the last 100 years. Change is ubiquitous. Many things are different almost on a day-to-day basis—families are transformed, advances in technology are bewildering, economic patterns are altered, and social trends are modified. Our public schools, however, always seem to be out of phase and continue to fall far short of our expectations for them.

Educators, parents, and the public generally agree that students should be achieving at a considerably higher level, while at the same time developing a stronger sense of responsibility and self-discipline. Indeed, many feel that our national well-being, if not our very survival, depends upon how well schools can fulfill their tasks. Consensus breaks down, however, when we begin formulating specific avenues for change. There appears to be a kind of naive belief that if we could just put our shoulders to the wheel, we could achieve almost any educational goal. This belief translates into pouring larger and larger sums of money and effort into our schools, passing numerous complex laws, instituting copious reform policies; conducting endless meetings; and producing voluminous studies. Just like fixing an electrical appliance by jiggling or kicking it, these quick-fix approaches are fatally flawed and will fail to improve educational levels appreciably over the long haul. The problem lies in the fundamental design of the educational delivery system, and because of it, new money, laws, and policies will produce only modest and inconsistent results.

Consider the situation in the city of Chicago. In 1983 only seven of the high schools in Chicago scored above the national average in reading. The average score for the city's high school students on the American College Testing (ACT) program tests was 28 percent, significantly below the national average. The dropout rate for those entering Chicago's public schools was between 43 and 53 percent. Yet the city of Chicago spends $600 more per pupil than the average of all schools in the state and more per pupil than 31 of the 50 largest school districts in the nation (Walberg, 1989, p. 803). Money will not solve Chicago's educational problems. Nothing short of radical reorganization of the city's schools will provide any more than a band-aid repair.

We have failed to solve our school problems because we have been looking for solutions in all the wrong places. The failure of public schools to keep pace with our changing society is inherent in the system itself. The ownership and governing structure of the school system are at the root of the problem, preventing those who might have the ability and will to provide us with the greatest improvement from doing so.

THE PROBLEM WITH MONOPOLIES

The fundamental problem with our public schools, the one most ignored by popular reformers, is that public schools are essentially state monopolies. Government owns and operates them; it dictates which students can attend which schools and to a large extent what they must study and how they are to be instructed. One of the fundamental laws of human nature is that monopolies rarely, if ever, operate in the best interest of their customers. Instead, they exert exceptional energy to maintain, promote, and expand their own influence.

Society acknowledged the undesirability of monopolies at least as far back as 1890 with the passage of the Sherman Act and again in 1914 with the Clayton Act. These acts continue to give the federal government the right to prosecute and break up businesses that form monopolies and engage in monopolistic behavior. Yet public education is a monopoly sanctioned and protected by that same government.

Government monopolies are big on spending money and slow on providing service. They serve their own ends first and the customers' second. Slow progress, long lines, rising rates, complicated forms, regulatory minutiae, administrative inflexibility, and gross inefficiency are all evidence of a monopoly's interest in self-preservation and self-enhancement.

The constant increase in postage rates has prompted some to take a serious look at the U.S. Postal Service as a governmental sanctioned monopoly.

A General Accounting Office survey reveals the organization spent as much as $10 million on conferences last year. What were the Postal officials talking about over the $100-a-plate dinners? Probably about how they could push another rate increase past the taxpayers to cover next year's conferences.

At one three-day session at the Phoenician Hotel in Scottsdale, Az., about 200 postal executives ran up a bar bill of approximately

$12,000. They were not, it should be noted, spending their own money. The taxpayers footed the bill.

There were also conferences in Hawaii and Florida. As governments tend to do, the conferences were scheduled in winter. However, the conferees in Hawaii did show a little restraint. Their dinners only cost $58. Why is it we never hear of a government conference in Alaska during winter where the conferees sit around and eat hamburgers?

The Postal Service also granted bonuses to every one—every one—of the service's 75 divisional general managers. Well, they were probably tired out from going to all those conferences so they needed a boost.

As Postal Rate Commissioner John Crutcher said, "Surely some of them [the commissioners] were so bad, they should have been fired instead of getting an award" ("First Class Fiasco," March 21, 1990, p. 4A).

It should not be surprising, then, that in spite of well-intentioned recommendations of national blue-ribbon commissions, public schools remain faithful to their bureaucratic origin. The power of well-intentioned school boards and administrators notwithstanding, it is too much to hope that the true top priority of any school will be to meet the interests of the parents and students they purportedly serve.

Most schools remain in a perpetual state of uproar over a myriad of minor changes. New forms, new policies, new texts, new emphases—all keep teachers and students off balance and busy. As with other governmental monopolies, the absence of meaningful external pressure encourages schools to exhibit an aggressive resistance to most change. When change does occur, it is snail-pace slow, uncertain, and unpredictable. It is often poorly implemented, leading not only to disruptions in existing programs, but also to disillusionment and reticence toward future change. In fact, recent changes in the public schools, precipitated by the critical reform reports that appeared in the 1980s, often handicap good teachers. Overly restrictive teaching and testing prescriptions, along with enormous loads of paperwork, exacerbate an already desperate situation. If you really want the inside scoop on regulations, ask a typical teacher. He or she will undoubtedly share with you several horror stories of stifling mandates and piles of extra paperwork.

WHO MAKES THE DECISIONS?

Public education in the United States is financed, owned, and operated primarily at local and state government levels. Local boards of education are responsible for setting school policy subject to federal, state, and local laws. They hire school administrators, teachers, and other staff to operate the schools and carry out their policies. School boards, in conjunction with school administrators, make almost all operating decisions affecting schools. They formulate budgets; allocate money among schools, departments, and programs; establish rules for student and teacher behavior; and plan for new programs and facilities.

In recent years, strong governors and legislators have led to a steady increase in state control. Legislatures and departments of education have the power to require specific courses of study, set the number of school days, determine school and classroom size, choose textbooks, and so forth. Local governments contribute less money and exert less control than they once did. The earlier stereotype of community-financed schools under community direction is rapidly becoming a thing of the past. The share of school revenues accounted for by local government has fallen from 82.7 percent in 1929–30 to 43.9 percent in 1986–87 (National Center for Education Statistics, p. 148).

The federal role in education has primarily been one of guidance and direction. The federal government has had its greatest impact on special areas of national concern such as in programs for the handicapped and regulations against discrimination. The government also encourages the development of specific programs and policies through the provision of special subsidies. Special science education programs, audiovisual media, and school meals have all to some extent been federally subsidized. The role of the federal government is growing and pressure from many quarters continues to encourage its further growth.

Governmental groups and agencies at all levels, in one way or another, make decisions regarding how much is spent on education, what kinds of education are offered, and how education is produced. Parents and students, the true customers, have very little influence on what they receive and virtually no control over the actual decision making.

The what, how much, and how questions are all answered with little or no parental or student input. While taxpayers have legal ownership and control through their elected and appointed representatives, they have about the same influence on the actual operation of public schools as they do in guiding the activities of the police department, post office, highway department, or the Pentagon. As a rule, bureaucrats run and operate governmental agencies with only sporadic and fleeting input from dissenting individuals and groups.

Decisions about how education is produced are especially shielded from parental and student influence by educators and governmental bodies. Resources available for education may be assigned in a number of ways. Thousands of decisions must be made about such things as the number of students per teacher; the amount of audiovisual equipment made available; the number and size of school buildings and grounds; the number and types of administrators and auxiliary personnel required; and the types and amounts of materials such as books, magazines, and supplies. It is important to choose the best mix, the one that produces the most learning for the dollar. Our public schools are simply incapable of identifying that mix.

Is it cheaper to produce a given amount of learning with

one teacher, 20 students, a state-of-the-art classroom with skylights, modern architecture, and elaborate audiovisual capability; or with a teacher, 30 students, a not-so-state-of-the-art classroom, and no media? The fact is, school administrators and legislators can only guess at the answer, and the incentives to find out are limited. We have been consolidating schools for years, resulting in larger schools and increased educational sameness. We still do not know if this or some other way is how schools should be organized for maximum efficiency.

Government programs are run by bureaucrats appointed by higher level bureaucrats, who in turn are usually appointed by politicians elected by voters. At the base of all this are the voters, many of whom, for perfectly good reasons, are ignorant about the issues and the candidates' positions on them. In fact, given the bewildering number of decisions all of us have to make on a daily basis, no one can hope to know everything about every issue on which he or she needs to decide. As a consequence, many meritorious proposals and excellent candidates for office are defeated and other undesirable ones are adopted or elected based on such tangential factors as emotions, bandwagon psychology, physical attractiveness, party loyalty, and name recognition. Contributing to such outcomes is the practice of educators with vested interests lining up behind those politicians who promise them the most money and best working conditions. It is difficult to be confident that the programs begun by government are in the best interest of anyone other than the politician and his or her major contributors from the last campaign.

Making decisions under the best of conditions is difficult enough, but the routine misunderstanding and concealment of costs and benefits associated with governments simply serve to complicate matters even further. Governmental actions have numerous and intricate effects, many of which would be hard to understand even if a voter wanted to be informed. Indeed, politicians and bureaucrats are themselves

frequently unaware of hidden benefits and costs and thus
become easy prey for special interest groups who do understand. Education, then, is like almost all other governmental
enterprises, controlled at the highest levels by individuals who
will never be able to really know what is going on or what
is needed. And even if those who control the schools had the
right information, there might be little interest in using it for
fear of upsetting the status quo, offending special interests,
and worsening their own situation.

BEHAVIOR OF THE PUBLIC SCHOOL MONOPOLY

No monopoly has absolute power. As a political entity, the
public school system to some extent must respond to political
pressure. Because public schools are financed by taxes, taxpayers are sometimes able to influence school policies, procedures, and objectives. Community influence sometimes can
be beneficial, but educators are just as likely to feel intimi-
dated and restricted by these influences as helped by them.

As public agencies, school systems can be and often are
pressured by individuals and groups of all persuasions. Public
schools have only a limited capacity to deal with the diverse
pressures exerted on them. Although forced to be all things
to all people, the system is crippled—crippled by forces deeply
embedded in the political structure of the system itself.
Funded by local, state, and federal tax money, schools are
controlled by agencies that for their own survival must listen
to numerous, often contradictory voices.

School officials have strong incentives to protect their own
interests. Their response to diverse demands is almost always
to act in their own best interest, and that means in the direction of preserving the system itself. Frequently, such action
is not in the best interest of education. Sound pedagogical
principles are often sacrificed in the interest of appeasement
and self-protection. Course requirements are sometimes

watered down or made impossibly difficult. Grades may be inflated to make student achievement look better than it is, or they may be lowered to demonstrate high standards. Discipline may become lax to minimize the risk of lawsuits alleging cruelty and discrimination, or it can be inhumanely harsh in the name of law and order.

Government's ability to operate efficiently and in the public interest is inherently limited because public employees have a built-in conflict of interest between their personal welfare and that of the taxpayers. Bureaucrats are far less careful when spending taxpayers' money than they would be if they were spending their own. They are generally insensitive to costs imposed on citizens via their actions since they personally bear little or none of the costs. "Following the book" almost becomes an end in itself. It is safer for them to have endless piles of forms filled out in triplicate. The fact that the excessive paperwork prevents them from providing the very service they are charged with providing is almost irrelevant. Ordinarily, they receive no special personal compensation or incentives for saving taxpayers time or money. In fact, making programs work more directly in the interest of taxpayers would impose nonmonetary costs on the public officials; they would have to spend more time and effort in discharging their duties. Since a government worker would receive no direct compensation for a meritorious act such as working overtime to help clients or simply working harder or smarter, he or she would not often be so inclined. Legislators and government officials, like the rest of us, are motivated by self-interest. The fact that they profess lofty goals and selfless ends does not alter the fact that their actions are strongly directed toward their personal self-interest.

Although the staffs of some schools have made valiant efforts toward making their buildings desirable places to be, they are not really forced to do anything to improve student satisfaction or provide increased instructional efficiency. Furthermore, individual educators are frequently hindered by regulations and procedures that discourage and often prevent improvement. The nearly 30 percent of our students who fail to graduate each year is ample testimony that the schools are failing to provide satisfying experiences for a significant portion of our students.

THE PROBLEM WITH EXPERTS

We are often led to believe that professional educators are experts who know exactly what constitutes the "right" kind and amount of education. Remarkable similarity of schools and academic programs is readily apparent across the nation, but students are incredibly different in their interests, goals, learning styles, and abilities. The simple fact is that no one can know for sure what is best for someone else. Yet, we go on year after year permitting educators to make our decisions for us.

School decision-makers at all levels do not know what varieties and amounts of education are best. Furthermore, there is often an inherent conflict of interest between their personal needs and the educational needs of their students. For instance, when asked to resolve our education problems, English teachers argue for more required English courses; mathematics teachers for mathematics courses; guidance counselors for more guidance time; administrators for bigger, more sophisticated facilities and equipment; and all educators for increased pay and smaller classes. The self-interest motive is strong for two main reasons. Our perceptions of any problem are unavoidably linked to who and what we are. If our only tool is a hammer, then all of our problems look like nails. Thus, for reading experts, the obvious solution to many educational problems is more and better reading programs. Professional educators and politicians are no more neutral and unbiased about what education should be than is the auto mechanic who presents you with an arm's-length list of suggested repairs.

How do we decide which courses students should take in school? What should their content be? What teaching methods should be used? What standards should be set? What credentials should teachers hold? A set of requirements, teaching methods, and education practices has emerged in our public schools as a result of informal and formal compromises among education experts. In true procrustean fashion, all students are forced through this more or less uniform program whether or not it fits their particular needs. Parental and student input into the decision making is minimal at best. Is our problem that education is too important to allow mere students and parents to make choices affecting themselves? Hardly! It is nothing more than the "expert syndrome" at work.

Unquestionably, some schools are more responsive to parental concern than others. More often than not, however, it is difficult for concerned parents to get more than sympathetic smiles from harried teachers or administrators. After all, your child is only one of several hundred. Requests for special consideration are often shifted from office to office. Everyone is sympathetic but no one is able to help.

Education remains a state monopoly. In spite of our best intentions and the recommendations of multiple blue-ribbon committees, our schools are simply not working in the best interests of their clients. If we really desire to make progress in education, we would be well advised to abandon our expensive and unproductive attempts at finding some national consensus for patching up the moribund public school monopoly. A radical change is clearly in order. The question is, what kind of change?

THE POWER OF CHOICE

Substantial change must be made in the American education system if we are to produce significantly stronger students and satisfy societal, parental, and student concerns. Deciding exactly which specific changes are needed and how to accomplish them has formed the basis of many lively debates. The one essential conclusion that must be accepted is that the government monopoly of education must be terminated. The monopoly problem must be dealt with successfully before we stand a reasonable chance of making truly significant changes in the system. As a nation, we are throwing billions and billions of dollars at the education problem without any clear direction as to what kinds of education we should produce or what the best means of achieving our goals are.

In the private sector, decisions as to which goods and services to produce are dictated by what consumers actually purchase. Consumer purchases are a signal to businesses to manufacture desired goods or provide demanded services. The problem of how much to produce is answered by how much consumers are able and willing to buy. How these goods are produced is determined as businesses choose the least expensive methods of production forced on them by their competition. The most efficient firm can undersell competitors and thus keep the pressure on them to adopt equally efficient production methods or risk going bankrupt. Firms scramble to copy the techniques of more successful firms or they risk being eliminated. Those unwilling or unable to keep up are purged and the overall efficiency levels of the industry rise.

Where is consumer choice in the public schools? What if an unusually mature student wants a curriculum different from the one laid out by the state department of education? What if a student needs a different teacher with a unique teaching style? Outside of school, our power for obtaining what we want derives directly from our ability to withhold our purchase from one supplier and to buy from an alternative source. This power of choice is absent in public schools, where educators are able to do things pretty much as they see fit. Students are captive clients. Public schools do not ever compete with each other. Short of a general rebellion on the part of local parents (it happens once in a while, say with a controversial textbook, teacher suspension, or a threat to the football program), it will be business as usual. Missing altogether is the hard-nosed system of competition seen in the private sector with its checks and balances keeping expenses in line and products selling at competitive prices. Altruistic goals notwithstanding, public schools frequently seem to operate more in the interest of teachers, school administrators, and other special interest groups than in the interest of individual parents and students.

Teachers and school officials are not bad people who are trying to "do in" students and parents or cheat the taxpayers. Educators are much the same as noneducators. It is simply too much to hand power to anyone and expect them not to use it to some extent in their own interest. How many of us take two when the sign clearly says "Take One"? How often do we drive over the speed limit, especially when we think that the "blue light special" is not around? Perhaps we should not behave this way, but we do. If you ask the superintendent of the local school district to draw up the budget and decide for himself how much money he needs to run a good program, do not be surprised when your taxes have to be increased to cover his budget request. The school system with the biggest budget, the most teachers, the largest student enrollment, and the most modern buildings is usually a source of envy. It serves as a model to be copied. Bigness confers both power and respect.

Even if school administrators wanted to achieve higher levels of efficiency, they may not know how. No one can know what teaching strategies and methods will produce the best results until they are tested in a competitive environment. School officials do not know what students and parents want in education. Since education is given away and school revenues come exclusively from taxpayers, schools can continue with existing programs regardless of levels of inefficiency and parental dissatisfaction. No signals provide feedback that would tip off an administrator or teacher that he or she is providing the right product in the most cost-effective manner. In the private sector the loss of customers provides that signal, a signal that forces the firm to pursue an alternative course of action. It is in the firm's interest to know what consumers want and to experiment with different methods of production to keep costs and prices at competitive levels. This entire competitive element is missing in public schools.

PUBLIC EDUCATION IS NOT THE ONLY MONOPOLY

Federal, state, and local governments have given monopoly power through licensing to many other groups, and consumers are worse off as a consequence. States license teachers, medical doctors, dentists, optometrists, morticians, lawyers, builders, beauticians, barbers, plumbers, realtors, and so forth. At least 800 occupations are licensed by at least one state in the United States (Rottenberg, 1980, p. 2).

At first glance, licensing would appear to guarantee high standards of performance on the part of those who must satisfy the requirements for the license. But what occurs in most situations is that the occupation being licensed gradually takes charge of the licensing process and uses it to restrict competition. The monopoly power they acquire through this process gives them the ability to control their prices and the quantity and quality of their services which translates into higher incomes for themselves. State and local governments permit members of these licensed groups to sit on the boards that administer the licensing arrangement, and they become strong lobbyists for new laws that further increase their power and enhance their welfare. The foxes are in charge of the henhouse, and the outcome is predictable.

Generally consumers are not aware of the higher prices they pay for permitting monopoly. After all, how would a patient know if a medical doctor is charging more or ren-

dering poorer service than would be the case if more competitors were allowed in the medical industry? The evidence
shows that not only do prices fall but quality of service usually
rises when more competition is forced on these licensed
groups.

Most states, for example, do not permit experienced dentists from other states to practice dentistry in their states
unless they pass an examination. Many of these out-of-state
dentists either choose not to take the examination or fail to
pass it and consequently are denied a license to practice. Only
15 states have reciprocity agreements that allow their dentists
to cross state lines without being tested. A study was done
comparing average dental prices in the 15 reciprocity states
with average prices in the nonreciprocity states. As expected,
prices were lower in the reciprocity group of states than in
the nonreciprocity group due to the increased competition
brought on by the more flexible licensing in the reciprocity
states (Shepard, 1978, pp. 187-201).

Similar results have been observed in other areas where
recent court decisions have ruled against practices that prevented competition. The price of legal services fell after the
U.S. Supreme Court decision permitting advertising in that
profession. From uncontested divorces to wills and business
incorporations, prices have fallen in the face of rising competition (Falk, 1978, pp. 1, 21). A further example is the
declining price of eyeglasses in the wake of the Federal Trade
Commission ruling that bans on eyeglass advertising, once
common in most states in the United States, are illegal (Benham, 1972, pp. 337-52).

The point is a simple one. Many of the problems with the
public schools stem from the lack of competition. Enhance
competition, and education costs will fall and service quality
will rise.

We are often lulled into tolerating monopoly because
professional experts never cease telling us of their high-
minded concern for our well-being. This expression of con-

cern is usually followed by support for licensing laws that have the effect of restricting competition. Unfortunately, whereas we have a healthy suspicion of the motives and actions of most of those with whom we deal, we often have few suspicions when relying on the advice of a professional expert such as a medical doctor or educator. We tend to buy the story and the monopoly continues. In most other areas of our lives, the existence of many competitors and substitute products serves to protect us from exploitation, but for education, competition is severely restricted. This absence of competition puts us at the mercy of our monopoly schools.

A case in point is the current situation with Jersey City's public schools. The state of New Jersey recently seized control of Jersey City's public schools, alleging that "the 28,000-student urban system is academically bankrupt and rife with corruption, mismanagement and patronage" (Associated Press, October 5, 1989, p. A13). More specifically, the state cited political intrusion in hiring practices; poor test scores; failure to provide a safe, clean environment for students; violations of bidding laws; failure to provide for handicapped children; and unauthorized use of state funds as some of the reasons for the takeover. Unfortunately, these and other, similar problems are not all that unusual.

In Atlanta, Georgia, a biracial group of citizens from all socioeconomic levels is attempting to improve "the quality of the membership of the Atlanta Board of Education" (Tucker, October 7, 1989, p. A21). In the first election the group chose to influence, the public returned the "mediocre-to-poor incumbents to office." The inept school board incumbents were reelected largely because of support from the local teachers' union and municipal unions. Their support came because at least one of the incumbents came out in support of collective bargaining for teachers. The message is clear in the Atlanta case: teachers and other public school employees can often be counted on to promote their own interests at the expense of students and parents. This is not an isolated incident. It occurs in one form or another across this country from school district to school district.

Fortunately, citizens' groups can be tenacious. They can increase their efforts and strive to win the next time around, and sometimes they are successful. But they will never win the war, only an occasional battle or skirmish. Teacher and administrator groups are relentless in preserving the status quo because their jobs are on the line. For the educator, education is a full-time concern. Citizens' groups are here today and gone tomorrow. If we have learned anything from government regulation, it is that over the long pull, the regulated industry will capture the regulators and use them to their own advantage (Kohler, 1986, p. 244).

What is needed is a shift of decision-making power from the expert to the person or persons most directly affected—students and parents. If students and parents had the power to choose schools and alternative curricula, educators would be forced to give more weight to their clients' concerns. The focus would shift from the educators' welfare to that of their clients—the students and parents. In other words, educators would find it to be in their interest to pursue the best interest of their clients.

Each year we train millions of students for a lifetime of work and leisure. The fact that conservatively 50 percent of our secondary students do not find school to be satisfying should be telling us something (Glasser, 1986, p. 2). Educators cannot possibly know what value any particular student or parent attaches to a specific course or program. Nor can they know what alternatives students must sacrifice when they take a prescribed course. Society has a legitimate interest in promoting some basic level of education for everyone, but that does not mean society should control all or most of it and permit its production to be monopolized.

All human beings are in pursuit of their own well-being. Exactly what constitutes our individual well-being, moreover, is a highly personal matter that can be defined only by us.

What is happiness for one may be misery for another. Collectively, we are constantly making many choices, choices reflecting the bewildering variation in our interests and tastes. We buy different types of cars, different styles of homes, different clothing, different music, and different gadgets. In a free society, there are as many different interests, desires, and lifestyles as there are individuals.

All of our individual decisions are made by balancing the benefits we expect to receive against the costs we know we will have to pay. Education is just one of those things, albeit an important one, that compete with many others in our decision making. No single optimum amount or type of education is right for everyone. Individual wants, abilities, and interests are so different that it would behoove us to see that educational decisions reflect these differences. In the next chapters we shall discuss how we might better provide education by allowing more individual freedom and responsibility.

It has become very clear to many Americans that government-run enterprises, be they the mail service, highway department, or schools, do not and cannot consistently operate efficiently and in the best interest of their clients. We all too readily assume that the government, being a public, nonprofit institution, will and can look out for society's best interest. Growing numbers of citizens are realizing just how untrue this is, not because public officials and workers are unscrupulous or inept, but because they are exempt from the competitive market forces that impose discipline and direction on the rest of society. Those familiar with Murphy's Law have long since realized that, as far as government is concerned, Murphy was an optimist.

Granting the need for some very basic level of education for all citizens and the importance of academic excellence for those who are so inclined, the nation's schools ought to be and can be changed. They must produce the kinds of results that individual parents and students desire, even though these results may not always be the kind that experts might recommend. The answer lies with eliminating monopolistic power in public education and enhancing the range of options available to parents and students. The consequences of such changes will be greater general satisfaction with schools, stronger student motivation, greater parental involvement, and improved efficiency in school operations. Education is too important to be left solely in the hands of professional educators.

Choice will
— greater satisfaction
— stronger student motivation
— greater parental involvement
— improved efficiency

Part 3

Improving Education Through Choice

Despite all the speeches, debates, studies, reports, and articles concerning public education, little consensus exists as to why we so consistently get such poor results from our schools. Even less agreement exists as to which specific reforms would ameliorate the myriad of educational difficulties we face. Alternatively, blame has been placed on teachers, administrators, students, and parents. General goals such as "excellence in schools" or "schools second to none" have been advocated. Blanket recommendations for more money, better teachers, and more buildings have been proposed. In spite of these efforts, significant progress toward the production of better schools has been spotty at best. Most states are currently engaged in education reform of some sort. Reforms often produce higher taxes, bigger budgets, more regulations, and larger administrative staff but rarely result in significant gains in student learning.

More recently some school systems are approaching the problem of reform from an entirely new angle. They are adding the element of parental choice. Although certainly not the elegant solution many would prefer, this element suggests a direction for providing significant reform through increased incentives and commitment from educators, parents, and students.

Chapter 9

Putting Choice into the Educational System

It is difficult to begin any discussion of the kinds of reforms we are proposing without running headlong into a dense junk-yard of bandwagons and buzz words. Incompletely, poorly defined, or inadequately tried approaches such as accountability, deregulation, restructuring, performance contracting, deschooling, and voucher plans have all pointed in the right direction; a direction away from centralized, bureaucratic, monopolistic control of schools. All of these efforts represent attempts to increase a sense of responsibility for all those who administer, teach or learn in our schools.

TYING REWARDS TO ACTIONS

In earlier chapters, we explored some of the givens of human behavior. We know that all people are different, that they have their own ways of learning, their own interests, and their own aspirations. We know that people will always seek that which is in their own best interest, however they envision it. We know that people will be more committed to something for which they have ownership; ownership in the sense that they have invested time, effort, and money, and have some degree of control. In short, commitment is directly related to the extent to which a person bears the cost and reaps the benefit. None of these human traits is either good or bad, they just are. They describe how human beings normally behave. Giving parents and students some significant say in where and what students will learn is the only way we can take advantage of these very normal human characteristics. Subjecting schools to an element of competition and market discipline will produce better schools as we channel the energy available in this normal behavior.

Parents who have to choose their child's school and have the right to remove that child cannot complain that they are powerless. When problems or disagreements arise, they will always have the option of selecting another school that is more compatible with their needs. Teachers and administrators will tend to become more diligent in identifying which combination of curricula, instruction, materials, equipment, and social environment is best for teaching their students. The better they become at making such adaptations, the better they will be able to attract students and the more money that will flow into the school. Schools will have built-in incentives to explore new learning directions, to discard those that do not work and expand those that do.

For a wide variety of reasons ranging from economic poverty to mental and physical disabilities, some students are more difficult to educate than others. Such problems may be solved by building added financial incentives into the choice system to insure that special problems receive special consideration. It would be easy to envision a scenario in which students with special educational difficulties will be a highly desirable element in a school. Some schools will no doubt even choose to specialize in providing for their needs and thus become even more proficient at meeting these needs.

In order for any educational system to work well, rewards must be securely tied to effort. Individuals responsible for costs must incur those costs, and individuals responsible for the creation of benefits must be allowed to share in those benefits. Specifically, each student must receive direct compensation for appropriate and productive behavior and incur costs for inappropriate and unproductive behavior. Each employee of the school system must benefit directly from his or her positive contributions and be penalized for failing to contribute appropriately. Such a system forces people to become more directly involved and responsible for their own decisions and will lead to a more effective education.

In a typical school, when a teacher fails to prepare adequately for a class, he or she personally gains by having more time for other things that are more pleasurable or important, and the students are consequently harmed by receiving something less than the most effective instruction. The incentives to just get by with merely adequate or minimal classroom preparation and performance can be powerful. For the most part, teachers are neither rewarded nor penalized to any significant degree based on how well they perform in their classes. Current efforts at merit pay notwithstanding, pay raises are normally across-the-board and tied to years of service and advanced course work. As appreciated as end-of-the-year recognition banquets and awards are, these forms of compensation do little to improve one's standard of living or encourage one to "get psyched up" to create and innovate in the classroom. To borrow from Chester Finn (1987), "success brings no prizes, failure no sanctions, mediocrity no response at all except intermittent alarms sounded by distant national commissions" (p. 2).

Teaching certainly generates intrinsic rewards for doing a good job in the classroom, but so do many, if not most, other jobs. In addition, school rewards can be infrequent, small, and uncertain. Thus, we cannot place too much confidence in the current reward systems to produce dependably higher standards for our schools. More recently, some reform efforts aimed at producing higher academic standards have in fact reduced the intrinsic rewards of teaching. Teachers have been inundated with straitjacket curriculum requirements, standardized tests, and mountains of paperwork required for documentation. Our schools are not without their fair share of excellent teachers and principals, but by and large the system encourages and produces mediocrity.

Lack of control and ownership can have a tremendous influence over how education is perceived. The care of school property is one revealing example. Since students and parents do not own school property, who loses when a student defaces a desk and is not caught? Although technically that student and his parents own a tiny fraction of the desk, it is not that student's property in any meaningful sense. The real losers are the rest of the taxpayers of the community, state, and nation, who are forced to ante up and pay to repair or replace the desk. Likewise, neither the student nor his parents have much incentive to improve school property; after all, someone else will get the bulk of any benefit that might ensue.

Similarly, school administrators and teachers do not lose personally if property is damaged or misused. Although much time may be spent in attempting to locate the culprit and in filling out forms, a broken window is ultimately resolved by a requisition for a replacement. Compare that with the possibility of a broken window in a private home. We have a strong incentive to prevent broken windows in our homes since we bear the entire cost. Most of us are extremely careful with our own money. If we expect to see markedly improved schools, we must create an educational environment with incentives more closely tied to individual behavior.

Private industry provides a good analogy for understanding this issue. If a private industrial plant pollutes the air by releasing toxic substances, the firm benefits by avoiding the costs of disposing of it and the public is harmed. They have an incentive to pollute. If the firm voluntarily cleaned up its operation, it would suffer higher costs and possibly threaten its own economic well-being. So how do we get the firm to clean up its act and the air? Of course we could make pollution illegal, but the costs to society are much higher than alternative approaches. Another way society could deal with this problem would be to "internalize" the cost of pollution by placing a tax on the waste. For every ton of harmful waste pumped into the atmosphere, the firm would be harmed through higher tax bills. The firm would now have a built-in incentive to reduce pollution. An alternative method of dealing with the problem might consist of a government subsidy or tax relief granted to the firm for each ton of waste *not* pumped into the air. Still another approach would be to assign property rights to pollution as the city of Los Angeles is currently doing. A fixed amount of pollution is permitted for the city, and each polluter is given a license to pollute up to his share of that total amount. Licenses are bought and sold, and in this way only the most efficient firms can afford to own a license. These systems would lead to a reduction in pollution because it is in the interest of the polluter to consider the cost since it falls directly on him.

In the past we have berated polluters in hopes they would stop polluting out of embarrassment or civic pride. Such attempts at changing behavior through moral suasion almost always result in failure as anyone who has tried to talk someone else into losing weight or giving up smoking can attest. When it is not in a person's interest to do something, as he or she perceives it, it is a definite uphill struggle to change his or her behavior. Putting the burden of the costs of pollution on the polluters themselves through some tax or property right scheme makes it in the polluters' self-interest to cease or reduce polluting. The result is "voluntary" reduction in pollution.

In order to achieve better results in education, we must similarly internalize costs and benefits by tying them more closely to performance. Even granting the bewildering differences in student abilities and interests, we can obtain better teaching and learning. Good teaching and effective school management need to be rewarded. Inherent penalties should be incurred by teachers and administrators who fail to educate youngsters appropriately. Good decisions should generate rewards and thus encourage still more good decisions. Opportunities for such rewards are virtually impossible within the present organizational structure of the school system.

CURRENT EXPERIMENTS WITH CHOICE

One of the most exciting reform ideas to gain public attention in recent years involves increasing parental and student choice of schools. School choice increases the level of ownership and control by parents and students as well as responsibility by school personnel. Essentially, this system allows parents and students to select a school that is most compatible with their interests and aspirations. Choice has always been available to those with sufficient income to afford private education or a more exclusive residential section or who were able to take advantage of parochial education. The growing interest in choice is reflected in the fact that the U.S. Department of Education has now published a book for parents on the subject of choosing a school (Weston, May 1989).

Choice systems seem to fall into three distinct levels. At the lowest level, parents and students could select only from public school options. While fraught with serious drawbacks, this system is surely better than the current forced assignment of students to schools regardless of school quality or student interest. At a higher level, parents and students could be permitted to choose between public and private alternatives. Under this arrangement they could choose any public *or* private school. Each school would receive the public money allotted to each student selecting that school. At the highest level, public schools would be privatized; that is, public schools would either be sold to private investors or abandoned. The distinction between public and private schools would disappear, as all schools would be privately owned. Parents and students would select the school of their choice, and tuition would be paid to the selected school by the government. Government would no longer own and operate schools, but it would retain a role of financing education.

CHOICE AMONG PUBLIC SCHOOLS

At the present time, most experiments with choice are at the first level, choices among public school options. Only a few school districts provide opportunities to choose private schools. Five states (Arkansas, Iowa, Nebraska, Ohio, and Washington) joined Minnesota in 1989 in providing some type of choice system. At least a dozen other states have considered or are considering giving parents and students more choice. Numerous cities and school districts are allowing varying degrees of choice. Several surveys reveal the extent of public choice in the nation's schools; for example, *Public School Choice, National Trends and Initiatives*, and *Survey of State Initiatives: Public School Choice*.

Proponents of public school choice continue to develop ideas concerning its efficacy. Arguments for this position have been extensively examined by Joe Nathan, Senior Fellow at The University of Minnesota's Humphrey Institute of Public Affairs (1989) and Mary Ann Raywid, professor of education at Hofstra University (1989).

Three main variations of level one public choice plans are currently in evidence.

1. Parents are permitted to select any public school within the state regardless of their school district. This approach is currently being tried in Minnesota.
2. Parents are given a choice among various undifferentiated public schools within a single existing school district.
3. Existing school districts encourage individual schools to spe-

cialize in some area such as the humanities, mathematics, natural science, or the arts. Such specialized schools are called magnet schools and parents can choose among them.

Three elements are essential for the success of any choice system. Parents must be allowed to choose the schools that are best for their children. A student's share of public school taxes must follow him to whatever school he chooses to attend and stay with him until he leaves or graduates. Schools must be empowered to make educational decisions.

Proponents insist that allowing parents to select the public school they think is appropriate for their child would definitely benefit both parents and students. Competition among schools would force them to pay more attention to the wishes of parents and students. Teacher and administration interests would be better meshed with those of their clients. Putting the power of choice into the hands of parents and students will force educators to promote the interest of students with a seriousness that is not currently present. Educators would have to meet the diverse needs of their students as a way of meeting their own.

The incentive structure of choice plans is potentially more conducive to student welfare than is the case under the prevailing school structure. Failure to meet client needs could cause a loss of students and revenue, leading ultimately to losses in wages and jobs. Schools having difficulty in attracting students could experience an enrollment drop and a corresponding drop in revenue. This loss could be a serious threat to the long-term economic health and survival of the school. School districts involved in choice must be willing to accept school failure as a possible outcome as some schools may indeed be unable to attract enough students and money to operate. The obvious intent is to permit financial pressure to build on teachers and administrators in those schools.

Choice generates a better pairing of student and parental needs and interests with educational programs without requiring consensus. No one is under obligation to find the one educational program that is right for all students. No single method of instruction must be adopted in all schools or by all teachers. Schools are free to find and use what works. Public schools are presently almost forced into treating all students as if they have the same abilities, goals, and aspirations. Choice can bring about diversity in educational options and methods, and that is healthy. It can also serve as a reliable testing ground for determining the viability of existing educational approaches as well as discovering new ones.

The limited experience we have had with public school choice in Minnesota, Boston, and Harlem shows real promise for the future of choice. Where students and parents choose schools, there is less vandalism, higher daily attendance, lower dropout rates, better student performance, and more positive attitudes on the part of teachers and students ("Real Choice," 1989; Nathan, October 1989).

While choice among public school alternatives shows real promise and is certainly a step up from our present no choice system, its potential is far more limited than many of its advocates may realize. Even though independent in some ways, schools would be operating within the same bureaucratic structure and are apt to fall back on old familiar ways of doing things.

Despite initial successes in trial runs and strong arguments put forth by its proponents, public school choice is severely limited by the fact that most plans leave the governing structure of schools unchanged. Public schools would still be owned, operated and controlled by the same administrative organization. In short, schools would remain a public monopoly. Education would still be provided by a single supplier, therefore, competition would be minimal and bureaucratic ineptness just as great.

An analogy might help us understand why it is hard to be overly optimistic about public school choice. Suppose there are 5 hardware stores in town and you owned all of them.

How much interest would you have in allowing store A to entice customers away from store B? Such an effort would surely represent a negative-sum game for you. You would not only incur the expense of store A's programs to attract new customers but also the cost of the loss of customers at store B. Your incentive would be to keep all stores operating by coordinating their policies to maximize your overall profits. Even though the town has 5 separate stores, the hardware business is a monopoly that will prosper at the direct expense of your customers.

A choice system limited to public schools resembles our hardware business. Although there is some element of choice, the public school system would continue to operate as a monopoly. Competition will tend to be mostly cosmetic—just friendly rivalry. Indeed, there is a strong aversion to allowing public schools to fail. Some public school choice plans, for instance, allow schools that lose students to retain a portion of the allocated funds. The St. Louis plan, for example, permits schools losing students to retain half of the funds assigned to those students (Uchitelle, 1989, p. 302). Such a policy could have the perverse effect of rewarding the very school from which students are fleeing. Clearly such a plan raises the tax burden on taxpayers and sends the wrong message to schools failing to meet the needs of their students.

Public school choice plans will no doubt be further inhibited by district policies that limit the actions of schools by denying them the autonomy required to better serve the diverse interests of their clients. With state and local governments still firmly in control of the schools, what freedom would a school have to depart from district policy? Could a single school raise teacher pay levels above other schools in the district? Could a school adopt a controversial textbook, hire an unorthodox principal, employ an uncertified teacher, or implement a strict discipline code? Public choice supporter Evans Clinchy has observed this obstructive behavior in districts already experiencing choice. He states:

In all too many instances the policy of diversity and controlled choice has been installed as a citywide desegregation measure only to languish as the entrenched bureaucracy dreams up all sorts of ingenious reasons why it should not and will not work, why surveys of parents and teachers should not be conducted, why decision-making authority should not be transferred downward from the central bureaucracy to the individual school (Clinchy, p. 293).

Public shools will continue to be run by politicians who are influenced by various pressure groups—many of whom would oppose any change that threatens the status quo. Myron Lieberman (pp. 234-240), well known public school critic, has pointed out that since 80 percent of the nation's teachers are unionized, union contracts will prevent the schools from having the flexibility they need to respond to parent and student wants. Others support particular programs in which they have a strong interest, giving little or no consideration to their overall impact on education quality. This is the educational equivalent of pork-barrel politics.

Public school choice systems do not change the basic control structure because they do not remove government from ownership and control. Given that the monopoly remains intact, public school choice proponents would seem to be entirely too optimistic with their claims. In assessing the merits of public choice plans, John Chubb and Terry Moe (p. 208) captured the essence of this concern by pointing out that "Choice becomes part of a big compromise among contending political powers—no one loses jobs, no bad schools are closed down, vested interests remain securely vested, the basic structure of the system stays the same."

CHOICE BETWEEN PUBLIC AND PRIVATE SCHOOLS

The second level of choice, the one that allows choices between both public and private schools, clearly would be superior to choice limited to public schools. With public and private school options, the range of choices would expand considerably and competition would be a lot keener. Under the current system, public schools in most areas face little threat from private alternatives. The public schools have to be incredibly weak or the private schools incredibly strong for private schools to pose any serious threat. With this second level of choice, public schools would face meaningful competition from private schools as well as other public schools. Many improvements in education would flow from this arrangement. After all, it is market discipline induced by competitive forces that holds the key to real school reform.

Having the government finance coupons or vouchers that can be redeemed for educational services at public or private schools removes the present major financial obstacle that deters many parents from choosing a private school option. Tuition charges at private schools, on top of public school taxes, are simply too much of a monetary burden for most parents, so they opt for the "free" public school.

In attempting to describe some potential outcomes of public/private choice in education, Amherst College professor Heinz Kohler (1990) has summed up the possibilities very well:

[M]any different types of schools would emerge; large schools and small ones, schools stressing the arts and schools stressing science, schools stressing general education and others vocational training, morning schools and afternoon schools, segregated schools and integrated ones. Instead of taking whatever a public school board decreed, parents could tailor their children's curriculum to their own tastes! They could spend a part of their certificates on a Monday-morning all-boy art school, another part on a Tuesday-to-Thursday-afternoon coeducational science school, and another part on a Friday all-black vocational school. Parents could buy whatever services they deemed best for their children.

There would be room, too, it is argued, for teachers and administrators to experiment and make greater progress in their fields.

Those who had a brand-new idea could open a school and test it out. They would not have to launch a full-scale political campaign to persuade the school board, other civil servants, or legislators of the soundness of their ideas. If successful, they would be swamped with applicants, have big revenues, and expand. Other, less successful schools would find their pupils and revenues evaporating and would have to conform to the consumers' choice or go out of business! This important feature of competition is entirely lacking in public schools. Because they operate on tax revenue, they can provide bad services and still survive (p. 583).

Chubb and Moe (pp. 219-225) have also come out in full support of public/private choice. They have outlined their version of this plan in some detail. Basically their proposal is similar to the voucher plan that Milton Friedman (1962) championed several decades ago. Their proposal has received extensive favorable reviews in recent months and should significantly influence public policy in education for years to come. Briefly, their plan would include the following elements.

1. The state would set minimum criteria for public or private schools receiving public money as well as establish requirements for graduation and teacher certification. Any school, public or private, meeting basic state standards could apply to accept students and receive public money.
2. Existing school districts could continue to run their public schools any way they choose.
3. The state would establish and fund a district Choice Office that would handle the administrative responsibilities. The Choice Office would receive all education money and dispense it to the schools enrolling the children.
4. Districts could govern their schools any way they choose, but they would be limited to the revenue they receive from the Choice Office. That revenue would be based on the number of children who voluntarily enroll in their schools. No add-on charges to the basic scholarships paid by the Choice Office

would be allowed by private or public schools. Citizens would be allowed, however, to raise taxes to supplement the amount coming from the Choice Office.

5. Each student would be free to attend any public school in the state or any private school that would accept him. An application process would be established with minimal restrictions on the schools and would guarantee each student a school.

6. Every effort would be made to provide transportation for needy students.

7. Each Choice Office would have a Parent Information Center to assist parents and students in choosing among schools and to process school applications.

8. Schools would have the autonomy to make their own admissions decisions and set their own tuition. Schools would also be allowed to expel students and deny readmission.

9. Each school would have the sole authority to establish its own governing structure and internal organization. There would be no state textbook selection committees, in-service training requirements, and so on.

10. Statewide tenure laws would be eliminated, although teachers would have the right to join unions and engage in collective bargaining.

11. The state would see that schools meet procedural requirements such as conforming to nondiscrimination laws but would not hold the schools accountable for student achievement. Parents and students would hold schools accountable through their freedom of school choice.

Just a few years ago, only a few hardcore optimists would have held out much hope for a public/private choice plan. Yet, today the signs are increasingly favorable. Because of the courageous and energetic efforts of state legislator Polly Williams and Wisconsin governor Tommy Thompson, for example, Milwaukee started the nation's first real experiment with educational vouchers in September 1990. Over the strident objections from the Milwaukee public school bureaucracy, the city will pay $2,500 to 400 low-income children toward tuition cost at several private schools (Fund, p. A14).

The second level of choice, when evaluated in terms of educational improvement, is preferable to the first level, which is limited to public school options since it reduces the influence of cronyism and special interest groups. But it lacks the real power of the third level (privatization), which offers the highest rewards in school reform and improvement. This third level will be explored in greater depth in the next chapter.

With very few exceptions, parents want the best for their children. No one cares more about your child than you do. If you do not take the responsibility for your child's education, neither will anyone else. No one knows more about your child's strengths and weaknesses than you do. No one knows more about your child's personality than you do. No one knows more about what motivates your child than you do. No one knows more about the kind of environment you want your child to experience than you do. No one knows more about the kind of philosophy you want your child subjected to than you do. The list is endless. And the beauty of choice is that schools can differ in philosophy, environment, disciplinary standards, dress codes, programs provided, homework requirements, grading standards, staff policies, teacher qualifications, facility standards, and so forth, in order to accommodate each child's requirements.

Chapter 10

Privatizing Public Schools: The Best Approach to Choice and Excellence

As important as universal education is, we all too often confuse the ends with the means. A public sense of responsibility to see that all citizens are provided with some minimum level of education does not necessarily mean that government at any level should own and operate schools.

In many other areas of life, government makes requirements of citizens and leaves it up to each individual to decide how best to meet that requirement. Liability insurance, for example, is required of most automobile owners, yet the insurance companies that provide the coverage are privately owned and operated. Automobile owners are free to pick the protection of their choice. The government's mandated insurance coverage does not simultaneously obligate the government to go into the insurance business. The federal government guarantees a certain amount of food for needy families, yet it does not own and operate farms, food processing plants, and grocery stores. Deserving individuals are given food stamps that can be redeemed at privately owned grocery stores. These stores in turn can present the stamps to the federal government for cash. The federal government, to take a third example, gives scholarships and guaranteed loans to worthy and needy college students, but, with the possible exception of the service academies, it does not own or manage federal universities. In each of these cases there is a tacit assumption that government cannot produce the needed service effectively and efficiently. As a society, we have wisely kept the government restricted to relatively few enterprises. Education is one of those enterprises that would have been better off with far less than the current level of governmental involvement.

Current efforts at providing parental choice among public schools and sometimes between public and private schools is a bold step toward meaningful educational reform. These efforts represent significant movement away from the lock-step homogeneity that presently defines our traditional schools. When parental choice and competitive schools are available, the levels of energy, variety, and learning expand rapidly. Limiting the role of government to the point that education is provided entirely by competitive private institutions would consistently generate these educational benefits.

THE PRIVATIZATION ALTERNATIVE

The inherent weakness of government ownership of various enterprises has become increasingly obvious. Privatization (government conceding ownership of various public institutions and enterprises to private organizations) is growing in popularity all over the world.

Privatization is on the rise because private firms can better serve the interests of customers and society than can government-run enterprises. The continuing disintegration of the iron curtain and the move toward greater individual freedom within the Soviet Union and its satellite countries attest to the growing recognition of this fact. Around the world private money is flowing into business endeavors once dominated by government. This broad trend toward privatization and governmental deregulation is encompassing both developed and developing nations.

Mexico's new president, Carlos Salinas, is trying to modernize Mexico's faltering economy by divesting the government of nonstrategic public enterprises. In 1982 there were 1,155 public companies in that country. Now less than 392 are government owned and the privatization process continues as hotels, sugar mills, airlines, and steel mills have been sold to private concerns (Ortiz, September 15, 1989, p. A11). The government benefits from an initial infusion of money from the revenues gained from the sales. The entire country gains from the fact that most of the enterprises sold were losing money. Once sold, they no longer require taxpayers' subsidies.

Even in the United States, governments are divesting themselves of fire departments, sanitation facilities, transit systems, and prisons. They have come to realize that privatization saves money and provides better quality service. Were it not for the lobbying efforts of the vested interests, primarily government employees, the movement would undoubtedly expand even more rapidly. E. S. Savas (1982) has written an excellent little book identifying public activities that could be privatized with great savings to the taxpayer. He has provided both theory and practical examples as well as guidelines for privatization.

PRIVATIZATION AND CHOICE IN THE GI BILL AND PUBLIC HOUSING

Having the government rely on privatization as a means of meeting its responsibilities is not without precedent. The federal government's approach to veterans' education after World War II and to public housing in recent decades represents an attempt to privatize those two functions. The GI Bill program was set up at the end of World War II to provide returning veterans with the educational opportunities they missed during the war. GIs were assigned a specified amount of money to attend any school of their choice—private or public. They were given the power to choose the school with the program most compatible with their individual interests. They were also free to transfer to other schools if their needs or interests changed. The government never owned or operated its own special schools for veterans. The GI Bill program has been recognized by almost everyone as a great success.

Conversely, in an attempt to deal with the very real problem of inadequate housing, the federal government has built, owned, and operated public housing projects for the poor for many years and has received extremely low marks for its efforts. The record, in fact, has been generally abysmal. Specifically, tenants have not received the type of safe, clean, and well-maintained housing they would prefer and the program has been handled very inefficiently. Housing quality is low and expenses to the government are high. Poor upkeep and high crime rates have resulted in the deliberate demolition of entire housing projects, some only a few years old.

Recently a new approach to providing housing was started by the Office of Housing and Urban Development. This office provides publicly funded housing credit to those in need. The credit can be applied toward rent for private housing. The poor, in search of housing, are thus able to select suitable privately owned housing and have the rent paid directly to the owner by the government. This plan leaves the power in the hands of renters rather than landlords or government bureaucrats and has resulted in a lower overall cost to taxpayers. The landlord cannot charge more than competitive rental rates and must maintain the property at high standards or tenants will take their vouchers to another landlord who will provide better or more housing for the same amount of money. The government does not have to build housing, repair housing units, or get involved in the day-to-day operation of rental units. This is a far superior system to traditional public housing projects.

THE NEW ROLE OF GOVERNMENT IN EDUCATION

Having the government sell its schools does not necessarily free it from financing them. Our national commitment to universal education will insure that government continues to finance most of the cost of basic education. Financing might work in much the same way as the food stamp program. Food stamps are provided to all those who qualify. The stamps can then be taken to any grocery store and exchanged for goods at prices set by competitive markets. The store is reimbursed in dollars by the U.S. government for the stamps collected.

In education, each parent could be given a learning coupon for each child. These coupons could be redeemed by the school or combination of schools in which the child is enrolled. The schools would in turn be reimbursed by the government in a dollar amount equal to the amount currently spent by the government for the average student.

Any difference between tuition charged and the dollar value of the coupon would be made up by parents and perhaps private scholarships. Competition between schools would control overall tuition levels and thus any additional cost charged. If parents felt that one school charged too much, they would be free to change schools the same way they change supermarkets when they think one is becoming too expensive.

Since the public would be picking up the tab, some limited controls would be necessary. Schools would be free to set their own policies (so long as laws are not broken) regarding such concerns as admission and retention policies, hiring and firing practices, methods of instruction, operating hours, types of equipment and materials used, tuition charged, and salaries paid. Students and parents could select any school as long as it complied with minimal government standards. States and localities would still retain the power to make certain education-related laws and set the amount spent per pupil. States would undoubtedly choose to require that all schools meet some minimum requirements. Such requirements, however, should be limited to absolute essentials. Over-regulation would simply turn private alternatives back into the inefficient public bureaucracy we have now.

States would also be concerned with making sure schools did not break existing laws against discrimination. Privatization should enforce both the letter and the spirit of laws governing equality of opportunity. Historical inequities and special educational problems might be remedied in a variety of ways. Minority or disadvantaged students, because of the increased expenses associated with helping them catch up, might be given coupons with larger financial value than non-disadvantaged students. These students would thus bring more money into their schools and become highly desirable and sought-after members of a student body. Schools might choose to educate them in smaller, better-equipped classes and would have the funds to do so. Special opportunities for travel and enrichment might also become part of enrichment programs. Administrators would also recognize that they might achieve greater gains for these students by not isolating them from the positive role models provided by stronger students. Special students, whether gifted, disadvantaged, or otherwise exceptional, might even be given special scholarships to further increase their opportunities.

NEW DIRECTIONS: FACILITIES AND FACULTY

For generations teachers and administrators have been able to imagine many ways to improve education, yet they have been frustrated by an inability to see these ideas implemented. Privatization would provide a much wider forum for successful ideas. Entirely new and currently undreamed-of possibilities for schools would open up. With the phenomenal growth of computerized networking, students anywhere in the country could have access to almost any expert or resource. Chemistry students in rural Iowa could receive special lectures from and interact with an expert in Boston. Students in South Carolina could take a "live" tour of the Rocky Mountains via VCR or computer with CD ROM.

Buildings, land, and equipment currently owned by our public schools could be sold for any use whatever. Many existing facilities would no doubt remain schools and be occupied by some of the same people who operate them now. Others might be bulldozed or turned to other uses. New schools would appear.

Schools might spring up almost anywhere and in almost any configuration. Nothing would prevent, for example, a shopping mall school in which students move from place to place to be taught by specialists much as they do now with private music, dancing, or art lessons. Students in depressed or rural areas might be bused to and housed overnight in special enriched facilities for a few days each week or several weeks each term. Gifted science and mathematics students from rural Georgia might spend two days each week in a special science laboratory at a college or science school in Atlanta. Many new options would be possible through the savings afforded by competition, scholarships, and special incentives for special students and the savings from greatly reduced administrative costs or special charges above the coupon value. Schools would be as diverse in their offerings as parents and students are diverse in their interests.

Privatized schools would hold real promise for the educational mavericks, those teachers who do not seem to conform to the status quo but probably do a splendid job. These creative and gifted teachers, who cannot conform to the rigid regulations of today's schools with their set curricula and elaborate lesson plans, have few alternatives. With this new system they will be free to attract their own students and start their own schools. And even if they choose to teach for other school owners, they will be prized and appropriately compensated for their efforts because the emphasis in a competitive, deregulated system is on *results*.

MAKING CHOICE AND PRIVATIZED SCHOOLS WORK

Any change as radical as privatization is going to take some real effort to make it successful. Probably the greatest challenge will be to keep from adding so many rules, regulations, and standards that the new system is little better than the old. We would be in effect rebureaucratizing the whole system. In order to give privatization a fair chance, several basic conditions must be met.

1. *Parents and students must have the freedom to choose any school they want.* They must ultimately be responsible for evaluating competing schools and selecting the one most compatible with their own interests, needs, and aspirations. The fact that some will undoubtedly choose wrongly should not be used to support the case that no one should be able to choose. We would do far better to educate the parents on how to choose rather than remove the option of choice. If a school once chosen does not live up to expectations, parents should be free to choose another.

2. *The money must go directly to the school selected.* Money provided for each student should go directly to the school itself.

The school would be able to bill the government on a weekly, biweekly, or monthly basis, thus permitting students to transfer if necessary or desirable. The potential loss of students and money is as important to the operation of this system as the potential gain of students and money. Ineffective schools will be reformed or go out of business. Effective ones will be rewarded.

3. *Each school must have the right to set its own tuition.* Schools must be free to set their own tuitions even if they are higher than the coupon amount. All schools would not necessarily charge more than the coupon amount, since they would be in competition with other schools to provide the most education at the lowest cost. Failure to minimize cost and tuition would put inefficiently run schools at a competitive disadvantage with other schools.

With schools free to set their own prices, we can expect that those which are currently exclusive and expensive will remain that way. But barring the institution of some sort of a means test (say, an income of less than $50,000 per year) as a condition for receiving a coupon, this will be unavoidable. People with more money have more choices in almost every area of life. This is a fact with which we will always live regardless of the type of school system we have.

The real advantages of choice will accrue to those with middle to lower incomes. For these families the options will increase. More of the beneficial aspects of currently exclusive schools will become available to these students.

4. *No school would be exempt from any antidiscrimination laws.* Under any system schools must comply with the same laws that regulate other privately run businesses. Using the choice system as a vehicle to deliberately resegregate schools would be impractical, socially unacceptable, and illegal. Choice will not resolve all of the current problems resulting from segregated living patterns, but nothing in the concept itself supports deliberate discrimination. Indeed, with a greater emphasis on ability and performance, there would be less tendency to discriminate on the basis of race, sex, or religion. Furthermore, nothing precludes society from instituting special incentive plans that encourage

schools to enroll and support students who are culturally, ethn-
ically, or economically different from the majority. Varying the
dollar value of coupons depending on social priorities could put
otherwise ignored minorities at a competitive advantage.

5. *Each school must have complete autonomy.* Although they
would have to comply with general laws and standards, power
would shift from state departments of education and existing
school boards to local school owners and administrators. The
degree of regulation at the state and federal level will always be
a threat. Privatized schools that are overly controlled by regulations may represent little or no improvement over public
schools.

6. *A wide variety of educational approaches and structures must
be tolerated.* Everyone must recognize that education and
schooling will be seen in very different ways by different people.
Aside from some minimum fundamental skills such as reading,
writing, and arithmetic, no one set of facts, skills, or attitudes
can be proven absolutely essential for all students. Nor has any
one universal method of instruction proven to be most effective
for all students. Each school must be free to establish its own
faculty, student body, institutional style, and delivery system.

   Teachers in competitive private schools would pursue the development of their skills with a new seriousness. The hunt would
be on to discover and implement what works, and woe be unto
those schools that consistently fail to produce results. Their failure to satisfy parents and students will lead to lean times and a
subsequent attitude readjustment. Who knows what fantastic
old or new instructional techniques and methods will eventually
prove to produce the best results? Successful techniques will be
tested and will survive. Those that do not work will die or be
modified. The incentive to innovate, research, and implement
better ways of producing learning will be there constantly.

7. *New schools must be allowed to form and disband relatively
easily.* Anyone who is willing to invest in a school—from existing
teachers and administrators to creative business people—should
be allowed to do so. Since school owners would have to put the
money up front to start their school, it will be the owners' money
at risk, not the taxpayers'. The merits of any school would rest

on its capability to attract and meet the needs of students. Schools failing to attract enough students should receive no more support or subsidy than any other failed business. Those who are able to provide the education that parents and students want and do it efficiently will do well. The real power rests with students and parents who can vote with their feet if the school does not satisfy them.

Parents would become better consumers of education. They would learn to evaluate their schools more accurately. They would gain valuable information from school failures as well as successes. The very fact that some schools are successful would indicate that these schools are meeting the demands of parents and students. Unsuccessful schools would demonstrate the opposite. No more taxpayers' money would be wasted on the continued operation of ineffective and unresponsive schools.

8. *Schools would not be allowed to form monopolies.* Schools would not be allowed to collude on pricing and management decisions, nor would they be permitted to merge to the point of creating a monopoly. The government would have the responsibility to maintain competitive markets here in the same way it does for all businesses. Current laws regarding unfair trade practices (false advertising, for example) would also apply.

WHAT RESULTS COULD WE EXPECT?

When Thomas Edison invented the first practical phonograph in 1877, it would have been impossible for him to even begin to anticipate where the recording industry would go. As brilliant as he was, how could he anticipate such things as synthesizers, CDs, digital cassette tapes, and stereophonic sound? In the same vein, those who are currently promoting the privatization of public schools can only begin to anticipate the changes and improvement in store for education.

Since private individuals would own each educational enterprise, their personal money would be at risk. Combining the freedom to set up private schools for profit with the pursuit of self-interest puts enormous pressure on the providers of education to be inviting, efficient, effective, innovative, and sensitive to customer interest—traits largely missing in the present school system. Instances of parents being forced to tolerate weak programs or woefully inadequate teaching would diminish. Schools would be forced to compete by providing the most educational value for the coupon.

Providing students and parents with a choice of schools serves as an even more powerful force for school reform than one might think. The reason is simple. A relatively small number of customers can have profound effects on the economic viability of any business. Every business needs a minimum number of customers to break even. New enterprises work very hard to reach that magic number. A business does not have to lose all of its customers before getting into financial trouble and risking bankruptcy. We are often surprised to see an establishment go out of business even though they still have many customers. It happens all the time. Let us assume that George Bush Elementary needs 500 students to break even financially. Anything less than this number will produce a loss, anything more a profit. If the number of students enrolled is 550, then 51 students (less than 10 percent of the student body) have the power to force the school to reform. If 51 students leave George Bush Elementary for another school, the school could no longer break even. Of course, if more than 51 students leave, the school's financial situation would become even worse and the pressure to reform more intense.

Just as other industries are constantly on the lookout for newer and better ways to produce, competition would force schools to imitate or even improve on the successful programs of successful schools, and the quicker the better. The benefits of workable plans thus would be disseminated rapidly throughout the educational establishment and tested with a level of commitment that is almost impossible to imagine within the public school system. Conferences and conventions would take on an entirely new air of seriousness. Somewhere out there is education's answer to Ray Krock or Sam Walton waiting to provide an educational approach that offers meaningful learning in ways that meet the needs of millions at a fraction of the current cost.

These exciting possibilities form a sharp contrast to the present static and often unmanageable practices that are prevalent in the public school system. In many school systems, change is seen as merely an unnecessary imposition and an unrewarded burden. Program variety is discouraged because it creates additional headaches for the administrators who must institute and monitor and for teachers who must implement.

With greater choice through privatization, the whole incentive structure would be changed. Changes would become a common occurrence and school faculties would have high stakes in making innovations work. The message would be clear: cause learning of the kind parents and students want or go broke. University of Georgia professor Dwight Lee (1986) has pointed out the importance of competition in improving educational quality:

[T]he most effective thing we could do to improve the quality of education in America is to make educators compete for the consumer's dollar. As long as educational consumers have to pay taxes to support public schools, and have little choice in the public schools their children do attend, our public school professionals will continue, whether consciously or subconsciously, to view their students as captive clients. Public educators have often taken advantage of their captive clients by paying less attention to the concerns of their customers and more attention to their own well-being (p. 26).

The spotty current efforts toward merit or incentive pay notwithstanding, little connection currently exists between teacher effectiveness and rewards for that effectiveness. If all schools were private, teacher and administrator compensation would be based on their contribution to the primary

mission of the school. A school's profit would be tied more
directly to the performance of the teacher in the classroom.

Competition would develop between schools for capable
teachers and administrators. Teachers capable of producing
outstanding results with their students would become more
valuable. Since effective teachers would be difficult to replace,
their value to their employer would become increasingly obvious. Undercompensated educators could seek employment
at competing schools where rewards more closely matched
performance. Ineffective teachers and administrators would
come under increasing pressure to improve or face low salaries or dismissal. No longer would schools be forced to hide
ineffective educators. Retiring on the job may no longer be
an option.

A significant acceleration of variety would lead to significant improvement in education. The diversity of educational
offerings would soar as parents and students would choose
schools and programs based on educational preferences reflecting their own uniqueness. Each school would undoubtedly seek to develop its own unique character. Arts, sciences,
classics, philosophies, or social graces could all serve to give
a distinctive emphasis on which to build a school. Parents
and students would select according to their personal
preferences.

But what of those parents or students who need help in
making a wise selection; who will help them? Since government already has an information gathering and disseminating
role, these efforts could be expanded to include education.
Community agencies and charitable organizations would no
doubt move in to assist those who desire additional educational direction yet lack the ability or experience to provide
it for themselves. Students who cannot obtain good advice
at home may find assistance from an educational counselor
provided by the "Y," Boy's Club, church, or perhaps some
altogether new organization such as an organization of retired
educators. Inexpensive reference books similar to those cur-

rently available for college and career selection will no doubt be published, giving pertinent information on schools and the important factors in making good selections. One such publication has already appeared in response to the choice plans currently available (Weston, Nathan, and Raywid, 1989). Schools will no doubt be evaluated and ranked in much the same way colleges and universities are today.

Each school would have a strong incentive to advertise its unique programs and thus provide additional information on which to base decisions. We see extensive advertising at the college level as competition for students increases. A single letter or telephone call will bring piles of pamphlets and brochures detailing programs and course options. Colleges and universities employ full-time personnel who prepare such information, distribute it to prospective parents and students, and advise those requesting it. Even more promotion would occur within a privatized system at lower levels.

Aspects of education that are currently ignored or examined only periodically would probably become hot topics. Methods of instruction would become open topics of debate among professionals and laymen alike. *Time, Newsweek,* and *U.S. News and World Report* would all carry the latest breakthroughs in educational research just as they now do with medicine, science, and technology. But progress would go beyond mere discussion. The most effective methods would win out over ineffective ones. Rewards would abound for those using the latest and best approaches. Presently, the incentives for change are very limited, if not negative. Today, new methods, regardless of how effective, initially create more work and stress without yielding any tangible benefit for the teacher or administrator. Under privatization the extra hours spent developing new teaching skills would lead to a tangible payoff.

Serious social problems such as the current concern over at-risk youth will not disappear with choice and privatization. What will happen is that more diverse methods for helping these students will be researched and implemented. Privatized schools will provide more alternative opportunities for disadvantaged students. The stakes in terms of a teacher's or administrator's well-being will certainly be higher. They will have even more incentive to develop solutions. Special schools, programs, and teachers will appear, and those offering the most effective solutions will set the pace for the rest of the field.

Meal programs and perhaps other special forms of services could be an important part of developing a worthwhile program. If children cannot learn now with inadequate nutrition, this will still be a problem with privatized schools and will require a solution. It is even possible that the level of nutrition would improve since the meals provided by private institutions would not be required to use the high-fat government surplus foods schools use now.

Where long distances between schools are involved, transportation may be necessary for insuring a true choice. No doubt arrangements will be made by some schools to cover transportation as part of a student's tuition. Schools may choose to own their buses, subcontract buses from independent companies, or subsidize fares on public transportation. Who knows what transportation opportunities will be developed for students who choose to commute long distances from home? Overnight stays might be one simple solution. Another might be a classroom built into a bus or train car. Students could finish first period while on the way to school and seventh period on the way home.

Another solution would be to have the local government issue a voucher for each student equal to the amount currently spent on each student for bus transportation. The government would then get out of the school transportation business. Alternative systems would arise in response to the potential opportunities afforded. Parents could spend their vouchers on taxis, buses (public or private), or use the money to pay for a portion of their private automobile expenses incurred in transporting their children to and from school.

Privatization of the nation's schools will cause the type and amount of education to vary greatly across the nation. Americans are a diverse people, pursuing many different goals. Although some goals are more popular than others, none can be proven absolutely right or wrong. Consequently, we should expect education to vary widely in terms of how it is defined and produced from community to community and from school to school. Nationally, a system of education giving parents and students free choice among privately owned and competing schools offers the best chance for our realizing the full potential inherent in our tremendous national diversity.

Chapter 11

Common Criticisms of Privatization and Choice

Converting to privatized schools represents a radical departure from the public school system as we know it. Many concerns have been raised regarding anticipated changes, concerns frequently expressed in defense of the status quo. We would like to present and evaluate some of the more common arguments. While it is impossible to predict all of the effects emanating from a privatized school structure, modest inference can provide sufficient grounds for forecasting some outcomes.

Most, if not all, of the complaints directed at the privatization plan for education have also been directed at other reform plans involving choice among public schools and choice between public and private schools. The complaints against privatization, however, are much more strident. The following list contains some of the more common criticisms followed by the authors' response.

1. Private schools may not give proper attention to socially important topics such as AIDS education, nutrition, or careers.
2. Privatization will cause some schools to become resegregated.
3. A system of private schools would be unfair to the poor and disadvantaged.
4. Many parents would not or could not make appropriate educational choices for their children.
5. Educational standards would surely fall under a privatized system.
6. Privatization would dehumanize the schools. Students would be viewed only as dollar signs.
7. Choice plans may be workable for cities and other densely populated areas, but they will never work in rural areas where students have to commute long distances.
8. Transportation would be a problem for many students and thus place a limit on their freedom of choice.
9. Many students and teachers could be hurt by the transition to a new system of privatized schools.
10. Some students are so disruptive or problematical that no school would admit them. What would happen to these students?
11. Fraudulent and dishonest school owners and teachers would take advantage of students and parents.
12. Why go through all this trouble since a privatized school system is no cure-all?

CRITICISM 1

Private schools may not give proper attention to socially important topics such as AIDS education, nutrition, or careers. Arguments as to whether or not students should be taught such special topics aside, the simplest way to handle the problem is to require all schools accepting government coupons or vouchers to teach the particular information desired. If we feel very strongly that all students should know about the dangers of AIDS, let us say, we could simply specify this and leave it up to each school to meet the requirement any way they want.

As an analogy, take the case of seat belts in cars. The federal government deemed it necessary that all automobile manufacturers selling cars in America provide seat belts and passed a law to that effect. The federal government did not find it necessary to produce and install seat belts in order to have this standard met. Or consider the federal government's ruling requiring that banks divulge to the borrower the annual percentage rate (APR) of interest they charge their customers. Banks in this country are privately owned and operated. Banks must comply with the law or risk serious penalties. The government merely monitors the process to make sure the interest rate education is given to each customer. In a similar manner, specified education topics could be mandated for all schools even though the schools would be private.

We might add parenthetically that every government regulation reduces freedom and productivity. We often fail to realize that government regulations carry a high price tag in terms of monitoring costs and increased product price. Citizens have a right to impose restrictions and regulations, but these should be used more judiciously than is currently the case.

CRITICISM 2

Privatization will cause some schools to become resegregated. Although some population shifting would undoubtedly take place, it is doubtful that schools would become any more segregated under a privatized school system. Many public schools are presently highly segregated because of housing patterns. Urban ghetto areas are good examples. Desirable or not, such a pattern is legal as long as deliberate racial discrimination is not the cause. Under privatization, minorities would be given tickets out of the presently segregated ghetto schools. By using both school tuition and transportation vouchers, the range of schools open to students in the presently highly segregated schools would expand greatly.

Schools would be required to abide by the law; they could not discriminate against students. Under a choice system, if a student elects to remain in a school in which he is in the majority, then that student is there by choice. On what basis can we argue that it ought to be otherwise?

Students under the present school system are assigned to schools based on where they live. For whatever reasons, many neighborhoods are highly segregated. Since schools, especially elementary schools, are typically located in neighborhoods, they tend to reflect the prevailing housing pattern. In some states a nonwhite parent with a child in a segregated school may have the option of transferring to a school in which he or she is in the minority. They may also choose a private school where they would have to pay the tuition and transportation cost to that school. Presently, most parents choose to do neither.

It is interesting that polls show a higher percentage of nonwhites supporting choice among public schools as well as voucher systems than whites. In a 1986 Gallup poll, respondents were asked the following question:

In some nations the government allots a certain amount of money for each child to any public, parochial, or private school they choose. This is called the "voucher system." Would you like to see such an idea adopted in this country? (p. 58)

Fifty-four percent of nonwhites answered positively against only 45 percent of whites (p. 58). In a 1989 Gallup poll respondents were asked: "Do you favor or oppose allowing students and their parents to choose which public schools in this community the students attend, regardless of where they live?" Sixty-seven percent of nonwhites favored such a practice, while 59 percent of whites supported it (p. 43). We could speculate that minority parents, at least those in the lower economic levels, see choice as a way to gain the leverage needed to obtain the education they want. Otherwise, they remain at the mercy of public school administrators. Perhaps someday the racial composition of schools will be no more an issue than is the percentage of minorities choosing a particular style of automobile.

CRITICISM 3

A system of private schools would be unfair to the poor and disadvantaged. Providing choices among private schools would help the poor and disadvantaged far more than it will the wealthy. Under the present system, the poor and disadvantaged possess the least power and fewest alternatives. They are limited to the often inferior schools to which they are assigned. Generally, schools in more affluent neighborhoods are significantly superior to those in the poorer areas. Where is the protection for the poor and disadvantaged under the present system? The poor cannot afford private schools, so they are trapped frequently in inferior public schools.

The recent struggle over choice in Milwaukee, Wisconsin, has emphasized this very problem.

The Milwaukee schools battle has become quite a spectacle. The parents who want to opt out of the public system are virtually all black, from relatively poor neighborhoods. They have watched a mostly white establishment promise reform, changes and better days ahead for years, while their children went down each day to the same failed schools and fell behind their suburban counterparts. Now this same establishment is using litigation and judges to sue the parents' alternative schools into oblivion and corral their kids inside the establishment's brick buildings. (Poor Schools)

Under a choice system, they would have realistic alternatives. They could choose to move to better schools or different schools. Choice, in itself, would guarantee a competitive environment that would make schools *want* to serve the poor and disadvantaged. The poor would gain control, and through control they could demand and get more of the kind of education they want. Power would shift from the educator producers to the parent/student consumers.

Earlier we pointed out that only a relatively few students could exert significant competitive pressure to make a school responsive to student and parental needs. The transfer of 10 or 20 percent may be all it takes to threaten a school's economic security sufficiently to keep their attention riveted on student and parental needs and concerns.

CRITICISM 4

Many parents would not or could not make appropriate educational choices for their children. Those who make this argument probably have one or two things in mind. They may be assuming that parents do not really care enough about the welfare of their children to make wise decisions or, even if they care, they are unable to make wise decisions. They assume that special knowledge is required to make appropriate decisions and that only an educated person would have that knowledge. We reject both assumptions.

Most parents of poor and disadvantaged students care very deeply about their children's future. It may not be easy to detect sometimes within the present school system because they are powerless and locked into particular schools and programs. What choices do they have? With the possible exception of severely disturbed parents, all parents want their children to succeed in life, even when they themselves have not. If given a real choice, we believe parents would vote with their feet and transfer if the schools their children attended did not provide a good education. This is what the record shows where choice has been implemented in some urban schools such as East Harlem (Fliegel).

As far as the second assumption about the inability of parents to make good decisions is concerned, this is nothing more than the vested-interest syndrome at work. The argument that only the educated can judge how good a school is, is patently untrue. Does anyone accept for a minute that only a mechanic can tell if your car is operating as it should? Or only a trained musician can tell when a chord is not struck properly? Or only an artist can appreciate the beauty of a sunset? Surely most parents know at an instinctive level whether or not their children are learning. Parents can generally tell if their children are enthusiastic about going to school. Children who are learning love to share what they are learning and demonstrate their newfound skills.

Furthermore, competition for students would guarantee some level of advertising. Schools would pour out all kinds of information about their programs. The reputation of the good schools would spread throughout the community as would the reputation of the poor schools. With choice goes power and with power any parent can reject weak schools and choose better ones.

Parents will undoubtedly make some unwise decisions. Certainly everyone makes poor decisions sometimes. All of us learn from our mistakes and use our newfound knowledge to improve the quality of our future decisions. Each positive and negative experience adds to the pool of knowledge available for future decisions.

A few parents, a very few, will not care about their children or be able to decide for them. The government will no doubt choose to set minimum standards as a basis for paying the vouchers, and this would provide some protection for the children of those few parents. Cases of criminal parental neglect are with us now and will remain with us. Perhaps under a privatized system the school staff will have more at stake in helping victims of neglect.

Under any circumstances, there must be allowance for a wide diversity of school types, programs, and options. All good schools will not be good in the same sense. Students are diverse in interests, abilities, and goals, and schools should reflect these characteristics.

It might be instructive to remember that we already have a limited choice system on the college level. Many children from poor or immigrant families choose colleges and graduate every year. Financial aid is available to the needy and this aid can be used at any college, public or private, as long as the college meets minimum standards. Parents and students are permitted to pick from hundreds of colleges across the nation, and the options available present so great a diversity in programs and standards that no one would assert that all colleges are equal in any sense. The information necessary to make the right decision is available from a wide variety of sources. Students and their parents are assisted in their difficult decision by teachers, counselors, commercial publications, clergy, neighbors, friends, and the colleges themselves through advertising.

CRITICISM 5

Educational standards would surely fall under a privatized system. High educational standards is one of those buzz phrases that everyone seems to understand in a vague sense, but even experts disagree on how these standards should be measured. By whatever measure, educational standards would rise under a system of private schools. Polls continue to show that many parents are generally displeased with the performance of our present schools. Under a privatized system those displeased parents would shop around for better schools, and their power to do so would be transforming. School owners would have a powerful incentive to provide students with the best possible offerings.

Some schools will no doubt maintain lower standards than others. But if the blue-ribbon commissions that have studied the American public school system for the past decade are correct, standards are already depressingly low for many of the nation's public schools. Under a privatized system, the educational level of the whole system would rise and this is where the focus should be, not on an occasional school here and there with low standards. Yet even weak schools will never be able to survive without the support of parents and students. After all, they maintain the right to leave the school that fails to satisfy them.

CRITICISM 6

Privatization would dehumanize the schools. Students would be viewed only as dollar signs. To argue that a private school system would dehumanize schools demonstrates a clear misunderstanding of the working of a market economy. We suppose that those who express this argument are concerned that privately owned, profit-making school owners would not care about student welfare: they would be indifferent to the needs and interests of their students. Such an argument is based on the false assumption that caring is a relevant aspect in quaranteeing school success. What is more to the point is whether the school meets the needs of the students. What is true is the frequent widespread dehumanization that is so evident in many of our public schools, all protestations to the contrary notwithstanding. Without some external discipline, educators cannot be counted on to act consistently in the interest of the students and parents they purportedly serve.

A market-oriented, competitive school system would force every successful school operator to be less self-centered. Only by catering to the personal interest of the student/client could he achieve his own interests. School people would quickly learn the lesson long ago mastered by successful businessmen: the better you serve your customer, the better you help yourself. Such a system guarantees the advancement of human welfare rather than just hoping that benevolence and altruism will somehow emerge to solve all of our problems.

CRITICISM 7

Choice plans may be workable for cities and other densely populated areas, but they will never work in rural areas where students have to commute long distances. Since many of the current experiments with choice have been conducted in urban areas, there is a temptation to believe that the system will be unworkable in less populous areas of the country. The assumption seems to be that where people are geographically spread out, it will be economically unrealistic for anyone to provide educational options for these people.

Living in small towns and rural areas has always had its drawbacks. This is why millions of Americans emigrated to the cities in the first place. Almost 75 percent of Americans now live in urban areas. Those who choose to remain in rural areas do so because for them the advantages outweigh the disadvantages. Limited shopping and cultural opportunities are compensated for by less crowding, greater personal safety, a slower pace, and a stronger sense of community.

Under the prevailing educational system, students have no real choice in either rural or urban areas. A private school choice system would not make it any worse for students in rural areas, and it definitely would increase the options many fold in urban areas.

We are not convinced that there cannot be more schools than we now have even in rural areas. The United States has been consolidating public schools for many years, eliminating small ones and forming fewer, bigger schools. There is some evidence indicating that the educational and economic advantages that many saw in consolidation are simply not there (Fox, pp. 273-296). A privatized system may provide a mechanism for reversing this trend and create more schools in urban and rural areas if this proves to be the case.

People who choose to live in rural areas have far more options than are commonly recognized. Small towns may have only one grocery store, one service station, one drugstore, one bank, and so forth, but any monopoly power that one might see there is illusory. These single sellers are held in check by the willingness of consumers to go out of town to buy. Excellent highway and communication systems encourage rural consumers to explore other opportunities. Shopping has become regional and, with the growth of television and shopping by catalog, national. The phenomenon of the shopping mall, in fact, depends on the willingness of the consumer to drive longer than normal distances. All stores in a county or group of counties are in competition with each other. It is nothing for many consumers to drive 50 or a 100 miles to shop.

A privatized school system would work more or less the same way. The competition would not be just between the two elementary or high schools in town, but between the schools in a county or region. Carpooling and special busing services would no doubt arise to facilitate such options. Of course, parents always retain the same rights they have today. One could remain in town and patronize the only school, or move to another place to live where there are more school alternatives.

Yet these counterarguments are far too provincial in scope. The tremendous boom in electronic options already presages opportunities that up to a few years ago could have been imagined only by dreamers and science fiction writers. Telephone/computer networking would allow an individual child or groups of children to learn from teachers and resources anywhere in the country. The current growth of laser disc technology is already allowing children to interact with teachers and other students far beyond their local communities. The Peach Springs School located on the Hualapi Indian Reservation in rural Arizona represents an excellent example. Isolated from other schools by 35 miles, the historically undereducated children of this region have access to resources unavailable even in some big city schools. Through the use of laser disc technology, they are able to interact with computers to strengthen their skills in areas such as language arts and science ("Laser Disc," Spring 1990, p. 8). Fax machines can provide exchange of test papers, essays, and many other essential documents. To limit our vision of rural education to a bleached out, ramshackle school building housing all grades is limited indeed.

Even if the worst case occurred and a local monopoly school was able to take advantage of parents and students by providing low quality education at high prices, the pressure would grow for another school or new alternatives to enter the market. Such a threat of competition is often all that is needed to keep a business operating in the interest of its customers. One final point: any group always has the right to form a charitable or humanitarian organization for any legal purpose. If the local school is truly inadequate and no alternatives are forthcoming, charitable groups could be encouraged to set up nonprofit alternative schools. Surely this would always remain an option and a check on any potential monopoly.

CRITICISM 8

Transportation would be a problem for many students and thus place a limit on their freedom of choice. Under a school system based on choice, transportation patterns would definitely change. How much and in exactly what ways cannot be predicted.

The current locations of the nation's schools were determined by school boards and school administrators often generations ago. Political factors frequently influenced these location decisions. Under a privatized system school buildings would be located with an eye toward the interests of students, parents, and limiting costs. The location configuration that would emerge may or may not be similar to the present one. Obviously the problem of getting students to and from school would be of immense interest to school operators as much as it is to any other business.

The fact of the matter is that parents probably should bear the cost of getting their children to and from school, and most could do that with little expense or inconvenience. Having to provide transportation over long distances would be a hardship for some, especially the poor. Some method of providing subsidized transportation for students would allow a much higher level of competition between schools and would work toward making schools even more sensitive to parental and student needs. But the necessity of providing for transportation does not require that the government own and operate buses.

One solution to the problem would be to have the government offer some form of transportation allowance to each parent equal to the current cost of running the government-owned school bus system. Parents could use this allowance in any way they choose to transport children to the school of their choice. By giving them a transportation subsidy, the government would, in effect, be opening up many more choices for students in both rural and urban areas. Such a plan would be preferable to having the government own and operate a transportation system. Under this allowance plan, parents would be encouraged to consider alternative schools knowing that all or a significant part of the transportation cost would be covered. We could anticipate many private entrepreneurs going into the school transportation business and the surfacing of many creative and economic ways of handling this problem.

CRITICISM 9

Many students and teachers could be hurt by the transition to a new system of privatized schools. Without a doubt some difficult adjustments will be a necessary part of the transition from a public school system to a privatized one. Risk and temporary discomforts are always a significant part of the price of progress. We cannot achieve excellence with the same people, doing the same things, under the same conditions, and in the same locations. Excellence and the status quo are incompatible. If we choose to pursue excellence, we must be willing to pay the price of change.

Most of the resources currently employed in the production of education will no doubt continue to be used, at least in the short run. The major change at first will be a change in ownership and incentives. School buildings will be bought by private investors and operated by teachers and administrators who already are knowledgeable and skilled. Behaviors would be altered, however, as a clear and decisive shift of control from professional educators to parents and students takes place.

Some teachers and administrators will no doubt need to relocate or find other lines of work. Many teachers who find job security within the current monopoly to be a powerful incentive for staying may choose to leave. This exodus will be easily balanced by an influx of former and prospective teachers seeking freedom, rewarding opportunities, and new challenges.

Borderline and incompetent teachers and administrators will find themselves forced to improve or find alternative work elsewhere. Some buildings would be closed and others built. In time many changes will occur as innovation and new technologies become profitable investments. It is hard to contain one's enthusiasm when contemplating the exciting changes that the unleashed forces of competition and market-driven activities will eventually produce for the educational system as a whole. The exact directions cannot be predicted other than to say education will improve in a multitude of ways.

In some situations, transition may be difficult for some students. Many students will no doubt initially choose to remain where they are; others will choose or be forced to relocate. Eventually, however, none of us will be able to imagine how a system ever operated otherwise.

Society is faced with a dilemma similar to the one it faced when changing from segregated to integrated schools or the one faced every day as it permits outmoded and inefficient businesses and factories to close. Assistance could be made available to those who are harmed because of the transition, but nothing should stand in the way of reform and the change that accompanies it. Progress will benefit everyone in the long run.

CRITICISM 10

Some students are so disruptive or problematical that no school would admit them. What would happen to these students? What is the fate of disruptive students currently in our schools? Depending on the area of the country and local policy, they have one of three fates. They can remain in school, learning little or nothing, and continue to disrupt. They can be expelled after a normally lengthy process. Or they can attend alternative schools that specialize in helping this type of student.

This third possibility, the alternative school, is showing real promise in assisting students who, for whatever reason, simply do not fit into the traditional public school setting. This promise should be even more encouraging when we consider that under a privatized system, people would actually compete to attract and help these students. We might even find the emergence of educational bounty hunters who specialize in finding dropouts and problem students and helping them to stay in school, learn, and graduate.

From the point of view of classroom deportment, schools ought to be able to demand at least the same level of civility required in institutions such as theaters and restaurants. In these businesses, those who refuse to comply with the proprietors' requirements are unwelcome but always have the right to change their behavior and return or select another theater or restaurant. If the restaurant requires a coat, tie, and sedate behavior, a customer may choose to go down the street to the raucous diner that does not even require shoes.

One of the problems that beset the present public school system is that every school is forced to accept all students assigned: the rude, unruly, disruptive, undisciplined, and dangerous alike. Teachers and school administrators have little or no control over whom they will accept or reject. Eliminating such students, once identified, is often a time-consuming and burdensome task. A private school would have and should have the power to reject such students far more efficiently.

We must accept the obvious fact that some students are uneducable under certain conditions and some few may be so under all conditions. Enormous incentives will exist within the private system to deal with all kinds of students, even the unruly ones, for there is profit in it for successful schools. But if some students refuse to conform to basic standards of acceptable human behavior, then they should be dismissed. If society wishes to keep them off the streets, let it find institutions other than schools in which to do so.

Fortunately, far more students will respond positively to discipline. Many schools will vie for their vouchers or coupons. An exciting outcome of a privatized system will be the restoration of order and discipline without which learning simply cannot take place. One of the cruelest things our public school system has done to students who want to learn is permitting the disruptive influence of those who do not.

Presently many students are in schools that do not want them but are forced to keep them anyway. Under a privatized plan almost all students would be wanted by someone. A great diversity of schools appealing to every stratum would emerge, with standards that vary across the entire spectrum. A student who cannot find a school that suits him from this list might even be able to encourage the formation of something entirely different.

CRITICISM 11

Fraudulent and dishonest school owners and teachers would take advantage of students and parents. Undoubtedly there will be fraudulent and dishonest school operators. Such people currently operate in almost every walk of life. Public schools are not without charlatans and hustlers as well.

Under a privatized school plan, school owners who break the law should be prosecuted the same as anyone else. If negligence or unlawful behavior leads to the wrongful injury of students and parents, the person who is at fault is open to legal action. Education would thus be no different than a department store that knowingly sold damaged or unsafe merchandise.

But the most effective mechanism in minimizing the problem of fraud is active competition. Schools will be concerned about their reputations. Honesty will be strongly encouraged because it will be in each school's best interest to be honest. Under the public school system, this aspect of competitive pressure is missing, to the detriment of student welfare. Students and parents have little recourse unless a problem reaches almost epic proportions.

CRITICISM 12

Why go through all this trouble since a privatized school system is no cure-all? No educational system imaginable is perfect. Privatization cannot cure all of our problems. But accepting the notion that privately produced education is no utopia is not an adequate basis for rejecting the concept altogether. Were school systems not presently flawed, no one would be interested in considering choice and privatization. Nature has imposed limits and restrictions on society. Resources and human abilities are always going to be less than we desire. There is no such thing as a perfect choice. The best we can do is make an optimum selection by trying to find the one best alternative from all possible options.

A private school system is the optimum way of handling education. It will deliver the most education for the money allocated. Some schools will undoubtedly cut corners, and some students will fall through the cracks. The mere existence of such deficiencies, however, should not lead us to conclude that a privatized system is undesirable. When this system is weighed and judged against the public monopoly of education, it is far superior. But it is no instant cure-all.

Chapter 12

A Final Note

At the present time, local and state governments own, produce, and give away elementary and secondary education. Regardless of the quality of their efforts or the results they produce, public schools have had little to fear in the way of competition. Any parent wanting to choose a private alternative has to pay twice, first through taxes and then through tuition. Aside from a few exclusive private schools where wealthy parents are willing to pay high tuitions, the only private schools that offer any real competition are church-related schools—most commonly the traditional Catholic parochial schools. Here the church is willing to subsidize the parents, thus keeping tuition low enough to attract students. In realistic terms though, most parents are simply unwilling to pay twice. Having to pay both school taxes and private school tuition effectively reduces the competition from private schools to an insignificant level.

Competition and client control must be incorporated into the educational system before any meaningful changes can be achieved, because, as with all monopolies, public school monopolies generally operate in the best interest of those who run them. The lack of competition is extremely costly to parents, students, and taxpayers in inefficiency, insensitivity, and inadequate education. Were competition less prevalent than it is in other sectors of the American economy, our nation would never have gained the political and economic power it enjoys.

In order to bring about positive and permanent change, we must alter the educational system in fundamental ways that totally redesign the incentive structure at all levels. Students must perceive it to be in their interest to get an education. No longer should they be allowed to blame the school or teacher they are "stuck with." They must be able to choose teachers who believe in them and want to make them winners. They should be able to avoid those who will not or can not help them achieve. School authorities and teachers must see that it is in their best interest to establish the most effective and cost efficient educational measures and techniques. Successful educators must be rewarded with income, prestige, job satisfaction, and comfort. Unsuccessful ones must face similar losses.

Financial rewards are certainly not the only incentives that drive teachers. Intangible rewards have always motivated teachers and will no doubt continue to do so, as is the case with many occupations and professions. Human beings, unfortunately, have not yet reached the stage where they can routinely be trusted to consistently sacrifice in behalf of others. No longer should we assume that all educators consistently do their best for all their students simply because they are dedicated to that purpose. We must face the fact that educators are no more called to their profession than plumbers are called to theirs or used-car salesmen to theirs. Like the rest of us, educators need the constant prompting and prodding, something only competition and compensation based on productivity can do consistently. The absence of competition all but insures that meaningful feedback from clients is unavailable to guide educators in better serving their students.

Most educators derive significant personal satisfaction from helping their students to learn and develop. Unfortunately, the system itself frequently works to deprive them of this benefit by overregulation. A rigid curriculum, too many classes, too many students, and inflexible, often contradictory regulations reduce teacher satisfaction from student learning and encourage teachers to "play the system."

By and large, schools are operated by competent people who care about educating children. Unfortunately, the system itself works against educators and students alike. Privatization holds real promise for making good educators even better and a mediocre educational system first rate.

We are well aware of the extreme difficulties involved in trying to privatize the public school system. Attempts to overthrow firmly entrenched bureaucracies always run head long into political and practical monsters. Every argument in support of privatization causes the bureaucracy to conjure up new objections. The educational bureaucracy correctly sees this new concept as a threat to its very survival. Teacher unions and education administrators are leading the fight against reforms that would change the governing structure of the schools. They have even opposed the relatively benign plans that permit choice limited to public schools.

Those who are responsible for our public schools will not yield their control without a struggle. Any progress toward educational reform must come to grips with the fact that reforms mean a reallocation of power and the threat inherent in this change. Chester Finn (1989, p. 32) expressed it very well in a recent article: "Choice augurs a rearrangement of power and authority relationships in American education, and the farther reaching and more comprehensive the choice policy, the more total the reallocation of power." The educational establishment stands to lose some or all of this power, and it should surprise no one that they are deeply troubled. Many of their arguments against choice are more reflective of their level of concern for personal welfare than an attempt to insure better education for students.

We believe that the struggle for the radical restructuring of American schools is winnable, but it can happen only if the public is informed and convinced of its necessity. With public support, pressure can be brought to bear on legislators, and the process can begin even in spite of entrenched opposition from the establishment. By harnessing the creative power of free markets and competition that have made our nation the envy of the world in so many areas, we can greatly increase our national capacity to produce educated citizens as well as developing national and international leaders in every field.

References

Associated Press. "N.J. Seizes Jersey City Schools, Charging Corruption, 'Abuse'." *The Atlanta Journal and Constitution*, October 5, 1989, p. A13.

Benham, Lee. "The Effect of Advertising on the Price of Eyeglasses." *The Journal of Law and Economics*, October 1972, pp. 337-52.

Berman, Paul. "The Next Step: The Minnesota Plan." *Phi Delta Kappan*, November 1985, p. 193.

Bloom, Allan. *The Closing of the American Mind.* New York: Simon and Schuster, 1987.

Blumenfeld, Samuel L. *Is Public Education Necessary?* Old Greenwich, Conn.: Devin-Adair, 1981.

Buchanan, James M. *The Limits of Liberty.* Chicago: The University of Chicago Press, 1975.

Buchanan, James M., and Gordon Tullock. *The Calculus of Consent.* Ann Arbor: University of Michigan Press, 1962.

Cavazos, Lauro F. "The Huge Problem in American Schools," a speech delivered before the Council of Scientific Society Presidents, Washington, D.C., December 6, 1988.

Chubb, John E., and Terry M. Moe. *Politics, Markets, and America's Schools.* Washington, D.C.: Brookings Institute, 1990.

164   References

Clinchy, Evans. "Public School Choice: Absolutely Necessary But Not
    Wholly Sufficient." *Phi Delta Kappan*, December 1989, pp. 289-
    294.
Cohn, Elchanan. *The Economics of Education*. Cambridge, Mass.: Ballin-
    ger, 1979.
Coleman, James S. "Do Students Learn More in Private Schools Than in
    Public Schools?" The Madison Papers, no. 4. Tallahassee, Fla.: The
    James Madison Institute for Public Policy Studies, 1990.
Committee for Economic Development. *Investing in Our Children*. New
    York: Committee for Economic Development, 1985.
Cooperman, Saul and Frank J. Esposito. *Public School Choice: National
    Trends and Initiatives*. Trenton, N.J.: New Jersey State Department
    of Education, 1988.
Crandall, Robert. "Import Quotas and the Automobile Industry: The Cost
    of Protectionism." *The Brookings Review*, Summer 1984, p. 16.
Cross, Patricia K. "The Rising Tide of School Reform Reports." *Phi Delta
    Kappan*, November 1984, pp. 167-172.
Detroit News Sunday Magazine. As cited in *Florence Morning News*,
    March 15, 1981, p. A4.
DeYoung, Alan J. *Economics and American Education*. White Plains, N.Y.:
    Longman, 1989.
Down, A. Graham. "Who Is Killing Excellence in American Schools."
    Presentation before the National Press Club, 1983.
Economic Report of the President. Washington, D.C.: U.S. Government
    Printing Office, 1989.
Everhart, Robert B., ed. *The Public School Monopoly*. Cambridge, Mass.:
    Ballinger, 1982.
Falk, Carol H. "Lawyers Are Facing Surge in Competition as Courts Drop
    Curbs." *Wall Street Journal*, October 18, 1978, pp. 1, 21.
Finn, Chester E., Jr. "A Call for Radical Changes in Educational Delivery."
    Education Digest, January 1987, p. 2.
Finn, Chester E., Jr. "The Choice Backlash." *National Review*, November
    10, 1989, p. 32.
Finn, Chester E., Jr. "The Radicalization of School Reform." *Wall Street
    Journal*, February 2, 1990, p. A14.
"First Class Fiasco." *Florence Morning News*, March 21, 1990, p. A4.
Fitzgerald, Randall. *When Government Goes Private*. New York: Universe
    Books, 1988.
Fliegel, Sy. "Parental Choice in East Harlem Schools." In Joe Nathan (Ed.),
    Public Schools by Choice. Bloomington, Ind.: Myer Stone Books,
    1989, pp. 95-112.

Fox, William F. "Reviewing Economics of Size in Education." *Journal of Educational Finance*, Winter, 1981, pp. 273–96.

Friedman, Milton. *Capitalism and Freedom*. Chicago: University of Chicago Press, Phoenix Books, 1962.

Friedman, Milton and Rose Friedman. *Free to Choose*. New York, N.Y.: Avon Books, 1980.

Fund, John H. "Milwaukee's Schools Open to Competition." *Wall Street Journal*, September 4, 1990, p. A14.

Gallup, Alec M. "The 18th Annual Gallup Poll of the Public's Attitudes Toward the Public Schools." *Phi Delta Kappan*, September 1986, pp. 43-59.

Gallup, Alec M., and Stanley M. Elam. "The 21st Annual Gallup Poll of the Public's Attitudes Toward the Public Schools." *Phi Delta Kappan*, September 1989, pp. 40-54.

Glasser, William. *Control Theory in the Classroom*. New York: Harper and Row, 1986.

Glenn, Charles. "The Significance of Choice for Public Education." *The Education Digest*, January 1986, p. 11.

William T. Grant Foundation Commission on Work, Family and Citizenship. *The Forgotten Half: Non-College Youth in America*. Washington, D.C.: William T. Grant Foundation Commission on Youth, 1988.

Hirsch, E. D., Jr. *Cultural Literacy: What Every American Needs to Know*. Boston: Houghton Mifflin, 1987.

Hood, John. "Education: Money Isn't Everything." *Wall Street Journal*, February 9, 1990, p. A10.

Howe, Harold II. "Education Moves to Center Stage: An Overview of Recent Studies." *Phi Delta Kappan*, November 1983, pp. 167-172.

Kearns, David T., and Denis P. Doyle. *Winning the Brain Race*. San Francisco: ICS Press, Institute for Contemporary Studies, 1988.

Kohler, Heinz. *Intermediate Microeconomics*. 2nd ed. Glenview, Ill.: Scott, Foresman, 1986.

Kohler, Heinz. *Intermediate Microeconomics*. 3rd ed. Glenview, Ill.: Scott, Foresman, 1990.

"Laser Disc Shines Brighter than the Arizona Sun." *Interactive Laser Disc*, Spring 1990, p. 8.

Levinson, Eliot. *The Alum Rock Voucher Demonstration: Three Years of Implementation*. The Rand Paper Series. Santa Monica, Ca.: The Rand Corporation, April, 1976.

Lee, Dwight R. "An Alternative to the Public School: Educational Vouchers." *Current*, October 1986, pp. 26-32.

Lieberman, Myron. *Beyond Public Education*. New York: Praeger, 1986.

Lieberman, Myron. *Privatization and Educational Choice*. New York: St. Martin's Press, 1989.

McKenzie, Richard B. *The Political Economy of the Educational Process*. Boston: Martins Nijhoff, 1979.

Maslow, Abraham H. *Motivation and Personality*. 2nd Edition, New York: Harper & Row, 1970.

Mueller, Van D. "Choice: The Parents' Perspective." *Phi Delta Kappan*, June 1987, pp. 761-762.

Nadler, Richard, and Tom Donelson. "Affirmative Reaction." *National Review*, September 15, 1989, pp. 28-29.

Nathan, Joe. "More Public School Choice Can Mean More Learning." *Educational Leadership*, October 1989, pp. 51-57.

Nathan, Joe, ed. *Public Schools by Choice*. Bloomington, Ind.: Myer Stone Books, 1989.

Nathan, Joe. "Results and Future Prospects of State Efforts to Increase Choice Among Schools." *Phi Delta Kappan*, June 1987, pp. 746-752.

National Center for Education Statistics. *The Condition of Education: Elementary and Secondary Education*. Washington, D.C.: U.S. Department of Education, Office of Educational Research and Improvement, vol. 1, 1988.

National Center for Education Statistics. *The Condition of Education: Elementary and Secondary Education*. Washington, D.C.: U.S. Department of Education, Office of Educational Research and Improvement, vol. 2, 1989(b).

National Center for Education Statistics. *Digest of Education Statistics*. Washington, D.C.: U.S. Department of Education, Office of Educational Research and Improvement, 1989(a).

National Commission on Excellence in Education. *A Nation at Risk: The Imperative for Educational Reform; An Open Letter to the American People*. Washington, D.C.: U.S. Government Printing Office, 1983.

O'Quinn, Cleve. "Lake City Voters Defeat New School Tax." *Florence Morning News*, March 7, 1990, p. A1.

Ortiz, Guillermo. "Mexico's Been Bitten by the Privatization Bug." *Wall Street Journal*, September 15, 1989, p. A11.

"Poor Schools." *Wall Street Journal*, November 14, 1990, p. A16.

Popham, W. James. "The Merits of Measurement-Driven Instruction." *Phi Delta Kappan*, May 1987, pp. 679-682.

"The Privatization Potential." *National Review*, November 10, 1989, p. 24.

Public School Choice: National Trends and Initiatives. Trenton, N.J.: New Jersey State Department of Education, 1988.

Raywid, Mary Anne. *The Case of Public Schools and Choice.* Bloomington, Ind.: Phi Delta Kappa Educational Foundation, 1989.

"Real Choice." *National Review,* September 1, 1989, pp. 12-13.

Rinehart, James R. and James F. Cummings, "Spending for Education—How Critical Have We Been?" *The Educational Forum,* May, 1965, pp. 461-466.

Rinehart, James R., and Jackson F. Lee, Jr. "The Optimum Level of Ignorance: Marginal Analysis in Education." *The Educational Forum,* (Winter 1988, 135-142.

Rottenberg, Simon. *Occupational Licensure and Regulation.* Washington, D.C.: American Enterprise Institute, 1980.

Savas, E. S. *Privatizing the Public Sector.* Chatham, N.J.: Chatham House, 1982.

Shepard, Lawrence. "Licensing Restrictions and the Cost of Dental Care." *The Journal of Law and Economics,* April 1978, pp. 187-201.

Silberman, Charles E. *Crisis in the Classroom.* New York: Vintage Books, 1971.

Stein, Herbert. "Who's Number One? Who Cares?" *Wall Street Journal,* March 1, 1990, p. A16.

Stern, Joyce O., ed. *The Condition of Education.* Washington, D.C.: U.S. Department of Education, National Center for Education Statistics, vol. 1, 1988.

Survey of State Initiatives: Public School Choice. Denver, Col.: Education Commission of the States, September 1989.

Tucker, Cynthia. "Groups' Effort to Better Quality of School Boards Gains Momentum." *The Atlanta Journal and Constitution,* October 7, 1989, p. A21.

Uchitelle, Susan. "What It Really Takes To Make School Choice Work," *Phi Delta Kappa,* December, 1989, p. 302.

U.S. Department of Education. *Elementary and Secondary Education Indicators in Brief.* Washington, D.C.: U.S. Department of Education, Office of Educational Research and Improvement, 1987.

Walberg, Herbert J., et al. "Reconstructing the Nation's Worst Schools." *Phi Delta Kappan,* June 1989, p. 803.

Weston, Susan Perkins, with Joe Nathan and Mary Anne Raywid. *Choosing a School for Your Child.* Washington, D.C.: U.S. Department of Education, Office of Educational Research and Improvement, May 1989.

Index

ABOUT THE AUTHORS

JAMES R. RINEHART received his Ph.D. in Economics from the University of Virginia in Charlottesville and has published widely on public policy issues, including education. He holds the positions of Professor of Economics and Director of the Center for Economic Education at Francis Marion College in Florence, South Carolina. The Center is affiliated with the South Carolina Council on Economic Education and the Joint Council on Economic Education in New York. Dr. Rinehart works as a consultant for numerous private and public agencies, and organizes and conducts in-service training programs for public school teachers. He also holds membership in many national professional associations and honor societies.

JACKSON F. LEE, JR., received his Ed.D. in Curriculum and Instruction from Duke University in 1972, specializing in science education. He is currently a Professor of Education at Francis Marion College. Since 1987 he has been Director of the Francis Marion College Elementary Science Leadership Program, which trains teachers and district science consultants. Dr. Lee has been a consultant to school systems and state departments of education, and has published numerous articles and manuals on a variety of educational topics. He co-authored *Providing for Individual Differences in Student Learning: A Mastery Learning Approach (1984)*.

Roger Boyle, First Earl of Orrery

Books by
KATHLEEN M. LYNCH

Roger Boyle, First Earl of Orrery

A Congreve Gallery

Travellers Must Be Content

The Social Mode of Restoration Comedy

ROGER BOYLE, FIRST EARL OF ORRERY

From a painting in the possession of Patrick Reginald Boyle, by permission of Mr. Boyle

ROGER BOYLE
First Earl of Orrery

BY

KATHLEEN M. LYNCH

THE UNIVERSITY OF TENNESSEE PRESS
KNOXVILLE

TO

E. L. R. and W. E. R.

Preface

The first Earl of Orrery was known in his lifetime as "the great man of Munster." The term was used sincerely by his friends, derisively by his enemies. Those who relied on his support and patronage praised him as one of the most accomplished noblemen of his time. Those who hated him or feared his influence or his pen branded him as a time-server and charlatan. Lord Orrery accommodated himself with apparent ease to changing political conditions, escaping the more serious hazards of shifted loyalties, but gaining less substantial rewards than many of his contemporaries. He enjoyed the personal friendship of both Cromwell and Charles II and served both masters well.

Orrery's death, at the relatively early age of fifty-eight, ended a career which had been crowded with activity. Of his uncommonly full life, versatility and adaptability are the most striking aspects. He was a brilliant soldier, an experienced politician, a vigorous pamphleteer, a graceful romancer, and the initiator of Restoration heroic drama. It must be conceded regretfully that the very diversity of his interests and the suavity with which he adjusted himself to other personalities increase the difficulty of categorizing the man Orrery. His own personality remains enigmatic. His surviving portrait, presumably painted when Orrery was in early middle age, betrays no secrets but suggests the wariness of the adroit fencer. "I should not have cared to cross swords with him," comments one of his descendants.

A full-length biography of Orrery must be considered overdue. The discursive *Memoirs,* published in 1742, of Orrery's first biographer, Thomas Morrice, afford an indispensable but inadequate and undocumented record of his life; and the *State Papers,* appended to the published *Memoirs,* cover less than a decade of Orrery's political career. T. Crofton Croker assembled material for a biography of Orrery but abandoned the project after he had written the first chapters. The first complete collection of Orrery's plays was published in 1937, ably edited, with a biographical introduction and critical prefaces, by Professor William S. Clark.

The manuscripts on which this biography has been chiefly based are widely dispersed. The larger collections were consulted in the British Museum, at Chatsworth, at Petworth, in the National Library in Dublin, and in the Harvard University Library. The important collection of the Private Papers of Margaret, Countess of Orrery, preserved among the Leconfield MSS., was broken up in 1928, when the major portion of these Papers was purchased by the National Library. Illuminating excerpts from this portion of the Orrery MSS. were published in 1941 by Mr. Edward MacLysaght in his *Calendar of the Orrery Papers.* The remaining Papers of this collection, which I discovered at Petworth in 1957, have recently been placed in the National Library on indefinite loan.

It has been assumed that the bulk of Orrery's official

correspondence was destroyed when Charleville House was burned in 1690 by a detachment of King James II's soldiers. It may be doubted, however, whether Orrery's more valuable manuscripts were left at Charleville after the death of the second Earl. Whatever documents Lady Orrery may or may not have loaned to the Earl of Anglesey, at his request, have disappeared. The missing correspondence of the period of the Protectorate may have been discreetly disposed of, perhaps by Orrery himself. The surviving manuscripts are sufficiently abundant to dismay, at times, even a biographer dedicated to the task of exploring them.

I have been aided in my research by grants from the American Council of Learned Societies and the American Philosophical Society. The John Simon Guggenheim Memorial Foundation not only awarded me a fellowship but also provided a generous financial subvention toward the publication of this book. I wish to acknowledge the kindness of the Duke of Devonshire, Earl Spencer, and Lord Egremont in permitting me to examine manuscripts in their possession. The Earl of Cork and Orrery, Mr. Patrick Reginald Boyle, and the Earl of Shannon have kindly permitted the use of family portraits and manuscripts. Thomas Wragge, Esq., librarian of Chatsworth, and Miss G. M. A. Beck, archivist at Petworth, have been singularly helpful. Many other persons have given me valuable assistance and advice. For his unfailing encouragement I remain deeply indebted to Professor John C. Hodges.

KATHLEEN M. LYNCH

Funchal, Madeira

Contents

Illustrations

Young Lord Broghill

Richard Boyle, first Earl of Cork, had reached the age of fifty-five when his eleventh child and fifth son, Roger, was born at Lismore Castle on April 21, 1621. Lord Cork had been honored with an earldom the preceding autumn and at that time had confidently taken as his motto: "God's providence is my inheritance." The record of the Earl's rise from obscurity to the status of the King's richest and most powerful subject in Ireland merits a distinguished place in the annals of famous self-made men.[1]

On October 13, 1566, Richard Boyle began life inauspiciously in Canterbury as the second son of Roger Boyle of Preston, near Faversham in Kent, and Joan, daughter of Robert Naylor of Canterbury. His mother, left a widow when Richard was only ten, managed to send him to Corpus Christi College, Cambridge, on a scholarship. He left the university to enter the Middle Temple; but finding his funds inadequate for the study of law, he became clerk to Sir Richard Manwood, Chief Baron of the Exchequer. At his mother's death, he resolved to make a fresh start in life. God took him by the hand, he believed, and led him to Ireland, where he arrived on June 23, 1588. A

1

young man of twenty-two, foppishly dressed, he had no material resources but the clothes on his back, twenty-seven pounds and three shillings in his purse, and the diamond ring and gold bracelet which his mother had given him.

Two years later Boyle became Deputy to Sir John Crofton, Escheator General of Ireland, and began to enrich himself in the process of carrying on his official duties in the investigation of forfeited lands and lapsed titles. Charged, rightly or wrongly, with embezzling funds, he was twice imprisoned. The beginning of his good fortune, he considered, was his marriage to Joan Apsley, a young heiress, who brought him valuable lands in Munster and connections with many influential families. A year later, however, she died in childbirth.

The Rebellion of 1598 further clouded Boyle's prospects. His lands were wasted; and he fled to England, where he resumed his studies in the Middle Temple and was soon offered employment by the Earl of Essex. Unfortunately, the old charges against him were renewed, and he was thrown into prison. With characteristic energy and eloquence, Boyle addressed a direct appeal to Queen Elizabeth, aroused her sympathy, and received from her an appointment as Clerk of the Council of Munster, under Sir George Carew, Lord President of Munster. The Queen's intervention Boyle regarded as the second rise in his fortune.

In 1601 Carew sent his much trusted Clerk to England to report the victory of the battle of Kinsale. Boyle was cordially received by the Queen and took advantage of the visit to purchase from Sir Walter Raleigh on excellent terms forty-two thousand acres of land in Munster. This important transaction he regarded as the third great favor which God, in his providence, had bestowed on him.

On July 25, 1603, Boyle married again. His second wife, Catherine Fenton, was the only daughter of Sir George Fenton, Principal Secretary of State for Ireland. This gentle lady, as good as she was beautiful, the mother of his fifteen children, Cork justly praised as "a most religious, virtuous, loving and obedient wife unto me all the days of her life" and the "crown" of all God's manifold blessings. She was equally devoted to her husband, whom she addressed in her letters as "my owne good selfe."

Boyle's older children were born in Youghal, where Raleigh had formerly resided. The ruined College of Youghal was rebuilt by its new owner as a stately residence, with two fine quadrangles and a terraced hillside garden. The house commanded a view of the roof tops of the town and Youghal's long white strand and harbor.

Boyle also rebuilt Lismore Castle, magnificently situated on a high cliff above the Blackwater. Many years later, when James II visited Lismore, he took one quick glance from the drawing room windows at the turbulent river, far below, and turned dizzily away. To this romantic residence, a few months before Roger was born, the Earl came by boat with his family. He expressed in his Diary his satisfaction in the new home, "where god bless us all."

Three of Cork's children died in childhood. For the others he arranged, as promptly as possible, splendid but, in some cases, not happy marriages. The children were all "promising," and several of them were to make names for themselves. Richard, Roger, Francis, and Robert were the four brothers who were to be closely associated during many years. Roger was nine years younger than Richard, Cork's eldest surviving son, a year older than Francis, and six years older than Robert, Cork's youngest son. Three of the brothers were to acquire titles. Richard, after succeeding to his father's title, was to be created Earl of Burlington, Roger became Earl of Orrery, and Francis became Viscount Shannon. Both Richard and Roger were to play important rôles in political life, and Roger was to win recognition as a brilliant soldier, a "learned Lord," and a man of letters. Robert was to achieve fame as a philosopher and scientist.

The most gifted of Cork's daughters, Katherine, was six years older than Roger. She was celebrated in her own time as "the incomparable Lady Ranelagh" and was undoubtedly one of the most remarkable women of her era. Although she belonged to no coterie and never attached herself to a Court circle, she exerted a considerable influence on leading statesmen of her time. She was her father's favorite daughter—"my Kate" he called her—and the favorite sister of Richard, Roger, and Robert, all of whom adored her and admired her and consulted her on all major and many minor problems in their lives.

By the date of Roger's birth, Lord Cork had not only amassed a fortune, but had altered and improved large areas of Munster, of which he had become owner, and had given employment to four thousand workers on his estates.[2] He was Ireland's "first capitalist." [3] His fortune had been made, as great fortunes usually are, by industry, thrift, and shrewd bargains. Those who were too hard pressed to deal with him on favorable terms no doubt suffered heavy losses. The poor peasants whom he employed toiled for a bare subsistence. On the other hand, he could be justly commended, as he was by Sir Francis Annesley, for having done more for Ireland than any other Englishman had done for forty years. Annesley remarked: "For my own part I protest if his estate were six times as much as it is, I should think him very deserving of it, for he employs the fruit of it altogether to the strengthening and beautifying the Commonwealth, and if all others who have advanced their fortunes in Ireland would do the like, this Kingdom would quickly flourish." [4]

Lord Cork rebuilt towns and built several new ones. His finest achievement in town building was Bandon, with its attractive wood and plaster houses, its six-arched bridge, its walls nine feet thick and forty to fifty feet high, its free grammar school and almshouses. Cromwell, at a later date, was so charmed with Bandon that he declared that if there had been an Earl of Cork in every province of Ireland, the Rebellion of 1641 could not have occurred.[5] Elsewhere Cork built castles, roads, and bridges, repaired churches, and founded schools (for Protestant children) and almshouses for the sick and old. On the farms he improved breeds of cattle. He established iron foundries in the Blackwater Valley and exported bar iron and artillery; smelted lead at Minehead; worked silver and copper mines; and quarried red marble. At Ardmore he set up a fish-curing establishment. Timber in the form of pipe staves fom the forests of Munster was one of his chief exports. He settled woolen weavers at Clonakilty and Cappoquin, linen weavers at Bandon and Youghal.

For his young children Cork had little leisure, although he provided handsomely for them, supervised their education with great care, and worried over their youthful follies. It was his custom to place his sons and daughters in infancy with country nurses, not bringing them home until they were old enough for lessons. This procedure must have been followed with Roger, who presumably, like his brother Robert, was inured "by slow degrees, to a coarse but cleanly diet, and to the usual passions of the air." [6]

Very little is known of Roger's childhood. He was still an infant when on July 9, 1621, his eldest sister, Alice, was married in the chapel at Lismore to Lord Barry, afterwards Earl of Barrymore. He was a child of three when Lord Deputy Falkland made a progress through Munster and honored Lord Cork with a visit of four days at College House in Youghal. In Cork's dining parlor the Lord Deputy ennobled Roger's twelve-year-old brother Richard, creating him Viscount Dungarvan; and Falkland's son Lucius and the young Viscount exchanged gifts.

Roger himself was ennobled at the tender age of six. On March 25, 1628, Lord Cork noted in his Diary that he had sent his sons Lewis and Roger to Dublin, with attendants, to be knighted.[7] On April 1 the ceremony took place in the presence chamber in Dublin Castle. Lord Falkland conferred on eight-year-old Lewis the title of Viscount Kinalmeaky and on Roger the title of Baron of Broghill.[8] Lord Cork must have considered that the substantial fees which he paid for these titles were well spent. A few weeks later, the Earl embarked for England with his wife, his eldest son, and his daughters Lettice and Joan. Lewis and Roger remained quietly at Lismore with tutors—one of Cork's chaplains and a Frenchman, François de Cary—from whom they received instruction in writing and in Latin and French.

The prolonged visit in England was a rewarding one for Lord Cork. His wife and daughters were

presented at Court by his most intimate friend, Sir
Thomas Stafford, son of Sir George Carew, former
Lord President of Munster. The Earl of Bedford, son
of Lord Russell, former Lord Deputy of Ireland,
loaned Cork his house in Northall for the autumn
months. Cork effected the marriage of Lettice to
George Goring, eldest son of Lord Goring, Vice-
Chamberlain to the Queen, and the engagement of
Joan to George, Earl of Kildare, of whom he became
guardian. A large loan to Charles I led to Cork's appointment as one of the Lords Justices of Ireland; and
he returned to Ireland in October, 1629, to assume the
duties of this post. His satisfaction in his new office
was marred by the unavoidable and ironic alliance
which it imposed with the other Lord Justice, an old
enemy, Lord Chancellor Adam Loftus. Another honor
was conferred upon the Earl in 1631, when he was
appointed Lord Treasurer of Ireland.

The greatest tragedy of the Earl's private life was
the death of his Countess, which occurred on February
16, 1630. He made the mournful entry in his Diary
under this date: "It pleased my mercifull god, for my
manifold syns . . . to translate out of this mortall
world, to his glorious kingdome of heaven, the sowle
of my dearest deer wife, who departed this world (to
my unspeakable grief) at the Lorde Calfeylds howse
in dublin." [9] Perhaps it was their mother's death which
determined his decision to enroll both Lewis, at the
age of eleven, and Roger, at the age of nine, at Trinity
College in Dublin. On the fifth of May the boys arrived in Dublin under the chaperonage of their sister
Alice, Lady Barrymore, and were admitted to the
college.[10]

It is probable that Cork's sons had very few contacts with other Trinity College students. They pur-

sued their studies at the college with private tutors, with some intermissions, perhaps until 1634. In the autumn of 1631 Lewis joined his father, his brother Richard, and the Earl's five sons-in-law in a lengthy progress through Munster, which included six or seven weeks at Lismore.[11] In the summer of 1633 Lewis was one of a number of young volunteers who joined Captain Thomas James, Captain of the *Ninth Whelp,* in an expedition against pirates off the Irish coast.[12] It is a safe guess that the boy welcomed such refreshing interludes in his course of studies.

A meager impression of the reactions of Lewis to college life may be gained from two letters which he wrote to his father in October, 1633. In the first he promises never to run into debt again, if his chamber and study may be finished, and laments that he possesses only eight pence in ready money.[13] In the second he gives a suitably expurgated account of his daily routine. The day begins and ends with private prayer. He spends an hour in the morning with Mr. Forster and in the afternoon is with him until nearly three o'clock. Before supper he reads history or associates with members of his family or his tutors. Sometimes he rides to Ringsend or borrows his brother Francis's falcon to go hawking. He keeps no ill company. He never walks, except in the college parks with Mr. Wilkinson or Mr. Forster, and seldom goes to town, except to church. He adds that he is enclosing his "poor discourse of earth and water" and will "shortly" send his discourses on the two other elements.[14]

On the still more youthful Roger this college experience seems likewise to have been wasted. Years afterwards, Lord Broghill confessed: "Amongst my many Faults, I know none which had a lesse Disputed Assendent over me, then a Detestation to Readeing and Studdy, in which vast unhappiness I continued till I went to see the World." [15]

The eldest son, Richard, at the age of sixteen, was already seeing the world. In 1628 he had been left with his tutor at Christ Church, Oxford. Homesickness cut short his university life. In the spring of 1630 he wrote to the Earl that he had "a longing desire" to see him; and the indulgent father permitted him to return to Ireland. Negotiations were soon begun to arrange Richard's marriage to Lady Elizabeth Clifford, daughter of Baron Clifford, afterwards Earl of Cumberland. But before an agreement had been reached, the King made the rather embarrassing proposal that Richard should marry Lady Anne Feilding, second daughter of the Earl and Countess of Denbigh and a Maid of Honour to the Queen. Richard was sent hurriedly to England to offer tactful objections to the King, who graciously permitted him to make him own decision. The relieved young petitioner commented: "I never saw a man express himself more sweetly and nobly than the King did in this business." [16] Richard then set out on his travels, first assuring "sweet clif" that he would not forget her.

From Paris Richard wrote home desiring his father's opinion of "the Queen's comedy," [17] Walter Montague's *The Shepherd's Paradise,* presented at Somerset House by the Queen and her ladies in January, 1633. He was in England in time for the Twelfth Night and Shrovetide festivities of 1634. On January 6 at Somerset House he saw Fletcher's *The Faithful Shepherdess,* which he found a "curious play." [18] On February 18 he had the pleasure of being one of the masquers [19] in the King's masque, Thomas Carew's *Coelum Britannicum,* which Sir Henry Herbert regarded as "the noblest mask of my time to this day, the best poetrye, the best scenes, and the best habitts." [20] The masquers were attired as ancient heroes in yellow mantles embroidered with silver, with plumed helmets.[21] Richard's expenses for this brilliant occasion were nearly six hundred pounds.

Lewis and Roger must have envied their older brother's experiences and longed for similar diversions. The year 1634 brought more varied activities for them, as well. The boy peers had the privilege of attending the opening of the Irish Parliament in that year. Lord Broghill, because of his extreme youth, marched in his robes third among the barons in the stately procession to St. Patrick's Cathedral of noblemen and churchmen.[22] That summer and autumn Roger made two trips in the *Ninth Whelp* to England, first to attend Richard's wedding to Lady Elizabeth Clifford at Skipton Castle and serve as a member of her escort to Dublin, and again to carry news of her safe arrival to Lord and Lady Clifford. He was back in Dublin on October 4.[23]

On December 15 Cork wrote to Lady Clifford: "Now Parliament is adjourned, we begin our journey towards Lismore to-morrow morning . . . and there god willing wee intend to keep a merry Christmas amongst our Neighbors, & to eate to the noble family of Skipton in fat does & Carps, & to drinke your healthe in the best wyne wee can gett." For some time Cork had been plagued by strained relations with Sir Thomas Wentworth, Lord Deputy of Ireland since 1631, who was now demanding that the Earl pay a heavy fine before receiving a "valid" lease for the College of Youghal. Despite his worries, Cork assured Lady Clifford that he was resolved to enjoy an especially merry Christmas with his entire family, trusting always to "Gods providence which never fayled mee." [24]

In 1635 Cork enrolled his sons Francis and Robert at Eton College. The Earl wrote at this time to Sir Henry Wotton, Provost of Eton, requesting his advice as to a governor and traveling companion for Lewis and Roger, whom he was about to send on a foreign tour. Wotton replied by dispatching to Ireland, with a letter of recommendation, Isaac Marcombes, a Frenchman by birth, in whose character and ability he had great confidence. Wotton wrote that Marcombes was "verie sounde in Religion and well conversant with Religious Men," that he had a good knowledge of literature and languages and spoke Italian as fluently as French, so that he would be an especially helpful guide in "that delicat Piece of the Worlde," Italy. Wotton had observed that Marcombes "seemeth in himself neither of a lumpish nor a light composition; but of a well fixed meane." [25]

Robert Boyle, whose tutor Marcombes subsequently became, was to have an equally high opinion of this traveler, soldier, and scholar, who "very well knew what belonged to a gentleman." Robert commented: "Scholarship he wanted not, having in his greener years been a professed student in divinity; but he was much less read in books than men, and hated pedantry as much as any of the seven deadly sins." He was eager to have his charges virtuous. A nice critic of words and men, he taught Robert "a very cautious and considerate way of expressing himself, which after turned to his no small advantage." [26]

Cork was ambitious for his sons. Lewis at sixteen and Roger at fourteen were old enough to derive much benefit from several years of study and travel in

Europe. The Earl concluded that Marcombes was qualified to give the two boys the discipline and training which might make it possible for them to be leaders of men. He informed the new tutor that "the only piece of poetry I ever thought worthie to commit to memory" was this:

> By skilful strokes of sword and pen
> A man may guide and govern men.
> Without their arte Man's man at most
> But skill in them makes man a hoste.[27]

Sobered by their father's prayers for God to "bless, guide, govern and protect them," Lewis, Roger, their tutor, and their older sister, Lettice Goring, took passage for England on February 13, 1636.

It was the custom of Marcombes to enclose letters by his pupils in his reports on their welfare and progress under his tutelage. Some of these letters may have miscarried or may have been lost at a later date. Enough of them have been preserved, however, to furnish an illuminating account of the European travels of two fashionable young gentlemen of that period.

The initial journey of three days to a small port near Chester was prolonged by a dangerous storm, which Marcombes considered "very profitable" for the badly frightened boys and a means of enabling them "heer after the better to know themselfs." [28] Roger briefly informed his father that they had "scaped a greate danger" and that sister Goring's coach was to meet them in Chester.[29]

To the relief of Marcombes, Lettice Goring left the party in Lichfield, and "beeing free from the trouble of travelling with women," [30] he was able to arrange a program of sightseeing. By way of Warwick, they proceeded to Oxford, where they visited the Bodleian Library, the most famous colleges, and the "fairest" churches. They spent a night at Eton College and took Francis and Robert on an excursion to Windsor Castle. They arrived in London too late to see D'Avenant's masque, *The Triumphs of the Prince d'Amour* at the Middle Temple on February 23,[31] although Marcombes had provided the lads with fine scarlet satin suits especially for this occasion. Had they seen the masque, they would have observed the Queen and her ladies dressed for novelty in citizens' clothes, and Lewis would have had a glimpse of Lady Elizabeth Feilding, whom he was to marry three years later.

The handsome scarlet suits were worn on the afternoon of March 5, when the boys were introduced to the Queen in St. James's Park by Lettice's father-in-law, Lord Goring. Sir Thomas Stafford, Roger reported, told them that they must also be presented to the King, but "oure clothes being of Scarlet he sayd that It was not fitting for Lent." Black suits were hastily procured, and in this more somber attire they had the honor of kissing the King's hand. They called on, but were disconcerted not to find at home, various noble persons whom Cork could claim as friends, including the Earl of Bedford, Lady Denbigh, Lady of the Bedchamber to the Queen, and Lord Northumberland. Roger expanded his letter from London by informing his father that Northumberland "is Admiral of the King's Navy." [32]

For the crossing to Dieppe the travelers were joined by Barnabas Scudamore, younger brother of Viscount Scudamore, English ambassador in Paris, and by Lord Savage's son. They journeyed to Paris by way of Rouen. At first the boys were homesick. They longed for beer from their father's cellar, mixed French wine with much water, and in fact, wrote Marcombes, had "scarce quenched their thirst since they left England." [33] They were already so much "distasted" with the prospect of a year's study in Geneva that their tutor feared to expose them to the "pleasing conversation" of the best company in Paris and hurried them away from the superior attractions of that too alluring city.

In Geneva, Cork's sons lived for more than a year in the house of Jean Diodati, a distinguished professor of Hebrew and theology at the University of Geneva and a cordial host to young English travelers. Charles Diodati, Milton's friend, had visited his uncle in Geneva in 1630, and Milton was to be the professor's guest in 1639. Marcombes allied himself with the Diodati family by becoming the second husband of Madelaine Burlamacchi Drelincourt, Jean Diodati's niece. [34]

As a "fortress of orthodox Calvinism," [35] Geneva did not appeal greatly to Roger, who wished that the religion of the Swiss Protestants were nearer that of the Church of England. Roger found Diodati himself "a learned man, and excellent Company." [36] His young hearers were impressed by some of their host's anecdotes, notably of his conversion of a courtesan when he was preaching in Venice.

Lewis was troubled by Cork's long silence of eight months, which he attributed to the miscarriage of his father's letters. On March 8, 1637, he informed his father that he and Roger were studying hard and, "as our teachers persuade us," making good progress. He begged to be assured "yt we are still happy in ye Love of soe deare & good a Father." [37]

In his sons' absence, Cork's quarrel with Wentworth

had reached its climax; he had been compelled to pay the outrageous fine which Wentworth demanded, and he had suffered a stroke of paralysis. During a winter's invalidism at Lismore, his daughter Alice had tenderly nursed him back to health. His sons were kept in ignorance of these trials; and when the long-awaited letter arrived, it was reassuring.

Lewis wrote again to thank Cork for his welcome letter and to explain several matters. His aversion to quenching his thirst with wine has apparently long since been overcome, and he offers apologies for excessive drinking, a vice which he now utterly loathes. His tutor's marriage has in no way hindered his duties toward his charges and must be regarded as "a particular accident," concerning himself only. Roger at sixteen is "already very nearly perfect in ye mathematiques . . . a good Horseman, Vaults well, & hath Italian enough for ye small time we have learn't." He is "not wholy soe fatt" as he was in Ireland and is already as tall as his father. Lewis, now eighteen, is "3 fingers" taller and hopes "to be distinguished from a dwarf at my returne." [38]

Boyle Smith, the boys' cousin, who had joined them in Geneva, wrote to Cork in a different vein, complaining of shabby clothes and insufficient funds and of Marcombes' absence at the time of his marriage.[39] Such grievances must be discounted in view of Marcombes' carefully guarded but adverse comments on the lad's conduct. The young man was "so noble" that he could "scarcely refuse" any good company. He made two journeys from Geneva to Lyons, losing all his money, concealing his losses, and borrowing a substantial sum from a merchant.[40]

In the spring of 1638, Marcombes wrote a long letter to the Earl of Cork from Genoa.[41] He had much to relate. He had left Geneva with Cork's sons and their cousin on September 30 of the preceding year, and they had traveled to Zurich. In Zurich they learned that because of the plague raging in the small cantons of Switzerland, they would be subjected to a quarantine of six weeks in the "cold Alps," if they attempted to enter Italy from that direction. Retracing their steps, they made a semicircular journey to Genoa through France, visiting on the way Lyons, Orange, Avignon, Aix, Marseilles, and Nice. The young lords admired the chief cities, fortresses and arsenals, and "all the rarityes" everywhere. They reached Genoa on December 1, and Lewis immediately fell ill of small-pox but recovered by the end of the month. He has promised to be more temperate in drinking but should be exhorted by his father on this subject. The "sad news" must be revealed that Boyle Smith died of smallpox on December 30. Marcombes tended him constantly through his illness, took care that "no papist, priest, or friar" entered his chamber, and pre-pared him for death. With much secrecy and con-siderable expense, Marcombes had managed to have Boyle's body put in a trunk and cast into the sea sev-eral miles from shore. He paid an Englishman to supervise this melancholy task, for Roger had suc-cumbed on Christmas Eve to the same disease and was very ill. Now that Roger was perfectly well again, the Italian journey was to be resumed.

Marcombes' next letter was written in May from Saumur, near Angers.[42] From Genoa he had traveled with Cork's sons to Lucca, Bologna, Ferrara, Padua, and Venice. Lord Feilding, Lord Denbigh's son, then Venetian ambassador, had been kind to the boys, and they had worn new black satin suits when he entertained them. On their return to Padua, Lewis became ill once

more, and it was evident that the heat of Italy disagreed with him. Nor did Lewis have very great affection for a country "soe full of superstition and
idolatry." The contemplated visit to Rome had to be
abandoned, "to the great griefe of my lord of Broghall," as well as of his tutor. From Florence they
turned north, spent a few days in Leghorn, went by
sea to Genoa, then to Marseilles and Montpellier. A
famous physician recommended a colder climate for
Lewis, and a journey by boat was undertaken on the
Allier River to its confluence with the Loire. They
must have passed Moulins, which Robert afterwards
visited and described with such enthusiasm as "a part
of the French Arcadia, the pleasant Pays de Forest,
where the marquis d'Urfé was pleased to lay the scene
of the adventures and amours of that Astraea, with
whom so many gallants are still in love, so long after
both his and her decease." [43]

The French journey was broken at Orléans, Blois,
and Tours, and at last Saumur was reached, where
the summer was to be spent. Marcombes reported that
Lewis was now well enough to do all his exercises, and
Roger had grown "mightily" and was a gentleman "of
a very good fashion." The young lords had learned
enough Italian in Italy to understand the language and
be understood by others; and they had seen "all that
could be seen for money & favor." In Saumur they
lodged in the house of a learned and agreeable Scottish
professor, Dr. Duncan.

The two boys wrote letters to Lord Cork from Saumur. Lewis mentioned that they had the use of Dr.
Duncan's library, as well as that of the late Protestant
theologian, Duplessis-Mornay. "We long for nothing," said Lewis, "but the honor of yor Lo^{ps} most pas-
sionatly desired l^{res}." [44] Roger was equally polite and

announced his intention of endeavoring "all I may" to prove an obedient son to "soe good, & soe noble a father." [45]

In November, 1638, the travelers reached Paris. A month later, Marcombes wrote a long letter to Cork [46] in answer to the Earl's demands that he should take a firmer hand with the young lords. Marcombes reminded their father that he could not treat his pupils as if they were but twelve or thirteen years of age. Although they fall something short of the "models of perfection" that their father prescribes, "when I compare them to other Gentlemen & yong Lords of their age, I am sure yt y^r L^p has matter of comfort rather then of any greef." It is impossible to govern with a father's authority young men who "have kept so long Companie with hunters and players and soe many other Gentlemen that will humour them in any thing & will let them know their Greatnesse, as my yong Lords have been used in Ireland." Marcombes is confident that the Earl may have "both honour and Comfort" in Roger, at least, because everyone who knows him loves him and speaks well of him. It is true that Lewis, despite many good parts, loves his pleasure and his own way a little too much, is inclined to drink too much, borrow money too freely, and say "things not altogether true." He is "much mended but not altogether cured." His "small errours" are imperfections of youth "which time and ye profitable conversation of y^r L^p will altogether cure." The sum of three hundred pounds which Cork has sent is very acceptable but will not last to the end of Lent, nor purchase new clothes for the journey to England. The boys continue their riding, dancing, and fencing but need to study history. They are "very religious" and never omit their Christian exercises.

Lewis wrote briefly [47] that he and Roger had new clothes and had acquired a coach and horses, coachman and footmen. They had paid visits and been called on by the two English ambassadors, Lord Leicester and Lord Scudamore. Lewis admits that he has sometimes played cards with his brother for trifling sums. He will do so no more, nor will he engage in gaming with others, "if I can conveniently avoid itt." He has never cared much for playbooks and romances; and since his father has forbidden them, he has not "looked on one."

In a letter written on the same date,[48] Roger effusively apologized for his neglect in writing, a neglect of which he has "thought oft much lesse" to be guilty. He is indeed grateful for his good education and Cork's liberal allowance, "solemn counsels," and fatherly affection. The boys have been supplied with new clothes, a coach, "and all other things necessary for those who have the honoure and happinesse to be youre L^{ps} sonns." Lord Leicester once visited them for half an hour; and Lord Scudamore has paid them three visits, always has them sit above him at the table, and always accompanies them to their coach. The capture of Breisach has been the greatest exploit achieved by the French for a long time. Marcombes is commended as "an honest and faithfull servant" to the Earl.

Roger acknowledges that he has sometimes played cards with his brother, after they have finished their exercises; but they have never quarreled on these occasions. He has read no "Playbooks Comical and Tragedicall" since leaving Ireland. If, on his return, his father finds him addicted to any vices, he may justly withdraw his affection, "the greatest misfortune I could have." Sometimes at Saumur Roger did read romances "to passe a few laesy houres" and to improve his French; but since his father has commanded him not to read them, that command "shall be to me an inviolable Law."

It must be suspected that Roger watered down the version of his lazy hours at Saumur to soften parental strictures. He was to remember that his taste for reading French romances was acquired during his youthful travels, for "makeing some Residence in France, I associated my selfe with Persons of my own Age, where I soone found, that he who was Ignorant of the Romances of those Times, was as fitt an Object for Wonder, as a Phylosopher would be, who had never heard of Aristotle, or a Methematician of Euclyd." [49]

In January, 1639, Marcombes wrote to Cork twice,[50] commenting in both letters on his fears that the boys' three suits would be torn or soiled before Easter. When they leave Paris, he will sell the coach and horses at a great loss. He notes that his pupils are well liked by the ambassadors.

Lewis wrote [51] of being invited on New Year's Day to see a play acted in English at Lord Leicester's house. He mentioned that in celebration of the capture of Breisach by Duke Bernhard of Weimar, a solemn Te Deum had been sung in Notre Dame.

Roger continued to be interested in Duke Bernhard, for whose reception in Paris, he wrote,[52] a royal welcome was being prepared. He refers to the New Year's play at Lord Leicester's house. Lord Scudamore has invited the two boys to accompany him to England, and it is their "extreame great desire" to do so and wait upon their father. Meanwhile, they are devoting themselves to their lessons. "Wee do follow our exercises so hard that we have not one spare oure, in the day, for in the morninge from six till ten we ride at the greate horse and runne at the Ringe, from 10 to 12 we fence, from 1 to 3 we dance, and the reste of the day we spende in readinge either summe Geographicall booke, or History or Italian."

In his last letter from Paris,[53] Marcombes stresses the fact that his pupils are serious students, although they do not indeed study "so much as those that will make profession of it." They devote much time to mathematics, "which my Lord of Broughill loves infinitely."

The boys and their tutor crossed the Channel with Lord Scudamore in "a good strong ship" and to their father's delight reached London on the fourth of March. Cork recorded in his Diary their arrival, adding: "for their safe retorn, god be ever humbly and heartily thancked and praised bothe by me and them." [54] The Earl was already in residence in Stalbridge, his new country home in Dorset, and here took place a great family reunion, which included all of Cork's children except his daughter Dorothy. Richard's wife, Lady Dungarvan, and Lady Barrymore had undertaken the heavy burden of keeping house for the hospitable Earl.

Before long, however, Cork considered it his patriotic duty to send his three eldest sons to aid the King against the rebellious Scots. The first Bishops' War was already launched, for the King's Scottish subjects had taken up arms to rescue their church from the dictation of the English bishops. At the beginning of April, 1639, Charles, who was insisting on the authority of the bishops, was in York with a very inadequate army and without funds to maintain it. Most of the young English nobility rallied to their King's support, and many of them raised troops to assist him. Cork gave Dungarvan money to raise and arm one hundred horse; and on the ninth of May, Dungarvan, Kinalmeaky, and Broghill left Stalbridge to join the King's forces. Cork wrote in his Diary: "God I beseech him, retorn them safe, happy and victorious, to my comfort." [55]

Rather in the mood of a Caroline masque, Sir John Suckling, at considerable expense, had equipped his own troop with scarlet coats and breeches, white doublets, and plumed hats. The war relapsed into a spectacle. Even Suckling, who cared little for war, was irked to have the English soldiers reduced to "walking up and down the Banks of Tweed like the Tower Lions in their Cages, leaving the People to think what we wou'd do if we were let loose." [56] Nor was he so frivolous as to be unaware of the King's serious loss of prestige. "Posterity," said Suckling, "must tell this Miracle, that there went an Army from the South, of which there was not one Man lost, nor any Man taken Prisoner but the King." [57]

The concluding ceremonies of this brief, abortive expedition were described by Sir John Temple in letters to Lord Leicester written from Berwick on June 11 and June 20.[58] On the sixth of June the King was informed that the Scots were within view of his camp. He went out to see them and with his perspective glass was able to distinguish their tents on the opposite side of the Tweed. The Scots requested that some English lords be sent to hear their grievances. A meeting was arranged between a group of Covenanters and the Earls of Essex, Salisbury, Holland, Berkshire, the Lord Treasurer, and the Secretary of State. The Scots spoke "plausibly" and were invited to a second conference. On the twentieth, articles of peace were "solemnly published" in the Scottish camp, although not received with much enthusiasm.

On June 24, Broghill returned from Berwick. After riding furiously all night, he arrived at Stalbridge at two o'clock in the morning, bringing the news that the King had concluded an honorable peace with the Scots and had dissolved his army. Lord Barrymore had not had time to arrive from Ireland with his regiment of one thousand foot.[59] The Earl of Cork, always reluctant to criticize the King, nevertheless expressed the private opinion that the King should not have dissolved his army so soon, "for it had been a more brave and safe work to have given . . . lawes with an Army and his sword drawne, then to have stood upon capitulations."[60]

By September negotiations were under way, sponsored by the King and Queen, for the marriage of Francis Boyle to Lady Elizabeth Killigrew, one of the Queen's Maids of Honour, daughter of Lady Stafford by her former husband, Sir Robert Killigrew, the Queen's Vice-Chamberlain. Lady Stafford had "set her heart"[61] on having her daughter marry Broghill, but for some reason this design was abandoned. Cork arrived in London on October 1 to spend the winter at the Savoy Palace, which Sir Thomas Stafford had loaned to him. The Queen soon took the opportunity of thanking him for furthering Francis's match, and he had the honor of kissing her "gracious" hands.

On October 24 Francis and Lady Betty were married in the King's chapel in Whitehall. The King gave a feast to celebrate the marriage, and Cork and three of his daughters sat at the royal table, "amongst all the great Lords and Ladies."[62] The King led the bride out to dance and, at the end of the dancing, led her to her bedchamber, where the Queen "with her own hands" helped to undress her. Cork gave a feast at the Savoy for the bridal couple and various mem-

bers of the Court. Three days later, Francis and Robert were sent abroad for travel and study, with
Marcombes as their tutor. Marcombes was convinced
that such discipline came none too soon for Francis,
who at seventeen had "tasted already a little drope
of ye Libertinage of ye Court." [63]

There was great rejoicing on November 17, when
Lady Dungarvan gave birth to her first son at the
Savoy. On December 12 the child was christened in
the chapel of Sir Thomas Stafford and was named
Charles in honor of the King. The baby's godparents
were the King, the Marquis of Hamilton, the King's
cousin, and the Countess of Salisbury. [64]

The year ended with a second fashionable wedding
in the Earl of Cork's family. On December 26 Lewis,
Viscount Kinalmeaky, married in the King's chapel
in Whitehall Lady Elizabeth Feilding, third daughter
of the Earl and Countess of Denbigh and a Lady of
the Queen's Privy-Chamber. The King gave the young
lady away and put a pearl necklace, the Queen's gift,
about her neck. When the feasting and dancing had
ended, their Majesties brought the bride to her bedchamber, where the Queen and the Maids of Honour
undressed her. Both the King and Queen "kissed and
rekissed" her and blessed the young couple, as did
Cork. [65]

Young Lord Broghill was, of course, involved in
these family festivities and in a variety of social pleas-
ures which his rank and his father's wealth made
available to him. At the same time, he was cultivating
literary tastes which his brothers did not share with
him. He was forming certain friendships, of which we
have little precise information, which were to have a
permanent influence on his life and his literary work.

Probably the most steadying of these friendships

was with Lucius Carey, now Lord Falkland, the "noblest" of King Charles's courtiers. Inevitably, Lord Cork and his children sought the society in England of persons whom they had known in Ireland. Indeed, Carey and Dungarvan had become acquainted in their boyhood at the time when Richard had been ennobled by Carey's father. The friendship continued and may have been invigorated by Carey's marriage to Lettice Morrison, whose father had held various posts in Munster. During the year before his death, Falkland was to correspond with Lady Dungarvan and was to indicate in his letters to her a special concern for Lady Katherine Jones, Broghill's favorite sister, then a virtual prisoner of Irish rebels in Athlone Castle.[66] Lady Katherine was the member of Cork's family whom Falkland most admired, and her regard for him was equally warm. After Falkland's death in the battle of Newbury, she was to plead with Sir Edward Hyde for renewed efforts to secure the peace between King and Parliament of which that "gallant Man," dying, had despaired.[67]

Lady Katherine once remarked that to her "great grief" she had discovered that "the entertainment of lords, ladies, and reasonable creatures, are yet several things." [68] As her father's hostess at the Savoy, she may have observed with alarm the more frivolous diversions to which Broghill succumbed. She no doubt welcomed his friendship with a young nobleman who was also a serious-minded scholar and patron of scholars. At Great Tew or in London Broghill must have been introduced to the "inspired traine" of men of letters for whom Falkland so cordially kept open house.

The poets and dramatists with whom Broghill at eighteen became acquainted were men older than himself and whose literary work was well known. He was always to regard with a certain reverence "my Elder Brethren, ye Poets in London," [69] whom he had first known as a would-be aspirant to fame, with a few manuscript verses, perhaps, to his credit.

Sir John Suckling, the wittiest and most gifted poet of the Court circle, became Broghill's most intimate friend. Both served the King in the Northern Expedition against the Scots in the spring of 1639, and they may have become acquainted at that time. Suckling was to celebrate Broghill's wedding with one of his finest poems, and in another set of verses on the same theme was to note slyly that "Brohall our gallant Friend," although jilted by his first love, could afford "a careless Smile" at that loss when eagerly leading his bride to the altar.[70] Broghill must certainly have seen in 1640 the production of Suckling's *The Discontented Colonel,* later revised as *Brennoralt.* Suckling's influence on the future Lord Orrery's work as a dramatist was to be greater than that of any other author.

We may wonder whether at this early date Broghill already displayed the "graceful temper, soft civility" for which Sir William D'Avenant praised him in his "Poem to My Lord Broghill," printed in 1657 and later entitled "Poem to the Earl of Orrery." [71] In 1657 D'Avenant was ready to affirm:

> *I shall patiently expect my best*
> *Renown from rich Reserves within your Breast.*

In 1639 the case must have been different, and, instead of receiving homage, Broghill may very respectfully have paid it to the new poet laureate. Broghill was much impressed by D'Avenant's Platonic plays, four of which had recently been produced and pub-

lished. Light-hearted spirits might scoff at Platonic
love; but Broghill was never to falter in his allegiance
to that extraordinary literary cult of which D'Avenant
had been made Court interpreter.

Broghill very likely read with approval the three
plays by his brother-in-law, Thomas Killigrew, which
had been printed by 1641. He must have found Killigrew the gayest of companions and been charmed, as
even Marcombes was, by Killigrew's "very sweet and
delectable" conversation.[72] He might not have relished
Marcombes' severe estimate of that young rake as
one "that plays ye foole allwayes through ye Streets
like a scoole Boy having allwayes his mouthe full of
whoores and such discourses, and braging often of his
getting money from this or ye other merchant without any good intention to pay." [73]

Two of Falkland's friends, Edmund Waller and
Abraham Cowley, were to furnish models for Broghill's occasional verses. Both Waller and Cowley wrote
effusive tributes to Falkland for participating in the
King's Northern Expedition; and Cowley went so far
as to suggest that Learning would rather sacrifice the
Bodleian or the Vatican than Falkland.[74] When Cowley's fortunes sank under Oliver Cromwell and he had
suffered imprisonment as a Royalist spy, Broghill encouraged him with a poem, "To Mr. Cowley on His
Davideis," [75] and possibly aided him in more material
ways. Cowley responded with his "Ode. Upon Occasion of a Copy of Verses of my Lord Broghills," in
which he expresses overwhelming gratitude for Broghill's "conquering Pen," drawn in his defense. He will
now be able to serve his Muse once more, since

Nothing so soon the drooping Spirits can raise
As praises from the Men, whom all men praise.[76]

At eighteen, however, Broghill was far from any such eminence. In fact, although he enjoyed the conversation of scholars and wits, he was perhaps equally attracted by the fashionable vices of a libertine Court. Many years later, he remarked to Lord Arlington that in "my yonger Dayes I have had mistresses & som times they were not inexorable." [77] His gaming debts soon reached the formidable total of one thousand pounds,[78] the amount of his annual allowance.

Broghill may not have been many months in London when he fell seriously in love with Frances Harrison, daughter of Sir Richard Harrison. She was one of the Queen's Maids of Honour and Elizabeth Killigrew's "chamberfellow." The courtship had been progressing favorably, and the wedding clothes had been ordered, when the young lady showed signs of wavering. It was rumored that Roger's brother Kinalmeaky, recently married, had "not kept his wedding night yet, as he is still under medical treatment" and that Mistress Harrison "seems to delay" for fear that Broghill might be equally "debaucht." [79]

Mistress Harrison had several ardent suitors; and of one of them, Thomas Howard, Broghill was so jealous that he challenged him to a duel. The rivals fought briefly, neither one being wounded, and the quarrel was soon made up. Cork's relief at this happy outcome is evident in the entry which he made in his Diary on January 20, 1640:

> This day as my son Broghill was at my table at dynner wth me, he was secretly called away by a messadg from Charles Riche, son to the earle of warwick, to answer a challenge he brought him from M[r] Tho. Howard, Son to the earle of Barckshier [Berkshire] ; whereuppon Broghill secretly avoyded the howse, bought him a sworde, and found Jack Barry, whom he made choice of to be his

second, and went bothe in Broghills coach, wth their
seconds, into the feilds, where they fought wth their
Rapiers, and bothe returned wthout any wound, onely
Broghill took away the frindg of Mr Howards glove wth
a passadg of his Rapier that went throughe from his hand
between his Arme and the syde of his boddy, without any
other harme, and theruppon their seconds parted them,
and made them frends; and soe they came home, supped
together; and all this for Mrs Harrison.[80]

Mistress Harrison's ultimate decision not to marry
Broghill gave Cork "very great satisfaction." Broghill's sister Mary commented that her father was always averse to this match, "though to comply with
my brother's passion he consented to it." [81] Despite
the Queen's entreaties to the contrary, Mistress Harrison chose to give her hand to Thomas Howard, declaring that she "had rather begg wth Mr Howard then
live in the greatest plenty that could bee with either
my Lord B^r[oghill], Charles Rich or Mr Nevill." Dorothy Osborne professed amazement at this decision,
since, in her opinion, Mr. Howard was not "a person
that can deserve one should necglect all ye world for
him." [82]

The night after his duel with Broghill Howard
danced in D'Avenant's masque, *Salmacida Spolia,* presented by their Majesties at the masquing house at
Whitehall. If Broghill was present at this entertainment, he must have seen under rather dazzling circumstances the young woman who was to console him for
the loss of Mistress Harrison and whom he was to
marry the following year. At a dramatic moment in the
masque, a varicolored cloud appeared in the sky, in
which sat the Queen, surrounded by ten martial ladies.
Among the ladies, dressed like the rest in a carnation
habit embroidered with silver, wearing a plumed hel-

met and armed with an antique sword, was Lady Margaret Howard.[83] The cloud floated gently to earth with its fair occupants, who withdrew from it to dance with the King's masquers. At Shrovetide there was a second performance of this masque, the last gay spectacle of the doomed Court.

It had become apparent that the rebel army at the Scottish border would not remain inactive. Charles bestowed an earldom on Wentworth, Cork's old enemy, and sent him to Ireland to raise subsidies and troops for a second northern expedition. Lord Northumberland was to command a new army against the Scots, and Wentworth, now Earl of Strafford, was to be Lieutenant-General. To equip and maintain an army large enough to be really effective, a Parliamentary grant was essential. The King summoned the Short Parliament to obtain the needed funds and when they were not forthcoming, rashly dissolved it. The day when Parliament was dissolved, May 5, Cork labeled "This doleful Tuesday." [84]

Other conservative Royalists besides Cork were dismayed by the King's highhanded ways. Northumberland loaned the King five thousand pounds but admitted that he could "Joy but little in my Charge." [85] He confessed: "It greeves my Soule to be involved in these Councells." [86] The King's situation impressed him as desperate. "It is impossible," he wrote to Lord Leicester, "that things can long continue in the Condition they now are in; so generall a Defection in this Kingdome hath not beene knowne in the Memorie of any." [87] Illness prevented Northumberland from assuming his distasteful command, and Strafford had to head the King's army. When the King reached York late in August, to be joined by Strafford, the Scots had already crossed the Tweed. Their occupation of Newcastle and Durham could not be prevented, and a peace had to be negotiated, "which I feare," said Northumberland, "will be the most dishonorable one for the King, that ever Prince gave to his Subjects." [88] Unable to pay his army, the King was compelled to summon the Long Parliament, which met on November 3.

There are brief references to Broghill in Cork's Diary during these troubled months. Broghill had been appointed commander of a troop of one hundred horse against the Scots; but he seems not to have taken the command.[89] On April 30 Dungarvan, Kinalmeaky, and Broghill attended the funeral in Westminster Abbey of Charles, Earl of Arran, only son of the Marquis of Hamilton and his wife Margaret, eldest daughter of the Earl and Countess of Denbigh.[90] On July 8 Broghill left London with his father for Stalbridge.[91] On October 13 Cork sent him to York with one thousand pounds in gold as a free gift to the King.[92] Already the campaign had ended, and the Treaty of Ripon was being concluded.

On January 27, 1641, Broghill married Lady Margaret Howard, second daughter of Theophilus, second Earl of Suffolk, by his wife Elizabeth, daughter of George Home, Earl of Dunbar. The young bridegroom was nineteen, his bride nearly eighteen. Lady Margaret was born in London in 1623.[93] At the age of seven, she lost her mother. Her father, before his death, had been honored with various Court appointments and had held the offices of Lord Warden of the Cinque Ports and Constable of Dover Castle. The marriage of the orphaned bride took place at the London house of her older sister Catherine, the wife of George Stewart, Lord d'Aubigny, third son of the Duke of Lennox.

Lord Cork was pleased with Broghill's marriage.

He added five thousand pounds to Lady Margaret's dowry of five thousand pounds and with the total sum purchased Marston Bigot, near Frome in Somerset, as a country residence for the young couple. The house was a pleasant one, and there were eight hundred acres of gardens, orchards, fields, and woodlands. Cork conveyed in a deed to Broghill the Castle of Broghill and three hundred acres around it to increase Lady Margaret's jointure.[94]

In his well-known *Ballad upon a Wedding*, Suckling paints a picture of Broghill's wedding as it might have appeared to a gaping country fellow describing it to a rustic companion. The bridegroom, richly dressed, is a splendid sight. The bride is as round and plump as a grape "that's kindly ripe." Her finger is so small that the ring would not stay on, her mouth so small that her teeth almost broke her words, though she speaks well.

> *Her Feet beneath her Petticoat,*
> *Like little Mice stole in and out,*
> *   As if they fear'd the Light:*
> *But oh! she dances such a way!*
> *No Sun upon an Easter-Day,*
> *   Is half so fine a Sight.*

> .   .   .   .

> *Her cheeks so rare a white was on,*
> *No Dazy makes Comparison,*
> *   (Who sees them is undone)*
> *For Streaks of red were mingled there,*
> *Such as are on a Katherine Pear,*
> *   The Side that's next the Sun.*

> *Her lips were red, and one was thin*
> *Compar'd to that was next her chin,*
> *   Some Bee had stung it newly.*

> *But (Dick) her Eyes so guard her Face,*
> *I durst no more upon them gaze,*
> *Than on the Sun in July.*

After the wedding ceremony, the feasting and dancing go merrily forward, and the bride is envied by every woman, the bridegroom by every man.[95]

In the year that followed this festive wedding, the author of the delectable ballad upon it died obscurely in France. The husband of the bride's sister was killed in the battle of Edgehill. The bridegroom whom "ev'ry Man" envied was to risk his life daily in defense of lands and honor. And the envied bride was to lose her first child during the siege of Lismore.

Broghill's future was to present more perils and difficulties than fall to the lot of most men. But his marriage was to bring him a generous measure of domestic happiness. His bride was to become, in the words of his brother Robert, "the great support, ornament, and comfort" of her family.[96] Broghill's manuscript verses on marriage have unfortunately been lost. Sir Thomas Peyton enclosed a copy of them in a letter to his sister-in-law, Dorothy Osborne, indicating that he admired them.[97]

Shortly after Broghill's marriage, the long trial of the Earl of Strafford began. Strafford had been accused of treason by John Pym and his followers in the House of Commons, who complained that he subverted the law of the kingdom by plotting to coerce Parliament with a northern army. The Earl's dignified defense could not dispel the prevailing opinion that the King intended to strengthen his own authority by bringing over from Ireland the army of Irish Papists that Strafford had raised and placing them under the Earl's command. The King's influence was further weakened by the fact that as a result of his unwise policies, two rival armies in the north were clamoring for their pay. When the House of Commons voted to assign to the Scots ten thousand pounds which had previously been set aside for the English forces,[98] the latter were resentful. This disaffection was fanned by members of the Royalist party in an effort to strengthen the King's position. Two groups of conspirators, one headed by Henry Percy, the Earl of Northumberland's younger brother, and the other by Suckling, worked separately, and to some extent in consultation with each other, in a design to bring forces from the north to assist the King.

Suckling's project expanded into the more dangerous of the two plots. When it became evident that Strafford must die, Suckling rather openly raised troops in the city to aid Charles in his ill-fated attempt to seize the Tower and free the Earl. Colonel Goring's shameless betrayal of both plots was disclosed in the House of Commons on May 5; and on the sixth, shortly before English ports were ordered closed, Suckling, Percy, and Henry Jermyn escaped to France. D'Avenant was captured but later released.[99]

It is possible, but not probable, that Broghill was involved in Suckling's plot. The communicative Goring did not include his brother-in-law's name in his list of conspirators;[100] nor did Percy mention Broghill in his letter of confession and apology to Northumberland.[101] At a later date, Cork warned both Dungarvan and Broghill against participating in Royalist intrigues.[102] It is difficult to imagine that Broghill could have been interested in saving the life of his father's most hated enemy. On May 12, the date of Strafford's execution, Cork noted tersely in his Diary that the

Earl of Strafford was beheaded on Tower Hill, "as
he well deserved." [103] Broghill lost in Suckling the
most brilliant of the companions of his youth. His
reaction to Suckling's flight and obscure death in
France is unknown. We must seek in his plays Broghill's tribute to this deeply valued friendship.

On July 21 Cork's "unruly daughter Mary" privately married, at the age of fifteen, the bridegroom
of her choice, Charles Rich, second son of the Earl
of Warwick. Mary Boyle had been in disgrace with
her father ever since her refusal to marry James
Hamilton, only son of the Earl of Clandeboye. After
Francis Boyle had been sent abroad with Marcombes,
Mary had shared a chamber with her brother's wife,
who "enticed" her to spend her time in reading plays
and romances and "in exquisite and curious dress-
ing." [104] She succumbed to the romantic courtship of
Mr. Rich, one of Mistress Harrison's cast-off suitors,
who wooed her at her bedside on his knees when she was
ill with measles. Lady Stafford, Francis Boyle's mother-
in-law, whom Mary regarded as "a cunning old woman,
and who had been herself too much and too long versed
in amours," [105] interceded in vain with Lord Cork in
support of this match. The refractory young lady was
hurried away in Broghill's coach to spend ten weeks
in seclusion in a little house near Hampton Court.
Here Dungarvan and Broghill "examined" their
younger sister and returned to Cork "highly unsatisfied" with her answers.[106] Eventually she broke down
her father's resistance, and he gave her a large dowry
of seven thousand pounds. His children's marriages
had been costly, and the Earl wrote to his Irish steward: "I shall come home like a spent salmon, as weak
and empty as may be." [107]

On September 21, soon after the adjournment of the Long Parliament, Cork left London with Broghill and Lady Broghill. He had decided to return to Ireland as a place of refuge from the civil strife that was grieving "all true English hearts." He also desired a more sober way of life for members of his family who had remained in England. Dungarvan and Kinalmeaky were already in Ireland; and the anxious father was receiving encouraging reports that Kinalmeaky had given up the "wenching, gaming, and Lasciviousness" [108] that he had been unable to resist in London. The young wife of Francis refused to accompany her father-in-law, to the distress of Marcombes, who decided to conceal from her husband as long as possible her unfortunate decision. Francis and Robert were safe in Geneva, breathing its pure air and enjoying its "good peace," at a time when the rest of the world seemed "altogether by ye eares." [109]

The Earl of Cork spent four days making a stately progress from London to Stalbridge. At Egham he was met by Lord Goring, the Countess of Holland, and Sir Thomas Stafford and his Lady. On September 22 Cork bade farewell to Sir Thomas for the last time. The following June the Earl was to receive from his old friend, then with the exiled Court at The Hague and Treasurer of the Queen's Household, a despairing letter, with the mournful announcement: "yor humble servant lives, and when I have said that, it's all." [110]

At Bagshot Cork was joined by Lady Kinalmeaky, who was to travel to Ireland with him. She was escorted by the Countess of Denbigh, the Countess of Richmond, and other ladies and gentlemen of the Court. There were several meals and a night's lodging for these guests, at the Earl's expense, before they returned to Oatlands. After a fortnight at Stalbridge, Cork proceeded to the new home at Marston, where other guests were entertained. The crossing to Ireland from Minehead was singularly calm and speedy; and on October 17 the Earl and his children landed in Youghal in time for morning prayers.[111]

2

The Art of War

In retrospect, Broghill compared the Irish Rebellion, which broke out in Ireland in October, 1641, to "a sudden storm of lightning and thunder." [1] Like other Munster landlords, the Earl of Cork, the most powerful of them all, had no advance warning of the impending tragedy, despite the fact that for fifty-four years he had lived chiefly in Ireland and had "made it a great parte of my Study to understand this kingdome and people in their owne true essence and nature." [2] No black clouds had been visible on the Irish horizon.

From John Whalley, his steward at Lismore, Lord Cork had had reassuring news of his family. Kinalmeaky, whose wild ways had so greatly worried his father, had promised amendment and had received Cork's gift of one hundred and fifty pounds. The garden, orchards, bowling green, and wilderness of Lismore were all in good order. The fine new pike pond had been completed, and a warmer bedchamber had been arranged for the aging Earl. [3]

Suddenly, only six days after the Earl and members of his family had landed in Youghal, [4] the Irish Rebellion broke out in Ulster. Unaware of the gathering storm, the Earl's party reached Lismore the evening

38

of October 19.[5] Several days later, there was a family reunion at Castlelyons, the residence of Cork's son-in-law, Lord Barrymore. The guests were at dinner when Cork was called from the table by a breathless messenger, who brought letters and the news that thousands of the Irish had been in rebellion for three days, were in arms everywhere, and had committed many outrages. Cork went through with the meal, then read his letters, and called aside Viscount Muskerry, who was among the guests and who "made light" of the report. The Earl could no longer conceal his concern, told his family the distressing news, and sent a warning letter to Sir William St. Leger, Lord President of Munster.[6]

On the eve of the Rebellion, Dublin had been saved, when Owen O'Conolly, a Protestant in the service of Sir John Clotworthy, betrayed a plan to seize Dublin Castle and murder the Lords Justices and the Council. But on the morning of October 23, the rising began, as scheduled, in Ulster; and dire accounts of its progress soon reached the Lords Justices. On November 11 the House of Commons received word from Dublin that without speedy relief from England, all the English Protestants in Ireland were likely to be destroyed and the kingdom lost.[7] On December 14 a letter was read in the House giving appalling details of brutal massacres everywhere in Ireland, except in Munster.[8]

Munster was, however, gravely endangered. Nearly all of its soldiers were withdrawn to guard Dublin, and St. Leger was left with a single troop to guard the province. Leaving the countryside unprotected, the terrified English settlers fled to their scattered garrisons and walled towns, to await a tempest which they were so feebly prepared to resist.

The English Parliament recognized the strategic importance of the ports of Munster and voted to send some assistance to that province.[9] Richard, Lord Dungarvan, was appointed Governor of Youghal and received arms to supply a troop of horse.[10] The Earl of Cork raised among his English tenants a troop of one hundred horse for Lewis, Lord Kinalmeaky, and another for Roger, Lord Broghill, and paid them out of his own funds as long as he was able to do so.[11] Kinalmeaky was sent to defend Bandon, Broghill to defend Lismore, and Cork himself undertook the defense of Youghal.

In December, St. Leger and his son-in-law, Murrough O'Brien, Baron Inchiquin, Vice-President of Munster, marched against Leinster rebels who were harassing Waterford and Tipperary and killed six hundred without the loss of one man.[12] But before the end of the month, Richard Butler, Viscount Mountgarret, the Marquis of Ormonde's brother, invaded Munster with a formidable army of fourteen thousand men, whose pikes "made as great a show as a spacious wood."[13] Clonmel, "the key of Munster,"[14] twelve miles from Lismore, was taken, the town of Dungarvan was betrayed, and only the strongest garrisons held out.

In January, 1642, "after a heavy and sorrowful Christmas," Cork wrote from Youghal to his son-in-law, George Goring, describing the plight of his province, "wherein are more cities and walled towns, and more brave harbours and havens than all the rest of the kingdom hath." The Irish inhabitants were three to one in the "poor weak town" of Youghal. Lord Dungarvan had been summoned to the aid of St. Leger. Walled up at Lismore, Broghill was restive and eager for action, for he was "full of hot blood and courage." Lady Broghill was expecting her first child.[15]

John Whalley informed Lord Cork that Broghill was "very industrious in the preparing and trayning of his troopes." [16] A firm believer in military discipline, Broghill was convinced that "none can expect to have a good Orchard, who has his Trees out of a bad Nursery." [17] When he heard that the enemy were approaching Lismore, he was ready to sally forth and give them one blow before they besieged him, provided he had one-third of their numbers; but if such a move should be "more folly than Valour," he would devote himself to defending the castle. "My Lord," he assured Cork, "fear nothing for Lismore, for if it be lost, it shall be with the life of him that begs your Lordship's blessing." [18] Broghill wrote frequent short notes to his father, begging, "though it much grieves me," [19] for much needed money and commenting compassionately on the sufferings of his soldiers.

Of the first siege of Lismore a graphic account has been preserved in a letter written by Broghill's chaplain, Urban Vigors, to Henry Jones.[20] The castle was besieged by the same force that had recently compelled the members of a captured garrison at Tallow to hang one another. The rebels quartered in the town of Lismore and placed their sentinels in the churchyard. On February 23 the castle was summoned. A gentleman rode up to it with a drummer before him and offered Broghill honorable terms and a safe convoy for his people. Broghill protested that he was unacquainted with such language and that his "absolute answer" was that he would live and die in the castle. After drinking a few glasses of wine and aqua vitae, the gentleman left. Being a "vigilant man," Broghill placed good guards, reassured hundreds of people who had taken refuge in the castle, and watched himself for three successive nights. Vigors observed: "my honourable Lady was newly brought to bedd of a Child, other wise I dare say, shee would likewise have watched in person, for shee is a Lady that truely feares God, abhorrs and detests Rebeles, and I know but few men in the land will shoote off a fowling peece better or neerer the marke then her Ladiship."

The first qualification for a good general, Broghill maintained, is great presence of mind in all emergencies. "The moments to obtain victory are few." [21] As the siege of Lismore continued, an effective stratagem occurred to him. He ordered all of the castle ordnance —harquebuses, muskets, carbines, pistols—shot off at once, and spread a report that reinforcements from England had arrived in the town. In dismay the rebels fled to the Blackwater and boarded boats at Affane. Broghill and his men pursued them, securing many prisoners, wagons, scaling ladders, and hundreds of stolen cattle.

Lord Cork was impressed by Broghill's resolution and resourcefulness and by the fact that his "good lady lay in at Lismore without the least discouradgment." [22] The child born under such adverse circumstances did not survive; but there were soon hopes of a second "lusty boy" to "recompence the loss of the first." [23]

Although Lismore had been preserved, conditions there continued to be rigorous. The native Irish were driving all cattle that they owned or could seize over the Blackwater; all ploughs were idle; no rents could be collected; and the inmates of the castle were threatened with famine. At night the flames from five hundred fires could be seen between the Blackwater and the town of Dungarvan.[24] Cork sent his son as much ammunition as he could spare, and Broghill declared, "we waste as little as any garrison in Ireland." [25] When their pay was reduced and his soldiers were on the verge of mutiny, Broghill quieted their complaints. He made what raids he could and longed to do "som gallant exploit," [26] but dared not stay long outside his garrison. "We make war," he perceived, "more like Foxes than Lyons," with twenty sieges for one battle.[27]

While Broghill was engaged at Lismore, Kinalmeaky, soon to die a soldier's death, was displaying great courage and enterprise in the defense of Bandon. In one bitter sortie, in which he lost no men, one hundred and four of the enemy were slain and fourteen prisoners taken.[28] But he had no pay for his soldiers and very little powder, and the rebels around Bandon multiplied "like Hydra's heads." [29] Cork's son-in-law, David Barry, Earl of Barrymore, took the field with his troop to defend his lands and tenants; and his charitable Countess sheltered, fed, and clothed many destitute families that had taken refuge at Castlelyons.

Divided loyalties were a source of added misery in such confused times. Inchiquin, although a Protestant, was Irish by birth and was already suspected of protecting and being protected by his many Catholic relatives and friends in rebellion.[30] Such charges were to plague him throughout his campaigns in Ireland.

The Earl of Cork, struggling to defend Youghal, lacked the vigor of his young sons and son-in-law. He was "full of distractions, not like the man he was." [31] Youghal was "very weak and ruinous," its walls much in need of repairs.[32] Before the Rebellion, Cork's rents had yielded him fifty pounds a day, whereas now he had less than fifty pence a week and had sold his plate to pay his soldiers. Sir Charles Vavasour's arrival in Youghal with one thousand foot on February 24 gave the Earl fresh hope. But the news of Vavasour's coming spurred the rebels to violent measures. They seized and hanged eight of Cork's English tenants and buried one woman alive.[33]

Immediately after landing, Vavasour joined St. Leger and Cork's eldest son, Richard, and took the castle and town of Dungarvan. The defection of Muskerry shortly afterwards was a painful blow. When Muskerry marched with four thousand men toward Cork to besiege the city, St. Leger hastened back to defend it. In April, Muskerry was routed outside Cork and lost about four hundred men and much of his equipment. He was again defeated in June.[34] He justified his rebellion by producing a commission from the King which Broghill examined and discovered to be a forgery.[35] During the siege of Cork, St. Leger, worn out and disillusioned, died on the second of July, and Inchiquin assumed the chief command of the English forces in Munster.

At the beginning of September, Sir Philip Percival's castle at Liscarrol, after a siege of thirteen days, surrendered on honorable terms to General Barry, who had besieged it with seven thousand foot, five hundred horse, and a train of artillery. On September 3 with greatly inferior forces, Inchiquin defeated Barry and recovered the castle in the hard-fought battle of Liscarrol. Barry lost seven hundred men, Inchiquin twelve. Four of Cork's sons fought bravely in this engagement, and Kinalmeaky was killed by a musket shot. As Kinalmeaky fell from his horse, Francis Boyle, at the risk of his life, seized the horse's bridle, in a vain endeavor to save his brother. On September 29 the Earl of Barrymore died from the wounds which he had received at Liscarrol. Both young noblemen were buried with military honors in the Earl of Cork's chapel in Youghal.[36]

In November, Dungarvan and his family and Broghill and Lady Broghill embarked for England.[37] Aid
for Munster was desperately needed, and no stone
must be left unturned to obtain it. In a letter to
Dungarvan,[38] Cork expressed his fears for the journey
and its outcome. Disregarding his orders, Dungarvan
and Broghill had chosen a pilot in whom their father
had no confidence. Scarcely had they left Youghal
harbor, when a "hideous Storme arose." The old Earl
acknowledged that he had knelt in prayer, begging
God to forgive his sons' contempt for his "just commands" and to bring them safely to shore. He now
solemnly entreated them to perform faithfully the
vows which they had made to him, lest the estate
should be lost which he had acquired for them with so
much labor, expense, and time. They must "be extreame carefull how you carry y'selves & what company you keep, for the tymes are so full of danger that
no honest man knowes whom to trust." Youghal had
food for only two months, and supplies must be hastened. "I shall not sleep quietly," Cork concluded,
"untill I heare from you at large, & therefore I pray
you wryte frequently and liberally unto me."

A fortnight later, Cork wrote again to Dungarvan,[39]
reminding him that no supplies of food had reached
Youghal since the outbreak of the Rebellion. Cork had
fifteen companies to feed, and without speedy relief
these would mutiny or starve. His only provisions
were salt beef, bread, barreled butter, and cold water,
which made "a rich Churchyard & a weak Garrison."
He grieved to see soldiers die daily who might have
done their King and country good service.

At the end of December, Cork received a letter
from his favorite daughter, Lady Katherine Jones.[40]
After withstanding a siege of twenty-two months at

Athlone Castle, she had accepted a safe conduct, scrupulously carried out, from the rebel commander, Sir James Dillon, and with her daughters and infant son had reached Dublin in safety. The sufferings which she had witnessed had made her decide to leave "this bleeding & well neare ruined Commonwealth." A report that her father was dangerously ill had troubled her greatly. The death of Kinalmeaky she must not lament, "encountered in soe just a cause, & so noble a way."

The King's desire to conciliate the now confederated Irish Catholics became increasingly apparent and increasingly disturbing to the English Protestants in Ireland. In January, 1643, Charles instructed the Marquis of Ormonde and the Earl of Clanricarde to confer with the Catholic leaders and give him a summary of their complaints. In March the two groups of commissioners met and dispatched their proposals to the King. Charles was eager for a truce that would at least bring back to England, to support him in his quarrel with Parliament, the English soldiers who had been opposing the Rebellion. The Irish Catholics held out the still brighter prospect of an Irish army of ten thousand men to defend his cause, if he would consent to a free Irish Parliament and unrestricted freedom of worship for Irish Catholics.

Meanwhile, Inchiquin and other commanders pleaded in vain with Parliament for pay and food for their half-starved soldiers. The Adventurers' Bill[41] had helped to increase the English forces in Ireland; but the necessary equipment for them failed to arrive. Inchiquin protested bitterly against the policy of sending over men without arms, which was useless, unless "these men shall with jaw-bones kill soe many rebbells." [42]

Cork continued to write to his absent sons. He bade them hasten home, since nothing was to be gotten in England but expense of money and time, and in Ireland they might do themselves "some good one way or other." [43] He complained of Inchiquin's lack of cooperation with him, warned them not to become involved in Lord Savile's dangerous designs, and urged them to "chaw the cudd" upon his former letters. [44]

Cork took the precaution of sending to England four trunks and his "red box of writings," which had "matters of great weight and value in them." [45] He instructed his English steward at Stalbridge to take particular care of the papers and of one hundred pounds which he had sent him and to keep his woods, orchards, gardens, walks, bowling green, and wilderness at Stalbridge in good order. His English rents were now his sole source of revenue, "for all that I have heere is wasted and gone." Cork was unable to write the letter in his own hand but signed his name with trembling fingers.

Inchiquin lacked strength for a spring offensive and resorted to some dubious intriguing with Muskerry, which aroused the resentment of Cork and his sons. Muskerry agreed to spare Youghal, if Inchiquin would not oppose his capture of Cork's castles of Lismore and Cappoquin. Inchiquin agreed not to interfere for a certain length of time, but he did strengthen the two garrisons. [46] The first fruit of this secret agreement was the burning of Lismore town early one Sunday morning. Cork's almshouses and most of the thatched houses and cabins were destroyed. Two almsmen and about sixty Irish tenants, including women and children, were killed and others taken away as prisoners. [47] On June 3 Sir Charles Vavasour and Francis Boyle retaliated by capturing the castle of Cloghleigh, where they put the entire garrison to the sword. But the following day, as the victors prepared to return to Castlelyons, a large body of rebels attacked them, killed and wounded a number of officers and thirty soldiers, and carried off Vavasour and other officers as prisoners. Cork recorded the defeat in his Diary, adding sadly: "God in mercie turn His heavy hand from us." [48]

Cappoquin was besieged late in June by Lieutenant-General Purcell. Although the castle received many shots, Captain Hugh Croker repelled the rebels, and about three hundred of them were killed or wounded. Among the slain was the officer who had led the invaders in the burning of Lismore town.[49]

After wasting the country around Cappoquin, Purcell, assisted by Muskerry, besieged Lismore. On another Sunday morning, the twenty-third of July, they stormed the castle and made a breech in the walls, which the defenders repaired. Quarter was offered but refused. The assailants were discouraged by constant heavy fire from the castle turrets and after eight days withdrew.[50] To Captain Broadrip, who had defended the castle so well, Cork sent as a reward a gift of five pounds, a riding coat, doublet, breeches, and his own cloak of black Waterford frieze lined with black taffeta.[51]

Dungarvan and Broghill landed in Youghal in July,[52] and Broghill at once returned to Lismore. As an aftermath of the siege of the castle, hay and corn which the rebels had left had to be salvaged. Raiding for cattle was resumed. Cork received an appeal for wood for the house and for a small lime kiln to provide lime for mending the castle walls. Cork's allowance of forty pounds a week was "too slender a purse" for Broghill's housekeeping.[53] In the midst of such endless demands on his vanishing resources, the old Earl died on September 15, 1643, and was buried in the curious, ornate tomb which he had built for himself and his family in St. Mary's church in Youghal. Dungarvan became second Earl of Cork.

Also on September 15 the articles of a Cessation of hostilities for twelve months, as ordered by the King, was signed by Ormonde and the Confederate Catholics. The uneasy peace was far from reassuring to the English Protestants in Munster, who now had to see the province drained of a large part of Inchiquin's troops for the King's service in England. One English regiment from Munster landed at Minehead on October 23 and a second soon afterwards at Bristol. It was at first assumed that the soldiers were Irish rebels, brought over to massacre the Protestants in England. Even when the facts were known, it was feared that an army of native Irish would soon follow, as indeed the King secretly intended. Charles appointed James Butler, Marquis of Ormonde, Lord Lieutenant of Ireland and sent him complicated instructions for securing the support of the Irish. A vehement reaction from the Parliamentary leaders to the King's procedures and suspected intentions was inevitable. On November 10 the House of Commons accused Inchiquin of treason for sending forces to England against Parliament.[54] On November 11 Parliament authorized the use of the Parliamentary Great Seal, which was subsequently entrusted to six of its commissioners.

Inchiquin had never received from the King a commission as Lord President of Munster, and in February, 1644, he arrived at Oxford to request that title. Unfortunately, Charles had previously promised the post to the Earl of Portland and believed that he should keep his word. Inchiquin left Oxford a resentful and discontented man.

In the affairs of Munster the King had relatively little interest. He was deeply involved in an intrigue with the Earl of Glamorgan, to whom he gave a secret commission to command the hypothetical army of ten thousand Irish soldiers and other forces to be supplied by the Catholic princes of Europe. The Irish army could not be achieved without granting demands, which the King himself recognized as excessive, on the part of the Confederate Catholics. Their agents waited on the King at Oxford at the end of March and were followed in April by Protestant agents, whose demands were equally extravagant and opposed in every way to those of the Catholics.[55]

As the Cessation continued and the situation of the English Protestants in Munster still further deteriorated, Inchiquin decided to support Parliament against the King. On July 17 Inchiquin, Broghill, and the other commanders in Munster sent a letter to the King from Cork to explain that they were taking up arms to defend their religion, their lives, and his interests. They were appealing to Parliament for aid and trusted that both the King and Parliament would recognize the justice and necessity of the Irish War. They reminded the King that the Irish had publicly proclaimed that they had his commission for what they had done. "We aim at nothing," they affirmed, "but Gods glory, your Majesties honour, and the safety of the English Nation." [56]

On July 18 the same officers sent a letter from Cork to the Houses of Parliament.[57] They alleged that they had submitted to the Cessation only to preserve their garrisons. They now put themselves under the pro-

tection of Parliament and were ready to prove their
loyalty by offering Parliament a chance to secure any
of their garrisons. The unhappy misunderstanding of
the King and Parliament had prevented the continu-
ance of their supplies, and the army sent to relieve
them had lived upon them. The rebels had taken advantage of the Cessation to send their wardens to
demolish castles, to place guards on the highways to
interrupt the markets, and to murder Englishmen who
left their garrisons to buy food. The "deluded" King
was prepared to grant the Irish "overswaying Votes."
A Franciscan friar, just executed, had confessed before
his death that he had agreed to betray the town of
Cork to Muskerry. No faith could be expected from
a people whose religion forbade them to keep faith.
In resuming their arms, the Protestants resolved to
perform their duty and "maintain that which is a
thousand times more deare unto us, our Religion."

At about the same date, Broghill implored his
brother-in-law, the Earl of Northumberland, the husband of Lady Orrery's sister Elizabeth, to use his
influence to secure aid from "that noble Assembly"
which had the Protestant religion so much at heart.[58]
Inchiquin wrote letters to his brother, Lieutenant-
Colonel Harry O'Brien,[59] and other officers [60] who had
left Munster to serve the King, requesting them to
return to Ireland in the service of Parliament, and
promising them advancement and good pay. He expelled Irish Papists from Cork, Kinsale, and Bandon;
and Parliament shipping soon filled all of the Munster
ports under his command.[61]

As newly appointed Governor of Youghal, Broghill
issued a series of terse orders designed to safeguard
the town against possible rebel action.[62] In accordance
with the policy followed in other Munster ports, he

required all Papists to leave Youghal at a certain date,
taking nothing but their clothes with them. Any looting
of the abandoned houses was to be punished by death.
The markets were to continue. All who subsisted on
charity must take ship for England. All able-bodied
adults must attend divine service regularly. For any
evasion of these orders, penalties were prescribed to
suit the severity of the offense.

For the time being, the Munster officers could do
little more than keep their garrisons together. Early
in November, a Dutch ship brought Broghill desperately needed provisions.[63] In November,[64] leaving Sir
William Fenton as his Deputy, Broghill went to London to plead for greater speed in the relief of his
province; and in December,[65] he presented his "humble
propositions" to the Committee of Both Kingdoms for
Irish Affairs.

Broghill managed to impress upon Parliament his
own merits and Munster's needs. In January, 1645,
the Committee for Irish Affairs sent a letter to
Inchiquin requesting him to give Broghill a commission
as General of the Horse in Munster, in recognition of
his "good service" in Ireland before the Cessation and
his "present care & diligence" in soliciting the affairs
of his province. The Committee expressed the hope
that "such merit may ever have all due encouragement."[66] Broghill returned to Ireland soon afterwards,[67] bringing with him Inchiquin's commission as
Lord President of Munster, ten thousand pounds, and
a promise that two thousand of the Ulster troops
would be transferred to Munster. Most of the money
was immediately spent on arms and food, so that in
a few weeks the troops were again living on chance
supplies.

Broghill's reaction to the worsening relations between the King and Parliament can only be surmised. His sister Katherine, now Lady Ranelagh,[68] wrote an eloquent letter to Sir Edward Hyde, imploring him, in memory of gallant Lord Falkland, to persuade the King to conciliate Parliament, while Prince Rupert's feats in the north (in the second Bishops' War) encouraged "a hearkening temper." It must be a Parliament, she observed, where its Houses are, of which the King's party called themselves members. "I beseech you," she begged, "stop their mouthes." [69]

In April, 1645, hostilities were resumed on a large scale. The Earl of Castlehaven invaded Munster with six thousand men and quickly captured Liscarrol, Cappoquin, Mallow, Doneraile, Castlelyons, Lismore, and nearly all of the other castles in co. Cork. On June 26,[70] Lismore, after a brave resistance by Major Power, was reduced almost to a ruin. The country was ravaged to the walls of Cork, where Inchiquin, whose forces were half the size of Castlehaven's, was compelled to shut up his army. Broghill went to England in June, "with a resolution, never to implore more aide, if not now cheerfully relieved." [71]

By the end of June, Castlehaven was gravely threatening Youghal. On July 5, a group of refugee ladies from Youghal arrived in Cork, including Lady Broghill, Lady Barrymore, Lady Smith, and "many other women of quality, together with their children and the best of their household stuff." [72] Captain Claxton brought them to Cork bay, where Lord Inchiquin and Sir William Fenton met them in Sir William Penn's pinnace.

The siege of Youghal lasted for many weeks. The rebels built a fort at the harbor's mouth and mounted ordnance there. They succeeded in blowing up the *Duncannon* frigate, one of two ships guarding the harbor. The same day they fired on a group of officers watching their maneuvers from a blockhouse on the quay, killing one officer, wounding others, and endangering Sir Percy Smith, Deputy Governor in Broghill's absence. Castlehaven intended to starve out the town, which for a month had no provisions for the soldiers, except what was forcibly taken from the distressed inhabitants. With difficulty Captain Penn and Captain Swanley brought in supplies by night.[73] On one occasion a thick Irish mist prevented the men at the fort from seeing the sails of three or four ships passing by.[74] In September, Broghill returned from England, bringing men, ammunition, and food; and early in December, Castlehaven raised the siege.[75]

Since Castlehaven attempted nothing more, the Supreme Council of Confederate Catholics sent Preston in his place. The two became rival generals, with separate armies, which they kept a few miles apart. Their failure to unite prevented their effective action, and both were recalled to Kilkenny. A small force left behind in the earth fort near Youghal surrendered after a three days' siege.[76]

The summer's campaign had brought the Parliamentary forces few victories. In May, Broghill had won a battle with his cavalry near Castlelyons.[77] Ballymartyr was besieged and captured in August and hastily burned, when Castlehaven "came on so fast with his forces." [78] By December, Inchiquin's army was in such straits that he hastened to London to appeal to Parliament once more for speedier aid. He left Broghill in Cork as his Deputy. Broghill wrote to Sir Philip Percival: "We have come to the crisis of our disease and must either immediately recover or die." [79]

Broghill had some knowledge of the King's attempts to obtain an Irish army. In those troubled times, intercepted letters and captured documents threw light in dark places. Glamorgan took advantage of the vague but large powers which the King had granted him to offer the Confederate Catholics more concessions than the King had intended or had dared to propose. When the Papal Nuncio, Rinuccini, arrived in Ireland in October, Glamorgan went further and drew up a secret treaty with him which, if put into effect, would make Ireland virtually a Catholic state. Unfortunately for Glamorgan, a copy of his original treaty sanctioned by the King came into Ormonde's hands and revealed Glamorgan's deviations from it. The King's favorite was soon forgiven, and Charles disowned the treaty. In accordance with the King's orders, Ormonde continued to treat with the Confederate Catholics for a peace, on more modest terms, which would bring them greater political freedom, the question of their religious freedom to be referred again to the King.[80] Ormonde's treaty had not yet been concluded when Broghill complained tartly to Sir Philip Percival: "My Lord Ormonde has now declared himselfe so publikely for yᵉ Roges yᵗ I wonder he sticks at any thinge henceforward yᵗ may advantage them." [81]

The English Parliament's army in Ireland was clearly in need of a leader of considerable stature and influence. Sir Hardress Waller suggested to Sir Philip Percival that Lieutenant-General Cromwell would be the happiest choice. Cromwell had shown a decided interest in the support of Munster and would make an excellent Lord Lieutenant.[82] Percival heartily agreed, since Cromwell's fame might "induce men to raise meanes of fit termes to relieve us from those who have so long and so heavily afflicted us." [83]

In the report which Inchiquin submitted to the Com-

mittee for Irish Affairs in January, 1646,[84] he stated
that Munster had been able to hold out during the
last two months only because of aid from Sir Thomas
Fairfax and contributions levied from some parts of
the country after the rebels went into winter quarters.
Two thousand foot and five hundred horse were
urgently needed. Early in February he informed
Lenthall, Speaker of the House of Commons, that
Youghal was threatened again by an army of fifteen
thousand, which had advanced within twelve miles of
the town. He would like to go back to his charge,
carrying nothing more than his sword, "if it bee
thought fitt I bee returned in that equipage." [85] In
March he reiterated the "absolute necessity" of his
return, with six thousand pounds which had been
voted for Munster's relief and the five thousand suits
of apparel which he had previously requested.[86]

Broghill in Cork had frequent conferences with Ad-
mirals Moulton and Penn for the purpose of planning
concerted action against the rebels. There were some
hours of social diversion, as when, on January 30,
Broghill and other commanders and their ladies were
entertained at a banquet on board Penn's pinnace in
Cork bay. In honor of his guests, Penn fired eight guns
when they arrived and seven when they left.[87]

The Irish forces suffered a serious loss that spring
when a Parliamentary squadron took possession of
Bunratty Castle, strategically located near Limerick,
and the Earl of Thomond declared for Parliament. In
April, when rebel troops near Bunratty drove away
cattle, burned houses, and murdered townspeople,
Broghill's soldiers routed the invaders and killed their
commanding officer. The rebels fled over the Limerick
River, some of them struggling through the water up
to the chin, with Broghill's men in pursuit. Broghill

burned most of Bunratty and wasted the surrounding country. In a letter to Inchiquin, still in London, Broghill commented that this victory kept six thousand Irish, ready to be shipped from Waterford, from going to the King. But he had been obliged to stop the "starving mouths" of his soldiers by distributing among them a meager twenty-seven pounds, which he had obtained from local residents "by many Orations and faire words." The week before, he had given his soldiers all the money which he and his wife possessed, which was twenty pounds in gold.[88] With more men and money, much more could be accomplished. Not long afterwards, Parliament paid him fifteen hundred pounds for his services.[89]

The Supreme Council of Confederate Catholics signed their treaty with Ormonde on March 28, appending to it an agreement to send six thousand Irish soldiers to the King on April 1 and four thousand more on May 1. It was already too late, however, for an Irish army to aid the King. A few days after the treaty had been signed, it was learned that there were no longer any English ports where an Irish army in defense of the King might safely land. When on July 30 Ormonde's Peace was at last publicly proclaimed, Rinuccini, the Catholic clergy, and the Irish general, Owen O'Neill, refused to accept it. A new Supreme Council was chosen by the Catholic clergy, Rinuccini was appointed its President, and Glamorgan agreed to assume the office of Lord Lieutenant. At the end of September, unwilling to risk England's total loss of Ireland, Ormonde reluctantly offered to serve Parliament, or, with the King's permission, resign his post.[90]

On June 26 Broghill took Blarney Castle.[91] The Munster forces were weakened and were again in danger of being thrust back into their garrisons and losing their markets. They might well be accused of rashness if they attacked an enemy more than twice their size. William Jephson lost over one hundred of his undernourished cavalry, who "dyed like rotten sheep." [92] On July 14 Bunratty was captured by rebels. Inchiquin brought back from England five thousand pounds, of which one thousand was spent for biscuit and salt to enable the army to march, and the rest for five weeks' pay for the soldiers.[93]

Broghill returned to England to beg for at least five thousand more foot and five hundred more horse to make possible a "thorough prosecution" of the war. He received a sympathetic hearing. His loan of nearly four hundred pounds to the army in Munster was repaid. He was promised six thousand pounds and one hundred cavalry and was given a commission as Commander of a brigade of four regiments, in recognition of his excellent service as Inchiquin's Deputy.[94]

Much of the promised aid failed to materialize. Robert Boyle, writing to Marcombes in October, praised his brother's "gallantry" and "unwonted success" while in sole command of the army in Munster, but added that when Broghill came to England to beg supplies, although liberally voted, they were "so slow in their despatch, that many think they have just cause to apprehend that the physic will not get thither before the patient be dead." [95] Broghill went back to Ireland with his commission, but with only two thousand, six hundred and eight-five pounds, "a contemptible sum," he objected, for "our distressed friends." [96] His elder surviving son, Roger, had been born in his absence and had been baptized on August 14 in Christ Church in Cork.[97]

On February 21, 1647, Lord Lisle, eldest son of Robert, second Earl of Leicester, landed near Cork, with reinforcements for Munster.[98] He had received a commission as Lord Lieutenant of Ireland for Parliament for one year only, nearly a year ago, but had lingered in England until little time remained for his active service in this office. Lord Lisle brought with him "paper commissions," as Lord Inchiquin bitterly described them, for Ireland to be governed by four commissioners: Inchiquin, Broghill, Algernon Sidney (Lisle's brother), and Sir Hardress Waller. When Inchiquin, feeling deeply insulted, refused to recognize these commissions, Lisle took violent measures. He sent Inchiquin's regiment out of Cork, called in all field officers from the garrisons, posted two thousand armed men at the closed gates of the town, and had Broghill's regiment drawn up, their pistols charged, at Inchiquin's door. The Lord President perceived that Broghill was in effect executing an office of which he himself retained only the name. Eighty officers went to Inchiquin's house to assure him of their support. He conferred with Lisle's council of war, stalling for time, until two hours after Lisle's commission as Lord Lieutenant had expired. He then informed Lisle that he now had the authority, as Lord President, to make Lisle and his council prisoners, if they declined to obey his orders. After brief and somewhat embarrassed consideration, the unwelcome "grandees" decided that it would be wiser to return to England and carry on the feud there. They were forced to secure a warrant from Inchiquin to leave, packed their trunks, and set sail from Cork on April 17.[99]

There had been some coldness between Inchiquin and Broghill ever since Broghill, when Inchiquin's Deputy, had prejudiced the Earl of Northumberland against the Lord President.[100] The coldness was now open hostility. Inchiquin tightened his hold on the

Protestant army in Munster, and Broghill presented articles of impeachment against him in London. In the midst of the jarring of these Munster men, Inchiquin wrote to Lady Ranelagh that his quarrel with the brother of a sister "who I know loves him" would never "lessen the honour I owe your Ladyship, which really, Madam, I shall ever nourish, being fixed upon no other Object or Ground but those Gifts which God has given you in much more than ordinary measure." [101]

Many other officers and gentlemen accompanied Lisle and his party to England. While at sea and delayed by a great storm, they were met by Sir Arthur Loftus, with the news that Parliament had revoked the appointment of Algernon Sidney as Governor of Dublin and given the post to Colonel Michael Jones, who had refused to serve as Sidney's Deputy.[102]

Early in May, Inchiquin was encouraged by the arrival of troops, arms, and provisions. He captured Dromana, Cappoquin, and Dungarvan, and Parliament voted him a letter of thanks.[103] He still needed more men for new garrisons, and for months his officers went without pay. Many officers fell sick for lack of proper food and because they were compelled to lie "naked on the cold ground." [104] Inchiquin resented the fact that it is "an impossible thing" [105] for a man Irish by birth to be an acceptable leader against the Irish, except when winning victories.

On July 28 Ormonde delivered to Parliament the sword of his office as Lord Lieutenant for the King and sailed for England. In August he presented a report to the King at Hampton Court in which he acknowledged the failure of his delaying tactics, both with the Parliamentary commissioners on the one hand and the Confederate Catholics on the other. He

had been compelled to put Dublin and the garrisons
which he still controlled into the hands of the two
Houses of Parliament, lest they be taken by the Irish
"and these places be lost to you eventually, when you
recover your rights." [106]

In the twelve articles of impeachment which Broghill
and Sir Arthur Loftus now brought against Inchiquin,
the Lord President was charged with favoring officers
who were not faithful to Parliament; protecting Irish
Papists, including priests; permitting public mass to
be said in Cork and Kinsale; and wasting supplies.
Inchiquin published a denial of most of the charges
and explained that concessions to the Irish had been
made only when Parliament might profit from them.[107]
Although Broghill's accusations "made a great impression against Inchiquin," [108] the latter had many
supporters, Parliament was sufficiently engaged with
graver matters, and the impeachment was dropped.

There were conflicting accounts of Inchiquin's activities. As Colonel William Jephson reported gains,
Broghill reported Jephson's losses, which "some say"
occurred while he was "bowling at Malloe." [109] Early
in September, Inchiquin was able to claim one of the
bloodiest victories of the war, when he stormed the
Rock of Cashel, destroyed its cathedral, refused any
quarter, and directed the massacre of three thousand
men, women, and children. He also routed Muskerry,
Glamorgan, and Owen O'Neill in two successive battles
near Clonmel. O'Neill fled, and Glamorgan was captured and given quarter.[110]

Doubts of Inchiquin's good faith persisted. A packet
of letters was intercepted in which Colonel Robert
Sterling and Captain Thomas Marshall, officers in
Inchiquin's army, desired various commanders to join
them against Parliament. Inchiquin was ordered to

send the officers at once to London to answer letters containing matters of such "high consequence." [111] In November Inchiquin won a decisive victory over Lord Taafe at Knocknanuss. He was thanked by Parliament for this good service, but at the same time crisply reminded that he had recently been granted ten thousand pounds and more equipment than the generals in the other provinces, and the war should be ended in the spring, if "effectually & unanimously carryed on by all." [112]

At the end of January, 1648, Inchiquin wrote to Lenthall [113] in the strongest terms to beg for supplies voted long since. His soldiers were in a "miserable and insupportable Condition," and many were dying of want. If help could not come, he would like to send back the soldiers who wished to return home and make whatever terms could be arranged for the "wretched English" who must remain. In February he strengthened his position by taking Carrick and other strongholds and levied substantial contributions from Kilkenny and Waterford. His private dealings with Colonel John Barry, a Papist, increased Parliament's distrust of his intentions, and he was advised to prevent Barry's "ill designs." It was expected that he would receive cordially the Parliamentary commissioners who were coming over with "ample power & instructions" to compose distempers in his army; and he must "abhor" all thoughts of making peace with the rebels.[114]

As Inchiquin's favor with Parliament declined, Broghill's increased. In February the House of Commons voted to pay Broghill two thousand pounds to satisfy a portion of his arrears,[115] and on March 17 he was appointed Master of the Ordnance in Ireland.[116] Preparations were soon under way to send him with reinforcements to Munster to supplant Inchiquin.

As Parliament was preparing to take action against Inchiquin, some of the officers in Munster were planning his overthrow. Suspicious of Inchiquin's behavior, these officers, with or without Broghill's knowledge, plotted to seize Cork and Youghal while Inchiquin was in the field with the army. They sent a ship to England for supplies, anticipating that when it returned, they could persuade the greater part of the Munster army to abandon Inchiquin. The conspirators were Broghill's uncle, Sir William Fenton, Colonel Edward Temple, Lieutenant-Colonel Phaire, and Major Purdon. The plot was discovered, and by the end of March, Inchiquin had imprisoned the four officers in separate garrisons.[117] Perhaps in the belief that Broghill must have had some share in his uncle's intrigue, Inchiquin also imprisoned Broghill's young children, who had been left in Ireland.[118]

On April 3, Inchiquin summoned to his quarters in Mallow ten officers, whose loyalty to Parliament he questioned, and told them that he had at length decided to oppose "this present pretended Parliament in England," dominated by an Independent faction, which he hoped to see "flat on their Backs" by Michaelmas Day. He would join Lord Taafe and all the Irish of Munster in an effort to re-enthrone the King and restore a free Parliament. If the officers would not join him, they should go to England. They refused their support and took refuge on board Admiral Crowther's ship, the *Bonaventura*. Crowther brought them to England and reported Inchiquin's defection.[119]

Broghill's own dilemma must have caused him many anxious hours. A Royalist at heart, he could not fail to resent the plight of his monarch, now the captive of a hostile army at Carisbrooke, "reduced from three Kingdoms to three roomes in a poor Castle." [120] After much deliberation, he had resolved to act as Inchiquin had already done and declare for the King. But Inchiquin's imprisonment of his relatives because they *were* his relatives made any alliance with Inchiquin, even in a common cause, peculiarly difficult.

Several courses were open to Broghill: he could decline to take supplies to Munster; he could take them to Dublin and persuade Jones and Monck to join him against Parliament; or he could make up his differences with Inchiquin, proceed directly to Munster, and give added support to the King's cause there. His love of Munster and the persuasions of Lord Holles and other friends of Inchiquin prevailed.

Sir John Denham wrote to Ormonde at St. Germain that Broghill had decided to consent to a reconciliation with Inchiquin, although he could not recognize him as his superior officer. If Ormonde, "the only person he will trust," would serve as mediator, representing the undertaking as his own project, Broghill would lay aside "all former animosities" and be ready to join with Inchiquin "in the common interest." Only Jermyn and Lord Colepeper were to be informed of Ormonde's rôle.[121] Ormonde replied to Denham that Broghill's overture was "as well received as he can wish" by the Queen and Prince Charles and should be kept "a secret to all but those he desires should know it"; Broghill's "owne way" would be observed in approaching Lord Inchiquin; and Ormonde would do his part "with great and particular inclinations to serve my Lord of Broghill." [122] For the time being, no definite steps could be taken. Ormonde had still to reach Ireland, and Inchiquin's current activities were far from conciliatory.

Parliament lost no time in proclaiming Inchiquin a traitor. His commissions were declared void, and his nine-year-old son, Lord O'Brien, who had been brought up in Colonel Jephson's house, was committed to the Tower.[123] Crowther was instructed to block up the ports of Youghal, Cork, and Kinsale and to transport to Dublin all of the soldiers who wished to desert Inchiquin and join the Leinster forces.[124] Little more could be done. Most of Inchiquin's soldiers stood by him; his harbors were well fortified; and he could not be ousted from his post.

At the end of May, Inchiquin's projected alliance with Lord Taafe and the Confederate Catholics became an actuality, and a Cessation which suited both parties was arranged.[125] Inchiquin waited impatiently for Ormonde's arrival from France with an army which would join his and Taafe's and pave the way for Prince Charles's coming. He loaned troops to Clanricarde and Taafe to reduce Coote in Connaught.

Six months of wearisome negotiations dragged on before Parliament could secure the release of Inchiquin's prisoners. On March 30 the Committee for Irish Affairs demanded to know the charges against them.[126] In the following months the Committee made frequent attempts to have Inchiquin's son exchanged for the captive officers in Munster "and likewise for the children of the Lord Broghill which are there." [127] It had been disturbing to learn that the prisoners had "suffered very much by their streight imprisonment." [128] Inchiquin was directed to permit them to write freely of the treatment which they received, for "according as he useth them there soe hee must expect his sonne must be used here." [129] Finally, on October 10, arrangements were completed to send Inchiquin's son to Munster, "wth the first opportunity of wind & weather," in the custody of Lieutenant-Colonel

Beecher, who was to return to England with Inchiquin's prisoners.[130] When Beecher arrived, Inchiquin
still refused to surrender one prisoner, Colonel William Knight, who had opposed his Cessation.[131]

Ormonde landed in Cork on September 29, 1648. He
had to pretend that he brought money as well as men
and that a squadron of the fleet would soon appear.[132]
Inchiquin's men, on the verge of mutiny, refused to
march until their wants were relieved. They lacked
brogues and stockings, and many were ill from a diet
"chiefly of rooks." Their discontent stemmed less from
aversion to peace than from despair of the King's business. Inchiquin was further discouraged by the fact
that the Irish had become "much more high in their
demands, as they conceive the King low in condition."
They insisted on having churches granted to their
clergy; some demanded a Catholic governor; and they
threatened to put themselves under another protector,
if the King should not yield to their terms.[133] The King,
soon to be on trial for his life, was more hopeful than
his Munster generals. The Earl of Leicester noted
with surprise the King's "strange conceit" that the
union of Ormonde and Inchiquin might save him; "he
hangs still upon that twigg." [134]

Prince Rupert arrived in Kinsale in January, 1649.
In one respect, his presence was embarrassing to
Inchiquin, for Rupert's servants and retinue attended
public mass in Cork every day; and Inchiquin was
obliged to ask Ormonde to drop "some little hint"
that this had been prohibited. Moreover, the Irish
soldiers who came with Rupert were "singularly in-
solent" to the English.[135]

For a time the fortunes of the Royalist armies in
Ireland improved. The King's execution, which occurred on January 30, 1649, spurred strong Royalist

sympathies among the native Irish. The Confederate Catholics had more confidence in Ormonde than in Rinuccini; and the latter left Ireland after his mission there had failed. Munster was quiet; and Ormonde and Inchiquin won significant victories in Leinster and Ulster. But on August 2 the fatal battle of Rathmines dashed Ormonde's hopes, when Jones totally routed Ormonde's army. This grievous defeat presaged the successful invasion of Oliver Cromwell, who at the end of March had accepted from Parliament the combined posts of Lord Lieutenant and Commander-in-Chief of the forces in Ireland.

Ormonde regarded the King's execution as an inhuman sacrifice and an overwhelming blow. He vowed to devote the rest of his life to revenge for the King's death; "to bear with all sorts of men for this purpose"; and to impose a curse on his sons if they should slacken in that duty.[136] He apprehended that Cromwell, "or some such John of Leyden," would now be elected by "the dreggs and scum of the House of Commons" to establish "a perfect Turkish tyranny." [137]

In Broghill's case, the murder of his sovereign was no doubt a major factor in his decision to try once more to patch up his quarrel with Inchiquin and to offer his service to the son of the royal martyr. Although Broghill was now living in "retirement" at his Somerset manor house at Marston, he was by no means inactive. It is highly probable that it was Broghill who sent to Munster in March "a gentleman from Somersetshire" to inform Inchiquin that "a considerable force" was ready to be transported from that county "to join with any that take arms against the present régime." [138]

By March it was known at the exiled Court of Charles II that Broghill would soon arrive there and

would accompany the King to Ireland. Lord Cork
wrote a letter of compliment to Ormonde to pave
the way for Ormonde's favorable reception of his
brother.[139] Broghill's sister-in-law, Lady d'Aubigny,
who had suffered severely for the Royalist cause and
was to die in exile shortly afterwards, also appealed
to Ormonde in Broghill's behalf. She earnestly requested that "your kindness to my brother Broghill
may not bee the lesse because beg'd from a stranger,"
especially since this favor is "so obligingly recommended by his Ma^ty." [140]

On April 20 the young King sent Ormonde explicit
instructions regarding Broghill. Convinced of Broghill's ability to serve him and cordially welcoming his
assistance, Charles wrote:

> Wee have received so full information of the good affec-
> tion of the Lord Broughell to the King our late father of
> blessed memory, and to us, and wee have likewise received
> such expressions of his desire to do us service, that wee are
> fully resolved to pardon whatsoever he may have formerly
> done amisse, and to consider him, for the time to come, as
> a person, upon whose loyalty and affection Wee may con-
> fidently rely, and the rather, because he intends shortly to
> wayte upon us in his way to Ireland. Wee intreate you
> therfore to have the like consideration of him, and to
> afford him your just favour & protection in such things
> as may concerne him in that kingdome, and particularly to
> receive his Lady (who intends imediatly to repayre
> thither) with civility & kindnes answearable to her qual-
> ity, and to the esteeme wee have of her, and to endeavour
> (as there shall be occasion) to doe all good offices, and to
> settle a right understanding between the Lord Inchiquin
> our President of Munster and the said Lord Broughell,
> which wee desire as a thing much conducing to our service
> in that Kingdom.[141]

In late March or early April, Broghill secured a
pass from the Earl of Warwick to visit the baths in

Spa for his gout. He left Somerset and arrived in London, completing the first stage of his journey. On April 8 the King's Secretary, Sir Edward Nicholas, wrote to Ormonde in cipher from Caen:

> The Earl of Cork saith he expects his brother the Lord Broghill here every day, and that he comes hither with intention to adhere to the King's friends in Ireland, upon some invitation from your Excellency. I believe he intends to go over thither, either with the King, or with my Lady Ormonde. I pray your Excellency to advise your friends by your next what you conceive fit to be done therein in relation to the King's service in regard of the great disaffection that is known to have been between the Lord Inchiquin (who hath deserved so eminently well of his Majesty) and the Lord Broghill.[142]

But an episode which seemed incredible to Broghill himself kept him in London, reversing his well-laid plans. His voyage was never made; and the King was to wait another decade for the assistance which Broghill still desired to give him.

Cromwell's Noble Lord

The year 1649, which began so gloomily with the
King's trial and execution, brought Broghill an un-
expected challenge. His forced, if partial, retirement
had been singularly irksome to a man who considered
suspense "the worst of evils." [1] Confident of his skill
as a military leader and of his power to sway Munster,
he was ready to hazard his life in the new King's service. To his astonishment, a contrary course was shortly
determined for him.

Of the miscarriage of Broghill's plans there is a
detailed and rather quaint account in the *Memoirs* of
his life written by his chaplain, Thomas Morrice. [2] No
sooner had Broghill reached London on his way to
Caen, than a messenger from Cromwell appeared at
his London lodgings to inform him that Cromwell intended to visit him when he was at leisure. Although
Broghill insisted that, as he was unknown to Cromwell,
he could not be the person Cromwell sought, he was
assured that he was. Thereupon, he agreed to wait on
the General, and the messenger departed. While
Broghill was "musing," Cromwell came to him and
said that the Commonwealth Council of State knew
of Broghill's intention to seek the exiled Charles Stuart

on the Continent and had given an order to commit
him to the Tower, but that Cromwell himself had a
great respect for him and wished to alter his purpose.
When Broghill protested his innocence, Cromwell produced copies of incriminating letters.[3] Forced to acknowledge the letters as his, Broghill requested advice.
Cromwell then recommended that Broghill should
serve under him as a general officer in the war against
Ireland, taking no oaths and agreeing only to fight
against the native Irish. Although Broghill asked for
time to consider this extraordinary proposal, Cromwell
compelled him to make an immediate decision.

For a man of Broghill's active temperament and
soldierly instincts, the decision to accept Cromwell's
terms was inevitable. Languishment of uncertain duration in the Tower—if not a worse fate—was an un-
bearable alternative. Broghill genuinely desired to
serve the King and managed to convince himself that
it was "a very great Providence" that he could be
preserved for this ultimate end. Meanwhile, he could
accomplish the project closest to his heart, the conquest of Munster for the Protestant interest there.
For the rest of his life, however, he was to be vulner-
able, and by no means insensitive, to the bitter charges
of "apostasy" which his numerous enemies were to
bring against him.

Broghill found himself able to keep the terms of an
agreement which demanded no oath of loyalty to
Cromwell's party. The General was soon to concede
gratefully that the surrender of the Munster garrisons
was largely Broghill's work. As their relationship continued, Broghill acquired a sincere regard for Cromwell, tempered by certain reservations. Privately and
discreetly, Broghill labored for the Royalist cause; but
Cromwell was aware of at least some of these activities

and accepted the situation. Indeed, Broghill became Cromwell's valued adviser and the much beloved friend of Cromwell's sons, Henry and Richard. For the next ten years of his life, Lord Broghill was to serve the Cromwell family conspicuously and well.

Cromwell sent Broghill to Bristol to await transportation to Ireland and secured for him five hundred pounds to meet his initial expenses.[4] Early in October, 1649, about two months after Cromwell began his Irish campaign, Broghill landed at Wexford. Commissioned by Cromwell, he assumed the colonelship of a regiment of twelve troops of horse, composed of officers and soldiers from Cork and neighboring towns. Deserving officers who could not yet have commands were assigned to one troop, with Broghill as their captain.[5] When he appeared at Cromwell's headquarters, Broghill halted his company, and they cried: "A Broghill! A Broghill!" Cromwell's men responded: "A Cromwell!" Having exchanged greetings, Broghill tactfully directed his men to shout: "A Cromwell!" Cromwell then had his men reply: "A Broghill!" "And so they joined." [6]

Broghill's arrival in Ireland occurred at an opportune moment in the autumn campaign. Although encouraged by Jones's defeat of Ormonde at Rathmines early in August and his own bloody but decisive victories at Drogheda and Wexford, Cromwell was temporarily depressed by heavy losses in his army from fighting and from the illnesses of large numbers of his soldiers. He assigned to Broghill the task of securing the submission of the principal garrisons in Munster, a duty which Broghill successfully accomplished in little more than a month. Cork had already capitulated when Broghill and Colonel Phaire came there to restore order. There had been some confusion and terror in the city, as Lady Fanshawe experienced, when she fled from Cork at three o'clock in the morning, "through thousands of naked swords." [7] At any rate, Cork was spared the usual atrocities of Irish warfare; and Kinsale, Bandon, and Youghal surrendered without bloodshed.

On November 14, Cromwell wrote from Ross to Thomas Scott, a member of the Council of State, that he expected Lord Broghill to do "very good offices" in Munster and recommended that he be granted "all his suite," two hundred pounds, to bring his wife to Ireland,[8] for "such a sum would not be cast away." He reported that he had made Broghill, Sir William Fenton, General Blake, and Colonel Deane commissioners for the temporary management of affairs in Cork harbor, now to become a victualing place for the Irish fleet. It must be understood, he added, that "this business of Munster will emptie yoᵉ Treasurie." [9]

On the same date Cromwell wrote to William Lenthall some details of the surrender of Youghal. On shipboard in Youghal harbor certain officers, who had been Cromwell's agents in Youghal, and the Mayor met a group of officers arriving in the harbor to demand the submission of the city and proposed terms of surrender. When Broghill declared that it would be for Youghal's "honour and advantage" to desire no conditions, his suggestion was adopted. Broghill, Fenton, and Phaire landed and "were received," wrote Cromwell,—"I shall give you my Lo: Broughalls owne words,—with all the reall demonstrations of gladnesse an overjoyed people were capable off." Cromwell concluded: "And by the endeavours of the noble person afore mentioned [Broghill] the garrison is put in good order." [10]

On the second of December, Broghill captured Dungarvan, where Cromwell met him. It was at Dungarvan that Lieutenant-General Michael Jones, worn out by the rigors of the campaign and the victim of a contagious fever, died on December 19. His body was brought on a gun carriage at midnight to St. Mary's church in Youghal and buried in the Earl of Cork's chapel. Standing by his grave, Cromwell delivered a solemn funeral sermon.

The day before his death, Jones requested a private interview with Broghill and told him that he believed Cromwell suspected them both and intended to destroy them; but if Broghill would join him, they would "set up" for themselves and drive Cromwell and Henry Ireton out of Ireland. Broghill begged Jones not to increase his high fever by such thoughts and recommended that they first wholly subdue the Irish.[11]

There is evidence that Broghill, as well as Jones, had been nursing Royalist hopes, and that the King's party believed that he might be persuaded to abandon Cromwell. As early as the previous summer, Ormonde had reached the conclusion that it might still be possible to secure Broghill's services for the King. On the eighteenth of July, Ormonde advised Secretary Long:

> In Munster I know no man of consideration, to worke by or upon, but the Lord of Broghill; & he is not cleare of suspition from the Rebells, nor I think apt to trust himselfe into the first brunt of a designe. If any of the westerne parts of England towards the Sea declare for the Kinge, & that persons proper to stir him up may be found, and sent to him, it may produce something from him, for I believe his wishes are for the Kinge. He may perhaps apprehend my Lord of Inchiquin cannot be made his freind; but I dare undertake to secure that feare, or his very interest, if he places it in any thinge my Lord of Inchiquin possesses, or can resigne, so it may be evidently useful to the Kinge: and for this I have warrt.[12]

In December Inchiquin informed Ormonde that he had recently received messages from Broghill to the effect that Broghill "does not act for them [Cromwell's party], nor by theyre Comission; that he will never disserve the King though he act in this Nationall Quarrel; and that though perhaps I may not beleeve it, yet he would be glad to doe mee personall service." Broghill had also offered to use what authority he had "to keep in those that I would have in." [13]

There were times when Broghill was painfully reminded of Cromwell's leading rôle in the execution of Charles I. Once when he was riding with Cromwell on one side and Henry Ireton on the other, the King's death became the subject of their conversation. Cromwell remarked that if Charles had followed his own mind and had had trusty servants, he might have "fool'd em all." Cromwell's party once thought of joining the King, but decided that it was safer to prevent the more powerful union of the King with the Scots. When Cromwell and Ireton intercepted a letter from Charles to the Queen in which he proposed an alliance with the Scots, they then determined to ruin him. At these disclosures, Broghill was silent but horrified.[14]

Cromwell was forced to abandon his unsuccessful blockade of Waterford and went into winter quarters in Youghal. He was gratified by the conquests in Munster but disturbed by the condition of his troops. "I tell you," he wrote to Lenthall, "a considerable part of your army is fitter for an hospital than the field. If the enemy did not know it, I should have held it impolitique to have writt it. They know it, yet they know not what to doe." [15] Broghill was singled out for Lenthall's particular attention:

His Lordship hath been eminently serviceable unto you, and I do earnestly and humbly desire he may be taken into consideration, his Lordship never having shrunk from

your interest, though under as great trials and necessities
as any man, he having his whole fortune under the power
of the enemy, which was in Ireland, and that little in
England so engaged that I dare say his wants were scarce
to be paralleled; and as yet his estate lies in those countries
which are under the enemy's power.[16]

We have the testimony of Broghill's youngest
brother Robert that Broghill's services to Cromwell
in Munster had interrupted the writing of his first
major literary work, his heroic romance, *Parthenissa,*
a portion of which Robert had read in manuscript.
This long-winded and never completed narrative,
which he was to publish in installments, was to occupy
its author for many years, during intervals of illness
and enforced leisure. In a letter to his "dearest Governor" written in December, 1649, acclaiming his
brother's recent Munster victories, Robert observed
that although Broghill had been "reduced to leave" his
Parthenissa, he had "happily emulated" the adventures of his hero, had proved himself "as good at reducing towns in Munster as Assyria," and had been as
eloquent "with masters of garrisons, as mistresses of
hearts." [17]

At the end of the 1649 campaign in Munster, Cromwell, attended by Broghill, Fenton, and other officers,
made agreeable excursions to Cork, Kinsale, and
Bandon. In Cork they received a "very hearty and
noble entertainment." [18] Cromwell admired Bandon,
which he praised as "a fine sweet town, and an entire
English plantation, without any admixture of Irish." [19]
His appreciation of the beauty of Ireland he shared
with Broghill. On a later occasion, standing on a hill
in Tipperary, Cromwell exclaimed: "This, indeed, is
a country well worth fighting for." [20]

On December 29 John Hodder wrote from Cork to

Lady Percival: "Lord Broghill lodges at my house, and he told me that he did not receive forty pounds out of his estate since the war." [21] But from a military point of view, much progress had already been made. Cromwell rejoiced that "a great longitude of land alongst the shore" [22] had been secured. The forthcoming spring campaign must reduce the inland fortresses.

Broghill could scarcely have been pleased when Ireton was appointed Lord President of Munster in January, 1650. For a second time Broghill had failed to secure this coveted post. However, in the same month, in satisfaction of his arrears, Parliament voted him the custody of Lord Muskerry's estate to the value of one thousand pounds annually, until the country where his own estate lay could be gained from the power of the enemy. [23]

On January 29, Cromwell took the field again. Broghill accompanied him on his march northward as far as Mallow, where he was left with a flying camp to protect Cromwell's rear. As ordered by Cromwell, Broghill captured old Castletown Castle, near Kildorrery, giving quarter for life to the private soldiers, but causing all the officers to be shot, "to affright those little castles for so persistently holding out." [24] He also secured a mountain stronghold belonging to Sir Edward Fitzharris.

Cromwell's son Henry landed in Ireland early in the spring, in command of a regiment of horse, and immediately joined Broghill. Together they defeated Inchiquin near Limerick, killing one hundred and sixty of Inchiquin's men and taking over one hundred prisoners, including three officers. One of the officers, a cousin of Broghill's, Colonel Randal Clayton, although condemned to death, was pardoned. [25]

With reinforcements from Cromwell, Broghill totally routed a church army at the battle of Macroom on April 10. Between five and six hundred of the enemy were slain and several prisoners of distinction and the standard of the church of Munster captured. In the pocket of the most important prisoner, the Bishop of Ross, Broghill found "some papers of singular consequence." From Macroom Broghill returned to the nearby castle of Carrigadrohid and summoned its garrison, which refused to surrender. His stern expedient for bringing the Governor to terms he described in a letter from Cork written on April 16:

> I gave orders that if the garrison in it [the castle] delivered it not up, we should hang the bishop before it. The former not being done, the latter was; and 'tis observable that immediately after the bishop was hanged, I came up and persuaded the governor after the execution to surrender me the castle almost upon the same terms he had refused to save the bishop's life, the only difference being that I gave him 16 arms to defend his soldiers from the Tories.
>
> The bishop was wont to say there was no way to secure the English but by hanging them. That which was his cruelty became his justice.[26]

On April 27, Oliver Cromwell began the siege of Clonmel. Discouraged by the city's resistance and the poor condition of his army, he sent messengers to Broghill with the news that he must raise the siege and retire in disgrace, if not promptly relieved, and begging Broghill to cease other activities and come at once to his aid. Broghill replied that he would not fail to reach Clonmel within three days; and he kept his word. At Broghill's arrival, Cromwell's whole army cried out: "A Broghill! A Broghill!" Cromwell came forward and embraced Broghill and congratulated him on his bravery.[27] The siege was vigorously renewed; and at last the city fell, after Cromwell had sacrificed two thousand men to gain it.

On May 22, shortly before leaving Ireland, Cromwell wrote a letter to the Governor of Dublin, stating that he had given permission to Lord Moore to spend six months at Mellefont and requesting fair and civil treatment for him.[28] This favor was probably solicited by Broghill, for Lord Moore's uncle had been the husband of Broghill's sister Sarah. On May 29 Cromwell returned to England, leaving Ireton as Lord Deputy and acting Commander-in-Chief of the army.

Broghill joined Ireton in conducting the prolonged siege of Waterford, which lasted from early June to the tenth of August. Waterford held out until Lieutenant Croker and his brother, Sergeant Croker, led a party which burned the suburbs and, concealing their small numbers under cover of the smoke, put all they met to the sword, secured the great guns, and marched to the western gate, which they opened to their fellow-soldiers. Broghill, always on the alert, with a small perspective glass descried Sergeant Croker and his men at the gate. "The town is ours," shouted Croker, brandishing his sword over his head.[29] It was during the siege of Waterford that Ireton, who, according to Broghill, was, like Cromwell, "not over knowing in books," spent almost every summer evening discussing theories of military strategy with Broghill, "to learn," said Broghill, "ye little I could teach him." [30]

Broghill's relations with Ireton, and also with Edmund Ludlow, were unfriendly. In June, 1650, when Ludlow was appointed Lieutenant-General of the Horse, Broghill felt slighted and voiced his sense of neglect. Both Ireton and Ludlow were aware of Broghill's merits but distrusted his loyalty and apparently resented Cromwell's regard for him. They debated whether Broghill "should be wholly laid aside, or whether something should be done to content him for the present," and decided upon the latter course. Broghill was appointed Lieutenant-General of the Ordnance in February, 1651.[31]

After nearly eight years of exile and illness in foreign countries, Broghill's older brother, Lord Cork, returned to Ireland at the end of May, 1651,[32] and resumed his residence in Youghal. Much of the country lay waste, and more of it must be wasted, although, as the commissioners of Parliament reported, the contributions required from the various counties already exceeded the value of the profits from the lands.[33] A round of family parties followed Cork's arrival, despite the hazards of travel which they involved. Cork noted in his Diary that on the third of June, in a journey to Castlelyons, he escaped being captured by a party of Irish horse "in the way I was to pass," only because Broghill, having been attacked by them first and being stronger than they imagined, "charged and defeated them." [34]

The difficult siege of Limerick was begun by Ireton on the same date. Warned by Ireton's chaplain that Ireton intended his ruin and had declared that "he must be cut off," [35] Broghill kept away from Limerick and busied himself taking castles and making forays. During the months of June and July, he was constantly in action, with scarcely a breathing space. He could boast that he never lost a battle; and his ingenuity was equal to all emergencies. Once, when he was unable to gain a seaside castle without a ship, he had a ship brought ten miles by land, manned it, and successfully stormed the castle. On another occasion, when a regiment of Muskerry's horse expected to charge him at the entrance to a narrow pass, where no more than three could go abreast, he chose the only alternative route, a bog a quarter of a mile long, had tarpaulin from the gun carriages spread across it, hastily got his men over, drew them up, and "after a handsome dispute," entirely routed the enemy. Immediately afterwards, he overcame superior numbers on a bridge in the town of Castlelyons, and the same day pursued and scattered another force that fled "faster than our wearied horses could follow." [36] The Protestant settlers in and near Cork greatly valued his services and begged to have him remain in their neighborhood throughout the summer.[37]

In July, in the battle of Knocknaclashy, Broghill nearly lost his life. He survived, as he did in several other crises, when the odds were heavily against him. There are detailed accounts of this battle in Cox's *Hibernia Anglicana,* Morrice's *Memoirs,* and a letter which Broghill addressed to Lenthall, which was afterwards published.[38] Muskerry's opposing army was three times the size of Broghill's. After a long pursuit, in tempestuous weather, with their provisions exhausted, Broghill's troops, divided into two wings, met Muskerry's in the middle of a plain. "Our word," said Broghill, "was Prosperity, theirs St. James; our signal white in hats, theirs green Fern." As the Irish advanced, their priests sprinkled holy water on them. A regiment of the enemy's foot met Broghill's right wing, which he commanded, "and we fired in each other's faces and mingled." Broghill charged and killed the leader that opposed him; but his own troop was charged in front, flank, and rear, "and their pikes galled us much."

As he went to the aid of his endangered left wing, Broghill was isolated and was offered quarter, which

he refused. There were shouts of: "Kill the fellow in
the gold lace coate!" and Broghill's horse received
three shots. Then a lieutenant of his troop, who was
shot twice and had his horse killed under him as he did
so, rescued Broghill. A fresh party of the Irish were
put to flight by stratagem. Broghill ordered his men
to shout: "They run, they run!" As the first rank of
the Irish looked back, those behind saw their faces and
assumed that they were running, "and so all that party
fled." The Irish lost six hundred men, including many
officers. "We relyed," Broghill commented, "on a
better strength then the Arme of flesh, and when their
strength failed them, ours did not fail us." After the
battle, Broghill collected many charms, which had
been worn about the necks of the slain. Some charms
were against death by sword, others by pistol or
musket. Most of the "miserably deluded" soldiers,
Broghill observed, had died from the weapon against
which they had a charm.

The defeated army had been on its way to relieve
Limerick. Ireton let the besieged know the result of
the battle by three peals of ordnance and three volleys
of small shot. Ravaged by plague and famine, Limerick fell on October 29, the day after Broghill and
Cork arrived there. Broghill's mind was afterwards
haunted by the plight of that city, where the living
could not bury the dead and resembled walking
skeletons.[39]

Cork was cordially received by Ireton, who offered
"to remove all rubs" in his business [40] when he met with
the commissioners. But on November 26 Ireton died
of the plague in the stricken city. He was succeeded as
Commander-in-Chief by Ludlow, who was to hold this
post until Charles Fleetwood arrived in Ireland as
Lord Deputy in October, 1652. The death of Ireton,

his most dangerous enemy, improved Broghill's prospects and served to increase his influence with Cromwell. When he met the commissioners of Parliament in Kilkenny in December, Broghill successfully pleaded his brother's interests, and in January Cork began to receive rents from his lands.

Broghill's daughter Katherine was christened at Blarney Castle on February 11, 1652.[41] Cork was present on this occasion and indeed was a frequent visitor at Blarney. In the summer and autumn the two brothers entertained the commissioners of Parliament to good purpose. Cork was assured of assistance in retaining his estates, and Muskerry's former estates were surveyed, so that Broghill might determine their true value.[42]

Early in the summer Broghill wrote to Inchiquin that the submission of Muskerry "will probably bring us peace." [43] Muskerry's last stronghold, Ross Castle, surrendered on June 27. Broghill had served as an intermediary with Muskerry for a treaty, which was slowly effected, since Muskerry "juggled" in all his overtures.[44] While Ross was being subdued, Broghill captured Drumagh Castle and fought a useful rear action. His successes were listed by the commissioners of Parliament as amongst the "Wonder workings of our God." [45] At the end of August, the commissioners informed the various commanders, including Broghill, that they considered that the danger of resistance was over, but warned that the Irish who had laid down arms must hold no meetings and must not travel without special license.[46] Finally, on September 26, Parliament declared the Irish Rebellion ended.

The end of the Rebellion marked as well the end of Broghill's active military career, which had continued intermittently for more than a decade of his relatively short life. His interest in the strategy of warfare never waned, and he was to draw heavily on his military experience in one of his most effective literary works, *A Treatise of the Art of War*.

In 1653 Lord Cork began the rebuilding of Lismore. On August 4 he was able to sleep for the first time in the room there which he had "reedified"; [47] and visits between Lismore and Blarney were frequently exchanged. On September 8 Parliament renewed Broghill's grant of Blarney Castle and other lands to the value of one thousand pounds a year, to be settled on him and his heirs forever, "as a Mark of the Parliament's Favour to him, for his eminent and faithful Services to the Commonwealth." [48] In October the commissioners of Parliament ordered Captain Robert Storey to guard against a possible landing by Prince Rupert and to take orders from Broghill, Phaire, and Wallis. [49]

After Cromwell had been installed as Lord Protector in December, 1653, he sent Henry Cromwell to Ireland to discover the attitude of the officers of the army there to the new government. The Protestant settlers, headed by Broghill, recognized Henry Cromwell as their true friend and urged his promotion to the rank of Commander-in-Chief. [50] The resettlement of Ireland was now slowly getting under way. According to Morrice, [51] it was Broghill who proposed the plan, which was adopted, of transporting the Irish gentry to Connaught and settling their confiscated estates on the adventurers and soldiers. The forfeited lands were surveyed and appraised, and those who received them drew lots for their shares. Broghill and Colonel Phaire were among the commissioners appointed to set out lands in various baronies in co. Cork for this purpose. [52] In April, 1654, the commissioners of Parliament ordered that the arrears of Broghill, Fenton, Foulk, and other officers should be paid out of half of the lands in co. Cork.[53] A few months later, Broghill's petition to restore certain enclosures on his English estates was granted.[54]

On September 3, Broghill took his seat for Cork in London in the first Protectorate Parliament. Whitelocke recorded gratefully in his *Memorials* that on September 6 "the Lord Broghill my noble intimate Friend" [55] made a speech in the House commending the treaty with Sweden and moved that Whitelocke should receive two thousand pounds in satisfaction of his expenses as Ambassador. In a speech on November 10, Broghill supported Cromwell, protesting a motion whereby Parliament would be authorized to pass bills into laws in certain cases without Cromwell's consent. "I could wish," said Broghill, "I could have redeemed that wound with a pound of the best blood in my body." [56]

There is a melancholy account of the distresses in Ireland, after peace had been secured, in a letter written from Youghal by Robert Boyle to his Somersetshire friend, John Malet, on January 22, 1655. Boyle lamented that "we inhabit but a Desert scarce peopled with any thing but fowre-legg'd or two legg'd Wolves." Taxes were "insupportable," and starving natives were contributing seven shillings a month for a single cow. The native Irish must be removed to Connaught, except for "the inoffensive Plowman," who would be permitted to remain. Yet "amongst all this Ruine and these Distractions," Boyle reported, Broghill had found leisure to print the first four parts of *Parthenissa*. The romance had been accorded in London "amongst divers of the Witts a very favorable Reception." [57] Two months later, Malet apologized to Boyle for his delay in writing, due to the fact that *Parthenissa* "required some of my time to entertain her with most serious observance of her excellent beauties." Surely nothing can be said against romances, Malet added, when Broghill is "their sanctuary." [58]

Henry Cromwell returned to Ireland the following July as Acting Commander-in-Chief, under Fleetwood as Lord Deputy. Fleetwood was soon recalled, and Henry Cromwell ruled virtually as Lord Deputy, although he was not granted his commission for that office until November, 1657. Shortly after the arrival of "Lord Harry," the Earl of Cork was entertained at Phoenix House, the Lord Deputy's Dublin residence. Lord Harry assured Cork that Broghill had especially recommended him to his care, and Cork would find him a "reall frend." On a later occasion, Lord Harry promised Cork that his family should no longer suffer "by those who hated us because wee did not comply with their desyres." [59]

In March, 1655, Cromwell appointed Broghill President of the Council in Scotland, with a salary of one thousand pounds a year.[60] Broghill's prospects were brightened, also, by a grant from Parliament of three thousand pounds for lands in Ireland for his arrears.[61] Then, as at all times, Broghill's chief interests were in Ireland; and it was with some reluctance and for one year only that he accepted his new post. He was in Edinburgh, discharging the duties of his presidency, for exactly twelve months. In August, 1656, he left Scotland to take his seat for Cork and Edinburgh in the second Protectorate Parliament.

In letters from Edinburgh to Thurloe and Cromwell, Broghill reported his struggles to achieve a strategic balance between the two rival parties in Scotland, the Resolutioners, opposed to Cromwell, and the Remon-

strators, some of whom favored him. Broghill found
their feuds and their fanaticism exasperating but managed to be courted by both parties. When he had
brought them to an agreement, they praised him for
doing the Protector "as much service as in winninge a
battell." [62] Broghill laid out intelligence money frugally
but to advantage, and prided himself on paying the
spies who gave him intelligence more than others
would give them for withholding it.[63] Severe attacks of
gout scarcely curbed his energy. He reduced the army;
introduced measures to improve trade and manufactures; established an exchequer court; and effected
other reforms. It was the conviction of Robert Baillie
that President Broghill was "a man exceeding wise and
moderate," who "gained more on the affections of the
people than all the English that ever were among
us." [64]

The scope and efficiency of Cromwell's spy system
impressed Broghill, and he modeled his own upon it.
He never encountered but one of Cromwell's spies, a
Jew, who once peeped through the arras in a room
where Broghill was walking with Cromwell. Cromwell
started to run at the intruder with his sword, then discovered that he was "a friend" to whom he paid one
thousand pounds a year for intelligence.[65] In his dealings with his own spies, Broghill was undoubtedly useful to Cromwell, although he also secured helpful
information for the Royalists. Since both the Commonwealth and Royalist parties employed the same
spies, there were elements of danger in these activities;
and Broghill became involved in at least one highly
embarrassing episode.

Sir Robert Walsh, a Royalist spy, was released
from the Tower through Broghill's efforts, on condition that he would procure intelligence for Broghill

from the exiled Court of Charles Stuart. In a curious "narrative" [66] Walsh related a private night meeting with Broghill in London, when they were interrupted, while "contriving a cypher," by a knock at the door. Broghill went out and spent three-quarters of an hour in another room with his intelligencer from Bruges, who brought him items of news from "the 3rd person about the King." Then Broghill gave Walsh fifty pounds from his own purse and hastened him away. Soon afterwards, unfortunately, Walsh was arrested and imprisoned in the Fleet. Incriminating evidence of these negotiations reached Cromwell. With some difficulty, Broghill cleared himself; but Walsh fell into disgrace with both sides.

During Broghill's absence from Ireland, the Earl of Cork cemented his friendship with Lord Harry Cromwell. Once when they went hunting together, Lord Harry's horse fell on him, and Cork quickly caught the bridle and saved his companion from being dragged. Lord Harry told Cork that he had urged Broghill to return to Ireland, "now that former enemies had promised to help us." [67]

In 1657 Broghill was active in the House of Commons as one of Cromwell's advisers. In January he opposed the Militia Bill, which imposed a decimation tax on all former Royalists. In defense of his point of view, he produced an ingenious assortment of legal, biblical, and historical arguments; [68] and after its second reading, the bill was rejected. When Cromwell inquired why Broghill attacked this bill, Broghill rejoined that its passage would have made three kingdoms rise in rebellion. Cromwell seemed impressed; but the major-generals who had promoted the bill hated Broghill "to the death" for his share in defeating it.[69]

During the spring months, Broghill was a prime mover in framing the "Humble Petition and Advice" which embodied an offer of kingship to the Protector. In April a Parliamentary committee, of which Broghill was a member, waited several times on Cromwell to discuss this proposal. Broghill marshaled his arguments with eloquence and vigor. It is better, he maintained, that the supreme magistrate be fitted to laws in existence than that they be fitted to him. A King has by law the power that a Protector has only from the authority that constituted him one. "What is good in it's own Nature [monarchy], is always good, and if by intervening Accidents it be a while clouded, yet at length it shines and overcometh, and all Men do desire to revert unto it." [70]

On May 8, although sorely tempted, Cromwell announced his decision against kingship. On June 26 he was once more inaugurated as Lord Protector. Arthur Annesley wrote to Henry Cromwell that the ceremony was conducted "with much magnificence and order." But "there were no bonfires . . . and it was observed that the L. Lambert and most of the martiall list absented themselves." [71]

After Cromwell had refused the Crown, Broghill approached him with a rather startling suggestion. With the concurrence of the exiled King and the approval of Cromwell's wife and the young lady in question, Broghill proposed a match between the King and Cromwell's daughter Frances. In a private interview with the Protector, Broghill said that he had heard strange news in the city which might perhaps offend Cromwell. The latter's curiosity was at once aroused; and Broghill explained "in a jocular way" that the news in the city was that Cromwell was going to marry his daughter Frances to the King. Cromwell then "with a merry countenance" asked: "What did the fools think of it?" Broghill replied that everyone thought it was the wisest thing for Cromwell to do. Looking "steadfastly" in Broghill's face and "a little tickled" with the project, Cromwell requested Broghill's opinion, and Broghill assured him that this would be "the best and safest" course he could take. The King would consider favorably any step that would end his exile, and with a King for a son-in-law and in all probability a grandson who would be heir apparent to the throne, Cromwell's greatness would be forever established. Cromwell listened attentively, walking up and down the room with his hands behind him, "pondering with himself." At last he told Broghill that the King would never forgive the murder of his father. Cromwell's guilt "lay so heavy upon him" that, to Broghill's regret, "that business broke off." [72]

In the midst of Cromwell's deliberations concerning kingship, Blake won on May 20 his great naval battle over the Spanish fleet in the harbor of Santa Cruz. In honor of this exploit, Broghill wrote "Verses to His Highness on his late Victory in the Bay of Sancta Cruse in the Island of Teneriff," in which he divided his praise between "undaunted Blake" and Cromwell's "resistless Genius." [73] Although the poem was never published, it is highly probable that Broghill presented Cromwell with a manuscript copy of it.

In July Broghill spent a weekend with the Protector at Hampton Court.[74] Cromwell increasingly sought the advice and support of Broghill and a few other congenial companions. For one of the rare glimpses of Cromwell among his friends, we are indebted to Whitelocke:

> The Protector often advised . . . with the Lord Broghil, Pierepoint, my self, Sir Charles Wolseley and

Thurloe, and would be shut up three or four Hours together in private discourse, and none were admitted to come in to him; he would sometimes be very chearful with us, and laying aside his Greatness, he would be exceeding familiar with us, and by way of diversion, would make Verses with us, and every one must try his Fancy; he commonly called for Tobacco, Pipes, and a Candle, and would now and then take Tobacco himself; then he would fall again to his serious and great Business, and advise with us in those Affairs; and thus he did often with us, and our Counsel was accepted and followed by him, in most of his greatest Affairs.[75]

By the end of August, Broghill was back in Ireland. In September he entertained Henry Cromwell in Munster and in October spent a week with him in Kilkenny.[76] His friendship with Henry Cromwell deepened, and in conversing with and observing him, Broghill made "every day new discoveries of eminent things in him" and was impressed by "his great guift in reading of men." [77] The "Humble Petition and Advice" had encouraged Cromwell to invite persons of his choice to become members of an "Other" House, replacing the House of Lords. Broghill received a summons to sit in this House; and on December 24 he returned to England.[78]

Broghill left Ireland with some misgivings, for recent disquieting news from England made Ireland seem "a very happy place." [79] He took his seat in the ill-fated "Other" House on January 20, 1658. The new assembly had been in session but a fortnight when, angered by the refusal of the House of Commons to transact business with it, Cromwell suddenly dissolved Parliament on February 4.

That same week, the Marquis of Ormonde came to London in disguise to explore the outlook for a Royalist invasion. Informed of his arrival, Cromwell told

Broghill, "there is a great Friend of yours in Town," [80] and gave Broghill an opportunity to warn Ormonde to escape. Cromwell was less inclined to spare Lady Ormonde, until Broghill proved to him that a letter which Cromwell had taken from Lady Ormonde's cabinet was in the handwriting of Lady Isabella Thynne, Ormonde's former mistress. Cromwell was not averse to a little "merry Drollery" at Ormonde's expense and permitted Lady Ormonde to keep her liberty and her estate.[81]

To Henry Cromwell's dismay, Broghill soon began to grow restless. He complained of his gout and talked of a year's retirement in Ireland. The Protector was an altered man, melancholy and pensive, "and seem'd to be afraid of every Body." Once when Broghill was riding with him in his coach from Westminster to Whitehall, the crowd halted it in so narrow a place that none of Cromwell's halberdiers could stand beside it. At the door of a cobbler's stall, which kept opening a little, Broghill saw something shining like a drawn sword or a pistol. He struck with the scabbard of his sword on the door and a tall man, leaping out, slipped away before the Protector's guard could seize him. Cromwell never rode that way again.[82] Eager to keep Broghill with him, Cromwell offered him comfortable accommodation at Hampton Court and promised that his attendance upon business should not be strained beyond his health.[83]

In letters of affectionate remonstrance, Henry Cromwell deplored Broghill's "terrifying" [84] proposal for retirement and warned him of the miscarriages that his presence in England would prevent. He regarded his friend's letters "even as my eyes" [85] and confessed: "My life would be very dull, were it not for your lordship's communications." [86] Henry Cromwell was frankly puzzled by Broghill's "surprizing impulse" to "throw up all," grieve His Highness, and leave his friends "alone to tug at all manner of difficulties." Henry argued:

> Do you not think others will creep in during your lord-ship's absence? And why, now you see his highness so well enclined, should you let him cool? And why do I thus patiently endure your absence, but for the greater end, which I think your lordship may effect in England? . . . Your lordship calls your life dull. Now, I cannot tell what life is more active, than to be always as your lord-ship, contriving helps for sudden difficulties and emer-gencyes. 'Tis the not being conversant with these things which makes a life dull, though perhaps more happy. . . . As for the state of publick affairs, 'tis true 'tis bad, but I believe it mends. And why should your lordship, whose courage and faith has been always eminent, now faint in the way, and dye like Moses upon mount Nebo, before you enter into the land of Canaan? [87]

Broghill seems to have doubted the prospects of "the game our masters are to manage." [88] Whatever his motives, he was in Ireland again before the middle of August. His new residence was Ballymaloe House [89] near Cork, where the Earl of Cork paid him a house-warming visit. [90]

Cromwell's struggle to control his army officers, which darkened the last months of his life, ended with his death on September 3, 1658. Broghill wrote a letter of condolence to Thurloe and expressed the be-lief that Richard Cromwell, succeeding his father, would be happy "if his friends stick to him." [91] The Protector's death was the subject of a notable letter which Lady Ranelagh wrote to Broghill on September 17. She reflected somberly:

> I must owne not to have received the news of his high-ness's death unmovedly. . . . He . . . who a few days

before shooke all Europe by his fame and forces was not able to keepe an ague from shakeing him. . . . If the common charety allowed to dead men be exercised towards him, in burying his faults in his grave with himselfe, and keepeing alive the memory of his vertues and great aymes and actions, he will be allowed to have his place amongst the worthyest of men. . . . I doubt his loss will be a growing affliction upon these nations, and that we shall learne to value him more by missing him, than we did when we injoyed him. . . . I confes his performances reached not the makeing good of his professions; but I doubt his performances may goe beyond the professions of those, who may come after him.[92]

Broghill was to live long enough to test the validity of his sister's prediction.

Through the autumn months Broghill lingered in Ireland, although Richard Cromwell earnestly desired his return to London, and Henry Cromwell was convinced that only Broghill could bring Richard's affairs to "a good consistence." [93] When Richard belatedly called a Parliament, Broghill expressed the view: "I cannot say, that will be our remedy; but I doubt if that be not, noe thing will be." [94] He exerted his influence to get "only good and sober men" elected to the new Parliament and was prevented by these efforts from attending its first sitting. However, in January, 1659, he was ready to take the first fair wind for England.

A month later, accompanied by Lady Ranelagh and her daughters, Broghill sailed for Bristol.[95] After passing Minehead, the ship violently struck a shoal and "scattered" the small party in the cabin. They commended themselves to God, expecting that at any moment the waves would come in and sweep them away. But Broghill's never failing courage and presence of mind saved their lives. He hastened on deck, just managing to avoid having his brains beaten out

by the beam of the detached rudder, calmed the terrified crew, and forced them to take down the sails
and mend the rudder. The ship struck no more, and
with "a good stiff gale" the travelers safely completed the journey.[96]

Lady Ranelagh's letters from London that spring
reflect her concern over Broghill's depressed state of
mind. As he appeared unwilling to make any plans,
she offered to take charge of his "2 poore boys" [97] for
the summer. She reported that Richard Cromwell was
"very obligeing" to Broghill, visiting him at his lodgings, telling him his thoughts "wth great freedome,"
sending for him when in need of advice, and offering
to make him a member of his Council; but Broghill
"seemes fastened in his resolutions of liveing pri-
vatly." [98] It may be surmised that Lady Ranelagh was
also referring to Richard Cromwell in her mention of
"ggg," by whom Broghill was "much courted" and
who manifested "a passionate affection" for him. This
attachment worried her, for she feared that Broghill
was building upon "a sinking interest." [99]

Broghill became alarmed by the growing opposition
of the army officers to Richard's authority. At a meeting of the Council of Officers on April 14, he spoke
boldly against their proposed test to purge the army
by forcing every officer to swear that the execution of
the late King was "lawful and just." Broghill protested:

> If you will have a test to purge the army, I think I have
> as good a right to propose one as any other man; and I
> shall therefore take the liberty to propose, that all shall
> be turned out of the army that will not swear to defend
> the Government as it is now established under the Pro-
> tector and Parliament. I . . . declare I am against all
> tests, and for the continuance of the liberty of the army;

but if you will have a test, I am for this. This is reasonable, because your being depends upon it; and lawful,
because it is to maintain that authority by which you sit.
If you will not pass it here, or do pass the other, I will
move for this test tomorrow in Parliament, where I am
confident it will pass.[100]

Desborough, who had made the motion for the test,
now withdrew it.

Not long afterwards, on Broghill's advice, Richard
dissolved the Council of Officers, delivering a brief
but dignified speech which Broghill had written for
the occasion. The army officers correctly guessed that
Broghill had engineered this affront; and several of
them, meeting Broghill, suggested that an address
should be made to Richard to discover who had advised such an action without the consent of Parliament.
Broghill quickly responded: "At the same time this
address is made, I humbly move there may be also
another address to know who advised the calling of a
Council of War without the consent or knowledge of
the Parliament, for if he be guilty who advised the
dissolution of the Council, he must be much more
guilty who advised the calling it." [101]

Broghill's efforts to steer Richard's course, although
persistent, were doomed to defeat. Against the advice
of Broghill, Fauconberg, Howard, and other trusted
friends, Richard took the fatal step, under strong pressure from the army officers, of signing a commission to
dissolve his Parliament. His enforced abdication followed; and the officers set up their own government.
Commenting on the passing of "y^t famelly interest
which is now vanishing from amogst us," Lady Ranelagh expressed her astonishment that by so sudden and
bloodless a revolution a free and full Parliament had
been dissolved and a chief magistrate laid aside "whose

father had such an interest in ye very Army by whose motion this was donn." [102]

It was whispered that Broghill had urged clapping up Fleetwood, Desborough, and other officers in the Tower, and "an evil eye" [103] was against him. Just in time to escape being arrested himself, he secured a pass and hurried away to Ireland, where he could rely on the support of the Munster regiments. On May 18 Lord Cork met him at Bennet's Bridge.[104] Lady Ranelagh had sped Broghill on his way and was relieved to entrust him to the care of Lady Orrery, who was "blessed wth a temper y^t . . . makes her easy to every body." Of her brother's turbulent career Lady Ranelagh remarked: "As he has had some Cares and troubles soe he has had very great mercys & deliverances, as he often striking upon ye sands & yet geting off safe being proofe enough of y^t." [105]

Not long after Broghill's arrival in Ireland, the Commissioners for Irish Affairs in Dublin were ordered to secure him. Against the advice of his friends, he obeyed their summons to appear before them, but brought his own troop of horse as a guard. By "artful reasoning" he persuaded the commissioners to consent to his return to Munster, with full command of the province, on condition that there should be no disturbance there.[106]

From now on Coote in Connaught and Broghill in Munster, like "wary" Monck in Scotland and Montagu with the fleet, spoke against, but acted for, the restoration of Charles Stuart. To this end, the rule of the clique of army officers in London had to be broken and the Rump Parliament set up by them in May, dismissed in October, and restored in December, had to be replaced by a "full and free" Parliament, including those members excluded in 1648. The im-

mediate prospects were bleak. Henry Cromwell, who
had held the title of Lord Lieutenant of Ireland during
Richard Cromwell's protectorate, was ordered by the
Rump Parliament to resign his post to the commissioners appointed by them. Before receiving the order
for his recall, he had already, on June 15, sent a dignified letter of resignation to Lenthall. He acknowledged that he could not promise "soe much affection to
the late changes, as others very honestly may" and
thanked God that he had been able to resist "the great
temptation" to withdraw his affection from the cause
in which his father lived and died.[107] Another blow for
Broghill was the arrival in Ireland at the end of July
of Edmund Ludlow as Commander-in-Chief of the
Irish army, with the rank of Lieutenant-General.
Ludlow proceeded to "new model" the army, replacing
many officers whose loyalty he suspected.

In June the King took definite steps to win Broghill's
assistance. As early as the preceding April, Edward
Villiers had informed Hyde, the King's Lord Chancellor, that, taking advantage of his interest with Lord
Belasyse, a member of the King's "Sealed Knot," he
had made "some progress in discoursing at distance
with Ld Broghall," whom he found more powerful in
the government than Lord Belasyse's nephew, Lord
Fauconberg.[108] Broghill's brother, Francis Boyle, who
was at The Hague, hinted that there were those of
the Protector's party who had resolution and power
to make "a greater change then the last," as
would "shortly apeere." [109] On the thirteenth of June,
Thomas Howard wrote to the King that Lord Broghill
desired the King to come to Ireland, and "he assures
me he will doo all things that may advance your Service." Either Howard or Francis Boyle would "very
suddenly" return with particulars.[110] Charles decided

that Edward Villiers, rather than Howard, should pay Broghill a visit, assure him of the King's favor, and offer to receive any message he might care to send. In communicating this decision to Villiers, Hyde explained:

> the King lookes upon lord Brahall as a Person who may be most instrumentall to doe him service there [in Ireland], and he does not beleeve he will have any aversion to it when ye Season shall be proper, & therefore the King very much desires . . . that you would make haste to Ireland, and that you would assure Lord Brahall of all that he can wish for from the King, if he will performe this Service, and that hee may likewise undertake to H. Cromwell that hee shall be gratified in all that he will propose and it will be in ye king's power, as soone as his Declaration shall be knowne, to send over men, money and Armes. And for this ye king hath ye absolute promise of those who are very well able to performe it.[111]

Somewhat regretfully Hyde recognized the necessity of Broghill's services. He wrote to Ormonde: "There is nothing like a good opinion of my Lord Broughill, and yet it is wished upon any occasion he might receive fair treatment." Hyde reminded Ormonde that Broghill's civilities to Ormonde's family had been "very extraordinary" and that to the influence of Lady Ranelagh, Broghill's sister, Ormonde owed the protection which he now enjoyed.[112]

It was probably Broghill whom Lord Mordaunt described to the King as "a person of fortune and interest" who was eager to serve him. This person, "as morall and religious, as wise," had abilities which made him courted by all parties and great influence upon those "who push for power"; and nothing of importance could be kept secret from him. He was "extreame cautious" to run no risk of discovery and would trust only one person to bring him to kiss the King's hands.[113]

That summer Nicholas Monck brought to his brother, General Monck, in Edinburgh a message from the King requesting the General to support the royal cause. Monck's chaplain, John Price, was first consulted and agreed that the King's message "must sleep in as few breasts as might be." [114] The private conference of the two brothers was inconclusive, for Monck was not yet willing to commit himself beyond exerting his influence to restore a Parliament.

Monck kept in touch with the officers in Ireland, urging their support in this endeavor. On November 23 he wrote from Dalkeith a cautious letter to Broghill, begging him to lay aside all thoughts of retirement until some more auspicious time, when Monck would gladly be his neighbor and lead a country life with him. Meanwhile, if there should be a Parliament, Broghill ought to be a member of it. "Truly my Lord," wrote Monck, "I honour you much, and am sorry to heare of yoᴵ Resolution to leave off publique imployment, which if such a Man as you should doe before thinges bee setled itt would be a meanes to leave things soe unsettled that it might putt us together by the Eares." [115]

At Coldstream—a "stream of good news"—Monck received an encouraging report from "the then growing Party in Ireland." [116] On December 13, taking advantage of Ludlow's absence in England, disaffected officers of the Irish army had seized Dublin Castle and arrested Colonel John Jones, Ludlow's Deputy, and his fellow commissioners. Dublin and all the other Irish garrisons except Duncannon had declared for Parliament and against the English army officers.

On January 1, 1660, Monck left Coldstream and

began his march to London in cold but sparkling winter weather, the Tweed so clear that his men could distinguish the colors of the pebbles in the water as they crossed it. As he advanced toward London, the inscrutable General kept his own counsel. His friends waited anxiously, hoping that, backed by his army, he would demand a free Parliament that would bring in the King. From Dunstable on January 27, Monck wrote to Broghill, commending him for "putting the army in Ireland into honest and sober hands." [117]

When Ludlow returned to Ireland, late in December, the Dublin officers refused to allow him to land near Dublin. He was received by the Governor of Duncannon and later recalled to London by the restored Rump Parliament to answer a charge of treason.[118] His power in Ireland was ended. There was still a senior Irish officer, Sir Hardress Waller, who was known to oppose a full and free Parliament. Perhaps suspecting a design against him, Waller took possession of Dublin Castle on February 15, but three days later was obliged to capitulate. He was held a prisoner at Athlone, but was eventually permitted to return to England.

On February 16, Sir Charles Coote and the officers under his command declared for a free Parliament which would admit the excluded members.[119] Two days later, Broghill and forty-three Munster officers issued a similar, more elaborate declaration, composed by Broghill. In his most persuasive manner, Broghill argued: "If the said excluded Members be re-admitted, they must be either the greater or the lesser Number in the House: If the lesser, where is the Danger of their Admission? If the greater, where is the Justice of their Exclusion?" [120]

Broghill and Coote [121] vied with each other in

private offers to the King to restore him in Ireland. Broghill's communication reached the King first. In the latter part of February, Broghill sent his brother Francis with a brief letter, quilted in the collar of his doublet, to the King at Brussels. Nine years later, when he was impeached in the House of Commons, Lord Orrery quoted the words of this letter, as he remembered them:

> If yo^re Matie on this humble invitation will be pleased to honor yo^re Protestant Subjects of Ireland by coming into this yo^re Kingdome wee solemnly engage ourselves as wee are Chrystians and Gent[lemen] to serve you with our lives and estates against all opposition, and by Gods blessing with the hazard of both to restore you to yo^re Kingdomes, for which be pleased to take the faythfull engagements of . . . Broghill, Charles Coot, Theoph. Jones, Richard Coot, Henry Medensis, Arthur Hill, John King, William Werden.[122]

The King received Broghill's invitation "with a great deal of joy" and was preparing to accept it when a better prospect was presented to him.[123] At the end of March, Sir John Grenville arrived in Brussels with most welcome proposals from Monck for the King's return to England.

Lord Cork and Robert Boyle witnessed Monck's arrival in London on February 3. On February 11 Monck demanded that a free Parliament should replace the Rump not later than May 6. This ultimatum, as Cork noted in his Diary, was greeted with bonfires throughout London; and "such expressions of joy . . . were not seen for manye yeares." [124] With extreme caution Monck took the successive steps which made the Restoration inevitable. His decision to recall the excluded members insured enough votes to bring the

Rump Parliament to an end. The excluded members
resumed their seats on February 21; and soon afterwards an act was passed making Monck Commander-
in-Chief of all the forces of the Commonwealth.
Between March 17, when the Rump was dissolved,
and April 25, when the Convention Parliament assembled, a Council of State had authority to issue
writs and transact all necessary business, including the
resettlement of the civil government in Scotland and
Ireland.

It was the interim Council of State which offered
Broghill the long-awaited prize of the Presidency of
Munster. On March 8, 1660, the Council of State sent
word to Broghill, Sir Charles Coote, Sir John Clotworthy, and Sir William Bury that they among others
had been appointed commissioners to manage the civil
government of Ireland, and their commissions would be
"speedily dispatched." [125] By an order of the preceding
day, Sir William Fenton, Sir John Percival, Sir William Penn, and William Hawkins were appointed
members of the Council of Broghill, Lord President of
Munster.[126] On May 11 Lord Cork sent Broghill his
commission as President.[127] The news of this appointment was received in Cork "with many demonstrations
of joy, expressed by bonfires, vollys of great shot from
the forts, &c." [128] Many years later, when the Earl of
Anglesey reproached Orrery for having served two
masters, Orrery observed that Anglesey had done the
same thing, and that when Anglesey was President of
the Council of State, he had sent Orrery a commission
as Lord President of Munster "under your owne
Hand by the name of Art. Annesley and under a
Greate Seale of England, which I think was none of
the Kings." [129]

An Irish Convention, with representatives from each county and borough, had begun meeting in Dublin on February 7. On February 27 Broghill was welcomed among its members "with great joy," after having been ceremoniously met "on the way" thither by various persons of quality.[130] The Convention deplored the "horrid violence" offered to the dignity of Parliament in 1648 and branded the late commissioners as "turbulent spirits."[131] On March 30 the Convention sent to two of its members, Sir John Clotworthy and William Aston, then in London, instructions to secure confirmation of grants of land made under the Cromwellian settlement to Lord Broghill, Sir Charles Coote, Colonel Michael Jones deceased, Dr. Henry Jones, and the children of the late Sir Charles Coote the Elder.[132]

As late as March, 1660, in his official correspondence with Thurloe, Broghill maintained that he was opposed to making Ireland "a back door" to let Charles Stuart into England.[133] In the meetings of the Irish Convention, however, he at last revealed his hand. From London Cork sent his brother the "excellent newes"[134] of Parliament's cordial reception of the King's letter and Declaration from Breda. A new chapter was now beginning in Broghill's life. With his singular adaptability to altered conditions, he was better able than most men to shake off the past and devote his remarkable energies to the present.

In so doing, he did not abandon old friends. Immediately after the Restoration, Broghill exerted himself to gain protection and assistance for Henry Cromwell. No doubt the latter was quite as ready to forgive Broghill for his Royalist activities as he was to assure the King and the Duke of York "(how hard, or needless soever it bee to beleeve mee) That few can wish their Royall persons, family, & Interest, more prosperity & Establishment than I do." [135] Broghill was never to have a friend of greater integrity and more winning modesty than Henry Cromwell. Nor did Broghill ever again enjoy so harmonious a companionship with any other Governor of Ireland.

Lord President of Munster

Broghill's satisfaction in his new office as Lord President of Munster was marred by his keen rivalry with Sir Charles Coote, Lord President of Connaught. With some reluctance Broghill and Coote entered into partnership to reduce Ireland, Coote securing the north and Broghill, "with great care and diligence," the south. The Dublin officers invited the two leaders to "repair to Dublin" and "much depended" on their "Judgment and prudent management of affairs." [1] In an intercepted letter from Colonel Marcus Trevor to Colonel Cromwell, written on April 18, 1660, which Ormonde opened and preserved among his papers, Trevor commented that the army in Ireland was aiming at "the ould fundamentalls of a settled Government," and "what little differences arise among us heare, have their springe from, and betweene, our 2 great ministers of state." [2]

Both Broghill and Coote had desired to be first in their offers to gain Ireland for Charles II, but Broghill had played his hand so cautiously that Coote had

received the first direct reply from the King. No
doubt both men aspired to the highly desirable office
of Lord Lieutenant of Ireland. When it was rumored
that Sir William Waller would be sent to command the
army in Ireland, Coote sent word to the King, by a
correspondent whose identity cannot be determined,
that he would not oppose the choice, if the King so
ordered; otherwise, he would never quit his post, "lett
ye other [Broghill] take this knowledge, as well as he
can." The same correspondent expressed the opinion,
presumably shared by Ormonde, that the Presidency
of Munster was an honor which Broghill by no means
merited, "for he y^t is false to one will not be true to
another, and it is certaine he has jugled extreamely in
ye Kings businesse," indeed throughout the Convention had been "extreame earnest & busye to putt hard
Conditions upon his Ma^tye." [3]

Broghill's name headed the list of commissioners
which the General Convention in Ireland appointed
in May, 1660, to attend the King in England. The commissioners were to offer congratulations to his Majesty
and gifts to him and his brother, and to request the
King to call a Parliament in Ireland, appoint a chief
governor, grant an Act of General Pardon, Indemnity,
and Oblivion, and authorize an Act of Settlement for
that kingdom.[4] On May 14 Charles II was proclaimed
King in Dublin. It was probably Broghill who penned
the "Humble Address" to the King from the officers in
and near Dublin. The officers professed their gratitude
that God had preserved the King in his person and
"wch we know is dearer to you in your religion," and
rejoiced that his Majesty not only observed his own
laws but was disposed to pardon all his subjects that
had broken them.[5]

On May 25 the King was met in Dover by a great

assembly of gentry, the "noblest," said the Duke of York, that he had ever seen. Broghill's brother, the Earl of Cork, took Monck in his coach to meet the King and saw the victorious General made Knight of the Garter. Cork himself took his place in the House of Lords as Baron Clifford and within a few weeks was appointed Lord Treasurer of Ireland. He wrote to Broghill "at large" of these joyful events and urged him to come over "speedily." [6]

Broghill lost no time in acting on such sensible advice. In the summer of 1660 he arrived in London, bringing with him not only the felicitations of the Convention, gracefully phrased by himself, but also a poem which he had composed "to express his joyful sentiments and those of the 3 kingdoms." [7] To his dismay Broghill received from the King an initial rebuff, which was soon explained, however, as a result of Coote's jealousy. Broghill's brother Francis, now Lord Shannon, learned from the King that Coote had claimed the honor of having been the first man who "stirred" for the King in Ireland and that Broghill had opposed his action and was at last persuaded "against his will" to join him. Fortunately, Broghill was able to send Shannon back to the King with the actual letter in which Coote had cautioned: "Remember my Lord you first put me upon this Design, and I beseech you forsake me not in that wch you first put me upon, wch was that of declaring for King & Parliament." [8]

The way was now paved for an auspicious interview, which Broghill hastened to obtain. The Lord Chancellor arranged the conference in a penciled note which he passed to the King at an August cabinet meeting. "I pray be pleased," the Earl of Clarendon wrote, "to give an Audyence to my Ld Braghall, who

will say many thinges to you of moment, and I thinke
with duty enough: if you will give him leave to attend
you tomorrow morninge at 8 of the clocke, I will
give him notice of it." The King wrote back: "You
give appointments in a morning to others sooner then
you take them yourselfe; but if my Lᵈ Braughall will
come at 9 he shall be welcome." [9]

A useful mediator in behalf of his brother was the
Earl of Cork, now Baron Clifford. On August 28 the
King honored Cork by dining with him and remaining
at cards at his house until two o'clock in the morning.
Cork had proposed that no other guests should be
invited, except by the King, "whereupon" Broghill
"was by him invited." [10]

On August 21 the King ordered a bill prepared for
Broghill to hold by royal warrant the office of Lord
President of Munster which had previously been
granted him by the Convention Parliament.[11] To this
office the post of Governor of co. Clare was annexed.[12]
On September 5 the King created Broghill Earl of
Orrery.[13] On October 26 the King signed a warrant
entrusting the immediate management of Irish affairs
to three Lords Justices: Sir Maurice Eustace (Lord
Chancellor), and the rival Presidents of Munster and
Connaught.[14] Each Lord Justice was to receive a salary of fifteen hundred pounds. In the course of the
next months Orrery was made Colonel of a regiment
of horse in Ireland, Captain of one troop in it, Governor of the city of Limerick, and Constable of Limerick Castle. He was granted the wardships of Folliott
Wingfield, heir of the late Richard Wingfield, and
Mary Stuart, heiress of the late Andrew Stuart,
third Baron Castle Stuart.[15] Laden with honors, he
returned to Ireland at the end of this eventful year.[16]

Shortly before Orrery's departure from London,

the King ordered published his eagerly awaited *Declaration* concerning Ireland, outlining the provisions to be made in a forthcoming Act of Settlement.[17] The *Declaration* clearly favored the Protestant adventurers and soldiers, upon whose continued support the King necessarily depended. Advised by persons "of quality and interest" in Ireland, among whom Orrery was presumably the most emphatic, the King made the dangerous assumption that there was a large enough proportion of undisposed forfeited lands in Ireland to satisfy all justifiable claims.

The Protestant adventurers and soldiers were first to be confirmed in the lands which they at present enjoyed and to receive reprisals and have arrears satisfied from forfeited lands. Soldiers, listed by name, who had served the King overseas were to be provided for later. Innocent Papists, who could prove their loyalty to the King's father or to the King, were to have their former estates or lands of equivalent value, but outside the corporations. Ormonde and his wife, now Duke and Duchess of Ormonde, and Inchiquin, now Earl of Inchiquin, were specifically named to be fully restored to their lands. Another category included Monck, now Duke of Albemarle, Orrery, Coote, now Earl of Mountrath, and several others who had been "early" in their dutiful addresses and had "made good their professions." Vague assurance was offered of further provision for all who merited it. Excepted from favor were the regicides and those who had opposed the King's restoration. A Parliament was to be called in Ireland and suitable bills prepared to execute these decisions. On the whole, the *Declaration* marked a triumph for Orrery, who had certainly impressed upon the King his own recent and valuable services, as well as Protestant claims in general.

Settled at Phoenix House in Dublin, Orrery led an arduous life, working out details for the projected Act of Settlement, with the preparation of which the King had entrusted him, and besieged by appeals for the restitution of lands. His voluminous correspondence with Ormonde, which was to extend over the next eighteen years, began auspiciously enough with Ormonde's thanks for "an excellent narrative" of Orrery's proceedings in Ireland. "You have served the King," Ormonde observed, "to the degree he expected and your friends and servants promised you would and have found time to gain esteem for me." [18] And in a subsequent letter, Ormonde acknowledged: "Your kindness to all my relations hath always anticipated any desire of mine." [19] Lord Cork in London "cautiously" discussed with the King the disposition of certain estates in Ireland and persuaded him to refer decisions to the Lords Justices.[20] Orrery took care, however, to ascertain and gratify the King's wishes and wrote confidently to Secretary Nicholas (who was to receive a substantial sum of money): "I think I may truly assure you that I am much mistaken if, what ever ye King pleases, I doe not get past in ye Howse of Com⁸." [21] Sir James Shaen, Register-General to the commissioners for executing the King's *Declaration,* requested from Orrery a list of persons for special pardons and also undertook to secure for Orrery himself the lands of Sir Hardress Waller, "before all is gone." [22]

The spectacle of the King's Coronation on April 23, 1661, was considered by Cork "the most splendid that has been I think seen in Christendome." [23] A few days afterwards, Cork kissed the hand of the King, "who used me with great Civilitye and exprest much to my brother Orrery," [24] and left the Court for Ireland. In Dublin the Coronation was celebrated with appropriate ceremonies which Orrery, suffering from one of his now frequently occurring attacks of gout, could not attend.

On May 8 the Irish Parliament began its first session. Orrery was unable to ride in the procession of dignitaries to St. Patrick's Cathedral; but he did take his seat at Chichester House as Lord Justice and Privy Councillor, "notwithstanding his infirmity of ye Gout." [25] At the end of July this Parliament was prorogued, after it had accomplished its chief business, the first draft of a bill of settlement to be presented to the King. Orrery was gratified when Ormonde reported the King's favorable response to this "yonge magna Charta." [26]

In March the King ordered lands in co. Clare assigned to Orrery, in recognition of his having been "eminently instrumentall and successful in the late happye work of our Restoration." [27] He also ordered that such foreigners as Orrery named should be admitted into the corporations to encourage trade and manufacture in those towns.[28] In the midst of his other activities, the indefatigable Earl found time to visit Munster and establish garrisons there, lay the foundation of his house at Charleville, and settle in Limerick forty Dutch families, whose efficiency in the manufacture of linen "did my Hart good." [29] In a few spare hours, snatched from his public duties, he completed his first play, *Altemera*.

Orrery received from Anglesey the cheering news that the Lords Justices were to be assigned ten thousand pounds in the Act of Settlement.[30] Less pleasing was the announcement of Ormonde's appointment in November as Lord Lieutenant of Ireland. On December 18 Mountrath's sudden death from smallpox removed one powerful rival and gave Orrery the brief

solace of sharing the government of Ireland, until Ormonde's arrival, with only one other governor, the
Lord Chancellor. This flattering increase of authority,
Orrery professed, was "a compliment I would have
declined; but the Council would have it, and so it
past." [31]

Although he had hoped to gain the office which Ormonde now received, Orrery managed to conceal his
keen disappointment. He wrote to Secretary Nicholas
that he was glad to be relieved of his post, and to be
relieved by the Duke of Ormonde would be "a double
Contentment." He could now return to that province
with the government of which his Majesty, in his "unlimited goodness," had honored him.[32] While await-
ing the arrival of Ormonde, Orrery planned a hall,
chapel, and stables for Phoenix House, to meet Ormonde's needs,[33] and for his own use in Dublin rented
Thomas Court for three hundred pounds a year. At
Rathcogan in Munster Orrery carefully supervised
the building of his stately country house, Charleville
House, of which he was the architect, and which was
to be his favorite residence for the next ten years.
This ill-fated mansion, shadowed by a gloomy prophecy, was to be reduced to ashes in the lifetime of Orrery's grandson, the third Earl.

In the spring of 1662, following his father's example, Orrery sent abroad his two sons, Roger and
Henry, for several years of study and travel under
the tutelage of Dr. Jeremy Hall. The boys had as
their traveling companion Folliott Wingfield, Orrery's
ward, whom he had recently married to his eldest
daughter Elizabeth.[34] On June 22 the King appointed
Orrery Sergeant-Major-General of the Army in Ireland.[35]

In May, 1662, the Act of Settlement was finally

passed by both Houses of the English Parliament. It was accepted by the King in September and was printed before the end of the year.[36] Orrery had considered it necessary, as well as tactful, to decline for the time being his own gift from the King of ten thousand pounds, in view of the number of persons whose bonds had been forfeited but who had obtained the King's pardon.[37] The passage of the Act must not be jeopardized. The King ordered Ormonde to give Orrery the promised sum,[38] but was later obliged to offer Orrery instead fifteen hundred pounds a year from forfeited lands.[39] Despite his original hope of settling all legal claims and also obtaining a large revenue for the King, Orrery must ultimately have shared Ormonde's conviction that "there must bee new discoverys made of a new Ireland for the old will not serve to satisfy these engagements." [40]

Orrery was probably the author of the long preamble to the Act of Settlement. Several pages were devoted to denouncing "the unnatural Insurrection" of Irish Papists in 1641 and their subsequent treacherous behavior, in contrast to the faithful service of "several of your Majesty's subjects," who "with much difficulty and hazard" had secured control of Ireland and invited the King to return to that kingdom.[41] The main body of the document followed the lines of the King's *Declaration* in the provisions for adventurers and soldiers and for Papists who could prove their innocence. In a list of persons to receive special favor, mention was made of the Duke of Albemarle, the Earl of Orrery, the (deceased) Earl of Mountrath, and several other former Cromwellians, who "for their Service and Sufferings in the War of Ireland" were to retain their estates. The Duke of York was to receive a large portion of the lands of the regicides.

For an estate vested in the King, Sir James Shaen was to receive eight thousand pounds "without further delay." Instructions were included for the commissioners [42] who were to execute the Act.

Orrery's pen was most useful to the King in clarifying the provisions of the Act of Settlement. His aid also proved to be valuable in "discovering" Irish lands with which to placate Cromwellian soldiers, reward favored persons, and increase the King's income. Orrery proposed to settle an Irish revenue higher by eighty thousand pounds yearly than any earlier sovereigns had received in times of peace.[43] Such a prospect naturally gratified Charles, who declared that he found Orrery "a very worthy and very able person," in whom he had perfect confidence.[44]

On July 27, 1662, members of the Irish Privy Council were sent to Howth to welcome the arriving Lord Lieutenant. Orrery, suffering from an attack of gout, could not go; and it was decided that the King's sword should not be carried before the other Lord Justice, the Lord Chancellor. The next afternoon Ormonde came to Dublin Castle, attended by the Lord Chancellor, members of the Privy Council, and other lords. Later, he went to Orrery's house at Thomas Court, where his patent was read and his oath administered. That evening there were bonfires and fireworks in honor of the occasion.[45]

Orrery's graceful speech,[46] on delivering the sword to Ormonde, was obviously intended for royal consumption. He remarked that the King's subjects in Ireland, who had been indebted to the King before for their "being," were now indebted to him for their "well being." The King, who had given the Act of Settlement, had now given his Grace to execute "that great Act." Ormonde was kind to come to this "ruin-

ous and disjointed Kingdom." He was entreated to
"pass by what wee did when wee were not our selves,
and to accept of what we now doe when wee are our
selves." Your Grace, said Orrery, knows "wee were
then unfitt for you and wee now know you onely are
fitt for us. We need all your goodness to forgett the
ill that is past, and all yoʳ abilities to act the good
which is to come." The address must be regarded as
an excellent example of Orrery's oratorical gift.

A pleasant chapter in Orrery's life opened with the
arrival in Dublin in the summer of 1662 of Mrs. Katherine Philips, "the matchless Orinda." The Duchess of
Ormonde and Lady Cork and her daughters gave Mrs.
Philips a cordial welcome; and Lady Elizabeth Boyle
became Orinda's "lovely Celimena" and Lady Anne
Boyle her "ador'd Valeria." Mrs. Philips soon made
the acquaintance of Lord Orrery, who impressed her
as a "man of great parts and agreeable Conversation."
Orrery read and admired her translation of a scene
from Corneille's *La Mort de Pompée*, sent her the
French text of the play, and "earnestly importun'd"
her to complete her translation, which she did at his
request. Orinda basked in the homage of this gallant
friend, "a man who had so lately commanded a Kingdom"; and Orrery found her Platonic affectations
equally congenial.[47] He sent her commendatory verses
on her *Pompey*, later prefixed to her published poems,
which charmed her by their "Elegancy on so undeserv-
ing a Subject." [48] Poetic flattery could scarcely soar
higher than his extraordinary tribute:

> *You English Corneille's Pompey with such flame*
> *That you both raise our wonder and his fame,*
> *If he could read it, he like us would call*
> *The copy greater than th' Original.*[49]

RICHARD BOYLE,
FIRST EARL OF CORK

From a painting in the possession of the Earl of Cork and Orrery, by permission of his Lordship

LISMORE CASTLE, LORD ORRERY'S BIRTHPLACE

Drawing from a print (1746) in the possession of the Earl of Cork and Orrery, by permission of his Lordship

MARGARET, COUNTESS OF ORRERY

From a painting in the possession of Patrick
Reginald Boyle, by permission of Mr. Boyle

OLIVER CROMWELL (1653)

*From a painting by Sir Peter Lely, by per-
mission of the Birmingham Art Gallery*

ELIZABETH, COUNTESS OF BURLINGTON,
AND KATHERINE, VISCOUNTESS RANELAGH

*From a painting in the possession of
the Duke of Devonshire at Bolton
Abbey, by permission of his Grace*

JAMES BUTLER, FIRST DUKE OF ORMONDE

*From a painting in the possession of the Duke of
Buccleuch, by permission of his Grace*

CHARLES II

From the frontispiece to Orrery's
A Treatise of the Art of War (*1677*)

ELIZABETH, COUNTESS OF NORTHUMBERLAND

From a painting by Sir Peter Lely in the possession of Lord Egremont at Petworth, by permission of his Lordship

CHARLES FORT AT KINSALE

From a drawing in the manuscript of Thomas Phillips'
Military Survey of Ireland (*1685*), *by permission of the*
National Library in Dublin

Orrery's initial venture in the field of heroic drama must have impressed Orinda. It is tempting to imagine that she was a delighted spectator at the private production of his first play, *Altemera,* the evening of October 18, 1662, in the hall of Thomas Court, where Orrery entertained Ormonde and "most of the persons of Honor in these parts" with "a noble Banquet and a Play of his own making." [50] Orinda, as well as Orrery, had the satisfaction that same month of witnessing the opening of a Dublin theater, the Theatre Royal in Smock Alley, "a new Play-house . . . which in my Opinion," commented Orinda, "is much finer than D'Avenant's," [51] and where she saw plays "in the newest Mode, and not ill acted." [52]

When Cork arrived in Dublin in December, he found Orrery confined to his Dublin house with an attack of gout and unable to participate in the festivities of the Christmas season. Ormonde entertained Cork and his family at a dinner and dance, and Cork gave a dinner, ball and banquet for all Ormonde's sons and Lord and Lady Cavendish. [53] Invalided but never idle, Orrery may well have been at work on his next play, *Henry the Fifth.*

Orrery sponsored the production at the new Dublin theater of Mrs. Philips's *Pompey* and advanced a hundred pounds toward the cost of Roman and Egyptian costumes for the actors. [54] Songs for the play were written by various persons, one by a Frenchman employed by Orrery; [55] and fashionable ladies memorized and sang them. The Earl of Roscommon wrote a prologue for the play and Sir Edward Dering an epilogue. The first performance took place the afternoon of February 18, 1663. [56]

A week later, on February 26, as the Earl of Cork noted in his Diary, Orrery's *Altemera* was publicly performed at the Smock Alley theater, before an audience which included Ormonde, Cork, and other notable persons.[57] The occasion must be regarded as a memorable one, for *Altemera* was the first English heroic tragedy, not adapted from a French source, to be publicly acted after the Restoration.

Political tensions soon blighted such promising theatrical ventures. "There is a Plot discover'd here," wrote Mrs. Philips, "but what to make of it I know not; and indeed 'tis so unlucky an Age for Plots that even those on the Stage cannot thrive: For the Players disband apace." [58] The plot to which she referred was a frustrated attempt on the part of disaffected Cromwellians to seize Dublin Castle and murder the Lord Lieutenant, as a protest against the alleged too lenient treatment of Irish Papists by the English commissioners who conducted the Court of Claims. Some seven-eighths of the Irish Papists who sought to prove their innocence had their lands restored; [59] and it was only too apparent that there would be a shortage of lands for the adventurers and soldiers.

Orrery had an effective spy system (still modeled on Cromwell's), and through one of his intelligencers was able to give Ormonde a fortnight's notice of the "damnable plot." In a letter to the King on May 23, Orrery took pains to inform his Majesty of this useful service and described his own effective suppression of dangerous fanatics in Munster.[60] He assured Ormonde that he was excluding from the town of Rathcogan, where Charleville House was located, all Presbyterians, Independents, Papists, and "any other sort of Phanatticks," admitting only "good old Protestants," and added that he was establishing there linen and woolen manufactures and "all other good trades." [61] He encouraged ship building; and Munster soon had

more shipping in its two seaports than all the other
seaports in Ireland.[62]

With Lord Kingston Orrery undertook the farming
of alehouses for a year and of the inland excise for
seven years.[63] The King issued a warrant, "as a speciall
mark of our Bounty & Favour," for Orrery to have
one-third of the "lapsed" money, forfeited by adventurers who had failed to pay their full subscriptions,
provided that he would pay one thousand pounds from
the first profits to Thomas Killigrew and Edward Progers, Grooms of the King's Bedchamber.[64] Clarendon,
whose grants in Ireland fell short of his expectations,
contended that Orrery's "Assurances to the Bedchamber Men, to help them to good Fortunes in Ireland,"
procured for him their defense and vindication "when
any Thing was reflected upon to his Disadvantage or
Reproach." [65] Orrery expressed profuse gratitude for
the new grant, which, however, he did not receive. The
least attractive aspect of Ormonde's character emerges
in his repeated refusals to endorse the King's repeated
orders to assign this gift to Orrery. Ormonde, who
himself, in the estimate of Pepys, owned "more acres
of land" than "any prince in Christendome," [66] found
it more expedient to set aside ten thousand pounds of
the lapsed money for the purchase of Phoenix Park
for the King and to let Orrery wait indefinitely for
his share.[67]

The Dublin plot, although suppressed, was regarded
as a danger signal of Protestant hostility to the Act of
Settlement; and it seemed prudent to devise an "explanation" of the Act in terms which would reassure
the adventurers and soldiers of their rights. Ormonde
turned to Orrery to work out details for a new Act,
to be known as the Act of Explanation. The task was
no easy one, and Orrery admitted to Secretary Bennet

that he had "tormented my Brayne to doe it, as much as ye goute has tormented my Feet." [68] He complained to Ormonde in a similar vein and confessed that "a hundred Times, I flung away my Pen & tore my Papers." But at last he lighted upon a plan, the "loose sticks" of which he bound "into a Faggot" to present to his Grace.[69]

Orrery's presence in England was deemed necessary to push the new Act; and in July, 1664, he took up his residence in London for a prolonged visit. Many other London visits were to follow, always welcomed by Orrery, always costly. The expenses of these journeys ranged from a minimum of two thousand, five hundred pounds to a maximum of seven thousand, eight hundred and seventy-five pounds.[70] Orrery returned home each time with some desired plum of the King's bounty and with promises, seldom fulfilled, of more favors to come. When it was rumored in Dublin that Orrery owed the King a large sum of money, Jeremy Hall, Orrery's steward, indignantly protested that Orrery ought to be "rather on the receiving than paying side." [71]

It was the King's custom, as Orrery meticulously notified Ormonde on each occasion, to provide a royal yacht to convey his "trusty" adviser to an English port and to transport him to Ireland at the end of his visit. When an attack of gout prevented one of Orrery's journeys, Lord Aungier remarked sarcastically that the opinion of "the great man of Munster" was "so indispensable to the King's affairs" that it had to be sent over by a friend.[72] His conferences with the King Orrery found highly satisfactory, for his Majesty appeared to be "hugely intent" on the settlement of Ireland and "extreme careful of his Protestant subjects." [73] Then, as always, Orrery tended to mistake the King's exceptional patience as a listener for concurrence in those Protestant interests so dear to the Lord President's heart.

In November, 1664, Orrery took his seat for Arundel in the English House of Commons. "Pressed" by the King, he attended most of the sessions of the House. Agreeable meetings with the King's ministers, with the Duke of York, and, best of all, alone with the King in his closet filled the remainder of those London days. Orrery kept an exact account of the number of hours of private audiences which the King graciously accorded him. When Orrery kissed the King's hand before returning to Ireland in the summer of 1665, the King did him the "unspeakable honour" of discoursing with him alone for nearly an hour and gave him "soe many Evidences & assurances of his Royal favor" that he was "soe dead foundred" he could scarcely get to his coach.[74] There were times when Orrery was "locked up alone" with the King for an hour and a half, or even two hours. "Noe man livinge," Orrery told Conway, "can be kinder to another then Mr. Church [the King] is now to Mr. Rogers [Orrery], advisinge with him, many houres in a weeke alone, on his most important & secretest Concernes." [75]

The King's personal friendship for Orrery aroused the jealousy of rival courtiers, none of whom, however high in royal favor, enjoyed Orrery's degree of intimacy with the King. It was perhaps as a well-informed, fluent, witty, and ingratiating conversationalist that Orrery won the King's friendship. Although Charles was a good listener, he was easily bored. Orrery could talk plausibly and delightfully on the most varied subjects and could adapt himself with perfect poise and good breeding to any occasion. He records in one of his letters that he had played a game of ombre with the King and the Spanish ambassador (Baron de Batteville) and had been "victorious over both." [76] Clarendon deplored the King's indulgence of the frivolous de Batteville; [77] Orrery, on the contrary, cultivated the ambassador, matched wits with him, and was able to outmatch him at the gaming table. The French ambassador Colbert reported to Louis XIV that the English Court possessed in Lord Orrery a "bel esprit, conseiller de Cromwell, grand ami du Chancellier, et créature de la Duchesse de Yorke et son parent, qui avoit plus de credit avec le Roy que touts les autres Ministres ensemble." [78] Colbert was even able to swallow the King's prodigious jest that the affable English Earl was "a Catholic in his heart." [79]

His London visit of 1664–1665 was an eventful period in Orrery's private life and family circle. His youngest daughter, Lady Barbara Boyle, was baptized on November 8, 1664, at St. Martin's-in-the-Fields. The following February his son Roger was married at Dorset House to Lady Mary Sackville, daughter of Richard Sackville, fifth Earl of Dorset, and Frances, Countess of Dorset. [80] Orrery welcomed the alliance and fortunately could not foresee that this daughter-in-law was to be the chief thorn in his otherwise happy domestic life. In March Orrery sent his son Harry abroad for a second time to continue his studies under Dr. Jeremy Hall. [81] Orrery was gratified, of course, by the royal favors which his older brother now enjoyed. The Queen Mother procured for Lord Cork the title of an English earl, the Earl of Burlington; and the King and the Duke of York helped to arrange the marriage of Burlington's daughter Harriet to Lord Clarendon's second son, Lawrence Hyde. [82]

For his continued work on the Act of Explanation, Orrery received from the King a grant of four thousand pounds.[83] On the Earl's son-in-law, Folliott Wingfield, the King graciously conferred the title of Lord Powerscourt.[84] On May 26 Orrery was sworn a member of the King's Privy Council.[85]

Orrery's views on the Dutch War are not known. The English victory over the Dutch navy on June 3, 1665, brought personal tragedy to the Earl of Burlington in the death of his second son Richard, on board the Duke of York's ship the *Royal Charles*. A single cannon shot killed Lord Falmouth, Lord Muskerry, and Richard Boyle; and Boyle's severed head struck down the Duke, who was standing nearby.[86]

On July 27 Orrery kissed the King's hand and began his homeward journey to Ireland.[87] He was soon deeply involved in the affairs of Munster, where he found the long morning and afternoon sessions of his provincial court in Charleville "as tiring as debating a bill of Settlement for Ireland in England." [88] He was much concerned over the plight of the half-starved Munster army, of which he commanded nearly a third.[89]

Meanwhile, Orrery's work on the Act of Explanation drew to a close; and he was confident, as he assured Lord Arlington, that the Act would serve the King's interest.[90] Arlington was to benefit substantially from the Act. In a succession of cordial letters to the King's powerful Secretary of State, Orrery made it clear that he was bestirring himself to secure for Arlington the "fine estate" of over sixty thousand acres of Lord Clanmalier,[91] as well as an additional ten thousand pounds from the Irish revenue. When the Act passed the Irish House of Commons in December, Orrery reported to Arlington that there was

only one vote against it, although, he feared, "many
negatives in heart." He had taken the greatest pains
to keep his friends "steady" for the bill and thanked
God that all dangerous opposition to it was now over.[92]
It was too late to correct the harm already done,
in the assignment of lands, through bribery, forgeries,
and patronage. Moreover, the general terms of the
Act, far from conciliating any party, disappointed the
adventurers and soldiers, who already felt cheated,
and dismayed the Irish Papists. No Irish persons not
yet adjudged innocent were to have their claims heard
in the future, so that about five thousand petitioners
were excluded from any possible redress. The adventurers and soldiers were to give up a third of their
estates or claims, in order to create a suitable fund
for reprisals. Certain individuals were singled out for
special favors. Fifty thousand pounds from the forfeited houses of the city of Limerick were to satisfy
the arrears of the Earl of Roscommon and the Earl
of Orrery; and Orrery was to retain all the lands
assigned him by the Act of Settlement. Ormonde was
to have fifty thousand pounds in lieu of further satisfaction of his claims. Among others who were specifically provided for were Inchiquin, Arlington, Burlington, and Sir James Shaen. It may be surmised that it
was Orrery who added the proviso that the "barbarous
and uncouth names" of most of the Irish towns should
be replaced in future letters patent by "new and proper
names more suitable to the English tongue." [93]
Orrery's expenses were always heavy. In the spring
of 1666 he complained to Ormonde that his "little
stock" of money was much depleted by his recent
journey to London and "the marriage of a daughter." [94] The marriage of his daughter Margaret to
Inchiquin's eldest son, William, Lord O'Brien, was

another important link in the carefully wrought chain
of his social connections. It became apparent that the
forfeited houses in Limerick would yield only a small
portion of the fifty thousand pounds which the King
had granted to Orrery and Roscommon; but the King's
additional gift to Orrery of the island of Limerick
was a welcome concession, and Orrery commended
the city as "one of ye noblest seats of a Town y^t I
ever saw." [95]

Louis XIV's declaration of war against England
in January, 1666, spurred Orrery to unremitting efforts to strengthen the defenses of Munster. Ambitious to win personal laurels and to achieve prestige
for the province which he governed, Orrery gave Ormonde no respite in his incessant demands for better
pay for the impoverished army, funds for repairing
Munster forts, and the raising of a militia as a safeguard against a possible French invasion or Irish rebellion.[96] His importunity in pleading for a militia
broke down Ormonde's obvious opposition; and with
apparent ease Orrery raised an effective force of two
thousand horse and thirty-three hundred foot,[97] which
an enthusiastic observer described as "not in feare
of any enimy." [98]

Between the lines of Ormonde's scrupulously polite,
self-justifying replies to Orrery's lengthy appeals for
military aid may be read the Lord Lieutenant's jealous
distrust of a rival whose influence he sought to curb.
He thanked Orrery for his "pertinent Reflexions," [99]
but wished that Orrery had not passed them on to the
King. "I doubt not," Ormonde grudgingly conceded,
"but I shall find those in yor L^{ps} Government in as
much if not more readinesse then any." His exaspera-
tion flared in the pointed remark: "Y^r Letters can
never be too long nor perhaps mine too short." [100]

In September, 1666, Ormonde made a stately ten days' progress through Munster, raising Orrery's hopes that the funds which he had so "fruitlessly" requested for the repair of the Munster forts would subsequently be forthcoming. The distinguished guest was met at the borders of Limerick by Orrery, many of the gentry of the province, and nine troops of horse who greeted his Grace with a welcoming volley. Such a proud display of the Lord President's authority was presumably far from gratifying to the Lord Lieutenant. Accompanied by Orrery and members of his family, Ormonde proceeded to Limerick, attended a service in the cathedral there and a Council meeting, and viewed the castle, where all the cannon were fired in his honor. At Charleville there was another Council meeting and a stag hunt in Orrery's park. The tour included visits to Cork, Kinsale, Blarney, Youghal, and Lismore.[101] In October Orrery, his wife, and several of his children paid a reciprocal visit to Ormonde in Kilkenny.[102]

At the sixth session of Charles's second Parliament, the "fatal bill" prohibiting the importation into England of Irish cattle was passed on November 23 by a margin of ten votes.[103] The King, greatly in need of a supply for the Dutch War, yielded reluctantly to the insistence of members of the House of Commons on the passage of this bill. Acrimonious debates had been carried on in the House with as much vehemence as if England's sole grievance was from Irish cattle. Swords were drawn, and a duel was narrowly averted between Ossory and Buckingham, which the latter provoked by "injurious national reproaches." [104] Lord Conway gloomily observed: "Ireland . . . is laid by and neglected. Under what sad fate we lie, or what evil stars are over us, I know not." [105]

By 1667 there were almost no lands undisposed of in Ireland.[106] Always a generous friend, Orrery sacrificed a thousand pounds in order to make up a deficit in a grant for Sir Heneage Finch.[107] Orrery had received no portion of his share of the fifty thousand pounds assigned to him and Roscommon by the Act of Explanation and had given up lands worth twice the amount.[108] Regretfully he ordered his son Harry home from his travels. Harry's annual allowance of five hundred pounds exceeded his father's income from an estate which had once yielded four thousand pounds a year.[109] It was an ironic fact that despite the King's frequent efforts to reward him, Orrery was a richer man in the service of Cromwell than in the service of Charles II.

Orrery felt keenly the injustice to Ireland in the passage of the Irish Cattle Bill. He was not, however, a man to indulge in vain regrets, once the bill was passed; and he hastened to find ways of compensating Ireland for what she had lost. He built a whole street in Charleville for linen manufacturers, furnished them with looms and other equipment, and considered himself pleasantly employed "amongst mechanicks." He also established a free school in Charleville, "y^t I may myself inspect ye Education of ye yonge Gentry of this Province, wch I looke on, as my Duty." [110]

The project which was to give Orrery more enduring satisfaction than any other was the restoration of the fortifications of Kinsale. It was his conviction that an expenditure of six thousand pounds would make the fine harbor of Kinsale the best port in the King's three dominions for sheltering merchant ships and endangered ships of the Royal Navy. Kinsale had the further merit of being "in the road of all the trade in the world." [111] Early in July, 1667, Orrery spent laborious hours exploring the rocky site of the decayed fortress, although "to gouty feet such rugged walks are not easy." [112] Later on, he carefully supervised his workmen, as they repaired the bastions of the fort and an old tower, fortified the blockhouse, raised a battery and fixed a boom. He announced himself ready to "pawn my Plate rather than necessary works shall stand still." [113] A personal letter from the Duke of York, signed "your affectionat freind, James," congratulated Orrery on bringing into "a good posture" a harbor "in which the safety of much wealth of this nation may suddenly be concerned." [114]

The disgrace and flight of the King's valuable but difficult Chancellor, Clarendon, distressed Burlington, who had married his daughter to the Lord Chancellor's son. Orrery refused to criticize the King for dismissing his chief Minister. He admitted that Clarendon had been "a true friend to Ireland"; [115] but their personal differences [116] softened the blow.

On November 30, 1667, after Clarendon's fall, Charles wrote to Orrery [117] in the most cordial and reassuring terms:

> My L^d of Orrery, I am so well persuaded of your particular kindness to me & so satisfied with the constant service you do me upon all occasions, as I had omitted to say any thing to you, till now upon the late change I have made, because I hope you are so much assured of my true friendship to you, as no alteration could shake me in it; for you may be most confident that you may stand upon your own legs & that you need nobody's friendship with me, nor ought to fear the ill offices of any man can have any effect to your prejudice. Therefore I will say no more at this time but conjure you never to doubt the constant kindness of
>
> Your very affectionate friend
> Charles R

The King's much cherished letters impressed Orrery as "more like what a Father would write to a son, then a King to a subject." As a proof of such intimacy, Orrery quoted to Conway the delightful close of one letter of invitation to England: "I will say noe more to you now, but only desyer you to com over against ye Sittinge of ye Parl^t, not only to serve me ther, but also to receive from my self full satisfaction, y^t I am your affectionat Frend, C R." [118]

After the fall of Clarendon, according to Morrice, the King offered to Orrery the high office which Clarendon had held. The offer may have been made in July, 1668, preceded by private conferences which Burlington and Orrery had with the Duchess and Duke of York.[119] Morrice relates that the Duchess of York summoned Orrery to her closet and talked to him for "nearly half an hour" about her unfortunate situation and the Duke's, since her father's disgrace. She alleged that she had no friend but Orrery whom she could trust and begged him to restore the Duke and herself to the King's favor. If Orrery would sue for the post of Lord Chancellor for himself, she and the Duke would give him their support. Orrery "told her plainly y^t he was but a decrepit Man," but he would serve them in other ways. He feared that the Duke's being reported a Papist hindered his popularity, whereupon she put her hand on a Bible and declared that he was "no more a Papist than she was." It would be difficult, Orrery demurred, to convince people that this was true. Soon afterwards, the Duke desired to see Orrery in *his* closet, begged him to accept the post of Lord Chancellor, and promised to be guided wholly by his advice.

The next morning Orrery was summoned to an interview with the King, who remarked on his brother's general unpopularity for having followed the late Chancellor's counsels. The King was relieved to know that York now intended to be "wholly advised" by Orrery, since there was no one else in the three kingdoms with whom he could trust his brother. Orrery reported his two conversations with the Duchess and the Duke. The King then begged Orrery to accept the chancellorship, as "the fittest man among all his subjects, not only for that Employment but to work upon his Brother." Because of his ill health, Orrery declined the post, even when offered a deputy. He agreed to advise York, while always making the King's service his first concern.

After taking a reflective turn or two in his coach in Hyde Park, Orrery went back to the King to suggest that York should at once beg the King's pardon and promise to be entirely guided by him. The King "thought that wicked Woman his Wife would not let the Duke be so submissive." Nevertheless, the conciliatory meeting was arranged, with Orrery as the flattered and successful peacemaker.[120]

The relations between Orrery and Ormonde became more strained. Ormonde respected Orrery's financial ability and skill in handling public funds. He resented, however, the King's favors to the Lord President, which Orrery could not refrain from reporting in detail; and he refused to authorize the large gift of the lapsed money and Orrery's share of five thousand pounds which the King had more recently granted to Orrery and Anglesey.[121]

To Orrery's constant requests for funds to settle the arrears of the soldiers in Munster and to repair the Munster forts Ormonde lent a reluctant ear; and only a trickle of money reached Orrery for these purposes. It was not in his power, Ormonde declared, to

furnish the means for "infallible Safety." [122] Hard
pressed to provide funds though he undoubtedly was,
Ormonde's resistance seems to have been chiefly motivated by his fears of a strong Munster as a threat
to his own authority. Nor was he wholly unjustified
in such fears. He was especially irritated because Orrery did not hesitate to send accounts of the plight
of Munster to the King and to the King's advisers in
England.

Orrery complained when a troop of his regiment
was ordered out of Munster and reminded the Lord
Lieutenant that Munster paid a third of the taxes of
the kingdom. "I was somewhat confident," he wrote,
"y^t y^{re} G^{ce} would have sent 3 or 4 Troops, rather than
have taken away one." [123] The bold and successful exploit of the Dutch fleet at Chatham in June, 1667,
caused Orrery to entreat the defense of Ireland with
added vigor. He urged placing beacons on all the sea-
coasts, strengthening the spy system, mustering all
militia troops, and hastening the pay of the army.[124]
"I am extreame sorry," he wrote, "y^t y^{re} G^{ce} should
thinke ye officers under my Go^{vt} more apt to take up
Rumours, & be unsatisfied, then thos in other Parts."
It was better for his officers to bring him their just
complaints than to "keepe them boylinge in their
Brests." He must redress what injustices he could and
represent to Ormonde what he could not.[125] It was
some comfort to assign all Dutch prizes for the pay
of the army.[126] The soldiers' great arrears were "past
my little Judgment to apprehend." [127] Ormonde's
project to pay them partly in corn would destroy the
tillage of Ireland; "but y^{re} G^{ce} knows best what is
fit." [128] Orrery pawned his last one hundred pounds in
gold to give each troop in his regiment five pounds and
"a fat beef." The poor fellows daily showed him their

naked feet, and he cheered them as well as he could; "but men cannot live upon words." [129]

Orrery's letters to Ormonde continued to be obsequious, and Ormonde's replies were stiffly courteous, as the rift between the two men deepened. Orrery admitted that he had been "pressed" by certain persons, whose names he would not divulge, to make accusations against Ormonde in Parliament; but he insisted that he would scorn such disloyalty. In March, 1668, Orrery requested Ormonde's permission to spend three months in England to settle a dispute concerning the estate of his elder son and to "forward the Designe" [130] of a promising match for his son Harry. Ormonde suspected that the real object of the visit was to attack the Lord Lieutenant and, if possible, effect his recall, although no one was "better able" than Orrery "to vindicate me." [131]

Orrery exerted his considerable gifts of eloquence to convince Ormonde of the warmth and loyalty of his friendship; and Ormonde found it difficult, but still possible, to discount such protestations. Ormonde's true opinion of the Lord President emerges in his letters to his son, Lord Ossory, in which he deplored Orrery's "notoriously known" infirmities of "vanity, ostentation & itch to popularity" and his peevish, malicious jealousy.[132] Orrery's "industry, ability, & ambition" made him the more dangerous enemy. "Besides," wrote Ormonde, "I fear these times do too much resemble those, wherein he was very active, & learnt his politiques." Despite Orrery's "thousand flatteries," Ormonde concluded, "I think he can hardly charme me out of my mistrusts." [133]

In April Orrery had the satisfaction of informing Ormonde that the King had ordered a frigate to come directly to Cork harbor for him.[134] A prolonged attack of gout delayed his departure; but on June 16, accompanied by Lord Roscommon and several other persons of quality, he landed in Minehead. The Lord President was "warmly" welcomed, as he landed, and went on to London the same day.[135]

In London Orrery promptly waited upon the King, the Duke and Duchess of York, and Lord Robartes, who was then Lord Privy Seal; and on these occasions there was "much discourse about Ireland." Rumors were soon afloat, one being that the Duke of Buckingham, himself aspiring to be Lord Lieutenant, had promised Orrery the post of Lord Deputy.[136] On August 10 Pepys met Orrery for the first time and was captivated by his courtesy. As Pepys waited at Goring House to speak to Lord Arlington, "my Lord Orrery took notice of me, and began discourse of hangings, and of the improvement of shipping; I not thinking that he knew me, but did then discover it, with a mighty compliment of my abilities and ingenuity, which I am mighty proud of; and he do speak most excellently." [137]

It is impossible to clarify a seemingly dubious transaction between Orrery and Sir James Shaen which, soon after the Restoration, deprived Ormonde of ten thousand pounds that he believed the King had intended for him.[138] Ormonde revived the old issue of this "mystery" without being able to solve it and added it to his grievances against Orrery. The latter was more profitably engaged. Confined to his London lodgings by gout, Orrery met there the commissioners for the Irish revenue; and on his advice, the commissioners accused Lord Anglesey, Vice Treasurer of Ireland, of squandering large sums in private warrants.[139] A meeting of the King's Privy Council was also held in Orrery's lodgings, when "Lord Anglesey so shuffled in his answers, that the King concluded him guilty of all the miscarriages charged upon him." After a session of three hours, the Council adjourned; but the King stayed for another hour and a half "in chearful discourse and kind entertainment of my Lord Orrery." [140] That October Orrery attended the King on a visit to Audley End.

Charles yielded to the pressures to which he was subjected to replace Ormonde, as well as Anglesey. The Lord Lieutenant was charged with having permitted Anglesey to pervert much of the public money, while the army remained greatly in arrears.[141] Warned of his probable removal, Ormonde recognized in the intrigue the hand of the Duke of Buckingham, and was convinced that Orrery's share in it would be revealed and "at length leave him a detected Jugler." [142] In fact, Orrery privately admitted to Conway that Mr. Gorgis (Buckingham) and Mr. Rogers (Orrery) resolved to give Mr. Carrig (Ormonde) "t'other heave." [143]

On February 14, 1669, Ormonde submitted his resignation as Lord Lieutenant, and Lord Robartes received the post. Sir Joseph Williamson noted in his Diary that the King did not make the change for lack of satisfaction in Ormonde but "for reasons arising out of his owne affaires." [144] There was general rejoicing among Ormonde's adherents, because it was evident that Robartes was not Buckingham's choice, nor was the appointment "pleasing" to Orrery.[145] The Duchess of Ormonde found some consolation in the dejection of both Buckingham and Orrery, who were as little satisfied by the change as if her husband had retained his office.[146] Concealing his disappointment, Orrery waited attentively on the new Lord Lieutenant; and on one occasion, Burlington, taking Richard Talbot with him, walked a long time with Robartes in his garden,[147] no doubt giving him appropriate advice on Irish affairs.

Orrery devised an ingenious cipher system for correspondence with his most intimate friend, Lord Conway. In this correspondence "Mr. Church" is the King, "Mr. Gorgis" Buckingham, "Mr. Carrig" Ormonde, "Mr. Welsh" Anglesey, and "Mr. Rogers" Orrery. Writing from Conway House, which Lord Conway had placed at his disposal, Orrery reported that Bridgman and Buckingham were now "sworn brothers," Arlington was melancholy, Anglesey had proved himself a knave, and Robartes was making "great professions" to Orrery's party. Robartes "has few Friends heere, & none wher he is goinge" [148] and is not likely to "trouble us past October." [149]

On June 1, 1669, Ormonde wrote acidly to Ossory that Orrery would shortly begin his journey to Ireland, "if the duke of Bucks can spare him." [150] Perhaps Orrery could not easily relinquish the excitement of the political game, for he was still in London on July 10, when he wrote to Conway very cheerfully that he "had need of as good legs as the best Ulster Footman has, to trott about as I have done of late." Robartes seemed to improve, when closeted with, and Orrery found him "a most honest, resolute gentleman." The King consulted Orrery on "his most important and secretest Concernes" and promoted a "strict friendship" between Bridgman, Buckingham, Osborne, and Orrery, of which Arlington was kept in ignorance. "Many good things" were brewing.[151] Meanwhile, the *Monmouth* yacht waited at Minehead for the coming of Orrery, "of which there is no more assurance, then the Jews have of yᵉ Coming of yᵉ Messias, or yᵉ Turks of Mahomett." [152]

Orrery gave up his intended summer holiday and remained in London. His enemies, headed by Arlington and Ormonde, had been marshaling their forces against him,[153] and in November he received a sum-

mons to the House of Commons to answer a charge of
treason. The charge was subscribed by Edward Fitzharris, who had been active in the Irish Rebellion and
whose lands had been given to soldiers and adventurers, and by Philip Alden, formerly a prisoner in
Dublin Castle. Orrery was ill of the gout but was
carried to the House on December 1. He was permitted to remain seated while making his defense,
which he did with such cogency and eloquence that he
impressed and satisfied the House. Burlington commented in his Diary on the skill with which his brother
"answered every article of the charge wch consisted of
ten." [154]

Orrery's defense was a masterpiece of verbal fencing. He asked the Clerk of the House to read the ten
charges one by one and demolished each in turn so
effectively that no detectable loopholes remained for
doubts of his innocence. To the charge that he had
favored the adventurers and soldiers, he made the
telling rejoinder that if powerful (as they were) to
make a disturbance, they were also powerful to keep
the peace. While he had been Lord Justice, there had
been no plot among the English, nor mutiny among
the soldiers. He denied having taken large subscriptions from the adventurers to "feed hungry courtiers."
The adventurers had voluntarily paid a penny an acre
to cover the expenses connected with having their
grants confirmed; and he and Lord Mountrath had
made up the large deficit involved. Far from instigat-
ing the Dublin plot of May, 1663, he had given early
notice of it to Ormonde. And he now paused to remark, with a touch of well-timed sarcasm, which could
not have been lost on his hearers: "Had I thrust the
English Interest into Rebellion & not headed them my
selfe I must have fought agst them with the Irish, And

I thinke few men that know mee would beleive I would be guiltie of such an Extravagancie."

Orrery made the point that he had "brought rogues to justice by means of other rogues." He had never converted any sums of the King's revenue to his own use without legal warrant, nor paid arrears to those who had opposed the King's restoration. He had given up one-third of his own lands (although exempted from doing so), in order to persuade others to do likewise. He solemnly denied the "great charge" that he had threatened that if the King did not confirm the estates of Orrery's party, "his Matie should be compelled to do it with fifty thousand swords." He must "absolutely and positively deny that ever I said those horrid sinfull and traytorous words and wish that the poynts of fifty thousand swords were in my heart if ever such a thought were admitted into it." He appealed to the King to confirm the fact that the first offer of aid to his Majesty from Ireland had been penned by Orrery and conveyed to the King by Francis Boyle, now Viscount Shannon; and he quoted from memory the words of that letter.

Orrery concluded by reminding the House that he had been "accused only of words, and all my acts have been contrary to the effect of the alleged words." As a noted legal authority had observed, "Words may make a heretic, but cannot make a traitor." If he had been charged with particulars, he could have answered "more particularly." He would now await the pleasure of the House, beseeching God "to direct you and to guide yo^re Voates as I am guilty or innocent of what I have been charged with." [155]

Orrery's confidence that the King would support him in this crisis was fully justified. Although Charles was not present at the trial, he refused to go to dinner

until he had heard how Lord Orrery "came off." [156]
On December 11 the King suddenly prorogued Parliament. It was manifestly his desire that Orrery's impeachment should be dropped. A suggestion, supported by a narrow margin of affirmative votes, that witnesses against Orrery should be brought over from Ireland, with the King's consent, was never carried out.[157]

Orrery was in England during Robartes's brief administration of the government of Ireland. Robartes was indeed "honest," as Orrery had found him, but tactless and unpopular. In January, 1670, he asked to be recalled, and Lord Berkeley of Stratton was named his successor. Burlington and Orrery spent many hours thereafter grooming Berkeley for his new post. Berkeley's admission that he considered Arlington his "great enemy" was a reassuring discovery. An afternoon at ombre with Berkeley, and "some of the lords," followed by an evening of serious business with Buckingham and Trevor, struck Orrery, though afflicted with gout, as a profitable, if taxing, disposition of his time. Orrery especially enjoyed private and flattering interviews with the King, which encouraged the delicious surmise, "if Promises are bindinge—well." [158]
By the King's order, Ashley, Berkeley, and Orrery effected the solemn tying of a "knot" of reconciliation between Lauderdale and Buckingham, after which ceremony Kingston, Buckingham, Lauderdale, Ashley, Berkeley, Trevor, Orrery, and Osborne were "as one man" and were "nothing but by common consent." [159]
Voluble and communicative by nature, Orrery was vexed when his letters to Conway were intercepted and copied, and he became obliged to limit his Court bulletins to "common Stuff." [160]

On receiving the King's permission to return to Ireland, Orrery could not resist informing Ormonde of the assurances of royal favor which were to sweeten his journey.[161] He left England in July, 1670, with Conway and Sir Frescheville Holles as his traveling companions.[162]

Berkeley, as had been hoped in certain quarters, was authorizing more lenient policies toward Irish Roman Catholics. It was Orrery's duty, as he saw it, to oppose such measures in Munster; and he vigorously set about purging garrisons of "crowds" of Papists that had invaded them and ordering the many convents that had sprung up in his absence pulled down. He was also compelled to remind Berkeley that the garrisoning of troops in Munster was entirely the Lord President's prerogative.[163]

Orrery had intended to return to London in October; but a fit of gout detained him in Ireland. He commissioned Frescheville Holles to take back to his father, Colonel Gervase Holles, "som bottles of usquebagh, to warme yor stomack this insuinge winter" and "som of our best black Fryse w^h is a warme & light Weare." A master of the language of graceful compliment, Orrery assured Holles: "If I knew any thinge els in this Cuntry worth yor Acceptance, I would make you a Present of it." [164]

After another winter in England, Orrery and Burlington traveled to Ireland together in the King's yacht, the *Merlin*.[165] Their arrival was preceded by the King's order to Berkeley to remit Orrery's Limerick rents for one year up to nine hundred pounds, "as a free gift." [166] The King further ordered that Harry Boyle should be made a lieutenant in his father's troop, although Berkeley had otherwise disposed of the post. Orrery wrote to Conway that he was still much involved in demolishing convents and prohibiting masses. He longed for a visit from his old friend, who could claim every member of the family at Charleville as his humble servant, "from ye Person y^t lyes in Quilts to thos y^t lye on Pease straw." [167]

In April, 1672, Berkeley was recalled, and Arthur Capell, Earl of Essex, became Lord Lieutenant of Ireland. Unaware of the blow which he himself was to suffer under the new administration, Orrery expressed appropriate delight in the appointment, assuring Essex: "We have long wanted a chief governor of your Lordship's principles and abilities." [168] Orrery had various causes of distress. In May he lost three good friends. Lord Sandwich and Sir Frescheville Holles were killed in the battle of Southwold Bay; and Secretary Trevor, one of Orrery's most loyal supporters, died of a fever.

Suddenly, on June 30, the Presidents' Courts in Ireland were ordered closed, and "the great man of Munster" was deprived of the office which he had so thoroughly enjoyed for twelve years. Orrery received a fortnight's advance warning of this action, had he so interpreted it, in a letter which Arlington apparently took pleasure in writing, explaining the King's concern over the Lord President's excessive precautions against Irish Roman Catholics, and requiring him to "forbear" harassing the militia and to admit Irish merchants more readily into the corporate towns.[169] Orrery at once wrote to the King that he had not harassed the militia, but merely ordered them to be ready to oppose his Majesty's enemies, and that he had removed only dangerous Papists from the corporations, and had never excluded any Papists who were traders by sea or linen or woolen manufacturers. But before the King could receive his letter, Orrery's office was suppressed. Essex bluntly informed Orrery of the King's order, which carried, however, the proviso that Orrery's "allowances for the Presidency should be continued." [170]

Deeply wounded by "this Marke of His Maj^ts Disfavour," Orrery told Essex that he longed for retirement and was in haste to take the necessary legal steps to surrender his patents.[171] Shortly afterwards, he wrote a lengthy "narrative" [172] of his misfortune to Sir Thomas Osborne, Treasurer of the Navy, calling attention to the fact that he had resigned not only the Presidency, but also his other offices, "y^t my Obedience might be ye more perfect, to his maj^ts Comd^s." He enclosed in this letter a petition to the King that in lieu of his salary, he might receive a single payment of eight thousand pounds, which would enable him to provide for his younger children.

The King's Roman Catholic advisers had scored a triumph over a Protestant adversary who obviously had the intention and probably had the power to keep Ireland firmly under Protestant control. The King was no doubt shrewdly aware that Orrery could no longer be serviceable to him in his bargaining maneuvers with Louis XIV. It was no longer possible to convince Louis that Orrery could be depended upon to lead the army in Ireland wherever his King commanded him.[173] Charles's personal friendship for Orrery remained undiminished.

Orrery retired to his small castle of Ballymartyr, near Cork, which he proceeded to fortify with six small guns removed from Charleville. It was a minor grievance that Essex soon required him to remove the fortifications of both houses, including even "5 little brass Drakes . . . wch we use to fyre, drinkinge his Maj^ts health on his Birthday or other sollemnityes." [174]

Essex was firmly opposed, as he told Arlington, to permitting "any private man to have possession of a regular fortified Place furnished with Guns." [175]

Orrery was unwilling to criticize the King and was too proud to complain to Essex or Arlington. But he found a much needed vent for his misery in a remarkable battle of words with Lord Anglesey.[176] The scratchings of those two envenomed pens make curious reading for an age far less accomplished than the seventeenth century in epistolary invective. Orrery resented Anglesey's unfriendly act in having given him the misleading advice that the stricter his measures against the Irish Papists, "the more acceptable you will be to the King." After the blow had fallen, Orrery included in his letter to the King some severe strictures against Anglesey and stated that he had broken off all correspondence with him. The dissensions of his courtiers were a never failing source of entertainment to a King who dreaded boredom, and Charles showed Anglesey the offensive letter. The consequence of that disclosure was a violent explosion of midsummer madness, as Orrery called it, which Anglesey hurled at his detractor.

In a letter to Orrery, Anglesey accused his opponent of having enjoyed an era of "prosperous wickedness" under Cromwell. Intoxicated by his "power to make Kings," Orrery had rendered kingship "lovely to an usurper," although Cromwell found the title "too hott to touch." Orrery had not corresponded with Anglesey until the former "began to savour Kingship in the right heire," after which conversion Anglesey had received many kind letters (yet extant) regarding the King's service.

Anglesey must now endure "with Christian patience" the same penance of Orrery's silence to which "some of my Superiors and many my Peeres," including Ormonde, Arlington, Shaftesbury, and Clifford, were very cheerfully submitting. Since Anglesey was enjoying "greater trusts from his Majesty and other great persons," he had no occasion to "prostitute" himself to court Orrery. It would be best to keep the quarrel a secret from Lady Orrery, "one of the most noble and vertuous Ladyes," and from her daughter-in-law, Lady Broghill. Orrery would do well, in the future, to convey his dispatches to the King through Lord Ranelagh, who, to be sure, had not exerted himself of late in Orrery's behalf. To conclude their dealings, Orrery should settle his debt to Anglesey of two hundred pounds.

In his reply to Anglesey, Orrery summoned all his powers of oratory and logic to the agreeable task of flattening his opponent. With cool composure and ironic emphasis, he reviewed their mutually chequered careers, finding the record more to Anglesey's discredit than his own. His resolution to have no more dealings with Anglesey was in accordance with the King's resolve to have no more dealings with Anglesey "in the Affaires of His Treasury in Ireland or of his Navy in England." Earlier offenses for which the King had graciously pardoned them both should not be revived by either. It had not been the "highest of the Ascendent" of Anglesey's greatness to be a recruit of an assembly which gave commissions to "fight against our persecuted Soveraign" and long refused to listen to a peace with him. It was under a Great Seal "which I think was none of the Kings" that Anglesey had sent Orrery a commission as Lord President of Munster, when Anglesey, as Arthur Annesley, functioned as President of the Council of State. This constituted actually "a little kind of superficiall Correspondency with me, before I relished Monarchy in the Right Line."

Although Anglesey must know best the causes why he was flung from some of his "elevations" about the middle of 1668, Orrery was "not intirely ignorant" of them. If Anglesey had failed to enjoy "prosperous wickedness" under Cromwell, this was no doubt due less to any want of desire on Anglesey's part than to Cromwell's often reiterated judgment that "som men were too crafty, too avaricious, & too pragmaticall to be admitted into public employm^{ts}." As to prosperity, Orrery's estate was "scarce what it was" in 1641, and Anglesey's, "I have bin told," was "somewhat augmented."

It was Orrery's hope to endure with "a Christian patience," equal to Anglesey's, the loss of a friendship which he had never really possessed. It had been reported from London that when the King suppressed the Presidents' Courts, Anglesey had bragged, "Now I am Quits with my Ld of Orrery, for all the Mischeifs he has done me." His post had been lost through no misdemeanor, nor had Orrery derived profit from it. It was Anglesey, by the way, who had a debt to clear with Orrery.

Since Anglesey had shown *his* letter, he must have been craving applause for "soe new, & hitherto unimitated a Mode of Drolery," which had pleased the Court exceedingly, "if laughing at it is an evidence of it." Although a novice in this "new Mode of writing," Orrery expected to improve with practice, with "such an original to copy from." With this final sally, Orrery put down his pen. As he did so, he must have indulged in the comforting reflection that his had been the last word in the argument and the best.

The King, My Master

Lord Orrery was the King's loyal servant through more than two-thirds of Charles's reign. From the Restoration to the end of his life, Orrery's letters are constantly embellished with deferential references to "the King, my Master." Orrery fervently declared: "God is my witness, never any subject loved his Prince more than I love him; w[h] I had rather my services than my words should assure him of." [1] The desire to be appreciated was strong in Orrery, and he dedicated his talents to the agreeable task of winning and maintaining the King's favor. It is true that he unflaggingly solicited the King's frequently delayed bounty, yet he valued more highly the honor of serving his sacred Majesty. Even Orrery's inveterate enemy, Ormonde, conceded that Orrery's affection to the King's service was "not to be shaken" and that his loyalty did not depend on the receiving of favors.[2]

Determined though Orrery was to rejoice over the King's restoration, he must have felt that some of Cromwell's qualities would have given Charles added stature as a monarch. To amuse and at the same time to advise the King was a tempting and challenging project which might serve both Orrery's personal in-

145

terests and his Master's welfare. A ready pen furnished the means.

During his extended London visits, Orrery had abundant opportunities to observe the lavish amount of time which the King squandered on his mistresses. The philandering of Orrery's youth was a remote memory, and in that age of dissolute courtiers, he presented the somewhat rare spectacle of a thoroughly domesticated and happy husband and father. Once Orrery ventured to talk seriously to the Duchess of Portsmouth of the kind of life she led, and she "wept very much" at his remonstrances.[3] But Orrery was far too tactful a man to upbraid the King on so delicate an issue. In his plays Orrery found a special vehicle for diverting amorous Charles with fictitious romantic intrigues, while at the same time advocating the nobler pursuits of responsible kingship.

Before his return to Ireland in December, 1660, Orrery had been commanded by the King to write a play for him, and even in the midst of his strenuous official duties he welcomed the assignment. Two years later, he was able to inform Ormonde, who was still in England, that he had "presumed to lay at his majts Feete" a copy of his first play, a tragicomedy (*Altemera*), which he had written in rhymed couplets, "because I found his majty relish'd rather, the French fassion of Playes, then the English." The experiment had succeeded beyond his hopes.

> I had just grounds to beleeve, at least Feare, that my Play would have bin thought fitter for the Fire then the Theater; but his majts mercy having condemn'd it only to the Latter; & then giveinge it to be acted, by Mr. Killigrew's Company; my old Frend Will: D'Avenant, apperd soe displeasd his Company mist it; That nothinge could reconcile me to him; but to write another purposely

for him; Therfore ye last, & this weeke, haveinge gotten
som few houres to my selfe from my publik Dutye; I
dedicated thos, to please my Particular Frend, And writt
this unpolished Draft of two Actes. . . .[4]

Not long afterwards, Ormonde received from Orrery
the "unpolished" draft of the rest of the second play.[5]

On February 26, 1662, the King wrote a most
cordial letter to Orrery in his own hand. To his thanks
for Orrery's "soe instrumental" services regarding the
Act of Settlement, thanks which, if fully expressed,
would not leave "roome in this sheete to say any thing
else," the King appended the gratifying news:

> I will now tell you, that I have read your first play,
> which I like very well, and doe intend to bring it upon
> the Stage, as soone as my Company have their new Stage
> in order, that the Seanes may bee worthy the words they
> are to sett forth. For the last I have onely seene it in my
> Lord Leui[ts] hands, but will reade it, as soone as I have
> leasure.[6]

In an undated response to the King's letter, Orrery
effusively thanked the King for this "unspeakable
honor," greater "than the highest performances of a
whole life could merritt." He was much pleased, he
declared, by the King's approval of his first play; and
since Ormonde had had only loose sheets of the second,
he would send the complete text of it in "one book"
to be delivered to his Majesty by Progers.[7] One of the
principal mysteries of Orrery's literary career is the
fate of this second play. It was a tragicomedy, based
in part on d'Urfé's *L'Astrée;* but its title is unknown,
and the manuscript has disappeared.

The arrival in England of Charles's bride, the
Portuguese Princess, Catherine of Braganza, in May,
1662, inspired Orrery to produce his "Verses to the

Queen," a poem in heroic couplets, which was never
printed but which must have been intended for her
indulgent perusal and the King's. Orrery had not witnessed the Queen's landing in Portsmouth, but his
soaring imagination had been more than equal to the
occasion. He affirmed:

> *Our ravished Fleete, beholding your bright Eyes*
> *Their wonder tell, in shoutes which clime the skyes.*
>
> .   .   .   .
>
> *Methinks I see you now with Joy survey*
> *This moveing forrest, rideing in the Bay.*

He made the rash promise:

> *Unheard of wonders English swords will doe*
> *Fighting for our Kings Glory, and for you.*

The spring voyage prompted seasonable compliments:

> *The Moneth of May shall allwayes be ador'd.*
> *In it our King was born, in it restor'd.*
> *And now in this blest Moneth, Heaven sends him you,*
> *Who hee more vallues then the other two.*[8]

Within the next decade, chiefly during periodic fits
of gout, Orrery composed five more heroic plays:
Henry the Fifth, *Mustapha*, *The Black Prince*,
Tryphon, and *Herod the Great*. *Henry the Fifth* was
perhaps already in D'Avenant's hands at the end of
1662.[9] *The Black Prince* was written at the King's
command and may have been sent to his Majesty in
installments. Orrery was flattered when the King "con-
jur'd" him to finish his manuscript, "which if he could
not do till he had a Fit of the Gout, He wished him a
Fit presently, y^t He might ye sooner finish it." [10] Bask-

ing in the warmth of such praise, the delighted author confessed: "if ever I writt any thinge fit for yᵉ Theatre, this Play is it." [11]

Orrery was in England from June 28, 1664, to August 14, 1665. During that interval he saw two of his plays, *Henry the Fifth* (August, 1664) and *Mustapha* (April, 1665), produced by D'Avenant's company; and another, *The General,* a revised version of *Altemera* (September, 1664), produced by Killigrew's. Orrery was in Ireland when his next play, *The Black Prince* (October, 1667),[12] was produced by Killigrew. During his extended London visit from June 16, 1668, to late July, 1670, he attended performances of *Tryphon* (December, 1668) and his first surviving comedy, *Guzman* (April, 1669), at D'Avenant's theater.

The burning of Killigrew's theater on January 25, 1672, was a serious blow to Orrery, for *Herod the Great* was ready for acting at that theater when the disaster occurred. An unidentified correspondent expressed the hope that "ye accident of burning of ye Kinges Theater will not be an occasion of yʳ lsp. concealing Mariamne from yʳ Servant" and begged Orrery to send him a copy of the manuscript.[13] The play was never produced. Its requirements in elaborate spectacle had been adapted to the facilities of the Bridges Street theater and could not be duplicated elsewhere. Orrery could scarcely have been consoled by the theatrical success of a rival tragedy on the same subject, Samuel Pordage's *Herod and Mariamne,* perhaps acted in the autumn of 1671 at D'Avenant's theater in Lincoln's Inn Fields and revived at Dorset Garden in October, 1673, June, 1675, and October, 1676.

Orrery was not in England when his second comedy,

Mr. Anthony, was produced by D'Avenant, probably before July, 1672.[14] He missed revivals of several of his plays: *Mustapha* (at Court, October and November, 1666, at Lincoln's Inn Fields, January, September, and October, 1667, and February, 1668); *Henry the Fifth* (at Court, December, 1666); and *The Black Prince* (at Bridges Street, April, 1668). He was in London for revivals of *Henry the Fifth* (at Lincoln's Inn Fields, July, 1668) and *The General* (at Bridges Street, April, 1669).

Henry the Fifth, the first of Orrery's plays to be produced in London, was excellently staged and brilliantly acted at Lincoln's Inn Fields on or shortly before August 13, 1664,[15] and had a run of ten successive days. Harris, as the King, wore the Duke of York's coronation suit, Betterton wore King Charles's, and all the other actors had new costumes.[16] Pepys admired "this most noble play . . . the most full of height and raptures of wit and sense, that ever I heard." [17] He saw the play revived at Court, two years later,[18] and once more at Lincoln's Inn Fields, with Betterton repeating his former triumphs as Owen Tudor.[19]

King Charles must have detected an appraisal of his own idealized character in Orrery's portrait of Henry the Fifth. Henry reflects with pride on his distinction as a lover:

> *When men name one who lov'd to a degree*
> *Ne're known before, they'l say he lov'd like me.*[20]

He easily wins the heart of Princess Katherine (Charles's Queen), and he is a model friend to his generous rival; but he is not so deeply involved in "private Gallantries" [21] as to forget that "English Swords" must be "led by an English King." [22] The

King of Portugal (Queen Catherine's father) is mentioned as having won a naval victory for King Henry
and is described as a "prosp'rous King, your Kinsman,
and your Friend," who has shown "his Friendship, like
his virtue, great." [23] At the end of the play, Henry
assumes the Crown of France, to which he is lawful
heir, receives the respectful homage of the French
nobility and officers of state, and makes the propitious
announcement:

> *English and French now but one people are:*
> *And both shall have my equal love and care.*[24]

The General, Orrery's revised version of *Altemera,*
was the second of his plays to be acted in London. It
received great applause when it was presented at
Court on September 14, 1664. Sir Heneage Finch
commented that the play was performed "in the
greatest and noblest presence wch ye Court can make,
before ye fullest Theatre, & with the highest applause
imaginable." [25] Following the performance, the whole
Court adjourned to Wallingford House, where Ormonde's son, the Earl of Arran, was married that
evening to Lady Mary Stuart, the youthful heiress of
the deceased Duke of Richmond and Lennox.

The verdict of Pepys was unfavorable when he attended a performance of the play on September 28 at
the Bridges Street theater. Pepys found *The General*
inferior to *Henry the Fifth* and "poorly acted, though
in finer clothes." [26] On October 4, at another performance, Pepys sat next to Sir Charles Sedley and was
much diverted by Sedley's whispered jests at the "dull-
ness of the poet and baldness of the action" and the
Platonic idealism of the rejected lover.[27] Pepys must
have failed to charge his memory with Sedley's flippant

witticisms, for when *The General* was revived in 1669, he described it as "a good play, that pleases me well." [28]

The General may be regarded as a dramatic interpretation, with romantic additions, of Orrery's diversified career. Clorimun (Orrery) is recalled from retirement to serve reluctantly as general of the army of an usurping King (Cromwell). As the soldiers welcome his return to them, Clorimun confesses:

> *My Joys, like theirs, shou'd now have been sublime,*
> *Had they not brought me to them by a crime.*[29]

He bides his time until in a "fitt Season" he may restore the rightful King, Melezer (Charles), to the Crown which he had lost. When Clorimun is imprisoned by the usurper in the Black Tower, he feels excused from further service to that tyrant. The soldiers, ever loyal to Clorimun, are eager to assist him in restoring Melezer. One of their commanders affirms:

> *Since in a Tyrant's cause wee prosper'd soe,*
> *In the true Kings our Swords shou'd Wonders doe.*
> *On the wrong side wee know how wee can fight.*
> *Let's prove now wee can doe it on the right.*[30]

Melezer has the glory (which Charles certainly never craved) of killing the usurper in single combat. The dying tyrant recognizes the justice of falling, after all his conquests, by a "single hand." As the play closes, the various commanders kneel before their King and offer the humble submission of his joyful subjects. The King responds with the gracious declaration of indulgence:

> *My mercy still shall be to those more great*
> *Which to it trust, and for it doe not treat.*
> *Past faults I'le never to Remembrance bring,*
> *For which the word I give you of your King.*[31]

Clorimun is sent off as general to a war in Sicily (Ireland).

Mustapha, the most popular of Orrery's plays, was produced at Lincoln's Inn Fields on April 3, 1665.[32] D'Avenant had provided new clothes for the actors and new scenes, had taken great pains to have the play "perfect and exactly perform'd," and derived "vast Profit" from its initial run.[33] The King, who had attended the first performance with Lady Castlemaine, had John Webb design scenes for a Court production,[34] which occurred on October 18, 1666. John Evelyn, who was present on that occasion, considered the play "exceedingly well writ." [35] Pepys was "not contented with it at all," when he saw *Mustapha* in 1665; but subsequent revivals altered his opinion, and he admitted that the more he saw the play, the better he liked it.[36] He admired the acting of both Betterton and Harris and considered that he had never seen such good acting as Smith's in the rôle of Zanger.[37]

In this play a noble general, beloved by the army, is martyred for his popularity. Mustapha, the older son of Solyman, is ordered killed by the Sultan, when the Empress, Roxolana, advised by a corrupt councilor, arouses Solyman's jealousy of his son's prestige. Mustapha dies bravely; thirty thousand soldiers mutiny to protest his death; and Zanger, his devoted half-brother, commits suicide. With mixed emotions, the Sultan banishes Roxolana and renounces the passion which had wrought such disaster:

Farewel for ever, and to Love farewel!
I'le lock my Bosom up where Love did dwell;
I will to Beauty ever shut my eyes,
And be no more a Captive by surprize:
But Oh, how little I esteem a Throne,
When Love, the Ornament of Pow'r, is gone! [38]

The Black Prince was acted at Bridges Street on October 19, 1667.[39] The King and the Duke of York were present, and the house, commented Pepys, was "infinite full." Pepys admired a fine dance in this play, but noted that there were "the same points and turns of wit," though "in excellent language," as in Orrery's previous dramas. When everyone had become tired of sitting, the reading of a letter "a quarter of an hour long" caused laughter and hisses, which indeed, said Pepys, if the King had not been there, would have put an end to the performance. When the Earl of Burlington saw the play a few days later, printed copies of the letter were handed out, and there were no more hisses.[40] A revival of *The Black Prince* the following spring impressed Pepys more favorably, although he slept through the earlier scenes.[41]

Through a maze of romantic intrigues and infidelities in *The Black Prince,* the Prince emerges as the conqueror of France and the favored suitor of the much courted Plantagenet. Alizia is restored to her former lover, King Edward, and Valeria regains the heart of King John. In the Prologue Charles is urged by the Genius of England to "once more invade the French" and show the world that

Our Charles, not theirs, deserves the name of Great.[42]

In the Epilogue the "trembling" poet and Prince anxiously solicit the King's favor. Although the Prince gained "immortal Honour" by his conquests, Charles had

> brought three Kingdomes to Remorse,
> And gain'd by Vertue more than he by Force.[43]

At the première of *The Black Prince*, Nell Gwyn, playing Alizia, is said to have captured the heart of King Charles. Looking directly at the royal box, she may have charmed the King when she declared that love

> Made Edward our victorious Monarch be
> One of those Many who did sigh for me.
> All other Flames but his I did deride,
> They rather made my Trouble than my Pride:
> But this, when told me, made me quickly know,
> Love is a God to which all Hearts must bow.[44]

It has been assumed that one of the most rewarding of the King's amours was initiated by Nell's arch interpretation of Orrery's graceful rhetoric.[45]

On December 8, 1668, Orrery, his wife, Burlington, and Lord Sandwich made up a theater party of four to attend the first and "much aplauded" performance of Orrery's *Tryphon* at Lincoln's Inn Fields.[46] Pepys thought the play admirable but complained that it had "the same design, and words, and sense, and plot" as all the rest of Orrery's plays, and "so many of the same design and fancy do but dull one another," as "every body else" agreed.[47] It is probable that on December 14 the King saw a Court performance of the new play.[48]

Tryphon is the most attractive of Orrery's usurpers and perhaps reflects the reluctant admiration which Orrery always felt for Cromwell. Although he had

performed violent deeds to attain the Syrian throne,
Tryphon is resolved

> *my Reign shall be so good*
> *As shall outweigh my want of right by Blood.*[49]

When the odds are against him, he bravely kills himself and "by his Death for all his Crimes has paid." [50]

The central issue of *Tryphon* is the vexatious question, provoked by Orrery's own troubled experience:
Is it right to serve an usurper? The subject is debated
at wearisome length, *pro* and *con,* by various pairs of
characters. Nicanor and Demetrius illustrate the various facets of Orrery's services to Cromwell. Nicanor
seems to represent the man that ideally Orrery might
have been, Demetrius the man that he was.

Demetrius, while disapproving of Tryphon's conduct, has remained faithful to him. He is not only in
high favor with Tryphon but serves him well and has
plausible arguments to combat the contention of
Aretus that

> *When e'r a Subject does usurpe the State,*
> *Any brave Hand has right to act his Fate.*[51]

Demetrius declares that his service to Tryphon has
been motivated by love to Syria (Ireland), not to
him,[52] that only Heaven has a right to punish
"Heav'ns Viceregent," and that

> *while his favour I so much possess*
> *My Pow'r will hinder any new excess.*[53]

The more scrupulous Nicanor refuses the office of
General, which Tryphon wishes to restore to him,
and will not wink at Tryphon's faults. He gives

Tryphon unflattering advice, which Tryphon values, but does not oppose his tyranny until fully justified. Aretus (Charles) is ultimately revealed as the grandson of the rightful King, preserved by Nicanor "from the Tyrant's Rage" during the time that Nicanor was "shut up in privacy." [54] Although he will not accept public office under Aretus, Nicanor is rewarded by the young King's grateful tribute:

> *The Way in which me to the Throne you bring,*
> *Is greater than to be your self a King.*[55]

Although *Herod the Great* was never acted, King Charles may have done Orrery the honor of reading the play in manuscript. The ruthless usurper, Herod, by "bold crimes" has reached "great ends." Like Cromwell, Herod pays the price for his black deeds by suffering an internal tempest (caused in Herod's case by jealous love) "above the Cure of Time or Art." [56] Herod's sleep is troubled by visions of those whom he has made ghosts, against whom he draws his sword. He loves Abner (Orrery), whose father he has killed, and gives him "Jewry's Government" (Ireland), which the bereaved Abner accepts "with sighs." [57] Eventually Abner redeems his honor by attempting to kill Herod and is mortally wounded by him. In describing Abner, Orrery paints a tenderly sympathetic portrait of himself:

> *He is, to give his Character in short,*
> *In War most fierce, most humble in the Court.*
> *Who merits favour, yet obtains it not,*
> *In him unask'd an Advocate has got.*
> *Respect for him he in all hearts has bred,*
> *Because it is not sought, but merited.*
> *Malice does fear such Vertue to pursue,*
> *Which makes him favour'd without Envy too.*[58]

King Saul was probably Orrery's last venture in heroic drama. The play was never acted and is of interest only as it reflects never forgotten crises in Orrery's own career. David, rather than Saul, is the leading figure, and David's dilemma prefigures Orrery's. In the service of Saul, like Orrery in the service of Cromwell, David wins martial triumphs against the Philistines (the native Irish), endures Saul's black moods, and will not oppose a tyrant who wields sovereign power and is "Heav'ns greatest Representative." [59] Saul, utterly unscrupulous, nevertheless, like Cromwell, has a conscience. He suffers "anxious Cares and watchful Nights,"

> *For that sweet Pow'r which Monarchs covet most,*
> *Ev'n in the fear of losing it is lost.*[60]

Saul nobly commits suicide, since

> *No hand but Saul's shall act his Tragedy.*[61]

Jonathan, like Henry Cromwell, is deeply devoted to both his father and his beloved friend David. He is sadly aware that

> *A strange infection thro' this Court do's run,*
> *Which wise Men see and seek in time to shun.*[62]

In the conduct of Abner Orrery evaluates another phase of his own experience. Abner is the loyal Captain of Saul's army but at Saul's death hastens to serve the new King, confident that

> *tho' our Swords were drawn for Saul, not him,*
> *We by confessing shall excuse our Crime.*
> *Brave Souls, like his, believe no fault so great,*
> *Which true submission cannot expiate.*[63]

These heroic plays, to which he owes his reputation as a dramatist, offer a valuable sidelight on Orrery's character. Their recurring images of formidable usurper, restored warrior king, and king-restoring general reveal Orrery's preoccupation with memories of the "one Action" which forever wounded his "past Fame." [64] Written when he was severely afflicted with gout, the plays provided for Orrery, in those painful illnesses, a kind of medicine for the soul. His conscience was eased, his monarch (he must have hoped) reassured by his successive portraits of a distinguished general reluctantly serving an usurper and joyfully thereafter bringing in the rightful king. Although Charles needed no confirmation of Orrery's loyalty, the plays kept steadily before the King a tactful reminder of the unique services of "the great man of Munster."

The image of militant kingship which Orrery persistently painted had little relation to the character of the ruling monarch but must have struck Charles as an appropriate image for public contemplation, presented with those novelties of a dramatic setting in which the King and his Court delighted. Charles enjoyed the spectacle and discounted the call to arms which ordinarily accompanied it.

Comedy proved a more suitable genre for offering the King and Court satirical glimpses of Cromwell's régime. In *Mr. Anthony* Orrery attacked the religious cant of the "saints" who flourished under Cromwell. The pious poses and stilted language of Cromwell's party had always been distasteful to Orrery, and he had certainly had many opportunities to observe the "sober steps and well weighed Justice" [65] with which "the Protector's Peace" had been ruthlessly enforced. The dupe in *Mr. Anthony* is a lascivious old man, Sir

Timothy, who is cured of "wenching at sixty" in a mock trial conducted by three shameless revelers in the sober garb of Puritan elders, "Chastizers of the Parish." The old lecher is branded by his accusers as "Spawn of the old Serpent" and is severely sentenced for his "Covey of vices," whose "several Fibers . . . grow from this one wicked Root, *viz.* Uncleanness." [66]

Orrery chose another literary medium for an unmistakable appeal to his Master to distinguish himself as a soldier king. In 1677 Orrery published *A Treatise of the Art of War,* dedicated to the King, and with a frontispiece representing Charles on horseback reviewing his troops. In his dedicatory epistle, Orrery assured the King of his enduring homage: "as . . . I paid my healthful Time to your Service, so now I would humbly endeavor to evidence to your Majesty, and to all others, that I dedicate my sickly Time to the same Duty, whereby all the Parts of my Life, would appear devoted to your Service." [67] In the midst of a detailed account of the discipline, equipment, and military strategy of a strong army, Orrery inserted his views on the "present fatal War" that the French had "kindled almost all over Europe," [68] in which they were likely to succeed, and which they were likely to continue until their enemies were weary of it. The French "daily improve in the art of making war," under the leadership of "a great and brave Prince," [69] who does well to make war in person against his enemies and who follows "the solidest Maxims of war." [70]

A second volume of the *Treatise* was to have followed the first, "if the 1st pleases your Majesty." [71] The fact that the project was not continued does not necessarily indicate the King's lack of interest in it. Nevertheless, Orrery failed in a cherished objective.

His broad hints that Charles should emulate Louis XIV on the field of battle aroused no latent ambition in Charles for military leadership. The King had chosen his course. He played a solitary game and went forward, undeterred, with the secret diplomacy which he found more effective than warfare.

Although a master of the art of compromise, Orrery had some difficulty in reconciling his inflexible Protestantism with undeviating service to a King alarmingly susceptible to French Roman Catholic influences. In a public life of shifting allegiances, Orrery remained unwavering and outspoken in his devotion to Protestantism in the country of his birth. He was never more in earnest than when he protested to Richard Talbot that "wherever the English & protestant Interest was concearned he beggd y[e] pardon of any private mans friendshipp." [72] As he grew older, Orrery became more tolerant of Dissenters, who, after all, were still Protestants and in that capacity serviceable. He even treated more compassionately the "misguided" Roman Catholics of Munster, with whose welfare he considered himself entrusted. His increasing concern for Roman Catholics as persons reflects the more humane side of Orrery's character. But his antagonism to Roman Catholic doctrines remained unabated, and he never relaxed in his tireless efforts to expose and suppress Roman Catholic plots.

Like so many others whose company diverted the King, Orrery could always enjoy the King's ear; but he never fully enjoyed the King's confidence. There is no evidence that "the most important secret" of the King's life, his undeclared Catholicism, which was successfully kept from the communicative Buckingham, was ever confided to Orrery. In the autumn of 1668 Pepys regarded Buckingham as "now chief of all men

in this kingdom." [73] But neither Buckingham nor Orrery had any inkling of a major incredible shift in the
King's policy.

The efforts of Henrietta, Duchess of Orleans, the
King's sister, to effect a secret treaty between Charles
and Louis XIV were crowned with success. On January 20, 1669, Charles wrote to his sister that a journey
to England on her part would further such an alliance,
for one must proceed "with all secrecy imaginable." [74]
On January 25 Charles summoned to a secret meeting
in his brother's closet York, Lord Arundell of War-
dour, both Catholics, Clifford, who was to embrace
Catholicism, and Arlington, who was to die a con-
vert. The King sought the advice of these counselors as
to methods for settling the Roman Catholic religion in
his kingdom and the most appropriate time to declare
himself a Catholic.[75] In March Arundell was sent to
France with the King's proposals, which Madame was
to convey to Louis XIV.[76] Charles made plain to his
sister that Buckingham knew nothing of his religious
intentions, "which he must not be trusted with." [77]
Arundell, Clifford, Arlington, and Sir Richard Bellings
served as commissioners in drawing up the secret
treaty, holding meetings for that purpose with the
King and the Duke of York.[78]

In April, 1670, Madame paid her brother a visit
in Dover, where the secret Treaty of Dover was
signed on June 1 by the four commissioners for England and by the French ambassador, Colbert de Croissy,
for France. The treaty was ratified by Louis on June
10. Its terms included the important stipulation that
Charles was to receive from the French King a large
sum of money for declaring himself, at the time of
his choice, a Roman Catholic. Charles granted Madame's deathbed requests, that same month, that Clif-

ford be made a Baron and Arlington an Earl. In Clifford's opinion Ireland was now "in a good hand," [79] since Robartes had been succeeded by Berkeley, who favored the Roman Catholics.

Buckingham was kept in a good humor by being permitted to negotiate the *traité simulé* with Louis, signed by Charles on February 2, 1671. The articles were the same as in the Treaty of Dover, except that there was no pledge of the King's Catholicism, which Charles repeated in a secret article.[80] Ashley and Lauderdale were two of Buckingham's assistants in preparing the sham treaty. Since Orrery, Buckingham, Ashley, Lauderdale, and several other enemies of Arlington were at that date acting "as one man," [81] it is probable that Orrery, in cheerful ignorance of the Treaty of Dover, had full knowledge of Buckingham's invalid transaction.

As late as the summer of 1672, Orrery seems to have had no suspicion of Charles's secret bargain with Louis XIV. Orrery was genuinely astonished by Arlington's warning that the King desired him to moderate his zeal against the Roman Catholics, a warning which was almost immediately followed by his loss of the Presidency of Munster. Clifford and Arlington showed Richard Talbot "great bundles" of intercepted letters from Orrery to Berkeley, in which Orrery had abused Talbot and "all the Roman Catholics." [82] Both Richard Talbot and his Jesuit brother, Peter, broke off their friendship with Orrery. In April, 1672, Ormonde told the Earl of Burlington that he had found in the fire in the King's bedchamber the charred fragments of a letter from Peter Talbot to Buckingham expressing doubts of Orrery's faithfulness to the King. Ormonde "saw Talbot written at the bottome but Peter was burnt but my Lord assured mee he knew well his hand." [83] It is not surprising that the suppression of the Presidency of Munster struck Charles as a suitable means of quieting trouble makers and furthering his profitable relations with the French King.

But Charles still had to reckon with an unaccommodating Parliament. The passage of the Test Act in March, 1673, forced the Duke of York to show his hand. Unable to take the Test, he resigned his offices and was sent, a reluctant exile, to Brussels.

Orrery once had a good-natured religious argument with the Duke, in which James acknowledged himself defeated. Always welcoming a good debate, Orrery asked the Duke why he was a Papist. James replied that without a "living infallible judge," which the Papists had and the Protestants had not, no one could be sure of any religion. Did the Duke believe, inquired Orrery, that there was such a thing as right reason? He did. Was an infallible judge of right reason needed? The Duke thought not. Then why must religion provide one? James had no answer and admitted that Orrery was "a cunning man in his Arguments." [84] Although Orrery kept on amicable terms with the Duke, who continued to "court" him, whenever the King and his brother disagreed Mr. Rogers (Orrery) "absolutely" stuck to Mr. Church (the King). [85] Nor did Orrery lightly use for the King the pseudonym of "Mr. Church."

By 1675 Orrery certainly knew from Danby something of the King's financial dealings with Louis XIV and probably suspected Charles's unconfessed Catholicism. The danger was too great to be ignored, and the King's course must be changed, if possible, before it was too late. Orrery adopted the expedient of addressing to the King a poetical epistle in which he deplored Charles's dubious entanglements with the French King.

This poem, preserved among Orrery's private papers,[86] is entitled "A Vision, which apeerd to a Member of the House of Commons on Tuesday Night the 9th of November 1675." As the poet lay on his bed, musing over the "denying Vote" (of supplies) passed (by the House of Commons) that day, the headless Ghost of the late martyred King appeared to him, commended him as "my Kings & Countrys Friend," and brought him "by airy paths" to the bedside of the present monarch. While the latter slept, Fame, as the Genius of France, poured poisonous words in his ear, advising him not to submit tamely to a senate that denied him "but a trivial sum" and to exert his divine right to tax his subjects, in order to safeguard his throne, his favorites, and his amours. The Genius continued:

> *Nor fear being Papist, 'tis a needful Thing*
> *To him who aymes to be a boundless King.*
> *When, or your Gold, or sword, the Pope does dread*
> *Hee's then your Slave that's the whole Churches head.*
>
> .   .   .   .
>
> *Tis more to awe that Priest, whom the Priests dread*
> *Then of thy petty Church, to be the Head.*

The royal Ghost then awakened his son and gave him contrary advice. He declared:

> *Nothing can worse with th' English Genius sute*
> *Then have their Kings strive to be absolute.*

If "to turn Papist" is the way to "arbitrary Sway," the change should disgust Charles.

Who is their [the Papists'] *Cheif, they are not yet agreed
But under Christ, our Church ownes you theire Head.*

.   .   .   .

*Romes Church, out of their Thrones does Monarks fling.
Our Church brings back a twelve Years exil'd King.*

Having delivered this warning, the Ghost put on
his head, and Fame, blowing her trumpet, flew back
to France. The Ghost recommended that the senate's
generosity should discourage the King from taking
"one pound a lawlesse Way" and concluded:

*O may itt never be poore Englands Fate
To become wise, when 'tis, alas, too late.*

With this parting reflection, the Ghost sighed deeply
and "vanished away."

The King was given a copy of "A Vision" and is
said to have been impressed by its "bold truths." [87]
The advice did not suit his purposes. His "senate"
was so little to his taste that he dissolved three Parlia-
ments within two years and ruled conveniently without
one for the last four years of his reign. Secret treaties
with France substantially increased his income, and
he held sensibly in reserve the trump card which he
had vaguely promised Louis that he would play at an
appropriate time.

Orrery had a difficult choice of directives. He was
too faithful to the King and too loyal a monarchist
to oppose the succession to the throne of the King's
Roman Catholic brother. He was too ardent a Protestant not to make strenuous efforts to curb in advance
the power in ecclesiastical matters of the next monarch.
Orrery's last political activity in England was in support of a bill which he drew up to hedge James's law-

ful succession with provisos which would insure Protestant interests. He earnestly begged Danby to promote such a bill, in preference to a new Test which would have maintained the *status quo*. Orrery felt wounded when his proposals were rejected and the committee on which he had been serving was dismissed. He informed the King that "he saw he was not guided by steady Counsels, and therefore desir'd to be excus'd from meddling any more in State Affairs." [88]

As his political influence waned and his infirmities increased, Orrery's resilience weakened. His services were no longer essential. He was incurably ill and indeed a "plain countryman" at last. Protestant Ireland, in defense of which he had long ago risked his youth, seemed shadowed by an impending crisis. He could not suppress the gloomy foreboding: "Our happiness will expire with the King's life." [89]

By a Person of Quality

Horace Walpole appraised Lord Orrery as "a Man who never made a bad figure but as an Author. As a Soldier, his bravery was distinguished, his stratagems remarkable. As a Statesman, it is sufficient to say that he had the confidence of Cromwell: As a Man, he was grateful and would have supported the Son of his Friend: Like Cicero and Richelieu he could not be content without being a Poet." [1] The triumphs of Orrery's public and private life could not be more aptly phrased, but Walpole's graceful dismissal of him as a man of letters must be challenged. It must be confessed that Orrery is more interesting as a man of action than as a writer. The man of action was nevertheless an accomplished writer. Orrery was a perceptive commentator on the stirring times in which he lived. His creative work, uneven as it is and marred by verbosity, at its best achieves the sort of flamboyant elegance which usually, but not always, distinguishes Dryden's plays.

As a writer, Orrery is more likely to be remembered for his versatility and fluency than for his depth. It may be doubted whether any man ever had a readier pen. The staggering bulk of Orrery's correspondence, quite apart from his other writings, makes the reader wonder how, like the heroines of Richardson, he found any time to live. Although Ormonde declared that "ye good L^d seldom covers his candle under a bushell," [2] Orrery often wrote anonymously. He may even have composed a number of unidentifiable documents of his period "by a Person of Quality."

To students of English literature Orrery is best known as Dryden's precursor as a writer of heroic drama. As Lord Burlington's unpublished Diary reveals, *Altemera,* Orrery's first play in date of composition, was also the first original heroic play to be publicly acted after the Restoration. *Altemera* was revised for the London stage as *The General* and long after Orrery's death was published under that title.[3] In a succession of plays which followed his first dramatic experiment Orrery further defined and popularized the new genre.

Sir William D'Avenant claimed the honor of having first discovered Orrery, "a great new World," but admitted:

> *You are the great discovery made by all;*
> *And it would seem as much fantasticall*
> *To say that you were found by me alone,*
> *As if I boasted that I found the Sun.*[4]

Equally extravagant was the homage which Orrery received from his younger contemporary, John Dryden, at the beginning of the latter's eminent dramatic career. In commendatory verses prefixed to Dr. Walter Charleton's *Chorea Gigantum* (1663), Dryden praised Robert Boyle's "great Brother," Orrery,[5] whom he already admired as a poet.

His third play, *The Rival Ladies* (acted in June,

printed in late October, 1664),[6] Dryden dedicated to
Orrery,[7] commenting that "this worthless Present was
design'd you, long before it was a Play; when it was
only a confus'd Mass of Thoughts, tumbling over one
another in the Dark." Dryden continued:

> . . . for this confidence of my Dedication, I have an
> Argument which is too advantagious for me, not to pub-
> lish it to the World. 'Tis the kindness your Lordship has
> continually shown to all my Writings. You have been
> pleas'd, my Lord, they should sometimes cross the Irish
> Seas to kiss your Hands; which passage (contrary to the
> Experience of others) I have found the least dangerous
> in the world. Your favour has shone upon me at a remote
> distance, without the least knowledge of my Person; and
> (like the influence of the heavenly Bodies) you have done
> good without knowing to whom you did it.

Dryden's Dedication indicates his awareness of the
conditions under which Orrery's "excellent Poems"
had been composed. "The Muses," Dryden noted,
"have seldom employed your Thoughts, but when
some violent fit of the Gout has snatch'd you from
Affairs of State: And, like the Priestess of Apollo,
you never come to deliver his Oracles, but unwillingly,
and in torment. So that we are oblig'd to your Lord-
ships misery for our Delight." It is evident that Orrery had attended a performance of *The Rival Ladies*
in the early summer of 1664, for Dryden mentions
the fact that his Lordship had "met" the play in
England and had had the "Goodness" not to dislike
it on the stage. The Dedication includes a defense of
the use of rhymed verse in tragedy, which Orrery had
much better commended by writing in it than Dryden
could do, he believed, by writing for it.

Paradoxically, although the initiator of Restoration heroic drama, Orrery was essentially a conserva-

tive writer. His closest contacts with men of letters had been many years before as a young courtier. Because Charles II liked rhymed plays in the French style, Orrery hit upon the happy, at any rate popular, expedient of writing in heroic couplets dramas which in many respects were not unlike the pre-Restoration Platonic plays which had delighted the Court of Charles I. Even in the use of the heroic couplet, D'Avenant had won earlier acclaim in his opera, *The Siege of Rhodes* (Part I, 1656; Part II, 1661). The originality of Orrery's heroic plays is chiefly limited to his consistent use of heroic couplets for serious plays presenting such achievements and conflicts of heroic love and valor as had already been featured in the blank verse tragedies and tragicomedies of D'Avenant, Suckling, Carlell, and other pre-Restoration writers of Platonic drama. Not only did Orrery admire these artificial dramatizations of the Platonic love ritual, but he detected in these plays, and especially in those of the gifted friend of his youth, Suckling, sources of tactful compliment to one's King which so sedulous a politician could scarcely afford to neglect.

Suckling's *Brennoralt* and *Aglaura,* both revived in 1661 and 1662, furnished the framework for Orrery's *The General,* the outlines of its principal characters, and a pattern of Platonic courtship. The hero of *The General,* like the hero of *Brennoralt,* is a discontented general, neglected by his King but at last richly rewarded by him. Unfortunate in love, each general fights a duel with a rival lover, to whom he nobly surrenders the lady. In both plays a disguised friend, who causes misunderstandings, perishes in a climactic duel scene. The heroine of *The General,* like the heroine of *Aglaura,* suffers from the King's (in *The General* the usurping King's) lustful passion for her, which she takes desperate measures to combat. Orrery is reminiscent of Suckling in his incredible flights of Platonic idealism, as in Clorimun's claim to fame, which Sedley found so preposterous:

> I'le save my Rivall and make her confesse
> 'Tis I deserve what hee does but possesse.[8]

On the other hand, Orrery could deviate (if less often than Suckling) from the high seriousness of the Platonic vein and could define "Platonicks" as "the subtlest sect in Cupids schoole." [9]

It is possible that Edward Howard, Lady Orrery's cousin, read Orrery's play in manuscript. On January 2, 1664, Howard's blank verse tragedy, *The Usurper*, was acted in London at the Bridges Street theater. In Howard's play, as in Orrery's, a noble general, popular with the army, although forced to serve the Usurper for a time, eventually, with the army's aid, brings in the rightful monarch. The true King generously offers indemnity for those whose "frailty and not malice" made them serve the Usurper. Howard's ruthless tyrant, except in his pursuit of a chaste lady, is clearly modeled on Oliver Cromwell.

Three weeks after the production of *The Usurper*, Burlington attended a performance of *The Indian Queen*,[10] in which Edward Howard's brother, Sir Robert Howard, and John Dryden had collaborated and which was the first Restoration tragedy in heroic couplets to be acted in London. In *The Indian Queen* the theme of a rightful sovereign's restoration (in this case a queen's) is again introduced. Burlington must have been particularly struck by echoes of *The General* in the duel scene in which the rival contestants are parted by an exacting mistress, who convinces her rejected suitor that merit, not possession, is the reward of love.[11]

Edward Howard cautiously hinted that Orrery's plays should be considered dramatic poems instead of plays, for reasons which Orrery himself would be best able to give.[12] Certainly *Henry the Fifth* may be thus classified. The only moment of violent action in this play is the brief duel in which King Henry fights with and disarms the eavesdropping Dauphin, whose sword he restores at Katherine's command. Orrery's chief concern is the Platonic conflict of love and friendship in which the rival lovers become involved. Katherine displays all the formidable tyranny of a Platonic mistress in the ambitious scene of hairsplitting argument in which her two suitors pay her homage and she upbraids Owen Tudor for being so true to friendship that he is false to love.

Although *Henry the Fifth* is weighted down with Platonic casuistry and is almost wholly lacking in dramatic action, Orrery's verse at times obscures these defects and rises above the level of competent mediocrity. His poetical style is seen at its best in the glowing couplets in which Blamount describes to the French Queen the conflict at Agincourt:

> *A while both Armies on each other gaz'd,*
> *Both at th' intended slaughter seem'd amaz'd.*
> *Could those who oft have bloody battels won,*
> *Stand long amaz'd at ills which must be done?*
> *Wars chearful Musick now fill'd every Ear,*
> *Whilst death more gaudy did than life appear.*
> *For various Ensigns did unfold such Pride,*
> *That all seem'd Bridegrooms there, and Death the Bride;*
> *The noble order in each squadron seen;*
> *The many Warriours of a haughty meen;*
> *The prouder horses chafing to be rid,*

Who breath'd the Combat as their Riders did;
Made all confess that War gave Death a grace,
And has its charms as well as beauty has.[13]

Inventions of martial spectacle always invigorated this soldier poet.

The success of D'Avenant's opera, *The Siege of Rhodes,* may have encouraged Orrery to choose episodes in Turkish history for his next play, *Mustapha,* and to make use, as D'Avenant had done, of a history of the Turks by Richard Knolles.[14] As in *Henry the Fifth,* Orrery rearranges and alters historical incidents and adds a generous infusion of Platonic love and rivalry. In temperament and in some of their reflections Orrery's Sultan and his Empress resemble the melancholy Solyman and his "tempestuous wife" in Part II of *The Siege of Rhodes.*

The complications of intrigue in *Mustapha* are more varied and more effective than in Orrery's earlier plays. Each of the major characters must cope with an agonizing conflict of loyalties which, after much self-scrutiny and argument, ends in heroic defeat. Such tempests of the mind are so exhausting, even for high-souled princes, that it is not surprising that Zanger concludes:

'tis a work more difficult and high
To help a Rival than it is to dye.[15]

Mustapha, heir to Solyman's throne and Zanger's half-brother, is not only Zanger's rival in love but has the added trials of his father's jealousy and his step-mother's plot to destroy him in order to save her son. He struggles valiantly against these towering odds; but the lament is wrung from him:

> *Fortune did never in one day design*
> *For any heart, four torments great as mine;*
> *I to my Friend and Brother rival am;*
> *She, who did kindle, would put out my flame;*
> *I from my Fathers anger must remove,*
> *And that does banish me from her I love;*
> *If, of these Four, the least a burden be,*
> *Oh how shall I support the other three?* [16]

The Empress Roxolana similarly weighs the multiple evils of her own predicament:

> *I in my perplext condition, must*
> *Become unnatural, or else unjust:*
> *Must leave a Son to Empires cruelty,*
> *Or to a gen'rous Prince inhumane be.*
> *My Husband, whom I love, I cruel make,*
> *Even against Nature, yet for Natures sake.*
> *His Son, by my contrivance, he must kill;*
> *Whilst I preserve my own against his will.*
> *The blood I save must answer for my guilt*
> *And wash away the stains of what is spilt.*[17]

Solyman, a monarch triumphant in war but "born to care," must demand the death of the son whom he has carefully nurtured for kingship and banish the queen whose perfect beauty has been his greatest joy. The widowed Queen of Hungary to protect her young son must court the exacting Empress, placate a worldly Cardinal, and reject and survive two noble suitors "who had no fault but love." [18]

The richness of spectacle, as well as the dramatic merits, of this tragedy contributed to its contemporary fame, and it became a stock piece of the Restoration theater. *Mustapha* was the last new play produced before the Plague closed the theaters, had a flattering initial run, and was the first play acted after the Plague and Fire. As late as 1694, Nahum Tate predicted that *Mustapha* would remain "a just Model of Tragedy, as long as the Stage shall last." [19]

Like figures in a stately dance, the characters move on and about the stage and are never too tormented to adopt graceful poses when they leave it. The violence of the fifth act is softened by stage effects and exquisite resignation. The Mutes advance, retire, advance again. Mustapha kills two of them, then, as his father enters, lays his sword at Solyman's feet and with filial deference announces:

> *Sir, to death I'le go.*
> *I am too guilty since you think me so.*[20]

After stabbing himself by his friend's body, Zanger has strength enough to bow politely to Solyman and reflect:

> *Lo, at your Feet, dear Friend, your Brother lies;*
> *And where he took delight to live—he dyes.*[21]

The characters are sufficiently lifelike to be credible, and their emotions are genuine and often moving. Sympathy cannot be denied to Solyman when he pleads:

> *Pity a father who must hate his Son.*[22]

Zanger is an engaging, if Platonic, lover. He finds love at first sight a delicious paradox:

> *Warm me, and quench me, for I freeze and burn*
> *And at one object both rejoice and mourn:*
> *What mean'st thou, Nature? Is it bad or good,*
> *Which makes this April-weather in my blood?* [23]

Mustapha, although not the "first Discov'rer" of the Queen's loveliness, is not to be outdone in worship by his friend:

> *You but the beauty of her face did find;*
> *I made the rich discov'ry of her mind.*
> *You of the borders of Elizium boast,*
> *Her mind is all the Inland to that Coast.*[24]

Imperious Roxolana offers a striking contrast to these gentle and courtly lovers.

Roxolana is more resolute than D'Avenant's Roxolana in *The Siege of Rhodes.* She is also a more fully developed character than Zempoalla in Howard and Dryden's *The Indian Queen,* whom she resembles in ruthlessness and energy of purpose. The Sultan's Empress revels in being "the partner of Supreme Authority." [25] She is capable of holding siege "against the whole Divan" and Solyman as well. But she deeply loves the Sultan who banishes her and the son whom her "guilty kindness" could not save. She has a magnificence which Zempoalla lacks, shuns the weakness of despair, and accepts her doom with regal dignity.

A mood of cynical disillusion is the most realistic element in Restoration heroic drama. Such a mood supplies the darker tones of *Mustapha* and adds a welcome starch to the play's somewhat wearing Platonic idealism. Corrupt statesmen are the frequent target of corrupt Rustan and also of Roxolana. The Empress holds herself aloof from the counsel of subjects,

> *For Slaves may govern whom they can perswade.*[26]

She coolly defends dissembling:

The Great should in their Thromes mysterious be;
Dissembling is no worse than mystery,
Obscurity is that which terrour moves;
The gods most awful seem'd in shady Groves.
And our wise Prophet's Text a rev'rence bears
Where it is hard and needs Interpreters.[27]

The Sultan expresses with eloquence his more deeply ingrained melancholy:

Did I in Winter Camps spend forty years;
Out-wear the Weather, and out-face the Sun,
When the Wild-Herds did to their Coverts run;
Out-watch the Jealous, and the Lunatick,
Out-fast the Penitential, and the Sick;
Out-wait long Patience, and out-suffer Fear,
Out-march the Pilgrim, and the Wanderer:
And there, where last years Ice was not unthaw'd,
(When in thick Furs, Bears durst not look abroad)
I with cold Armour cover'd, did maintain
Life against showres of Arrows, and of Rain?
Have I made Towns immur'd with Mountains yield;
Sent haughty Nations blushing from the Field?
And must I, at one cast, all that forego,
For which so oft I desperately did throw?
They steal my Laurels to adorn my Son;
Who can but dream of Fields that I have won? [28]

The Black Prince did not deserve and did not achieve the popularity of *Mustapha.* As Pepys objected, Orrery repeated "the same points and turns of wit" [29] that had served him in his former productions. As in *Mustapha,* but less poignantly, a King, jealous of his son, finds his sorrows greater than his power. As in *Henry the Fifth,* two rivals visit their mistress to learn from her their "destiny"; and the rejected lover receives from her lips the "obliging" disclosure that she will give him friendship, though she cannot give him love. As in *The General,* a disguise is adopted in the hope of separating lovers. Delaware's belated reading of a letter written by Plantagenet's deceased husband ends the play on a suitable note of Platonic sacrifice and proves that at last he has reconciled himself to being unhappy rather than unjust.

The second act of *The Black Prince* opens with a masque which the Court ladies present to honor King Edward's French captive, King John. Pepys considered this masque a pleasant innovation but "a little too long." Two floating clouds appear, containing women and men "richly apparell'd," who sing as the clouds descend. The masquers step from the clouds to dance on the stage, then return to them to continue singing until the clouds have ascended "to their full height" and the King's palace is revealed. King Edward notes with jealousy the impression which on this occasion the "bright Plantagenet" made on the Prince:

> *For I observ'd, during the masking Night,*
> *The Prince on her did alwayes fix his Sight,*
> *And often from his breast a Sigh would steal*
> *Which as his Looks his Passion did reveal;*
> *But that which made my Trouble much more great*
> *Was, when her Sight did with the Prince's meet,*
> *A bright Vermillion in her Face would rise:*
> *Then with a Sigh she would cast down her Eyes;*
> *What stronger Prooff could either of them show*
> *That he lov'd her, and that she lov'd him too?* [30]

It is tempting to imagine that Orrery may have been recalling an episode of his youth, when D'Avenant's masque, *Salmacida Spolia,* was presented at the Court of Charles I and the youthful beauty whom Orrery was to marry, Lady Margaret Howard, made a brilliant appearance among the masquers.

Tryphon, although again featuring in too abundant detail Orrery's favorite themes and situations, has a fair amount of dramatic action and some moments of genuine tragedy. From a welter of Platonic debate two strong personalities emerge, Stratonice, the most practical and sensible of Orrery's Platonic heroines, and the usurper Tryphon. Ruthless though he is, Tryphon has noble traits. He confesses to Seleucus that he is compelled to admire Stratonice the more because

> *My perfect Love meets with the like Disdaine.*[31]

As his enemies approach to murder him, he chooses to act himself what the Gods have decreed. Drawing his dagger and "viewing" it, he concludes:

> *My Hand is yet of this bright Sceptre sure,*
> *Which for my Sufferings is a certain Cure:*
> *Thus arm'd I will my Enemies outbrave,*
> *And, spight of Fate, deserve a glorious Grave.*[32]

For briefer intervals, *Tryphon* has something of the tragic dignity of *Mustapha.*

In *Herod the Great,* in accordance with his usual disregard of historical accuracy, Orrery enlarged upon and altered certain episodes in Jewish history recorded in the historical works of Flavius Josephus.[33] These episodes he fitted into a complex pattern of intrigue which provided more activity and less argument than his other plays. Each act contains at least one scene of theatrically effective action.

The increasing popularity of scenic effects in heroic drama spurred Orrery to attempt a magnificence of

spectacle in this play which doomed it to remain un-
acted. Only the Bridges Street theater, which burned
just as *Herod the Great* was ready for production
there, could have adequately represented Orrery's ambitious settings. The "obscura grotta" which that
theater possessed, which Orrery had previously introduced in *The Black Prince,* was to have been used
several times in *Herod the Great.* The scene in the
third act, where Herod reposes under a "magnificent
pavilion," was to have accommodated various ghosts
in white, blood-stained garments, who dance antic
dances with black javelins in their hands.

Professor William S. Clark attributes Orrery's
greater emphasis on wicked characters and evil actions
in *Herod the Great* to the influence of Settle, whose
Cambyses had recently had a highly successful run
at D'Avenant's theater.[34] But Orrery may have been
more impressed by the successive models of wickedness which Dryden had achieved in *The Indian Queen,*
The Indian Emperor, and *Tyrannic Love.* Among the
the books in his library Orrery listed "All Dryden's
Plays." [35] Despite refreshing innovations in *Herod
the Great,* the claim must be disputed that this play
"bears little resemblance" to Orrery's previous work.[36]
As in *Mustapha,* the bitter rivalry of father and son
and the dissension of a tyrant and his Queen are major issues. Antipater's rising from a vault for his fatal
duel with his father is a reminiscence of Suckling's still
popular *Aglaura.* Once more, Orrery features one of
his favorite characters, an usurper who struggles to
maintain his authority and who is judged and punished
for his crimes.

In Roxolana Orrery had already shown insight into
the character of a strong-minded, ruthless woman.
Solome resembles Roxolana in her decisive, imperious

ways. She assures Sohemus that Brother, King, Husband are "empty Names to one that loves like me." [37] Undaunted in defeat, she commits suicide on the throne which will not be hers, for

> *though to live in Thrones my stars deny,*
> *Yet spight of all I in a Throne will die.*[38]

The contrasting virtue of the Queen is portrayed with equal skill. Relieved of much of the incubus of a Platonic courtship, the Queen offers vigorous and impressive opposition to Herod's tyranny. She amply illustrates her noble contention:

> *What is it can resist a Soul resolv'd?* [39]

With persuasive eloquence she reminds Antipater that surrender to his father is his only honorable course:

> *Ah Prince, why do you thus mispend your Breath?*
> *'Tis a much milder Fate to suffer Death*
> *Than live to see him our bright Vertues blot:*
> *Since Merit cannot change him, words will not.*
> *In his ungrateful guilt still let him lye,*
> *But let us in our Innocency dye.*[40]

Herod arouses compassion by the acuteness of his inward conflicts. His violent acts alternate with gloomy meditations, when he walks "stern and silent in his private Rooms." [41] Herod is tormented by jealousy of his wife and son and has some troubled thoughts concerning the "sin" of usurpation. He admires in his Queen a generous heart that "will rather break than bow." [42] Like Othello, when he kills the Queen he "must sigh for what I will destroy." [43] As he gazes on her dead face, he pays her the superlative tribute:

> *Thus Night's dark Veils the Face of Heaven o'erspread,*
> *When to th' other World the Sun is fled;*
> *No King's Revenge like mine the Glory had,*
> *To make at once so many Beauties fade.*[44]

As in *Mustapha*, a vein of cynicism runs through this play and toughens its fiber. Antipater, although a chivalrous lover, defines incest as

> *but a Term of Art*
> *A name with which the Priests keep Fools in aw,*
> *For no such thing is found in Nature's Law.*[45]

Herod scoffs at belief in the supernatural:

> *The dead ne're to the living durst appear;*
> *Ghosts are but shadows painted by our fear.*[46]

He considers that "whining Virtue" is "much more troublesome than Vice" [47] and regards justice and laws as

> *too Pedantic things,*
> *To act the vengeance of offended Kings.*[48]

Orrery's verse in *Herod the Great* has a force and flexibility which, for once, he sustains throughout the play. His heroic persons all appear "in brighter Shapes" than they could ever have lived,[49] but as heroes might aspire to live. Their speeches, even in the agonies of death, are polished jewels. A fine example of heroic grandiloquence is Herod's outburst of jealous rage against his Queen:

> *If to my Love another she prefers,*
> *I'll tear out both her Lovers Heart and hers.*
> *Then I'll in Flames reduce them both to Dust,*

Flames, which shall be as burning as their Lust:
And when those Thrones of Love to Ashes turn,
I'll mix their guilty Ashes in one Urn:
There we shall see what charming Fires are bred
In Hearts united, when those Hearts are dead.[50]

When dying Sohemus threatens to haunt Herod after death, the tyrant's extraordinary energy blazes in his retort:

Would every Foe of mine all hope had lost,
But that of frighting of me with his Ghost.
Guards, to his Grave bear that perfidious Man;
There let him tell my Secrets—if he can.[51]

The complete degeneration of Orrery's talents in *The Tragedy of Zoroastres* remains an unsolved mystery. According to a note in the original manuscript, preserved in the British Museum, the play was "written in 1676." [52] It was never acted. Orrery laid the work aside in an unfinished state, and most of the still feebler fifth act apears to have been written by another author. From various historical sources [53] Orrery derived the career of his villain hero, the magician Zoroastres, around whose sinister career he wove his customary complications of love and rivalry.

The popularity of several recently produced dramatic operas [54] may have persuaded Orrery to decorate his tedious plot with even more lavish spectacular effects than he had devised in *Herod the Great*. The only character with any real vigor is Zoroastres, who compares himself to Tamburlaine and threatens an invasion of the heavens. Many of the couplets are metrically defective, and the best are pedestrian efforts.

Orrery's *King Saul* remained in manuscript for about a quarter of a century after his death. This tragedy was printed in 1703 and 1739,[55] and according to the 1703 title page was the work of "a Deceas'd Person of Honour," published "at the Request of Several Men of Quality who have highly Approv'd of it." [56] With a few deviations and additions, Orrery modeled *King Saul* on the biblical narrative of major episodes in the lives of Saul, David, and Jonathan. Platonic courtship has disappeared and is replaced by the celebration of marital happiness. The characters have little individuality, and the verse is merely adequate. Spectacular effects are not lacking but are subdued to the somber tone of the tragedy.

In the writing of comedy Orrery won no laurels; and it may be doubted whether he ever had any genuine interest in that genre. Since anti-Platonic raillery in *The General* may be regarded as the best sample of his lighter vein, some regret may be felt over the loss of Orrery's second play, featuring an anti-Platonic hero. When Orrery submitted to Ormonde the first two acts of this play, he briefly outlined its contents, indicating that it was to be a Platonic tragicomedy with a considerable infusion of anti-Platonic comedy. He commented:

> The Plot is such, that I wish you could but as much like ye rest of ye Play as I flatter my self your G: will like that, when by the Finisshing of what is begun, you will know it; And that yor G: may have som gess at it; I will tell you heere, that Acores is Romira in Disguise. In the speeches & Discourse, of Duels honnor, Jellosy, Revenge, Love & Envy, I have carefully declyn'd sayinge any thinge, I had ever heard, or read, on any of thos subiects; that if ye conceptions of them should not please you, the newness of them might. The Humour of Hilas, of wh: yor G^r will see som Touches, in the beginninge of ye second Acte, shall be enterwoven, if yor G: dislike it not, in every one of the Three remayninge; Tho I dispaire

to make my Hilas, as famous on the Theater, as the
Marquis of Urfé has made his, in the Romance; for be-
sides his Genius'es beinge exceedingly above myne, his
Hilas was not limitted to numbers, & Ryme, as mine is.[57]

Orrery's Hylas may well have been portrayed with
both sympathy and grace. The first Earl of Cork's
sons had visited as youthful travelers "the French
Arcadia, the pleasant Pays de Forest," [58] where
d'Urfé had laid the scenes of *L'Astrée*. In that attractive setting Orrery may first have read and admired the famous French romance. It is quite probable
that he was able to dramatize the lighthearted adventures of a witty, sophisticated Hylas more successfully than the farcical antics of his subsequent comic
heroes.

Whatever the merits of this lost comedy may have
been, Orrery's next venture in comedy was indeed, as
Pepys remarked, "very ordinary." Pepys quoted ap-
provingly Shadwell's comment that Orrery "was trying what he could do in comedy, since his heroic plays
could do no more wonders." [59] For *Guzman* Orrery
chose a Spanish setting, no doubt because such settings
were currently fashionable. He followed Dryden's example in *An Evening's Love, or The Mock-Astrologer*
in having his hero Francisco play the rôle of a fake
astrologer who exploits susceptible victims. Despite
its Spanish setting and Spanish names, *Guzman* illustrates the familiar pattern of Elizabethan and Jaco-
bean realistic comedies of London life and owes an
unmistakable debt to two of Ben Jonson's comedies.
The title character, like Jonson's Bobadill in *Every
Man in His Humour,* boasts, with a profusion of
picturesque oaths, of his skill in fencing, but either
runs away from duels or is ignominiously kicked and
cuffed by his opponents. Francisco resembles Jonson's

Face in *The Alchemist* in his busy manipulation of his various patrons. *Guzman* apparently had a lukewarm reception on the Restoration stage.

In *Mr. Anthony* Orrery again descended to the level of rather tiresome farce. The characters are stock figures of pre-Restoration and Restoration comedies of intrigue: an elderly lecher, exposed in adultery, a masterful wife, an amorous pedagogue-parson and the old nurse who is his compliant mistress, a trio of clever tricksters, two sets of intriguing heroines, and two cowardly bullies. The scene in which the two timid duelists, Anthony and Cudden, reluctantly fight each other, one armed with two crabtree cudgels and the other with bow and arrows, was sufficiently novel to be noted by Downes,[60] perhaps because the excellent comedians, Nokes and Angel, played these respective rôles. The fools and rogues who comprise Orrery's cast are sometimes demolished in well-turned, witty phrases; but the constant emphasis on cowardice and absurd buffoonery grows wearisome. Orrery's Muse was an aristocratic one, and his favorite dramatic medium of expression was the refined heroic couplet. *Mr. Anthony* quickly faded into obscurity, and Orrery attempted no more comedies.

For his contemporaries Orrery's reputation was enhanced by the publication in generous installments of his *Parthenissa*, the only substantial heroic romance achieved by an English author. When the taste for heroic romances had waned, Horace Walpole remarked harshly that Orrery's lengthy yet unfinished narrative would "content the most heroic appetite that ever existed!" [61] But in the era of the matchless Orinda unsated heroic appetites did exist. It may be assumed that John Malet was not the only reader whose correspondence suffered because the "excellent beauties" of

Orrery's heroine were so engrossing. Orrery rightly considered his feminine readers his most faithful patronesses. He dedicated the earlier volumes of his romance to Lady Northumberland and Lady Sunderland, the sixth and last volume to Princess Henrietta, Duchess of Orleans, and the "six volumes compleat" to Lady Northumberland.

For more than twenty years Orrery devoted a portion of his gouty intervals to the amours and military adventures of the four Platonic heroes who talk their leisurely way through *Parthenissa.* The French heroic romances of La Calprenède and Georges and Madeleine de Scudéry served Orrery as respected models; but the adventures of his heroes, although in a pseudo-historical setting, were essentially his own invention and fictionalized, at times, episodes in his own life. On first reading in manuscript the earlier chapters of his brother's romance, Robert Boyle had discovered striking resemblances between Broghill's conquests for Cromwell in Munster and the martial exploits of Parthenissa's gallant lover Artabanes.

Parthenissa proved to be a perfect medium for endless conflicts of Platonic love and honor. Unrestricted by the limits of a five act heroic play, Orrery created a series of narrators who take turns in regaling their captive but eager auditors with the complicated histories of their lives. The narrators could have been multiplied indefinitely, the auditors remaining frozen in their courteous listening attitudes.

In Parts I–IV of *Parthenissa,* published in 1655, Orrery interrupted the adventures of Artabanes and Parthenissa, related by Artabanes, with the adventures of Perolla and Izadora, related by Symander, and the adventures of Artavasdes and Altezeera, related by Artavasdes, and concluded with another segment of the history of Artabanes. Part V of the romance, published in 1656, introduces as a fourth narrator Callimachus; and Part VI, published in 1669, carries the story of Callimachus and Statira to their separation and imprisonment. In dedicating Part VI to the Duchess of Orleans, Orrery explained that although he had once intended to end Statira's story in this volume, "the Vicissitudes of her Fate were so many, and so various, that I could not confine it within so narrow a compass." [62] In the 1676 folio edition, comprising Parts I–VI, there are over eight hundred closely printed pages.

Orrery aroused the curiosity of contemporary readers in the stately opening sentence of *Parthenissa*:

> The sun was already so far declin'd, that his heat was not offensive, when a Stranger, richly arm'd, and proportionably blest with all the gifts of Nature, and Education, alighted at the Temple of Hierapolis in Syria, where the Queen of Love had settled an Oracle, as famous as the Deity, to whom it was consecrated. [63]

Much of the action of the romance is a narrative of past events. In a yew and cypress walk near the Temple, the stranger, Artabanes, Prince of Parthia, tells the story of his courtship of Parthenissa and his triumphs in warfare to the attentive Callimachus, Prince of the Priest of Venus. Callimachus is also entertained by episodes in the life of Artabanes's friend, Artavasdes, Prince of Armenia, and by the narrative of Symander, Artabanes's servant, who, for good measure, adds to the love story of Perolla and Izadora the adventures of Scipio and Hannibal in Africa.

At the beginning of Part II Artabanes rescues from bandits another visitor to the Temple, who proves to be Artavasdes. While the friends, both wounded, rest in adjoining beds, Artavasdes continues his history, from the point where Artabanes had left it. His mistress, on the basis of false evidence, had believed Artavasdes unfaithful and had married his rival, Prince Pacorus. Too late, she had learned the truth and had sadly banished Artavasdes, who has now come to the Oracle for advice. Artabanes, in his turn, continues his narrative as far as Parthenissa's flight to escape an unwelcome marriage. He has reached this crisis when lightning flashes suddenly fill the Temple, as an indication that the Oracle is ready to pronounce the fate of the two "generous lovers."

A portion of the second book of Part IV is devoted to colorful pageantry. There is a splendid procession to the Temple, including two hundred religious men wearing garlands of roses and myrtles and bearing images of flaming hearts in each hand; fifty white bulls; fifty white heifers crowned with anemones; one hundred young men in white; fifty maidens in white carrying turtledoves; and fifty maidens carrying swans in silver cages. The beautiful virgin who is to deliver the prophecy is followed by Callimachus, Artabanes, and Artavasdes. As the melancholy lovers kneel before the statue of Venus, the Oracle makes the cryptic prediction that a phoenix will rise from Parthenissa's ashes, and Artabanes will be blessed in its flames; and Artavasdes will soon be rewarded. Naturally enough, Artabanes is plunged in despair. Resuming his master's story, Symander carries it forward to the suicide of Parthenissa, who has taken poison to escape marrying Arsaces, King of Parthia. Artabanes, with difficulty restrained from killing himself, has been persuaded by Symander to consult the Oracle.

Callimachus has been patiently waiting to tell how he too had lost a mistress. A leisurely ride with his new friends to the city of Hierapolis gives him the desired opportunity. Callimachus is the unacknowledged son, exiled in childhood, of Nicomedes, King of Bithynia. After losing his first mistress, who marries Mithridates, his father's enemy, Callimachus falls in love with the beautiful Statira, Mithridates's daughter by a former marriage. While exploring the "inland seas" of Greece, Callimachus rescues Statira from a pirate lover, is shipwrecked with her, but manages to get her safely back to her father. She is plighted to Ascanius, King of Cyprus, and filial duty prevents her from marrying Callimachus, whom she loves.

Callimachus pauses briefly in his narrative, and the three riders dismount to rest under some trees by the river. They observe a boat ascending the river from which a young gentleman and two veiled ladies disembark. The ladies strikingly resemble the lost mistresses of Artabanes and Artavasdes, and one lady is overheard mentioning the fact that she has lost a lover and is deserved by a living prince. The strangers have apparently come to consult the Oracle. Although Artabanes and Artavasdes have no other objective in life than reunion with their mistresses, with whom their destinies are inextricably interwoven, they now move quietly away to a shadier spot, and Callimachus relentlessly goes on with his story.

Perhaps Orrery found some resemblance between the tragic predicament of Henrietta, Duchess of Orleans, married to a hated husband, and the unhappy Statira, betrothed by parental authority to an unloved prince. In his Dedication of Part VI of *Parthenissa* to the King's sister, Orrery commented that Henrietta had "ordered" him to write this section of the romance and that he had chosen as a model for the most virtuous Princess of Asia "the most accomplisht" Princess of his own age.[64]

In Part VI of the narrative, Callimachus relates his

further services to Statira. Both are captured at sea
by Nicomedes but released, and Callimachus saves the
life of Mithridates. Ascanius, reported dead, returns
to claim his bride, immediately after Callimachus has
at last married Statira. The rivals duel, Statira refuses
to break the marriage vows which she has just made,
and Mithridates imprisons his daughter and his new
son-in-law.

Here *Parthenissa* breaks off abruptly. Crueler blows
seem to await Callimachus, when the secret of his
parentage is disclosed. Artabanes and Artavasdes are
left so near and yet so far from the mistresses from
whom they had been banished. Indeed, the strange
ramifications of heroic romance are such that Orrery
might well have spent another twenty years unwinding
the clue of this labyrinth.

Orrery's lovers are subjected to the severest discipline of Platonic courtship. Every Platonic mistress is
aware that she wields powers of life and death over
her admirers. If she is cruel, a lover is likely to tear
the "plasters" from the wounds which he has acquired
in her service, whereupon she "enjoins" him, in "few
but powerful words," [65] to live, and he dares not dis-
obey. She may even do him the signal favor of tearing
off some of her linen to stop the "spring of blood"
from his side. Her sovereign beauty reduces him to a
state of "trembling respect." Monyma's paleness,
when rescued from a wild boar, is "well repaired by
the reflection of some falls of carnation-feathers which
shadowed her face." [66] As Parthenissa (her lover assumes) dies from the poison which she had taken, "the
beauties of Vermillion" in her face "resign'd their
Empire to the colour of Innocence." [67] Statira's landing in Thessaly, after her shipwreck, is compared to
"Venus's ascension out of the sea." [68] A lover readily

makes his way through a thousand swords to protect such heavenly charms. Callimachus seriously proposes to present Statira with "the Universe, or perish in the duty of attempting it." [69] When she marries him, he gives her his hand "prostrate at her Feet; and should have done it in a more humble and acknowledging Posture, if any such had been." [70]

Rival lovers abound and provoke duels which, however, must be stopped at a lady's command. A rival's life must be saved, sometimes more than once. Artavasdes concludes ruefully, after repeated services of this kind, "if I remain near Pacorus, I am eternally destin'd to preserve him, and if I go from him, I must lose that sight which preserves me." [71] Nevertheless, his sufferings for his mistress "were too much my duty, to be my trouble"; and he is comforted by the knowledge that " 'tis more noble to merit Altezeera without possessing her, than to possess her, without meriting her." [72] A mistress may be lost because of her obligations of filial duty, in which case love must give way to a "high friendship." [73]

The scope of so extended a narrative encouraged personal reminiscence. Orrery's preoccupation with the predicament of serving an usurper is reflected in a long debate between Ventidius and Artavasdes. Ventidius argues in favor of dethroning a king; but Artavasdes maintains that a king cannot forfeit his authority, "being answerable for his Actions to none but the gods." [74] Unhampered by the restrictions of the stage, Orrery gives nearly as much space to the warfare of Parthians, Armenians, and Romans as to the trials of Platonic love and friendship. Memories of the military achievements of his young manhood crowded in upon the invalided romancer. Orrery's heroes, like the youthful Broghill, win numerous victories against greatly superior numbers and with remarkably small losses. Orrery lingers over the glorious spectacle of troops in battle array. Multitudes of colors blow in the wind; arms and swords glisten; spirited horses neigh; and military music incites the soldiers to drown it by their shouts.

Although in his Preface to Part V Orrery described *Parthenissa* as "the idle Fruit of some idle Time," the romance was clearly a labor of love. If the modern reader will calmly and unhurriedly read on to the end of Part VI, his patience will in some measure be rewarded. He will be compelled to admire the ingenuity with which Orrery introduces fresh adventures and picks up the threads of the old, repeats with variations the successive steps of a Platonic courtship, dispatches his heroes to wars of conquest to accumulate new credits of merit and brings them back just in time to rescue their distressed mistresses. The highly idealized characters are impressive in their perfectly disciplined lives. A mistress who, after shedding some tears when forced to resign a lover, puts on her "usual looks" [75] must command respect. Orrery's prose has decorative values and is well suited to the atmosphere which he seeks to create. The almost impossible Platonic sentiments seem more credible because of the graceful and dignified language in which they are expressed.

Orrery completed three parts of another romance, of quite modest proportions, entitled *English Adventures,* "By a Person of Honour," [76] published in 1676. Ten copies of this romance are listed among the books in Orrery's library.[77] His primary objective may have been the entertainment of the King, for all Platonic scruples are thrown overboard. The tale is a disillusioned account of intrigue and unchastity. "Love which terminates in Marriage," remarked Orrery, "is not of

the essentials of my History." [78] Isabella has a number
of rival lovers, marries one, and is unfaithful to two
others. The King, whose mistress she becomes, dis-
covers her infidelity but takes her back when she pleads
innocence and kisses his hand "with her accustomed
grace." [79] A King, Orrery gibes, may be "of an humor
to value a gallantry in Love, more than the Conquest
of a Province; an injury in the first, is engraven in
Brass, while a service in the last, is written but in
Air." [80] The small volume has been remembered because it attracted the attention of Thomas Otway, who
derived the plot of *The Orphan* from the history of
Brandon in Part II.

The last major labor of Orrery's "sickly time" was
the first volume of *A Treatise of the Art of War*. In
the elaborate Dedication of this book to the King, Orrery stated that he had already prepared "the chief
materials" for a second volume, which would deal with
"the greatest, the most useful, and the most intricate
parts of the Art of War." He was convinced that generals can compose more instructive commentaries on
warfare than ordinary historians. If the King would
order all his commanders to present accounts of their
military strategy in writing, their actions would probably be more circumspect. Such accounts would furnish
valuable guidance to others, since "wise Councels are
still within the Power of wise Men; but Success is not."
No profession in the world is more built on reason
and sound judgment than the military profession. It
must be granted, however, that the only legitimate
purpose of war is "the obtaining of a good and lasting
Peace." [81]

The completed portion of the treatise is divided
into seven sections, dealing with the discipline of soldiers in garrisons, camps, on the march, and in battle.

Orrery is vigorous and persuasive in exposition and as precise in details as Defoe was to be, twenty years later, in his proposals for a military academy in *An Essay upon Projects*. Defoe was to reaffirm Orrery's conclusion that "the best way to prevent a War is, that our Neighbors may see we are in a good condition to make it." [82] Better pay, longer training for officers, better provision for old and maimed soldiers should be provided. Soldiers should be more strictly disciplined and should become accustomed in peace to the hardships of diet and lodgings of war.

There is abundant evidence in the *Treatise* of Orrery's love of detail. He advises that pikes should be sixteen and a half feet long, made of staves of seasoned ash with iron heads and sides covered with iron plates. He is equally precise in describing the proper diet of garrisons, the dimensions (illustrated with diagrams) of various kinds of camps, the order in which soldiers should march, and the formations in which they should fight. He praises the Greeks and Romans, whose "old-fashioned Plate" we have merely "hammer'd into new" [83] and commends a number of modern generals who have conducted glorious campaigns.

His own successful experience had taught Orrery the basic principles of good military leadership. He advises that a general, if unfortunately forced into a battle against his will, should conceal his apprehension. He should prevent chase or pillage until the enemy has been totally routed. Speeches before a battle should be confined to histories and romances, for only a "deep silence" [84] makes it possible for the words of command to be heard and punctually obeyed. Breaches will be made in the course of an engagement which only the immediate and resolute leadership of the general can repair. A general must not too hastily think the enemy routed, nor too slowly order the pursuit; and it is as essential for him to make the best use of a victory as to know how to gain it.

Orrery claimed for his essay the distinction of being the first entire treatise in English on the art of war. Historians of military strategy have commended it as an authoritative work of the period.[85] At least one of Orrery's proposals, that public provision should be made for old soldiers, was not unheeded. In 1680 the foundation stone of Kilmainham Hospital was laid in Dublin and in 1681 that of Chelsea Royal Hospital in London.

Orrery's miscellaneous prose works must have reached a formidable total. It is tiring to imagine the volume of his correspondence. Of the letters which he dispatched by "every post" a great number have been preserved, but as many or more may have been lost. In every political crisis Orrery's fluent pen was pressed into service. He was probably the author of numerous pamphlets signed first by his name. Equally often, perhaps, he remained discreetly anonymous.

His controversy with Peter Walsh in the early 1660's is a fair sample of Orrery's technique in political pamphleteering. In the autumn of 1660, Peter Walsh, an active Roman Catholic agent, addressed to Ormonde *A Letter desiring a just and mercifull regard to the Roman Catholicks of Ireland.* Walsh's main argument was that "many thousands of Protestants," including Protestant leaders in Ireland, had been "far more hainously criminal" against both Charles II and his father than "the most wickedly principled of the Roman Confederates of Ireland." [86] The attack stung Orrery in a sensitive spot, and he published two replies: one, *An Answer to a Scandalous Letter,* printed under his own name; the other, *The Irish Colours Displayed,* which appeared as "a Reply of an English Protestant to a late Letter of an Irish Roman Catholique."

In *An Answer* Orrery alleged that the Irish Papists had always been rebellious, the Protestants but once "in these last unhappy and unnatural troubles." [87] Despite Charles I's clemency toward the Papists, they had perpetrated in his reign the worst of rebellions. If Cromwell had not curbed them, what might they not have done? Most of the Protestants of Ireland served under the usurpers only "to bring the Irish Papists to those terms which without the force of English swords they would never have been brought unto." [88] The Papists had banished Ormonde and had hung their loyalty to their King "on the Popes sleeve." [89]

In *The Irish Colours Displayed,* addressed as *A Letter* had been to Ormonde, Orrery sought to extinguish his opponent with a mixture of sarcastic invective and polished oratory. He compared *A Letter* to "a brass penny in a heap of Rubbish, that before you find it almost puts out your eyes, and after you have it, 'tis hardly felt in your hand." [90] He would like to believe that a golden age might arise in Ireland out of the iron age that had lasted some hundreds of years, just as "a fair and gentle morning" sometimes succeeds a furious storm at sea.[91] Differences in habits, language, and religion between the Irish and English must be taken into account, as must the inevitable lack of sympathy between a conquered people and their conquerors. "I cannot hope," wrote Orrery, "to live so long as to hear *Jam cuncti gens una sumus* plaid by the Irish Harp, though I know it was sung by some English in their discourses about the beginning of the late

Kings Reign, but never I think by any Irish, and with
how sad Notes it then ended in the Close some men I
hope may still have leave to remember." [92] If the
Protestants in Ireland had been estranged from Ormonde by "unhappy revolutions," they now returned
to throw themselves in his arms, as lovers do into
those of a mistress whose "forced or feigned smiles
to a rival" had separated them.[93]

Walsh attacked Orrery's answers in two more
pamphlets, *The Irish Colours Folded* and *P. W.'s
Reply to the Person of Quality's Answer.* Walsh referred pointedly to "the defection of those that had
betrayed their trust and his Majestie's Interest in
Cork, Youghall, Kinsale, and the rest of the strong
holds in Munster. Who these were, is known to all
parties in that Nation . . . and they were not Irish
nor Catholicks." [94] Orrery is described as a witty and
malicious gentleman, an "Enchanter" who has labored
in vain to charm Ormonde. Taking due advantage of
the transparent anonymity of the "unknown Author"
of *The Irish Colours Displayed,* Walsh accused "a
Person of Quality of this Gentleman's own good
people" of "known, undeniable, reiterated Apos-
tacy." [95] Although Walsh lacked the stature of a really
dangerous adversary, Orrery must have found him a
troublesome thorn in the flesh.

From time to time Orrery flattered his king and
others with lavish poetical tributes. These effusions,
commented on elsewhere in this volume, are no better
and no worse than similar occasional pieces by contemporary poets. Such compositions were fashionable
and suited the taste of the age. They solicited the
patronage of those to whom they were addressed and
were a profitable investment of leisure hours. Orrery's
"Verses on the Death of Mr. Abraham Cowley, and

his Burial in Westminster Abbey" were published in the
1688 edition of Cowley's poems. Extravagant as they
seem to modern taste, these verses were acclaimed by
Orrery's contemporaries. Cowley's fame inspired Orrery's ingenious conceit that the great Fire of London
had not dared to approach the "majestic church"
where the "King of Wit" lies buried.

> *It at an awful distance did expire,*
> *Such pow'r had sacred Ashes o're that Fire.*[96]

Orrery's last illness prevented the completion of his
Poems on Most of the Festivals of the Church. He
had regretted having cast away so much precious time
on "airy verses" and had resolved to take leave of
that sort of poetry and devote his "converted
Muse," in the future, entirely to sacred subjects.[97]
Unfortunately, the converted Muse produced only a
conventional religious manual. The final stanzas, com-
memorating the martyrdom of Charles I, were found
among Orrery's papers after his death. His eulogy of
the martyred King may be regarded as Orrery's ultimate act of atonement for those years during which
he had not served the Stuart cause.

At Castlemartyr

The home which Orrery chose for his semi-retired life and where he was to end his days was the old castle of Castlemartyr, earlier known as Ballymartyr. Like other Irish castles, it had had a grim history. In 1583 the aged mother of its seneschal had been hanged from its main gate. It had often been plundered and had been partly destroyed in the Parliamentary war. The surrounding countryside Orrery considered pleasant "for all recreations." Castlemartyr was not far from the sea. It was near the well-governed town of Cork and also near Kinsale, which Orrery believed had the finest of all harbors. Orrery spent twenty-nine hundred pounds enlarging and repairing the castle to make it "English like" and "a good house for my younger son." [1] He also impaled a deer park.

In the summer of 1672 Orrery suffered from a prolonged ague. "It flattered me once," he wrote to Essex in August, "with a beleife it was leavinge me, but twas a Flattery only." [2] He had the limited satisfaction of continuing as Major-General of the Army in Ireland, Governor of co. Clare, and Constable of Limerick Castle. Essex politely requested his advice as to the disposition of troops in Munster, since "your Lo^p . . .

understands that Province so very well." [3] Both deplored the fact that too many companies of soldiers
had been ordered to England, leaving Ireland, and
especially Munster, poorly garrisoned. Both lamented
that the fortifying of Kinsale must be stopped, for the
eleven thousand pounds which, according to Orrery's
estimate, were needed for that project could not be
obtained. Essex secured from the King moderate compensation for Orrery for his guns and agreed to press
for one large sum in lieu of his pension, because of his
"soe ready compliance" [4] in surrendering his patents.

Orrery followed the custom, which he had adopted
with Ormonde, of writing to Essex by almost every
post. He suggested the congenial precaution of making
use of his cipher, "the best in the world," which even
"a great master in that art" had been unable to de-
cipher.[5] It was comforting to report to the Lord
Lieutenant that the letter to the King, in which Orrery
had explained his reasons for excluding from the corporations Roman Catholics who were not merchants,
had brought a favorable reply from Arlington. The
King considered that Orrery had "well justified" himself and would soon write a letter in his own hand
which would be "much to my satisfaction." [6]

A correspondence of a very different nature severely
taxed Orrery's patience in the last months of 1672.
His outrageous daughter-in-law, Lady Broghill, in-
jected into his happy domestic life a note of discord
which he endured with singular forbearance. Since
leaving Orrery's house, where they had been under
no expense, Roger and his wife had spent three extravagant years in London, and Lord Broghill was now
heavily in debt. On her return to Ireland, Lady Broghill clamored for a separate maintenance, while she
daily wrangled with her well-meaning but weak young

husband. Lord Orrery came in for a share of her vituperation, and she announced to her husband that she wished his father were dead. The letters in which Orrery meticulously examined her strictures must be regarded as models of persevering tact.

Orrery offered his recalcitrant daughter-in-law "friendly advice." He assured her that he would not desire her not to wish him dead, since he would never press her to anything so much against her inclination; but he urged her not to speak thus publicly, and particularly before her husband, who had not cast off a son's duty. The best way to have her husband's kindness would be to deserve it by affectionate and dutiful conduct. She had learned her rudeness "from the carriage of noe daughter of myne." She had provoked her husband to the extent of making him declare that if he had had a knife, he would have stabbed himself with it; and when he confessed that he would have been happier to have married a kitchen wench that loved him, she had replied: "& that had bin fitter for you." [7]

Lord Broghill wrote that his father's censure had troubled his wife very much for three or four hours; but soon she was "as merry as ever" and preparing to dispatch another undutiful epistle.[8] In her next letter she denied the kitchen wench insult and insisted that her husband should "take my advice before any others." [9] The question is, replied Orrery, whether your Lord or you tells the truth. And he reminded her that she had promised to obey her husband rather than have him obey her. He hoped that her heart might be changed, so that he might again call himself her most affectionate father-in-law and servant.[10]

Orrery urged his son to come with his wife to Castlemartyr and affirm in the presence of his parents what his wife "so positively denies." Lady Broghill would be treated with all civility and kindness and receive advice in easy and moving terms. Lady Broghill declined the offer. Her husband then mournfully reported to his father the inflammatory preface to the kitchen maid remark: "Shee sitteing at one End of ye table & I att ye other, I spouke to her in these termes, pray my Deare Come kisse mee, She makeing noe answer I repeated them over three or foure times, where upon shee tooke up a bibell y^t lay on ye table, & swore, as I understood her, y^t Shee would never come kisse mee." [11]

With the officials duties chiefly removed, Orrery yielded to the temptation to create unsolicited outlets for his abundant energy. He kept Essex regularly supplied with requests and complaints in all matters pertaining to Munster, seeking always in an advisory capacity to exercise some portion of his former authority. He expressed concern for the soldiers of Limerick, who could wait for ammunition but could not do without food. Funds should be found to make the castle of Cork "significant." Garrisons were poorly manned; fortifications were everywhere decayed; trade was sadly reduced; a disease was prevalent among cattle "greater than has been known in the memory of man"; [12] no Irish harbor was strong enough to shelter merchant ships or men of war from the Dutch. He must beg reimbursement for the money which he had spent out of his own purse in serving the government and a license to go to England to inform his Majesty of Ireland's needs.

At the end of January, 1673, Orrery received a most welcome letter from the King, cordially summoning him to the next session of Parliament.[13] This was followed by warrants from the King for the payment of his arrears, including a sum not exceeding nine hundred pounds as a "free gift" for the year's value on his estate.[14]

Orrery was preparing with alacrity to obey the King's summons, when he was stricken with a peculiarly violent attack of gout. For forty days, as he told Essex, he could be moved only when lifted in a sheet by four men.[15] When at last he was able to leave his chamber, he still required the support of two servants. During his illness, his fears for Ireland were accentuated by "the melancholly Fumes of ye Gout." [16] He compared Ireland to a body sick of many diseases; if but one were cured, it would die of the rest.

From the seclusion of Castlemartyr Orrery noted anxiously the proceedings of the March session of Parliament. He regretted that the House of Commons had forced the King to cancel his Declaration of Indulgence and had substituted for it a Test Act which would restrict office-holding to members of the Anglican church. He could not approve giving Irish Papists provocation for another uprising. Moreover, he was viewing Protestant Dissenters with an increasing tolerance, as the prospect of the Duke of York's succession to the throne became less remote. It would be necessary for all Protestant sects to unite in a common cause, bracing themselves to withstand the probable encroachments of a Roman Catholic régime.

Essex replied to Orrery's lengthy communications affably but concisely. It is evident that Essex felt none of the personal antagonism which, thinly disguised by courtly phrases, pervades Ormonde's letters to his Munster rival. Essex had a keen sense of the dignity of his position and would tolerate dictation from no one. He prided himself, however, on treating all men impartially. He was not jealous of Orrery's intimacy with the King and was Orrery's advocate for all favors which he considered reasonable.

Essex accepted with composure, as he accepted the Irish climate, the steady flow of Orrery's grievances. He reflected that the climate and air of Ireland seemed to incline all people to a "murmuring Kind of humor." [17] As the chief Governor of Ireland, he was determined to exercise the resolution which he failed to find in the King; and even with the King, he did not hesitate to use a firm hand. When he learned that his Majesty intended to give Phoenix Park to the Duchess of Cleveland, Essex protested with vehemence. All the nobility and gentry of Dublin would be "disgusted" to have their only place of recreation in the city removed, and he could not advise the King to take so "unpopular" a step.[18]

In October, 1673, Orrery was at last well enough to make the long postponed journey to London. Another session of Parliament was beginning, and both the King and Lord Latimer, recently appointed Lord Treasurer, begged Orrery to come over. Established at Warwick House, Orrery declared himself, as a man retired from active life, out of his element in the noise and confusion of politics. Nevertheless, he was soon diligent in conferring with the King's ministers on Irish affairs and his own. He was troubled by the growing rift between King and Parliament. The King was too ready to prorogue a disobliging Parliament, and Parliament was deficient in its duty to the King. When frosty weather confined "all us Gouty fellows to our Chambers," [19] Orrery's advice was still required, and he received "most gratious assurances" [20] of the King's favor.

A false rumor, which indeed he may have fanned, went about that Orrery was to be appointed Secretary

of State.[21] He disclaimed at all times an interest in
any post that would keep him permanently in England.
There were too many conflicts of interest to evade, the
Court was too dissolute, the "leg work" too strenuous
for a gouty man, the price of advancement too high. It
was wiser to be a much desired, frequently returning,
visitor. His power as the great man of Munster was
dear to Orrery; and even after he had lost the Presidency, he clung to the residue of the prestige which
that office had given him. A cheerful invalid, he made
a virtue of necessity and persuaded himself that he
preferred his "little Hermitage" in Ireland to all the
employments of the world.

As requested, Orrery sent reports to Essex on the
events of the brief but stormy session of Parliament in
the winter of 1674. He heard both Buckingham and
Arlington defend themselves before a skeptical House
of Commons. Buckingham fumbled; but Arlington
made "a very greate and elegant discourse." [22] It was
common knowledge, to be sure, that Arlington's star
was setting, although he escaped impeachment.

The Treaty of Westminster was very generally
welcomed, since it ended the highly unpopular second
Dutch War of the Restoration. Orrery had a special
cause of rejoicing, for forty-one companies of soldiers
were now released for service in Ireland, three of them
for Limerick.[23] Orrery's private affairs, too, appeared
in a more favorable light, as they always did when he
had the King's ear. The King confirmed his order of
1664 for Orrery to receive four thousand pounds, half
of this amount to cancel a debt to the Crown.[24] Orrery
was to be excused a year's value on his estate.[25] His
lands in co. Cork were to constitute the "Manor of
Castlemartyr," and provision was made for the government of the manor.[26] The lapsed money was to be

levied at last and paid to Orrery in two equal installments in November, 1674, and May, 1675.[27]

Shortly before his return to Ireland, Orrery scored
a considerable personal triumph. He was granted a
commission, signed by the King and countersigned by
the Lord Treasurer, now Earl of Danby, restoring all
the power which he had had as Lord President in the
military affairs of Munster. He was to preserve the
quiet of the province, act against rebels and traitors,
and function as Deputy in the Lord Lieutenant's absence. Orrery had gone to Windsor with the Lord
Treasurer, had had an interview with the King in
Lady Suffolk's lodging, and the same evening had received the King's order from the Lord Treasurer.[28]
The King acknowledged "our good opinion of yoᴿ
faithfull Services done unto us, and our Crown" and
his "speciall Trust and Confidence in yoᴿ wisdome
Courage and provident Circumspection." [29] Equipped
with this "little expected" mark of his Majesty's favor,
Orrery had proceeded to Bath to visit his eldest
daughter, Lady Powerscourt, who was recovering
from a serious illness. He was back at Castlemartyr in
late August.

A few days before he received Orrery's glowing account of the King's favor, a rumor, which he could
scarcely credit, reached Essex that Orrery was to be
permitted to raise a militia in Munster. Essex lost not
a single post in protesting to Secretary of State
Coventry against such a step. It was difficult enough
for the Lord Lieutenant to maintain his authority
without having to contend with Orrery as "yᵉ great
Patrone of yᵉ Protestant Interest." If Orrery should
raise a militia in Munster, Essex would be blamed if
one were not called in the other provinces, although
the present army was quite adequate, unless there

should be an invasion. The Cromwellians, with whom Orrery had "some little remains of Creditt," would be a dangerous faction in the militia, yet they could not be displaced without arousing Protestant resentment. Orrery would acquire such popularity both in Ireland and in the House of Commons that Essex's government might not be able to survive. If Orrery had already been granted a commission, it must be invalidated. The Lord Lieutenant's opposition, however, must be a carefully guarded secret, for it would be fatal if Orrery should "blaze it abroad." [30]

When informed that Orrery's commission had indeed been granted, Essex sent off a succession of urgent epistles to various friends. He admitted to Arlington that the majority of Protestants in Ireland were "vehemently sett upon" a Protestant militia, "a most pernicious thing," against which he was "utterly resolved." Some means should be found of attaching an order to the commission which would prevent Orrery from taking any action without "a particular command from the King." [31] Essex wrote in a similar vein to Sir Arthur Forbes, to his brother, Sir Henry Capell, to Coventry again, and to the Lord Treasurer. He resented the fact that he had not been consulted before a decision was made. He would be "no Lord Robarts," [32] wearying of his post, and must insist on the removal of this threat to his good government.

The Lord Lieutenant's persevering efforts were successful, and the commission was stopped. There is no evidence that Orrery was aware of the fact that Essex was a prime mover in blasting his hopes. Orrery did receive a rather cool letter from Essex, objecting to the general practice of seeking posts in Ireland without applying for them directly to the Lord Lieutenant.[33]

A malicious report had been circulated that Orrery was actually in possession of his third of the lapsed money which the King had ordered to be levied for him. The Earl of Dorset, Lady Broghill's father, acting upon this surmise, demanded the fulfillment of Orrery's written agreement to settle six hundred pounds per year from this grant on Lord Broghill and his younger children.[34] Again a victim of gout, Orrery begged Essex's aid in securing the lapsed money, for "my own crazy body"[35] reminded him daily of his financial obligations. The prorogation of Parliament until the next April deepened Orrery's gloom. " 'Tis seldom seen," he commented, "that long Prorogations make men meet in better humour."[36]

Munster affairs kept Orrery more hopefully occupied in the first months of 1675. Cork was flourishing, a "most loyal corporation," with only one Papist. The town had a good number of ships and was building more. No other Irish town, with the exception of Dublin, was more serviceable to the Crown.[37]

The pursuit of outlaws, known as Tories, engrossed much of Orrery's time and brought him a rather flattering friendship with one of them, the gallant young captain of a band of robbers, Owen oge Carthy. Carthy, although a Tory and a Papist, was not, Orrery assured Essex, a murderer. The youth insisted on surrendering to Orrery personally, as he would not trust his life to any other hands. Orrery had seldom seen "a stronger, activer fellow." He appeared wearing a sword and embroidered silver belt, but Orrery made him disarm. A real admiration for the young adventurer may be detected in Orrery's account of him:

I scolded him sufficiently for ye life he had lead, & made him I hope sensible of his Crymes, for he sighed often, &

tho to extenuate them, he began to say that he had not
offended any of yᵉ English, yet I stopt his speakinge, &
assured him I would be as much his Ennemy, if he opprest
any of his majᵗˢ Irish subjects who lived peaceably. . . .
He confess'd he feard nothing but to be taken a sleepe,
& owned yᵗ to have lived yᵉ life he lately did was as bad as
Death.³⁸

Orrery and Essex held contrary opinions of the
proper way to handle Tories. Orrery preferred to
guarantee that they would be pardoned as soon as they
had brought in other Tories; Essex made it his rule to
offer no promises in advance of service. Orrery was
convinced that his method was both more humane and
more effective and grieved, when he left Munster for
London, that "my Tories" must "goe a Toryinge
again." ³⁹

In April, 1675, Orrery requested a six months' leave
of absence and permission to take his son Henry to
London. The King had written a "most gracious"
letter in his own hand, requesting Orrery to come over
for the current session of Parliament, and had ordered
a ship to transport him. Parliament was prorogued
soon after Orrery finally reached London and did not
meet again until October. During the intervening
recess, many schemes were afoot to resolve the alarming differences of the two Houses. Orrery could not
"guess the outcome" and could only conclude that
"what is to be shund is much more visible then what is
to be imbraced." ⁴⁰

Orrery composed an elaborate narrative of his London visit, entitled "Some Memorials of my Journey
into England, the Year 1675." ⁴¹ From the Lord
Treasurer he had received an account of a bill for a
new Test, to be taken by all Parliament men of both
Houses and in all public employments, who must

swear that they would not attempt any alteration of the Protestant religion now established in the Church of England, nor of the government in church or state as by law established. The Lord Treasurer had sponsored the bill and had persuaded the King to favor it, and it had passed the House of Lords, after some sharp debates. Orrery spent two long evenings locked up with Danby, arguing "till it was broad day" against the bill and urging Danby to stop supporting it. The Lord Treasurer seemed much dejected by lack of money, the division of the two Houses, the too great expenses of the King, the Court factions against himself, "and one thing more," he added with a sigh. Danby's sigh and the silence which followed it may have aroused in Orrery painful apprehensions of the King's apostasy.

Orrery argued that the bill would never pass Commons,[42] the King would be disappointed, and the Lord Treasurer would be disgraced. Danby listened attentively to the plea of a "true friend" for "moderate indulgence" to Dissenters, who would suffer as much as the Papists from this bill at a time when their support was most needed, in view of the dangers of Popery. Orrery outlined to the Lord Treasurer a more moderate, face-saving measure, not involving Parliament men, which could be substituted for the present bill.

Orrery had arguments, as well, with his nephew, Lord Ranelagh, and Lord Conway, who hoped to enlist his support for an Irish Parliament, to be called on short notice, to obtain money for the Crown by the imposition of certain taxes. Orrery had never favored draining Ireland of funds to be expended in England, and he refused the substantial bribe which Conway offered him.[43] An old friendship was thus weakened, never to be fully restored.

In July Essex went to England for a visit which proved to be of nearly a year's duration. Aware that there were plans under way to remove him, Essex wished to vindicate himself to the King and, if possible, secure support from the Crown for his program of reform. He had to cope with the difficult problem presented by the unending flow of the King's gratuities, for which neither money nor land was available. Essex commented grimly on the state of his Majesty's third kingdom: "This Country has bin perpetually rent & torne since his Majesties restauracion, I can compare it to nothing better than flinging ye Reward upon ye death of a Deer among a pack of Hounds, where Every One pulls & tears what he can for himselfe, for indeed it has bin no other then a perpetuall scramble." [44]

Like Orrery, Essex was vexed by the sudden demand for an Irish Parliament. He discredited the report that his friend, William Harbord, and his own brother had begged for this, a report which must make "my Lord Conway & Lord Ranela laugh in their Sleeves." [45] He had some share in the counsels concerning a new farming of the Irish revenue, which had been entrusted to Ranelagh, and was allowed to assist in selecting the new Farmers. In October he was reassured by the King's willingness to allow an advance of sixty thousand pounds for Ireland's needs, including the civil and military lists. Two months later, he perceived only too clearly that both Ranelagh and Danby intended to "draw as much money as they can from Ireland and employ it in England." The army in Ireland would remain in arrears. Essex complained that he could see the King only with Ranelagh and the Lord Treasurer. He had vigorously but vainly opposed the policy of those two lords and had advised the King "according to my conscience." [46]

When Essex returned to Ireland at the beginning of May, 1676, it was doubtful whether he could remain in office much longer. That he was not recalled for another year was due to a balance of power between rival candidates for his post. A plan to stall for time by appointing Orrery, Conway, and Granard [47] as Lords Justices, in order to bring in Conway as Lord Lieutenant, was abandoned in favor of a more ingenious plan, designed to tempt the King, to make Monmouth Lord Lieutenant, with Conway as his resident and very active Deputy. Meanwhile, Ormonde's supporters were campaigning in his behalf to restore him to his former command. Orrery's share in these intrigues remains obscure. All that can be safely assumed is that under no circumstances would he have been an advocate for Ormonde.[48]

Orrery was disaffected by his failure to loosen the King's ties with France and to gain protection for the Dissenters. He observed with concern the Duke of York's distaste for the Presbyterian party; and Orrery's long sessions with Danby had failed to alter the Lord Treasurer's policies. Orrery made himself "useful," [49] however, to the new Farmers of the Irish revenue in helping them settle matters of payment.

His personal problems caused Orrery added anxiety. Precise arrangements were made for the payment of his pension in amounts of eight hundred and thirteen pounds and fourteen shillings per year, until he should receive eight thousand pounds in one payment.[50] But the lapsed money was still not levied, although the King had ordered a year ago that it should be collected in installments at the end of every three months "at furthest." [51] Orrery's steward, Jeremy Hall, listed the sums which Orrery had *not* received. Of the lapsed money there had been "nothing as yet but expense."

Other grants had been reduced. The expenses of Orrery's journeys to London made a dismal total.[52]

On July 6, 1676, Orrery left London for the last
time. After an unsuccessful operation, he had become
a permanently crippled man. A chalky substance had
been removed from his foot, and the wound had not
healed. "He never walked again," comments his first
biographer.[53] On the eve of Orrery's departure, London presented a rather ominous aspect. There was a
mounting terror of the growth of Popery. The King
had ordered the closing of St. James's Chapel, where
the Portuguese ambassador held mass. In a letter to
Essex, Orrery wrote: "I never saw ye people in such
Feares as they are inn. They keepe Guards in all
Places, as in Time of Warr." [54]

Essex was fully justified in his distrust of Ranelagh's
management of the Irish revenue. After his return to
Dublin, Essex discovered that Ranelagh was proposing
to pay only part of the army, reserving for other uses
some of the money designated for the army's needs.
In this juncture, Essex sought sympathy where it certainly was to be had, for concern for the "poor soldiers" was a passion with both himself and Orrery.
The correspondence of the two men reflected a new cor-
diality. Essex noted that Orrery had "eminently served
his Ma^ty." [55] Although the advice would have been
forthcoming in any case, he pressed Orrery for helpful
reports on the Munster garrisons. Essex was dejected
by the fact that he could not live a single day without
care in his high office. The hitherto self-assured Lord
Lieutenant begged Orrery's opinion, "freely without
Ceremony or flattery," [56] as to whether he was right or
wrong in his dealings with Ranelagh, and read with
much satisfaction Orrery's confirmation of "the reg-
ularity of my proceedings." [57]

For a time Orrery paid his troops with his own money, so that they would not have to leave their garrisons, in order to support themselves. Many soldiers lacked arms and without swords by their sides looked very much like Tories. The citadel of Cork was without a single musket bullet. Kinsale had sunk to the status of "the bleakest Garrison of Ireland." [58] Orrery wrote these alarming reports in an almost illegible hand. He refused to subject his correspondents to the discourtesy of a dictated letter, unless an uncommonly severe attack of gout made it impossible for his fingers to grasp a pen.

Orrery made an earnest appeal to Ned Progers to choose "some favorable hour" to beg the King to grant the lapsed money, promised long since. The prospective gift had been reduced by two thousand pounds; and Orrery had spent one thousand pounds in "prosecuting my right," and had promised the Lord Privy Seal three thousand pounds of the remaining total. Although nine thousand pounds were to have been received by May, 1675, there had been another delay, due apparently to the influence of Ormonde, whose own grants Orrery had never opposed. The King's will in this "unhappy affair" must of course, be "punctually" obeyed.[59] In March, 1677, the King issued an emphatic but ineffectual warrant that there should be no more delays "to make good our bounty." [60] Orrery fared better in securing annual payments on his pension, but he never received the eight thousand pounds in a single payment which was to have been his reward for so readily resigning his Presidency.

In all Orrery's voluminous correspondence, there is no word of complaint against his Master's broken promises. Orrery professed that he owed all that he had or was to the King, and "therefore to ye last Gasp all I have I will lay at his feet." [61] The terms of his pension he left to the King, for "whatever shall please his Maj^ty shall please me." [62] The King's wishes must always be "a law to me." [63]

At the end of September, 1676, Orrery made his will.[64] He appointed Lady Orrery executrix and also guardian of their youngest and only unmarried daughter, Lady Barbara Boyle. The Castlemartyr property was bequeathed to Lady Orrery for her life-time and at her decease to Henry Boyle. Lady Katherine Boyle, Orrery's third daughter, had been recently married to Captain Richard Brett of Richmond, Surrey, a cousin of Alexander Brett of Whitestanton, Somersetshire.[65]

The affairs of his elder son were a source of continual harassment to Orrery. All his children received generous allowances from their father.[66] Broghill's was one thousand pounds a year, and he also had his pay as Captain of a troop of horse. Nevertheless, his debts steadily increased, and he could not, or would not, pay his wife the annual sum required by the terms of her marriage settlement. The Earl of Dorset remonstrated with him, requesting possession of the last deed of jointure, enough money to bring Lady Broghill to Ireland, and the regular payment of her allowance.[67]

Lady Broghill took the more effective measure of demanding Orrery's intercession with his son. Resuming her correspondence with her father-in-law, she wrote to him one of her violent letters, protesting that Broghill withheld her allowance and she was without funds. In his usual patient, leisurely manner, Orrery reviewed with her Broghill's situation. Her husband was over four thousand pounds in debt, a contributing factor being her many expensive journeys to England and the necessity of maintaining two families. Orrery had "chided" his son and had undertaken to put his affairs in a better "posture." Broghill was to reduce his expenses and live a retired life. He was to hasten to Lady Broghill the money which he owed her, and she was to receive in the future two hundred pounds a year for her personal use. Always a tender-hearted father, Orrery felt compelled to remind this unloving wife that although he was offended with Broghill for his unworthy conduct, "yett I cannot devest my selfe of ye Affection I have for him, nor forgett he is my sonn & my Eldest." [68]

During much of the following year, Orrery was involved in arguments with Lady Broghill and her parents. He explained to Lord Dorset that Broghill was on the brink of ruin. Two thousand pounds of Broghill's debt must be paid at once, and paid out of money which had been settled on Orrery's younger children. The amount of the lapsed money had been reduced again, and Orrery could not hope to clear more than three thousand pounds of it. The six hundred pounds a year of lapsed money which had been settled on Broghill and his younger children must now be reduced to four hundred pounds; and as soon as his debts were cleared, Broghill must pay back to his father two hundred pounds a year of this, over a period of ten years. Orrery would send Lady Broghill the rest of her allowance and her traveling money. [69] He found it hard, as he wrote to Lady Dorset, to ruin his younger children, who had always obeyed and pleased him, for a son who disobeyed him. He had laid out twenty thousand pounds in improving his estate for his elder son. [70]

Orrery reminded Lady Broghill that she had been

under no expense when she and her husband lived at Charleville House, and their allowance was ample when they went to live by themselves. He was prepared to pay her two hundred pounds a year for herself and a housekeeper. But she must live in a retired way and without company for three years, until her husband had been extricated from his troubles. Would she agree to keep such "rules"? [71]

Lady Broghill's parents were displeased because Orrery would give them only a copy of the last deed of jointure; but Lady Dorset did apologize for her daughter's "foolish, frantic expressions." [72] It was agreed that Lady Dorset should bring up her grandson Charles, and Orrery should provide a home for Broghill's young heir, Lionel, and Lionel's sister, Lady Mary Boyle. Orrery promised that Lady Broghill should reap the good effects of a few gestures of tractability, "for my wife and I are Persons that will not bee outdone in Reall affection by any of our Relations." [73]

At the end of April, 1677, the long expected recall of Essex occurred, and Ormonde was appointed Lord Lieutenant for a third time. Essex admitted to Orrery that his term of service had been "very uneasy." But in five years he had not, he believed, wronged any men, and he had "much kindness for this kingdom." [74] Essex demonstrated, before he left Ireland, a particular desire to secure for Orrery a suitable increase in the payments of his pension and to serve him in a variety of ways. When a commission for a captaincy became available, he gave the post, without any prompting, to Henry Boyle, "whom I doe really looke upon as ye hopefullest young Gentleman in ye Kingdom." [75] In the midst of his grief over the plight of his elder son, this handsome tribute to "my son

Harry" gave Orrery the keenest delight. Essex's good opinion of Harry, Orrery declared, "is soe welcome a thing to me, as I know few things in this World could be more soe, but by his Actions, & services to yor Ex^{cy} to merit it; w^h I more then promiss my self, he will constantly endeavour." [76]

Orrery continued to disagree with Essex as to the best methods of administering justice. The former Lord President of Munster found it difficult to stop serving the sinners of Munster *in loco parentis*. It was with a heavy heart that he saw even Papist offenders depart for Dublin to be judged in accordance with Essex's "rules." Orrery related to Essex at some length the hoax played by a thirteen-year-old girl, Ellen Barry, who, at the instigation of a priest, posed as the ghost of a dead young man, in order to prove the existence of Purgatory and alarm the English Protestants.[77]

After making a public confession of her crime before the Bishop of the diocese and some of the clergy and gentlemen of the county, the terrified girl had fled. Essex regarded the episode as an instructive lesson to the Papists that "their false Religion supports itself only by cheats & delusions." [78] Orrery's concern was for Ellen herself. Having revealed the deception, she dared not return to her friends and must starve or beg, unless some provision were made for her.[79]

Orrery informed Essex of the ruinous condition of the fort at Bantry, which was the only stronghold of the English in the northern part of Munster. The soldiers at Kinsale had no straw to sleep on, nor blankets to cover them; and their guards had no candles, and only such firewood as Orrery provided for them. The miserable soldiers of one unpaid company had mutinied, and their ringleaders must be disarmed but should at least keep their red coats, for which they had paid. Whenever he could do so, Essex supplied the requested aid. Orrery fully sympathized with Essex's irritation over one insurmountable problem: Ranelagh's failure to pay the army. It seemed to be the policy of Orrery's "worthy" nephew "not to pay but to put off." [80] Ranelagh's "frivolous" pretenses were unmasked, when it was promised that payments would henceforth be made on time, but the undertakers would deduct twelvepence in the pound. [81]

Orrery had been at work for a year on his last major literary effort, *A Treatise of the Art of War*. To Essex, to whom he gave, as a parting gift, a copy of this work, Orrery explained his purpose in writing it. He had not been able to forget witnessing the extermination of an encompassed regiment near Kildare, when Berkeley was Lord Lieutenant. Little was generally known of "intrenched incompassings," or indeed of the history, principles, and maxims of warfare. For many years he had kept notes of what he had learned about war from experience, from books, and from discourse with others. Cromwell and especially Ireton had learned what he could teach them. Several commanders had urged the publication of his essay, and the King had allowed it to be dedicated to him. In acknowledging the gift, Essex commented that it would be "of great use to ye soldiers of his Majesties Dominions." [82]

With ceremonious courtesy Orrery and Essex exchanged compliments, as Essex prepared to leave his post. Orrery declared: "you have governed us justly, wisely, & God has blest y^r go^vt with Peace and you return with honour & a good Conscience, to y^re owne cuntry." [83] He would always retain "a grateful memory" of Essex's "greate and constant care" of the pay of the army.[84] And he had "an indelible Sense of all yor Favours to me, & myne." [85] Essex found some solace in the fact that he left the army with their March pay in their hands and had signed warrants for their June pay. In the face of perpetual obstacles, he had tried to be a patron to the army, "wch I have always lookt upon as it were ye unum Necessarium to bee here taken care off." [86]

Before Ormonde arrived in Dublin in August, 1677, Burlington had effected a truce between his brother and the incoming Lord Lieutenant. As he cautiously informed Essex, Orrery decided to make a suitable reply to any overtures by Ormonde and to grant him a "proportional Returne" of friendship.[87] He apologized for being too crippled to come to Dublin, sent his two sons to welcome the Lord Lieutenant, and offered to obey all commands with which he might be honored with "that perfect Duty" which he owed to the King's service and to Ormonde himself.[88] Ormonde thanked him for his great civility and at once assigned him the task of studying the ramifications of the Irish revenue and preparing bills for an Irish Parliament. Orrery doubted if he could be of any use to a person of "such greate Experience, & of soe Excellent a Judgm^t as yor G^{ce} is happy in." He pointedly observed, however, that from time to time Essex had honored him with important transactions and sometimes commanded "my insignificant opinion." [89]

Orrery accepted his current assignment with his usual readiness and was pleased by Ormonde's approval of his proposals. He foresaw that the army could not be paid monthly, even with the deduction of twelve-pence in the pound. It would be difficult to increase the King's revenue, when so much of it was not being applied to the benefit of the King's government in Ire-

land. Careful thought must be given to a consideration
of two weighty subjects: what the intended Parliament
might reasonably grant to the King, and what might,
in return, be expected from the King's bounty.

On November 4, 1677, the Prince of Orange married the Duke of York's eldest daughter, Princess
Mary, to the joy of the English Protestants. With
considerable diplomacy the King managed to negotiate
this marriage, while retaining his profitable alliance
with Louis XIV. In one of his merry letters to the
Earl of Rochester, Henry Savile complained that the
Dutch visitors who came to England for the royal
wedding left "clowds of dullnesse" behind them when
they returned home. The Princess of Orange took to
Holland with her as members of her household such
"beauties" as England afforded. Savile noted that
there had been much suing for places of honor on the
part of "the old Ladyes and the young beggerly
bitches." [90] Orrery's second daughter, Margaret,
Countess of Inchiquin, was named a Lady of the
Bedchamber. She was to spend the rest of her life
in the service of the young Princess. Lady Inchiquin's
youngest son, James, was perhaps already under Orrery's hospitable roof. Orrery was to take pride in
educating the boy, and by a codicil to his will was to
leave him a legacy of one hundred pounds a year. [91]

It was a great satisfaction to Orrery when, in the
early spring of 1678, after a lapse of over six years,
the work on the fortifications of Kinsale was resumed.
Orrery dispatched expresses to the two men with whom
he had made contracts for the work, and two days later
they came to Castlemartyr to discuss the plans with
him. Ormonde had requested twelve thousand pounds
for the project, and the money did actually come in
at the rate of three hundred pounds a week. Orrery

thoroughly enjoyed his frequent conferences with Captain Archer, an Irishman and a Papist, to be sure, but a brilliant engineer, who had taught him some things about fortification which he had not learned from "the ablest Masters of Europe." [92] He sat up late examining plans and making sketches himself which he discussed with his son Harry, who "has an Inclination," he noted, "to learn all that belongs to Warr." [93] Under the exhilarating influence of towers and bastions (on paper), the tone of Orrery's correspondence became more cordial. He sent Ormonde a copy of *A Treatise of the Art of War,* remarking gracefully that Ormonde had a double title to the book as "ye first General who gave me a Commission to be an officer and ye last Gen^{ll} I have ye honour to serve under." [94]

The fact that he had to be carried about in a chair did not deter Orrery from a three days' trip to Kinsale in July to observe the progress on the new fort. The roughness and hilliness of the journey and much getting in and out of a small boat "sett ye gouty humour on worke"; but Orrery's physical pain was outweighed by the joy of examining everything himself. He considered the wall work "the best and handsomest" he had ever seen and was convinced that no harbor in the world would be "so well defended." [95] Invited to name the fort, Ormonde christened it Charles Fort.

Ormonde remained unyielding in the matter of the lapsed money. He declared that he must wait to be guided by better judgments and by the King's instructions. Anglesey, perhaps seeking to repair their broken friendship, told Orrery what the latter had long suspected, that Ormonde "made a doubt on the King's order where there was no colour for it." [96] The Lord Lieutenant was always a little uneasy because he was aware that Orrery knew of his grants to a large number of clamorous Papist relatives to whom he had been "kind by obligation." [97]

In the autumn of 1678, thanks to the alleged Popish Plot and the wild rumors which rippled from it to Ireland, the militia in Munster was ordered settled, although not in the manner that Orrery desired. In a long, complaining letter, written on November 29, Orrery reproached Ormonde for letting more than two months go by, after the "horrid plot" was detected, before the militia was set up, and then employing the slow and inefficient services of the Commissioners of Array. The baffled commissioners had sought Orrery's advice. "But I love not," said Orrery, "to intrude where I am not called." No man, indeed, was better acquainted with persons and situations in the western counties than himself; and although preferring retirement, he would welcome all invitations from Ormonde merely to give advice, instead of playing the active rôle to which he had been accustomed as Lord President. Although he had thought of going to England in these "cloudy" times, "the universal applications of the poor Protestants" were keeping him in Ireland. The safety of Protestants seemed so precarious that "every country Gentleman & Protestant out of a Garrison goes to bed in Fears." [98]

Orrery followed this letter with a much more explicit one, addressed to Ormonde and the members of the Irish Privy Council, in which he desired "full, legall and cleare" authority to act as Major-General of the Army in any emergency. Might he judge and punish rebels without referring their cases to the Lord Lieutenant and Council? He had formerly exercised such powers. [99] In subsequent letters he offered further complaints. He especially deplored Ormonde's timing for raising the militia. The proclamations requiring Papist clergy to leave the kingdom and Papist laity to be disarmed would have had more weight if the militia had previously been set up to enforce obedience.[100] Orrery's protests were rather curtly dismissed. The Lord Lieutenant and Council informed him that the militia in Munster was being organized in exactly the same fashion and with the same likelihood of success as in the other parts of the kingdom.

Ormonde was much irritated by Orrery's incessant criticism and by his "diffusing" his opinions among ministers, courtiers, and Parliament men. Orrery had used the Popish Plot as a pretext for complaining of the lack of protection for Protestants in Ireland, had found Ormonde tardy in applying remedies, and had disapproved of every step which Ormonde had taken.[101] The Lord Lieutenant wrote sarcastically to Orrery that the fears of Protestants in Munster "seem to be greater then in any part of the Kingdome; from whence I do not hear, but y^t Protestants, y^t live out of Garrisons, lye down quietly, & rise safely; & I pray God, that they and their posterity may ever do so." [102] Orrery's proceedings ill supported his renewed professions of friendship. Yet this wily adversary elicited from Ormonde a kind of carping admiration. In a letter to Sir Robert Southwell, Ormonde pondered:

> I know not well w^t stile to give to my L^d of Orrery's dispatches, for the subject of them & the expressions in them may be varied by so skilfull a contriver, & w^n he pleases, take the figure of faithfull advice from a sworne Councellor, & then with as little pains as goes to ye running of a plot in a play, by shifting sides & disguises it may rise up in the shape of a formal accusation. In short take all he writes . . . together & you will find something of

the Councellor, of the friend, of the Accuser, & a great deal of the Libeller.[103]

Orrery's motives were undoubtedly mixed. The almost endless ramifications of the Popish Plot, so generally credited, made it seem the part of prudence for Ireland to have a militia well officered, well trained, and alerted for a possible invasion from France, supported by Irish Papists. Orrery felt that he was the best qualified man, as he probably was, to control the Munster militia. Under cover of stressing Ireland's danger and the failure to take proper precautions, he could also deal blows at Ormonde's administration and increase his own prestige as protector of the Protestant interest in Ireland. It is not clear which motive was uppermost. Moreover, although he had borne them cheerfully, Orrery was afflicted with the frustrations of a long invalidism. The constant activity which his temperament imposed on him must now be channeled into small streamlets. His last letters to Ormonde make melancholy reading.

One cross which Orrery bore with surprising serenity was the continued truculence of his daughter-in-law, Lady Broghill. He personally undertook the payment of her allowance and the custody of his grandson Lionel and his granddaughter Mary. Lady Broghill grudgingly thanked him for sending her money, a favor which "was more then I expected." She made a virtue of "being plane" and protested: "I cannot help saying I think never any gentlewoman was ever kept as I have bin." But she did concede: "If y^r Ld^{sp} doe us the favour to undertake our afares I doe not question but to be well dealt with." And the supreme compliment was wrung from her: "I wish y^r Ld^{sp} could bee in both countryes." [104]

Orrery took pains to assure Lady Broghill that her young children were well cared for. He found Lionel "of a very good Disposition, tractable, apt to learne," and quick to mend any faults for which he was "gently checked." [105] The fond grandfather had "putt Lionel into a vest Coat & Crabatt & hatt cocked up wth a plume of Ribbins soe that he looks like a young hector & is very well pleased he does soe." Miss was now running about and beginning to prattle. She was more "humersome" than her brother, "but that by Degrees & gentle usage will I hope wear away." [106] Somewhat softened by these beguiling reports, Lady Broghill admitted that "by all that come out of Ireland" she had heard of Orrery's kindness to her children.[107]

It became painfully apparent that Lord Broghill, now hopelessly in debt, was totally unable, as well as apparently unwilling, to make any provision for his wife. In May, 1679, Lady Dorset decided to initiate a suit in Chancery to secure legal confirmation of the allowance which had been promised to Lady Broghill at the time of her marriage. Orrery did not oppose this step and trusted that before Michaelmas the legal counsel on both sides might work out some agreement.[108] He was spared the knowledge that the suit would drag on for nine long years and cause his widow endless vexation.

Two months before his death, Orrery reviewed once more with his elder son the latter's dismal prospects. Broghill now had a debt of six thousand pounds, his whole estate was in the hands of creditors, and "few wise men" would care to have dealings with him. Orrery had confidence, however, that in seven or eight years he would be able to straighten out for his son even such "intangled" affairs. Lord Broghill could count on the unwavering support of a devoted father, who could "never thinke well of any that shall slight you." [109]

Orrery cemented his friendship with the Duke of Newcastle by helping to negotiate a fashionable marriage for the Duke's only son, Lord Ogle. On March 27, 1679, Lord Ogle married at Petworth Lady Elizabeth Percy, the twelve-year-old granddaughter of Lady Northumberland. Orrery was elated over the "happy union" of "my dear Master" and "my Mistriss," [110] although the only union achieved was the joining of great fortunes. Lady Sunderland commented devastatingly on the sixteen-year-old bridegroom: "My Ld. Ogle dos prove the sadest creature of all kindes that could have bine founde fit to be named for my Lady Percy, as ugly as anything young can be." [111] The continued interference of Orrery's relatives in the affairs of the child bride caused her great misery, which Orrery did not live to see. At about the date of Lady Percy's marriage, Henry Boyle married Lady Mary O'Brien, the youngest daughter of the first Earl of Inchiquin. Lady Broghill, so often harsh in her judgments, considered her new sister-in-law "a very pretty good humered young lady." [112]

The last year of Orrery's life was shadowed by storm clouds of English politics. The disclosure of his enforced involvement in Charles's secret alliance with Louis XIV compelled Danby to resign his treasurership in the spring of 1679. By dissolving one Parliament and summoning another, the King was able to save his unpopular minister from the consequences of impeachment, although not from imprisonment in the Tower, where Danby was to languish for five years. Orrery's concern over Danby's fall, although genuine, was probably mitigated by a conviction that he himself would have managed better, would have avoided commitments with the French King, and would certainly have contrived to keep clear of the Tower (as indeed Orrery had always successfully done).

On the advice of Sir William Temple, the Privy Council was remodeled. With Shaftesbury as President of the Council and the principal Whigs of both Houses serving as Councillors, it was hoped that the new Parliament would be sufficiently mollified to give the King stronger support. Orrery's name was conspicuously absent from the new list of Councillors, a fact which undoubtedly grieved him. He must have been aware, however, that his removal and that of other loyal members of the King's Privy Council was a piece of political maneuvering on the King's part, designed to win the support of his enemies. The King still desired Orrery's presence; and as late as May, 1679, when Orrery was too ill to make the journey, a man-of-war was waiting to transport him to England.[113]

Hungry for English news, Orrery begged his Somersetshire friend, Sir John Malet, a member of the House of Commons, to write to him by "every post." Orrery had hoped to come to England in May; but the insecurity of his Protestant neighbors made him decide not to abandon them in such troubled times. "Popery," he reflected, "is a prodigious Religion, & therefore I hope it will be disabled from doinge thos ills, w^h ye Principles of it oblige the professors of it to act." [114] The letters to Malet, although brief, indicate a warm and rewarding friendship.

Orrery resumed correspondence with Essex, now First Lord of the Treasury and a member of the influential triumvirate of ministers of which Lord Halifax and Lord Sunderland were the other members. Somewhat wistfully Orrery begged of Essex permission to write "from time to time" of Irish affairs.[115] When the new Parliament was prorogued at the end of May, Orrery trusted that the two Houses would meet "in a calmer Temper" [116] at their next session. Opposed as he was to the Exclusion Bill which had just been passed by the House of Commons, he presumably hoped that some variation of his own scheme for limiting James's authority, after he became King, might be worked out. Orrery advised against sending Irish troops to assist in subduing the rebellion in Scotland. On September 9 he wrote to Essex for the last time to report an alleged plot to smuggle French arms into Ireland and to express his concern for the safety of the King, "whom the God of Heaven longe longe preserve." [117]

In the final exchange of letters between Orrery and Ormonde, civility continued to be blended with sarcasm. In January, 1679, in an unfinished, unsent letter, Ormonde found relief for his irritation at Orrery's conduct in the blunt accusation: "There is no one thing don by mee by the advice and with the concurrence of the Councell (that I can call to minde) that has met with y^r approbation, or that has scapt y^r censure." [118] In a revision of this letter, adopting a milder tone, Ormonde informed Orrery that he would still receive his advice as "a very seasonable help," although Orrery had not very favorably interpreted, nor "very candidly" represented, the main transactions of Ormonde's government.[119] Orrery replied that he had to say what he thought, "since I am master of my Obedience but not of my beleefe." It was always his policy to obey his superiors, although he might sometimes wish that they had taken other measures. He hoped that he might live to deserve Ormonde's "less unfavorable opinion." [120]

In April Orrery was gratified to be entrusted with the quartering of twenty-one companies of a newly landed regiment, whom he paid out of his own purse. He was further gratified by Ormonde's approval of his arrangements and asserted that in the long run Ormonde would be convinced of his loyalty. His "whole temporal interest," he reminded the Lord Lieutenant, was "embarked in the same vessel" as Ormonde's.[121] The correspondence ended with pleasant, if perfunctory, professions of esteem on both sides.

On July 7 Orrery examined his wife's household accounts and for the last time signed a statement that he had done so.[122] Lady Orrery's half year's housekeeping allowance, which she never exceeded, was four hundred and fifty pounds, and she received an additional one hundred and fifty pounds for keeping her accounts. Orrery's half year's income at this date was nineteen hundred and sixty-nine pounds. About two-thirds of this amount was required for the running expenses of a household of sixty-six persons.[123] On September 18, Orrery added a codicil to his will, increasing his wife's bequest to include the unpaid portions of his pension and the money in lieu of lapsed lands, if obtained.[124]

Orrery's final illness began in September, 1679, with a severe attack of gout, accompanied by new and dangerous symptoms. A friend described "our major Generalls deadly distemper" as "a suddene & violent decay in nature." [125] In the last month of his life, although no longer able to write letters in his own hand, nor even to sign his name, Orrery reported to Ormonde, to Archbishop Boyle,[126] and to other correspondents no less than three Popish plots, none of which, as Ormonde investigated them, could be confirmed. His old adversary, Ormonde conceded, "left no man behind him his Equall" in the art of detecting plots.[127]

Orrery died on the eve of a temporary resolution of those political and religious problems which were to cause much bloodshed in Ireland before the end of the next decade. The Parliament which met on October 7, a few days before Orrery's death, was at once prorogued, was subsequently adjourned for a year, and was dissolved in January, 1681; and Charles's last Parliament met briefly the following March and was soon dissolved. For the remainder of his reign, in return for ruling without a Parliament, Charles was to enjoy ample subsidies from Louis XIV and was to live comfortably without the Parliamentary balance of power which Orrery had advocated in the time of the Cromwells and in which he had continued to believe.

The day before Orrery died, the news of his death reached England prematurely. His devoted sister, Lady Ranelagh, dispatched cordials to her brother that same night, "as not beleeving him dead." [128] Shortly before his death, Orrery "spoke much" of a sect of reformed Protestants in Piedmont, whose piety he greatly admired.[129] His concern to safeguard the future of English Protestantism, which had long preoccupied him, ended only with his life. On October 16 he was released from further waiting for God's time and the King's.[130] He was buried on October 18 in the ornate tomb of his father in St. Mary's Church in Youghal.

For the last seven of his fifty-eight years Orrery had lived in semi-retirement. We must view with compassion the nagging invalidism of those last years, which distorted his weaknesses: his vanity; his supersensitiveness to criticism; his delight in inflicting criticism on Ormonde, his arch enemy; his insistence on having at least a finger in every political pie. Orrery must be judged in the light of his fruitful achievements, when he played for high stakes, in his "healthful time."

His many faceted personality is elusive. He was one man to Oliver Cromwell, another to Cromwell's sons, still another to Charles II. To Ormonde, as Ormonde complained, he was several different men in a single letter. Unscrupulous where his interests were threatened, he was plagued by a conscience, which he soothed with idealized pen portraits of himself. In the final estimate of Orrery's life and work, we must not forget the bold and brilliant campaigning of his youth, his generously given services to great men who needed them, and his adventuring in new fields as a man of letters.

Epilogue

Immediately after Lord Orrery's death, there was a scramble for his offices. Lord Ossory, Ormonde's son, who had the advantage of being in London, recommended that Orrery's post of Major-General should be void and that Burlington should have Orrery's other posts; but the King demurred.[1] Ormonde was in equal haste to divide the spoils. The day after he received the news of Orrery's death, Ormonde wrote to Henry Coventry, Secretary of State, that he was signing a commission for Captain Edward Brabazon to have Orrery's troop and Lord Granard his foot company. The governorship of the city of Limerick could not be "in better hands" than Sir William King's. The posts of Major-General and Constable of Limerick Castle might remain vacant "for the present"; and the governorship of co. Clare might either fall or revert to the King or to "pretenders to reversions of pensions." [2]

The King, to his credit, disrupted these well-laid plans and promptly ruled that the money yearly paid to the Earl of Orrery, in lieu of his government of Munster, should not be transferred to the payment of any other persons until the pretenses to it of the

Earl's children had been determined.[3] In April, 1680, Ormonde received from Charles letters patent confirming Lady Orrery in her right to her husband's annual pension, granted him in return for his surrender of his Presidency and his "many faithful services" to his sovereign.[4]

Early in February, 1680, the Earl of Anglesey wrote to Lady Orrery in a rather peremptory tone to request all the literary remains of her husband. He affirmed that on "the 12th day of August 1664" Orrery had agreed to hand over to him portions of a history of Ireland which he had begun to write but had laid aside, his *Parthenissa,* some essays "of divine matters," and "passages of his own life" which Orrery was then writing. Anglesey offered Lady Orrery the bait of his assistance in her efforts to obtain the long overdue lapsed money. His own projected history of Ireland, he anticipated, would secure "hon^ble^ mention of your family to posterity." [5] Of course, Lady Orrery was well aware of the feud which had developed between Anglesey and her lord since 1664. She may or may not have handed over the papers. All that is known is that her husband's notes on Irish history, as well as Lord Anglesey's, have disappeared, as have Orrery's autobiographical notes, although the latter may have served as a basis for Morrice's *Memoirs.*

By June, 1680, Lady Orrery, a most competent businesswoman, had discharged all her husband's debts.[6] But the financial distresses of her elder son, Roger, now Earl of Orrery, were beyond her power to repair. "God knows," she observed sadly, "how much my hart is troubled to see how neer errecoverable ruin my Sonn is." [7] It was almost impossible to raise Roger's drooping spirits. His almost despairing letters were among the many burdens which the widowed

Countess was required to bear. Dejected as he was by financial anxieties and tormented by spiteful letters from his wife, Roger's only solace was his mother's concern for him. "Noe Sonn in ye world," he wrote, "can boast of haveing a better Mother then I have." [8]

Lady Orrery spent the autumn of 1680 with her sister, the Dowager Countess of Northumberland, at Northumberland House in London. She soon had the pleasure of a reunion with her daughter Margaret, who had obtained a leave of absence from her official duties at The Hague. That winter Lady Orrery paid an extended visit to her daughter Katherine in Richmond. Lady Katherine Brett's household offered the attraction of two very young granddaughters. Margaret Brett had been recently born and had been named for her grandmother.[9]

A sorry episode in the lives of the Bretts reached its climax the following summer. Richard Brett, apparently aided by his wife, succeeded in bringing about the secret marriage of Lady Northumberland's granddaughter, Lady Ogle, widowed at the age of fourteen, to a gentleman of considerable wealth, Thomas Thynne of Longleat. The wedding ceremony took place at Syon House in the presence of Captain Brett, who gave the bride away, Lady Katherine Brett, Lady Orrery, and "two or three more." [10] It was reported that Richard Brett received a handsome sum for effecting the match.

The marriage was never consummated. On her wedding day, Lady Ogle learned that Mr. Thynne had been guilty of a pre-contract with another lady. It was a nine days' wonder when Lady Ogle managed to escape from her grandmother's house, leave England, and take refuge in Holland, where she remained until after Mr. Thynne's death.[11] Lord Anglesey tried to soothe her resentment against Captain Brett; but she persisted in the conviction that she had been "betrayed & solde" [12] by him. The King took her part, and Richard Brett, although a favorite with his Majesty, was temporarily under a cloud.

In the midst of Lady Ogle's troubles, Lady Katherine Brett died suddenly in Richmond on September 3, 1681, at the age of twenty-eight.[13] Captain Henry Boyle, in a tender letter of condolence, attempted to comfort his grieving mother. His solicitude must have touched her, for he wrote: "That w[ch] wee are to doe who are spared a little longer is by our Respect and Duty towards your La[sp] to supplye in some measure with a fewe, that w[ch] was due from us all." [14]

Soon after her daughter's death, Lady Orrery went to live with her sister, Lady Northumberland, at Syon House. There she was to remain, except for brief visits elsewhere, during the last eight years of her life. This choice of a permanent residence could not have been lightly made, for Lady Northumberland, if contemporary gossip can be credited, was a formidable hostess. There is no evidence, however, that Lady Orrery, generally admired for her equable temper, found the atmosphere of Syon House oppressive. Lady Northumberland, domestic tyrant though she may have been, loved her sister and her sister's children. To Lady Northumberland's scrupulous care of them we owe the preservation of Lady Orrery's family papers.[15]

Further trials were in store for Lady Orrery. Early in 1682 Roger became seriously ill. His hope faded that he might undertake military service abroad; and a fleeting hope that he might gain strength enough to try as a "last Remedie" [16] the climate of Montpellier was also relinquished. He died on March 29, leav-

ing his eldest son, Lionel, under the joint guardianship
of Lord Burlington and "my dear mother," and entrusting to his mother the education of his daughter,
Lady Mary Boyle.[17] The senior Dowager Countess
steeled herself to make the best use of her afflic-
tions, "no matter how ruged the way is to everlasting
Bliss." [18]

In July Lady Orrery returned to Ireland for the
marriage of her youngest daughter, Barbara, to Arthur Chichester, third Earl of Donegal. Burlington
congratulated his sister-in-law on her "very prudent
choice" for his niece.[19] Only a few months after her
marriage, Barbara died of a fever at the age of
twenty. Lady Ranelagh had written in haste, but in
vain, to prescribe for "poor Lady Donegal" the remedy of Jesuit's powder which had saved Lady Suffolk's
life.[20] The Archbishop of Tuam conjectured that God
had made Lady Orrery "an Example for all to imitate
in their highest tryalls of patience." [21]

Roger's widow was the one person who sought to
increase the troubles of her mother-in-law. As her
lawsuit dragged on, Mary complained in many an
angry scrawl that "common justice, civility, and hu-
manity" had not been paid her in anything concerning
her and her children, and she was "far from being
so great a fool" as to have any hazard imposed on
her that it was in her own power to avoid.[22] Burlington found her charges against him insupportable and
endured her "vexatious letters" only in order to be
of service to the senior Dowager Countess.

Lady Orrery returned to Syon House with Lionel
and Lady Mary Boyle; and Lionel was placed in the
care of Lady Northumberland's chaplain, "a very sober man and a good scholar." In the autumn of 1683
Lady Inchiquin paid a welcome visit to her mother,

which ended tragically in Margaret's fatal illness and death. She was buried in London on December 27 at St. Martin's-in-the-Fields. A pathetic inventory of her few possessions was made by her husband. She died deeply in debt, and her jewels were in pawn, including a ring which she had bequeathed her mother.[23]

Within a period of three years, Lady Orrery had lost four of her six children. Little is known of her eldest daughter, Elizabeth. Yet much may be inferred from a brief letter in which Lady Powerscourt told her mother: "When I hear you are well, I am so delighted I never care for other news."[24] The love and sympathy of her surviving children undoubtedly sustained Lady Orrery. Unfortunately, public events of a most distressing nature, succeeding her domestic losses, gave her no respite from anxiety and grief.

In February, 1685, the news of the death of Charles II caused "consternation" among his Protestant subjects in Ireland. King James II lost little time in sending Richard Talbot, now Earl of Tyrconnell, to Ireland, in command of an Irish regiment and with authority to inspect and report on the army there. The appointment of Henry Hyde, Earl of Clarendon, as Lord Lieutenant was of little real significance, for Tyrconnell was permitted to assume undisputed control of Irish affairs. It was soon evident that Tyrconnell's immediate objective was the complete new modeling of the Irish army. Protestant officers were to be dismissed as rapidly as possible, on belated charges that they had served under Cromwell or shown other signs of disloyalty, and were to be replaced by Catholics. Among those allowed a limited reprieve was Captain Henry Boyle, perhaps because of his father's friendship with the Duke of York and his own popularity in Munster.

A curious interview took place between Tyrconnell

and Henry Boyle in Dublin in the summer of 1685.
Henry reported in one of his letters [25] that he was
summoned to sit by Tyrconnell's bed in the latter's
bedchamber, everyone else was sent out, and the doors
were locked. Tyrconnell spoke first of "the great
friendship" he had once had with Lord Orrery, the
cause of its rupture, and the aid which he had rendered
Orrery in securing the confirmation of his pension. He
continued: "And now that I have told you this Harry
Boyle, lett mee begg you to believe that all the friendshipp & service I ever had for y^r father, I have for you,
give mee y^r hand, pray believe mee, for by God tis
true, & God dam mee if I do not serve you wth all the
truth & power & Interest I have." He gave Henry a
choice of the place where his troop might be quartered,
and Henry replied: "My Lord all quarters are alike to
mee if they may bee for the King's service." Tyrconnell remarked that Henry was a modest man and
added: "you know the people soe well, & are so well
beloved in ye Countrye that noe man can have better
intelligence than you have, & none so fitt to serve the
King." If it would be "an ungrateful Employm^t" to
disarm, as he would have to do, disaffected friends
and neighbors, Henry might, on thinking the matter
over, delegate this labor to someone else.

Two days later, Henry waited on Tyrconnell a
second time. He requested permission to quarter his
troop in the "very stubborne" town of Bandon and
agreed to purge the town of disaffected men. He then
hastened to Bandon and accomplished this distasteful
task within two days. But Henry considered this mission "the hardest game I ever had to play." He was
"almost ashamed" to receive Tyrconnell's favors,
which he attributed to the influence (already waning)
of the Earl and Countess of Rochester.

In June, 1686, James gave unqualified support to

Tyrconnell by appointing him Lieutenant-General and Commander-in-Chief of the Army in Ireland. Six months later, Tyrconnell succeeded Clarendon, with the title of Lord Deputy. Henry promptly lost his post, the oldest Captain of Horse to be turned out. Burlington pondered his nephew's predicament, but could not believe that anything would be accomplished by Henry's coming to England just to kiss the King's hand.[26]

Meanwhile, the interference of Lionel's mother in the affairs of her son was complicating the lives of both of the boy's guardians. Lionel was now making the grand tour of the Continent with a tutor of whom his mother disapproved. Mary wrote a devastating letter to the tutor, his offended reply to which he enclosed in a letter to the senior Countess, who decided to suppress it.[27] Eventually the young Earl was brought home, and Lady Ranelagh, always resourceful in solving her family's problems, arranged to have Colonel John Cutts instruct him in the art of war, that he might be ready for military service in Ireland as soon as he could be useful there.[28]

In January, 1688, Henry Boyle sent Burlington a melancholy account of worsening conditions for the Protestants in Ireland. Kilkenny had received an Irish garrison, and Lismore was "threatened" with a like fate. Castlemartyr was daily thronged with persons from all parts of Munster "pressing me to do something for them before they are destroyed by the vast numbers of soldiers raised in all their neighborhoods." Henry hoped that his friends in England would not let him be forgotten, "while I stand in the gap here," and hinted that he could raise a regiment of horse to serve the English interest and the Protestant religion "whenever the word is given me." [29]

In June, 1688, the senior Dowager Countess of Orrery lost her long-drawn-out lawsuit with her daughter-in-law concerning Mary's allowance. The surviving evidence seems to indicate that Mary had made excessive demands and had refused to acknowledge sums which she had actually received. Nevertheless, although resenting the undue severity of the decree, Lady Orrery was not to be tempted by such "farr off and such uncertain expectations" as the possibility of a new lawsuit and perhaps a new chancellor.[30] Henry considered the decree "hard and unreasonable." He wrote consolingly to his mother: "She is certainly very much to blame that makes you pay so dear to bee ridd of her wrangles, but on the other side I thinke y^r Ld^{sps} Ease and quiet ought to be preferred before any thing in this World." [31]

There was unmistakable evidence of increasing political tensions in England in the summer and early autumn of 1688. These developments must have been noted, with mingled alarm and hopefulness, by English Protestants in Ireland. When the solicited invasion of England by William of Orange occurred in November, Henry Boyle was already in England and was among the first of James's subjects to welcome the Prince. In his retreat from Salisbury toward London, King James halted at Andover; and it was at Andover, on the night of November 24, that Prince George of Denmark, the second Duke of Ormonde, the Earl of Drumlanrig, and Henry Boyle, after supping with the King, left the royal camp to join the Prince at Axminster.[32] Henry Boyle must have felt convinced that in this national crisis he could take no other course. It is probable that on December 17 Henry was in William's party at Syon House, whence the Prince sent three lords to London to demand that James leave the city. A week later, James II escaped to France.

That same winter Henry returned to Munster to

play his part in the ominous conflict there. Large numbers of Protestant refugees had already fled to England, and Henry's wife could no longer safely postpone her departure. She wrote to Lady Orrery [33] that her countrymen had all turned soldiers. The newly raised Irish companies had recently cut down all the best trees at Charleville and most of those at Lismore to make pikes. Her husband had "a great many gentlemen with him," his life was in danger, and she left Ireland "with a very heavy heart."

Scarcely had William and Mary been proclaimed King and Queen, when Tyrconnell received word that James was bringing troops to Ireland.[34] James landed in Kinsale on March 12 and was welcomed in the town of Cork by his Catholic general, Justin Macarthy, whom he left in command there. The entire county of Cork was soon at Macarthy's mercy. Castlemartyr was plundered, and for a time Henry Boyle was held a prisoner in Cork.[35] By April only two Irish towns, Londonderry and Enniskillen, remained in Protestant hands.

At James's Irish Parliament, held in Dublin in the spring and summer of 1689, the Act of Settlement was repealed and over two thousand absentee Protestant landowners were attainted. The continued defense of Londonderry provided one ray of hope for exiled Protestants and became an engrossing topic in their letters. Many hearts were lightened when the Irish assailants of the city finally raised the siege early in August.[36]

In May Henry Boyle was in London, "in constant attendance at the Bell in Westminster," [37] pressing claims for his lost estates. He succeeded in obtaining an appointment as a major in Lord Cavendish's regiment of horse,[38] and on July 10 received orders to march that regiment to Kendal and thence to an embarkation point for Ireland.[39] Henry's last letter to his mother was written on August 10 from Hogshead in Lancashire, a "barbarous" part of the world, where no man's meat nor horse meat could be obtained, and where he was to wait for further orders. On the eve of a separation which indeed was to be permanent, he once more "humbly" begged his mother's blessing.[40]

Lady Orrery died at Syon House in August and was buried in Isleworth on August 24. Her widowhood had been marked by many sorrows, which she had borne with singular dignity and courage. She had lost four devoted children and had been constantly harassed by an unloving daughter-in-law. The lapsed money which she hopefully bequeathed to two of her grandsons [41] had never been paid. She had just said farewell to her deeply loved surviving son, who had embarked on an uncertain and dangerous campaign. Had her personality been less vigorous, Lady Orrery might have welcomed death as a release from insupportable burdens.

In the two years following Lady Orrery's death, the armies of King William III gained control of Ireland. In the battle of the Boyne on the first of July, 1690, King James's forces were completely routed, and from the scene of his crushing defeat James fled to France. Henry Boyle, promoted to the rank of Lieutenant-Colonel, fought gallantly in that famous battle, in which his commanding officer, the Duke of Schomberg, risked and lost his life. The fall of Limerick in September, 1691, ended the conflict in Ireland. Forty years earlier, the fall of that city had been a decisive event in Cromwell's conquest of Ireland.

Throughout William's campaign in Munster, the pillaging and burning of Protestant strongholds and great houses had continued. On August 26, 1690, "at twelve o'clock at night," Lionel Boyle sent a desperate appeal to the royal camp near Limerick for assistance to ward off an attack on Charleville House. The young Earl had seen a party of two hundred horse preparing "to powder down upon us to-night or to-morrow." If the house could be saved, he would offer it to the army for winter quarters.[42] In some fashion the danger was averted; and for the time being, Charleville House was spared.

In October James's natural son, the Duke of Berwick, with a detachment of soldiers, took possession of Charleville House. The Duke had dinner there, then ordered the house burned, and stayed to see it in ashes.[43] Thus an old prophecy was fulfilled. Many years before, in the time of the first Earl of Orrery, the "mad Quaker," John Exham, had stood by the door of Charleville House and cursed the handsome mansion. The Earl's servants would have seized the poor fellow, had not Orrery compassionately intervened to save his life; whereupon the grateful prophet declared: "The evil shall not be in thy days!" [44]

After the fall of Limerick, Henry Boyle returned to England to become Cornet and Major in the second Troop of Life Guards.[45] In 1693 he commanded the regiment of Schomberg's third son, the Duke of Leinster, in Flanders,[46] where he probably fought in the bloody battle of Neerwinden. On November 7, 1693, Burlington sent Colonel Congreve the "sad news" of Colonel Boyle's "being dead in Flanders, where he died of a burning Feaver." [47] Henry had expressed the desire that if he died near Youghal, he should be buried in the Earl of Cork's tomb, "at the feet of my dear father Roger Earl of Orrery." [48]

In 1691 one of Orrery's grandsons, William O'Brien, third Earl of Inchiquin, married a Maid of

Honour, Mary Villiers, his cousin, the sixth daughter of Sir Edward Villiers, Knight Marshal. The young Lady Inchiquin had an added claim to royal bounty because of the faithful services of her husband's mother as Lady of the Bedchamber to Princess Mary. Their Majesties gave her a dowry and appointed her husband Governor of the town and fort of Kinsale, "as a Person of whose curage Loyalty and experience We are well satisfyed." [49] Lionel Boyle, third Earl of Orrery, was also the recipient of royal favors. By 1699, although "at great Charge and Expences," he had obtained from King William "a gracious Letter for the Recovery of my Right of the forfeited Subscriptions, commonly called the lapsed Money." [50]

Charles Boyle, the fourth Earl of Orrery, served as a major-general in the army, was sent as an envoy to Flanders, and held the offices of Lord of the Bedchamber and Lord Lieutenant of Somerset. He had both scientific and literary interests. He encouraged the scientific experiments of George Graham, who invented an astronomical instrument which he named "the Orrery" in honor of his patron. Charles Boyle's literary tastes found expression in his contribution to the Phalaris controversy, his edition of his grandfather's plays, his revision of one of them, *Altemira,* and his original comedy, *As You Find It.*

Colonel Henry's son, Henry Boyle, first Earl of Shannon, became an influential Whig statesman. For twenty-three years he was Speaker of the Irish House of Commons, and he was nineteen times one of the Lords Justices. He was also Chancellor of the Exchequer and a Commissioner of the Irish Revenue. Trinity College gave him an honorary degree, and Sir Robert Walpole eulogized him as "King of the Irish Commons."

The first Earl of Orrery would have been gratified

by the accomplishments of his grandsons. But it is doubtful whether he would have admired the less turbulent climate of their lives. For he had explored with tireless zeal the art of war, both in practice and in theory, and had adapted the art of the courtier in perilous times to diverse personalities. Both arts he had served with a fluent and vigorous pen. If his rewards had not been proportionate to his opinion of his talents, he had had the satisfaction of weathering many a dangerous storm in a most dramatic epoch of English history.

Notes

The following abbreviations have been used: Add. MSS (Additional Manuscripts, British Museum, London); HMC (Reports of the Royal Historical Manuscripts Commission); PCC (Prerogative Court of Canterbury Will Book, Somerset House, London); PROD (Public Record Office, Dublin); SO (State Papers, Domestic, Signet Office, Public Record Office, London); SP 16—SP 29 (State Papers, Domestic, Charles I, Interregnum, Charles II, Public Record Office, London); SP 63 (State Papers, Ireland, Public Record Office, London); SP 77, SP 104 (State Papers, Foreign Entry Book, Public Record Office, London); TCD (Trinity College, Dublin).

1
Young Lord Broghill

1. See Dorothea Townshend, *The Life and Letters of the Great Earl of Cork* (London, 1904), on which the account of Lord Cork's life is chiefly based.

2. Brian Fitzgerald, *The Anglo-Irish* (London and New York, 1952), 31.

3. *Ibid.*, 28.

4. *Ibid.*, 38.

5. Denis Murphy, *Cromwell in Ireland* (Dublin, 1902), 242.

6. Robert Boyle, *Works* (London, 1772), I, "An Account of Philaretus during his Minority," xiii.

7. Lismore MSS. 26, f. 131.

8. Broghill is a townland in the barony of Orrery.

9. Lismore MSS. 26, f. 204.

10. *Ibid.,* f. 213.

11. Townshend, 223.

12. SP 63. 254. 52.

13. Lismore MSS. 17, f. 165.

14. *Ibid.,* f. 166.

15. Roger Boyle, Earl of Orrery, *Parthenissa, A Romance. The Last Part, The Fifth Tome* (London, 1656), Preface.

16. Lismore MSS. 17, f. 108.

17. *Ibid.,* f. 129.

18. *Ibid.,* f. 183.

19. *Ibid.,* f. 196.

20. *The Dramatic Records of Sir Henry Herbert,* ed. Joseph Quincy Adams (New Haven, London, and Oxford, 1917), 55.

21. *The Poems of Thomas Carew,* ed. Arthur Vincent (London and New York, 1899), 226.

22. *The Earl of Straffordes Letters and Despatches,* ed. William Knowler (London, 1739), I, 283.

23. Lismore MSS. 27, f. 39.

24. *Ibid.,* 18, f. 45.

25. *Ibid.,* f. 99.

26. Robert Boyle, *Works,* I, xix.

27. Cork MSS.

28. Lismore MSS. 18, f. 117.

29. *Ibid.,* f. 116.

30. *Ibid.,* f. 123.

31. *Dramatic Records of Herbert,* 56.

32. Lismore MSS. 18, f. 123.

33. *Idem.*

34. Donald C. Dorian, *The English Diodatis* (New Brunswick, New Jersey, 1950), 307.

35. *Ibid.,* 131.

36. Thomas Morrice, Memoirs of the most remarkable Passages in the Life and Death of the Right Honourable Roger Earl of Orrery, MS. 473 in the National Library, Dublin, f. 2.

37. Lismore MSS. 19, f. 33.
38. *Ibid.,* f. 37.
39. *Ibid.,* f. 10.
40. Add. MSS. 19,832, f. 43.
41. *Ibid.,* ff. 41–43.
42. *Ibid.,* f. 44.
43. Robert Boyle, *Works,* I, xx.
44. Add. MSS. 19,832, f. 45.
45. *Idem.*
46. Lismore MSS. 19, f. 76.
47. *Ibid.,* f. 74.
48. *Ibid.,* f. 75.
49. Orrery, *Parthenissa, The Fifth Tome,* Preface.
50. Lismore MSS. 20, f. 87 and f. 103.
51. *Ibid.,* f. 86.
52. PROD Lismore MSS. The present writer discovered this and several other letters to Cork by his children in a heap of manuscripts brought from the cupboards at Lismore Castle and deposited in the Public Record Office in Dublin.
53. Lismore MSS. 19, f. 114.
54. *Ibid.,* 27, f. 254.
55. *Ibid.,* f. 261.
56. Sir John Suckling, *Works* (London, 1709), 116.
57. *Ibid.,* 117.
58. Arthur Collins, *Letters and Memorials of State* (London, 1746), II, 601 and 603.
59. Lismore MSS. 27, f. 266.
60. *Ibid.,* 20, f. 99.
61. *Ibid.,* f. 7.
62. *Ibid.,* 27, f. 278.
63. *Ibid.,* 21, f. 136.
64. *Ibid.,* 27, f. 280.
65. *Ibid.,* f. 283.
66. See Kenneth B. Murdock, *The Sun at Noon* (New York, 1939), 234–235.
67. Clarendon MSS. 23, f. 114.
68. Robert Boyle, *Works,* VI, 523.

69. SP 63. 323. 150.

70. Suckling, *Works*, "Upon my Lord Brohall's Wedding," 27.

71. Sir William D'Avenant, *Works* (London, 1673), 275–286.

72. Lismore MSS. 21, f. 7.

73. *Ibid.*, 22, f. 109.

74. Abraham Cowley, *Poems* (Cambridge, 1905), "To the Lord Falkland," 19.

75. This poem has been preserved among the Bath MSS. at Longleat.

76. Cowley, *Poems,* 406–408.

77. SP 63. 319. 203.

78. Lismore MSS. 27, f. 333.

79. See letter of January 2, 1640, from Robert Reed to Thomas Windebank, SP 16. 441. 18.

80. Lismore MSS. 27, f. 286.

81. *Autobiography of Mary Countess of Warwick,* ed. T. Crofton Croker, Percy Society Publications, 76 (London, 1848), 5.

82. *The Letters of Dorothy Osborne to William Temple,* ed. G. C. Moore Smith (Oxford, 1928), 99.

83. D'Avenant, *Salmacida Spolia* (London, 1640).

84. Lismore MSS. 27, f. 10.

85. Collins, 627.

86. *Ibid.,* 652.

87. *Ibid.,* 654.

88. *Ibid.,* 661.

89. Lismore MSS. 27, f. 295.

90. *Ibid.,* f. 296.

91. *Ibid.,* f. 306.

92. *Ibid.,* f. 314.

93. She was baptized on February 11 at St. Martin's-in-the-Fields.

94. Lismore MSS. 27, f. 321.

95. Suckling, *Works,* 31.

96. Robert Boyle, *Works,* VI, 53.

97. See Peyton's letter to Dorothy Osborne of September 22, 1653, in *The Letters of Dorothy Osborne,* 93.

98. See Samuel R. Gardiner, *History of England From the Accession of James I to the Outbreak of the Civil War, 1603–1642* (London and New York, 1894–1896), IX, 308.

99. *Ibid.,* 357–360.

100. John Rushworth, *Historical Collections* (London, 1721), IX, 253.

101. *Ibid.,* 255–257.

102. Egerton MSS. 80, f. 15.

103. Lismore MSS. 27, f. 328.

104. Mary, Countess of Warwick, *Autobiography,* 4.

105. *Ibid.,* 9.

106. *Ibid.,* 12.

107. Lismore MSS. 22, f. 51.

108. *Idem.*

109. *Ibid.,* 21, f. 26.

110. *Ibid.,* 23, f. 8.

111. *Ibid.,* 27, f. 345.

2
THE ART OF WAR

1. Orrery, *The Irish Colours Displayed* (London, 1662), 2.

2. Egerton MSS. 80, f. 33.

3. PROD Lismore MSS.

4. See Chap. 1, n. 111.

5. *Idem.*

6. Morrice, ff. 10–12.

7. *The Journal of Sir Simonds D'Ewes,* ed. W. H. Coates (New Haven and London, 1942), 118.

8. *Ibid.,* 283–284.

9. *Ibid.,* 122.

10. *Ibid.,* 127 and 165.

11. Egerton MSS. 80, f. 31.

12. HMC, *Fifth Report* (London, 1876), Appendix, 346.

13. TCD MS. F. 3. 11, no. 21, f. 65.

14. *Memoirs of the Verney Family,* ed. F. P. and M. M. Verney (London and New York, 1904), I, 231.

15. *A Collection of the State Letters of the Right Honourable Roger Boyle* (London, 1742), 1–3.

16. PROD Lismore MSS.

17. Orrery, *A Treatise of the Art of War* (London, 1677), 11.

18. Add. MSS. 4227, f. 115.

19. Lismore MSS. 22, f. 137.

20. TCD MS. F. 3. 11, no. 21, ff. 61–77.

21. Orrery, *Art of War,* Dedication.

22. Egerton MSS. 80, f. 33.

23. Lismore MSS. 23, f. 135.

24. *Ibid.,* 22, f. 163.

25. *Ibid.,* 23, f. 75.

26. *Ibid.,* f. 10.

27. Orrery, *Art of War,* 15.

28. Egerton MSS. 80, f. 31.

29. Lismore MSS. 22, f. 144.

30. *Memoirs of the Verney Family,* I, 238.

31. *Ibid.,* 232.

32. Orrery, *State Letters,* I, 7.

33. Egerton MSS. 80, f. 31.

34. HMC, *Fifth Report,* Appendix, 346.

35. Morrice, f. 16.

36. Lismore MSS. 27, f. 369.

37. *Ibid.,* f. 372.

38. Egerton MSS. 80, f. 14.

39. *Ibid.,* f. 11.

40. PROD Lismore MSS.

41. On March 19, 1642, the King approved this bill, which released two million and a half acres in Ireland for English "adventurers" who provided funds to raise troops for Ireland.

42. Thomas Carte, *The Life of James, Duke of Ormond* (Oxford, 1851), V, 373.

43. Egerton MSS. 80, f. 15.

44. *Ibid.,* f. 39.

45. Shannon MSS.

46. Carte, *Ormond,* III, 119–121.

47. Lismore MSS. 27, f. 386.

48. *Ibid.,* f. 387.

49. *Ibid.,* f. 388.

50. *Ibid.,* f. 389.

51. *Ibid.,* f. 390.

52. *Ibid.,* f. 389.

53. PROD Lismore MSS.

54. *The Journals of the House of Commons,* III, 307.

55. For an account of these developments, see Samuel R. Gardiner, *History of the Great Civil War, 1642–1649* (London and New York, 1894), I, 245–250, 333–335, and II, 158–162.

56. *A Letter From the Right Honourable the Lord Inchiquin and other the Commanders in Munster, To His Majestie* (London, 1644).

57. *A Manifestation Directed to the Honourable Houses of Parliament in England* (London, 1644).

58. Add. MSS. 25,287 (Broghill's Letterbook), f. 32.

59. Add. MSS. 46,927, f. 1.

60. Included in *A Letter . . . To His Majestie.*

61. Carte, *Ormond,* III, 125.

62. Add. MSS. 25,287, ff. 13–16, 19–20.

63. *Ibid.,* f. 21.

64. *Ibid.,* f. 22.

65. SP 21. 8. 19.

66. *Ibid.,* 19. 187.

67. SP 63. 261. 64.

68. In 1643, when her husband succeeded to his father's title, Lady Katherine Jones became Countess of Ranelagh.

69. Clarendon MSS. 23, f. 114.

70. Tanner MSS. 60. 1., f. 217.

71. Add. MSS. 46,928, f. 18.

72. "Admiral Penn, William Penn, and their Descendants in the Co. Cork," in *Journal of the Cork Historical and Archaeological Society* (2nd Series, 1908), vol. 14, 108.

73. Tanner MSS. 60. 1., f. 217.

74. "Aphorismical Discovery of Treasonable Faction," in *A Contemporary History of Affairs of Ireland from 1641 to 1652,* ed. J. T. Gilbert (Dublin, 1879), I, Part I, 96.

75. Add. MSS. 46,928, f. 33.

76. "Aphorismical Discovery," 96–97.

77. Charles Smith, *The Ancient and Present State of the County and City of Cork* (Dublin, 1774), II, 157.

78. Add. MSS. 46,928, f. 25.

79. *Ibid.,* f. 34.

80. See Gardiner, II, 167–168, 175, and III, 33–56.

81. Add. MSS. 46,928, f. 34.

82. *Ibid.,* f. 32.

83. *Ibid.,* f. 38.

84. SP 63. 261. 64.

85. Tanner MSS. 60. 2., f. 413.

86. *Ibid.,* f. 552.

87. "Admiral Penn, William Penn, and their Descendants in the Co. Cork," 179.

88. *The Treaty with the Earl of Southampton . . . The Ship Called the Sovereigne taken by Captain Moulton . . . Also how the Irish Rebells fell on Bunracy with fire and sword and were after Routed by the Lord Broghill* (London, 1646).

89. SP 63. 260. 22–27.

90. See Gardiner, III, 55–57 and 155–161.

91. Add. MSS. 46,930, f. 31.

92. *Ibid.,* f. 39.

93. Carte MSS. 67, f. 299.

94. SP 63. 262. 63–67 and 83–89.

95. Robert Boyle, *Works,* I, xxxii.

96. Add. MSS. 46,930, f. 105.

97. See Register of Christ Church, Cork, 1643–1668.

98. *Sydney Papers,* ed. R. W. Blencowe (London, 1725), 14.

99. Richard Bellings, *Desiderata Curiosa Hibernica* (Dublin, 1772), II, 293–303.

100. Add. MSS. 46,931, f. 105.

101. *Ibid.,* 47,017, f. 371.

102. *Sydney Papers,* 16.

103. *Two Letters Sent From the Lord Inchiquin Unto the Speaker of the Honourable House of Commons* (London, 1647).

104. Add. MSS. 46,931, f. 128.

105. *Ibid.,* f. 55.

106. Carte MSS. 21, f. 409.

107. *Articles Exhibited to the Honourable House of Commons* (London, 1647).

108. Add. MSS. 46,931, f. 133.

109. *Ibid.,* f. 116.

110. *A Great and Glorious Victory Obtained by the Lord Inchiquin* (London, 1647).

111. Tanner MSS. 58. 2., f. 522.

112. SP 21. 27.

113. Carte MSS. 67, ff. 147–148.

114. SP 21. 27.

115. *The Journals of the House of Commons,* V, 465.

116. *Ibid.,* 503.

117. Carte, *Ormond,* III, 356–357.

118. Broghill's eldest daughter, Elizabeth, was five years of age, his son Roger, two. The date of birth of his second son, Henry, is unknown.

119. Carte MSS. 67, ff. 150–152.

120. *Sydney Papers,* 32.

121. Carte MSS. 22, f. 53.

122. *Ibid.,* f. 65.

123. Clarendon MSS. 31, f. 54.

124. SP 21. 27.

125. Carte MSS. 22, f. 99.

126. SP 21. 27.

127. *Ibid.,* 26. 158.

128. *Ibid.,* 24. 251.

129. *Ibid.,* 26. 166.

130. *Ibid.,* 25. 44.

131. William Knight, *A Declaration of the Treacherous Proceedings of the Lord Inchiquin against the Parliament of England* (London, 1648).

132. Carte MSS. 63, f. 548.

133. Clarendon MSS. 31, f. 274.

134. *Sydney Papers,* 48.

135. Carte MSS. 24, f. 248 and 259.

136. *Ibid.,* 23, f. 110.

137. *Ibid.,* f. 480.

138. *Ibid.,* 24, f. 105.

139. *Ibid.,* f. 10.

140. *Ibid.,* f. 403.

141. *Ibid.,* f. 483.

142. *Ibid.,* ff. 390–391.

3
CROMWELL'S NOBLE LORD

1. Add. MSS. 46,928, f. 34.

2. Morrice, ff. 18–23.

3. See Sir James Ware, *The History of the Writers of Ireland,* rev. Walter Harris (Dublin, 1764), Book I, 169–170. According to Ware, Broghill had received in his retirement a letter from the exiled King stating that "he had provided two small Ships to carry him to Ireland, that he knew what Influence Lord Broghill had on the southern Protestants, and only wanted his Company." Broghill had replied that he would soon be with his Majesty.

4. On July 7 the House of Commons voted to grant Broghill this sum. See *The Journals of the House of Commons,* VI, 254.

5. Sir Charles Firth and Godfrey Davies, *The Regimental History of Cromwell's Army* (Oxford, 1940), I, 587–588.

6. Morrice, f. 26.

7. Lady Ann Fanshawe, *Memoirs* (London, 1907), 55.

8. On December 4 the House of Commons voted to grant Broghill this sum. See *The Journals of the House of Commons,* VI, 328.

9. Tanner MSS. 56, f. 140.

10. *Ibid.,* f. 142.

11. Morrice, ff. 34–36.

12. Carte MSS. 28, ff. 205–206.

13. Clarendon MSS. 38, f. 169.

14. Morrice, ff. 30–33.

15. Tanner MSS. 56, f. 150.

16. *The Letters and Speeches of Oliver Cromwell,* ed. S. C. Lomas (London, 1904), I, 514.

17. Robert Boyle, *Works,* VI, 50.

18. James Caulfield, *Cromwelliana* (London, 1810), 73.

19. Murphy, 240–241.

20. *Ibid.,* 261.

21. Add. MSS. 46,932, f. 9.

22. Murphy, 249 n.

23. *The Journals of the House of Commons,* VI, 344, 444.

24. Murphy, 250.

25. Bulstrode Whitelocke, *Memorials of the English Affairs* (London, 1732), 447–448. As advised by "the cheife officers," Cromwell spared Clayton, regarding him as "one that is furnished with large abilities for the service of his country." Cromwell later (May 10, 1651) requested Parliament to take off the sequestration on Clayton's estate. See Tanner MSS. 54, f. 62.

26. Murphy, 324.

27. Morrice, ff. 24–25.

28. Murphy, 344. In 1653 Lord Moore recovered his estates.

29. Morrice, ff. 27–30.

30. See Orrery's letter to Essex of July 20, 1677, Stowe MSS. 212, f. 272.

31. Edmund Ludlow, *Memoirs* (Oxford, 1894), I, 264.

32. Burlington, Diary, I.

33. Tanner MSS. 54, f. 46.

34. Burlington, Diary, I.

35. Morrice, f. 39.

36. *Ibid.,* ff. 41–42 and Tanner MSS. 54, f. 76.

37. Add. MSS. 46,932, f. 23.

38. See Sir Richard Cox, *Hibernia Anglicana* (London, 1689), Part II, 67–68; Morrice, ff. 49–50; and *A Letter from the Lord Broghill to the Honourable William Lenthall Esq., Speaker of the Parliament of England* (London, 1651).

39. Morrice, f. 45.

40. Burlington, Diary, I.
41. *Idem.*
42. MS. Firth c. 5, ff. 163–164.
43. Tanner MSS. 53, f. 78.
44. MS. Firth c. 5, f. 76.
45. *Ibid.,* f. 96.
46. *Ibid.,* f. 131.
47. Burlington, Diary, I.
48. *The Journals of the House of Commons,* VII, 316.
49. MS. Firth c. 5, f. 234.
50. SP 25. 75. 586–588.
51. Morrice, f. 51.
52. John P. Prendergast, *The Cromwellian Settlement of Ireland* (London, 1865), 86.
53. MS. Firth c. 5, f. 296.
54. SP 25. 75. 537–538.
55. Whitelocke, 604.
56. Samuel R. Gardiner, *History of the Commonwealth and Protectorate, 1649–1656* (London, New York, and Bombay, 1903), III, 204.
57. Add. MSS. 32,093, f. 318.
58. Robert Boyle, *Works,* VI, 634.
59. Burlington, Diary, I.
60. SP 25. 76. 199.
61. *Ibid.,* 75. 760.
62. *A Collection of the State Papers of John Thurloe, Esq.* (London, 1742), IV, 559.
63. *Ibid.,* V, 18.
64. Robert Baillie, *Letters and Journals* (Edinburgh, 1775), II, 408.
65. Morrice, ff. 62–63.
66. SP 77. 31. 449–452. See also Clarendon MSS. 56, ff. 82–111.
67. Burlington, Diary, I.
68. Tanner MSS. 52, f. 186.
69. Morrice, ff. 63–65.
70. See Somers, *A Second Collection of Scarce and Valuable Tracts* (London, 1750), 128–129 and 150–153.

71. Lansdowne MSS. 822, f. 120.

72. Morrice, ff. 52–55.

73. Leconfield MSS.

74. Wilbur C. Abbott, *The Writings and Speeches of Oliver Cromwell* (Cambridge, Mass., 1947), IV, 586.

75. Whitelocke, 656.

76. Burlington, Diary, II.

77. Broghill to General Montagu, November 6, 1657, Thurloe, VI, 600.

78. Burlington, Diary, II.

79. Broghill to General Montagu, November 20, 1657, Thurloe, VI, 622.

80. Morrice, f. 60.

81. *Ibid.,* f. 62.

82. *Ibid.,* f. 66.

83. Thurloe, VII, 115.

84. *Ibid.,* 72.

85. *Ibid.,* VI, 811.

86. *Ibid.,* VII, 72.

87. *Ibid.,* 56–57.

88. *Ibid.,* VI, 622.

89. When Parliament renewed on June 5, 1657, Broghill's grant of lands in Ireland to the value of one thousand pounds a year, specific mention of Ballymaloe House was included. See *The Journals of the House of Commons,* VII, 544.

90. Burlington, Diary, II.

91. Thurloe, VII, 399.

92. *Ibid.,* 395–396.

93. *Ibid.,* 490.

94. *Ibid.,* 573.

95. Burlington, Diary, II.

96. Lady Ranelagh to Lord Cork, February 18, 1659, Lismore MSS. 30, f. 95.

97. *Ibid.,* 31, f. 2.

98. *Ibid.,* 30, f. 99.

99. *Ibid.,* 31, f. 2 and f. 4.

100. F. P. G. Guizot, *History of Richard Cromwell and the Restoration of Charles II* (London, 1866), I, 114.

101. *Ibid.,* 121.

102. Lismore MSS. 31, f. 15.

103. Robert Boyle, *Works,* VI, 122.

104. Burlington, Diary, II.

105. Lismore MSS. 31, f. 15. Thirty-one letters by Lady Ranelagh in the Spencer MSS. throw further light on her character.

106. Ware, 173–174.

107. Thurloe, VII, 683.

108. Clarendon MSS. 60, f. 340.

109. *Ibid.,* 61, f. 19.

110. *Ibid.,* f. 87.

111. Hyde to Villiers, June 20, 1659, Clarendon MSS. 61, f. 154.

112. Carte MSS. 30, ff. 485–486.

113. *Ibid.,* 213, ff. 361–363.

114. Francis Maseres, *Select Tracts Relating to the Civil Wars in England* (London, 1815), II, 711.

115. Orrery MSS. (Harvard University), MS. Eng. 218. 22 F.

116. Maseres, II, 746.

117. HMC, *Various Collections* (Dublin, 1909), VI, 438. After reaching London, Monck urged Broghill to come to England; but Broghill felt too much involved in affairs in Ireland to do so. See Broghill's letter to the Earl of Manchester, April 2, 1660, quoted in William Drogo Montagu, seventh Duke of Manchester, *Court and Society from Elizabeth to Anne* (London, 1864), I, 396.

118. See *A Letter from Sir Hardress Waller and several other Gentlemen at Dublin, To Lieutenant General Ludlowe: With His Answer to the Same* (London, 1660).

119. *The Declaration of Sir Charles Coot, Lord President of Connaught and the Officers and Soldiers under his Command* (London, 1660).

120. *A Declaration of the Lord Broghill, and the Officers of the Army of Ireland in the Province of Munster* (London, 1660).

121. Coote sent Sir Arthur Forbes with a message to the King, to which he received a reply, written on March 16,

enclosing blank commissions. See Thomas Carte, *A Collection of Original Letters and Papers* (London, 1739), II, 314.

122. SP 63. 326. 67.

123. Morrice, f. 80.

124. Burlington, Diary, III.

125. SP 25. 99. 226.

126. Add. MSS. 46,937, f. 32.

127. Burlington, Diary, III.

128. Letter from Dublin signed "519," Thurloe, VII, 909.

129. Orrery to Anglesey, November 28, 1672, Leconfield MSS.

130. *A Declaration of the Convention of Ireland* (London, 1660).

131. *Idem.*

132. HMC, *Eighth Report* (London, 1881), Appendix, I, 99.

133. Thurloe, VII, 859.

134. Burlington, Diary, III.

135. Sloane MSS. 4159, f. 74.

4

LORD PRESIDENT OF MUNSTER

1. *A Perfect Narrative of the Grounds & Reasons Moving Some Officers of the Army in Ireland To the Securing of the Castle of Dublin for the Parlament, On the 13. of December last* (London, 1660).

2. Carte MSS. 30, f. 572.

3. *Ibid.,* 48, f. 4. Ormonde kept an undated, unsigned copy of this letter.

4. *Ibid.,* 59, f. 49.

5. Rawlinson MSS. B. 35, ff. 19–20.

6. Burlington, Diary, III.

7. Morrice, f. 81. This poem has not been preserved.

8. *Ibid.,* f. 82.

9. *Notes which Passed at Meetings of the Privy Council Between Charles II and the Earl of Clarendon, 1660–1667,* ed. W. D. Macray (London, 1896), 8.

10. Burlington, Diary, III.
11. Egerton MSS. 2551, f. 69.
12. *Thirty-Second Annual Report of the Deputy Keeper of the Public Records* (London, 1871), Appendix I, 206.
13. Rowley Lascelles, *Liber Munerum Publicorum Hiberniae* (London, 1824), Part I, 9.
14. SP 63. 304. 89.
15. *Thirty-Second Annual Report,* App. I, 200, 202, 204, 205.
16. Burlington, Diary, III.
17. *His Majestie's Gracious Declaration For the Settlement of His Kingdome of Ireland, and Satisfaction of the several Interests of Adventurers, Souldiers, and other His Subjects there* (London, 1660). The text is included in Carte MSS. 66, ff. 493–512.
18. Carte MSS. 48, f. 9.
19. *Ibid.,* f. 14.
20. Burlington, Diary, III.
21. SP 63. 307. 73.
22. Orrery MSS. (National Library, Dublin), I, f. 18.
23. Burlington, Diary, III.
24. *Idem.*
25. Carte MSS. 64, f. 470.
26. Add. MSS. 37,206, f. 26.
27. SO 1. 4. 447.
28. *Ibid.,* 533.
29. SP 63. 307. 200.
30. Leconfield MSS.
31. *The Rawdon Papers,* ed. Edward Berwick (London, 1819), 158.
32. SP 63. 307. 264.
33. Add. MSS. 37,206, f. 42.
34. SP 29. 54. 52.
35. *Thirty-Second Annual Report,* App. I, 219.
36. Morrice's claim cannot be supported that Orrery personally discredited at the council table at Whitehall the arguments against the Act of Settlement of Roman Catholic agents sent over from Ireland. The Protestant commissioners who

accomplished this task in the spring of 1662 were Michael Boyle, Bishop of Cork, Cloyne, and Ross; John King, Baron Kingston; and Thomas Piggott. Orrery probably supplied the ammunition. See Morrice, ff. 84–88, Cox, *Hibernia Anglicana,* Part II, 5, and Carte, IV, 89–91.

37. Add. MSS. 37,206, f. 102.

38. Leconfield MSS.

39. *Idem.*

40. Carte MSS. 48, f. 21.

41. See *An Act for the better Execution of His Majesties Declaration For the Settlement of His Kingdome of Ireland, and Satisfaction of the Several Interests of Adventurers, Souldiers, and other His Majesties Subjects there* (Dublin, 1662), 1–8.

42. Orrery had secured for his former secretary, William Fitzgerald, the post of Sole Examinator to the commissioners. See SP 63. 142.

43. SP 63. 307. 232.

44. Leconfield MSS.

45. Carte MSS. 220, f. 472.

46. Sloane MSS. 1008, f. 185.

47. Katherine Philips, *Letters from Orinda to Poliarchus* (London, 1705), 65–67.

48. *Ibid.,* 72.

49. *Poems by the most deservedly Admired Mrs Katherine Philips, The Matchless Orinda* (London, 1678), "The Earl of Orrery to Mrs. Philips."

50. *Mercurius Publicus,* No. 43 (from October 23 to October 30, 1662).

51. *Letters from Orinda to Poliarchus,* 78.

52. *Ibid.,* 96.

53. Burlington, Diary, III.

54. *Letters from Orinda to Poliarchus,* 119.

55. *Ibid.,* 120.

56. Burlington, Diary, III.

57. *Idem.* Orrery's editor, William S. Clark, unacquainted with Burlington's unpublished Diary, conjectured: "Perhaps the presentation at Thomas Court was not the only acting of

Altemera in Dublin." See *The Dramatic Works of Roger Boyle, Earl of Orrery,* ed. William S. Clark (Cambridge, Mass., 1937), I, 105.

58. *Letters from Orinda to Poliarchus,* 164.

59. Philip Wilson, "Ireland under Charles II," in R. B. O'Brien, *Studies in Irish History* (Dublin, 1903), 79.

60. SP 63. 313. 168.

61. Add. MSS. 37,206, f. 123.

62. Add. MSS. 28,053, f. 48.

63. Burlington, Diary, III.

64. Carte MSS. 43, f. 202.

65. *The Life of Edward Clarendon . . . Written by Himself* (Oxford, 1759), 59.

66. *The Diary of Samuel Pepys,* ed. Henry B. Wheatley (London and New York, 1902–1909), VIII, 130.

67. Carte MSS. 143, f. 112.

68. SP 63. 316. 98.

69. Add. MSS. 37,206, f. 165.

70. Orrery MSS. (Dublin), II, f. 244.

71. *Ibid.,* III, f. 308.

72. SP 63. 328. 145.

73. *Ibid.,* 317. 2 A.

74. *Ibid.,* 319. 116.

75. *Ibid.,* 348. 54.

76. Add. MSS. 37,206, f. 168.

77. *The Continuation of the Life of Edward, Earl of Clarendon Written by Himself* (Dublin, 1760), 40.

78. HMC, *Buccleuch* (London, 1889), I, 437.

79. Sir John Dalrymple, *Memoirs of Great Britain and Ireland* (London, 1733), II, 39.

80. Burlington, Diary, III.

81. SP 104. 174 A. 63.

82. Burlington, Diary, III.

83. SP 63. 318. 87–88.

84. *Ibid.,* 319. 314.

85. Leconfield MSS.

86. Pepys, IV, 403.

87. SP 63. 319. 116.

88. *Ibid.,* 162.
89. *Ibid.,* 122.
90. *Ibid.,* 203.
91. *Ibid.,* 185.
92. *Ibid.,* 244.
93. See *An Act for the Explaining of some Doubts arising upon an Act* . . . *for the better execution of His Majesties gracious Declaration for the Settlement of His Kingdom of Ireland* (Dublin, 1665).
94. Add. MSS. 37,207, f. 29.
95. Stowe MSS. 744, f. 122.
96. Add. MSS. 37,206, f. 41 f.
97. SP 63. 321. 114.
98. *Ibid.,* 58.
99. Carte MSS. 48, f. 45.
100. *Ibid.,* f. 49.
101. Burlington, Diary, IV.
102. SP 63. 221. 18.
103. Burlington, Diary, IV.
104. *Rawdon Papers,* 219.
105. *Ibid.,* 229.
106. SP 63. 347. 9.
107. *Ibid.,* 321. 114.
108. *Ibid.,* 322. 3.
109. *Ibid.,* 34.
110. *Ibid.,* 140.
111. Add. MSS. 37,208, f. 82.
112. *Ibid.,* f. 55.
113. *Ibid.,* f. 82.
114. Add. MSS. 4162, f. 216.
115. SP 63. 347. 40.
116. Clarendon received only six thousand pounds from Irish lands and blamed Orrery for his disappointed hopes. See Clarendon, *Life,* 136.
117. Carte MSS. 69, f. 129.
118. SP 63. 333. 52.
119. See Burlington, Diary, IV. On July 8, 1668, Burlington and Orrery spent "half an hower in private" with the

Duchess of York at St. James's. The following afternoon the two brothers waited upon the Duke in his closet.

120. Morrice, ff. 97–100.
121. Add. MSS. 37,208, f. 131.
122. Carte MSS. 48, f. 106.
123. Add. MSS. 37,208, f. 7.
124. *Ibid.,* f. 20.
125. *Ibid.,* f. 122.
126. *Ibid.,* f. 126.
127. *Ibid.,* f. 140.
128. *Ibid.,* f. 130.
129. SP 63. 323. 42.
130. Add. MSS. 37,208, f. 191. Henry Boyle was married at a much later date.
131. Carte MSS. 69, f. 131.
132. *Ibid.,* f. 415.
133. *Ibid.,* 70, f. 419.
134. Add. MSS. 37,208, f. 207.
135. SP 29. 241. 148.
136. Carte MSS. 220, f. 396.
137. Pepys, VIII, 73.
138. See Carte MSS. 47, f. 549, and 49, f. 641.
139. *Ibid.,* 68, f. 181.
140. Lord Conway to Major Rawdon, September 29, 1668. See *Rawdon Papers,* 233–234.
141. Carte MSS. 48, f. 307.
142. *Ibid.,* f. 166.
143. SP 63. 325. 20.
144. SP 29. 271.
145. Carte MSS. 48, f. 335.
146. Ormonde MSS., MS. Letters of Elizabeth, Duchess of Ormonde, I.
147. Burlington, Diary, IV.
148. SP 63. 325. 20.
149. *Ibid.,* 27.
150. Carte MSS. 48, f. 352.
151. SP 63. 348. 54.
152. Matthew Wren to Pepys, July 17, 1669. See SP 29. 263. no. 15.

153. See Carte MSS. 48, f. 335. Ormonde had hoped that Orrery's absence in Ireland would give him "opportunities to undeceive the King in relation to him."

154. Burlington, Diary, V.

155. This summary is from Orrery's memorandum of the proceedings against him. See SP 63. 326. 67.

156. Morrice, f. 105.

157. William Cobbett, *Complete Collection of State Trials* (London, 1810), VI, 919.

158. SP 63. 348. 86.

159. *Rawdon Papers,* 239.

160. SP 63. 327. 38.

161. Add. MSS. 37,208, f. 211.

162. SP 29. 277. no. 69.

163. SP 63. 329. 28.

164. Bath MSS., Portland Papers, II, 1613–1772, f. 202.

165. SP 29. 290. no. 2.

166. SO 1. 8. 37.

167. SP 63. 330. no. 165.

168. Stowe MSS. 200, f. 17.

169. SP 63. 331. no. 89.

170. *Ibid.,* no. 114.

171. Stowe MSS. 200, f. 124.

172. Add. MSS. 28,053, ff. 48–54.

173. In 1669 Charles had given this assurance to the French ambassador Colbert.

174. Stowe MSS. 200, f. 273.

175. *Ibid.,* 215, f. 24.

176. See Leconfield MSS. for Anglesey's letters to Orrery (May 21 and July 23, 1672) and Orrery's reply (November 28, 1672).

5
THE KING, MY MASTER

1. SP 63. 317. 222.

2. *Ibid.,* 313. 147.

3. Morrice, f. 112. When Morrice's *Life* was printed (1748), this anecdote was omitted.

4. Add. MSS. 37,206, f. 54.

5. *Ibid.,* f. 74.

6. *Ibid.,* f. 108.

7. *Ibid.,* f. 109.

8. Leconfield MSS.

9. For this reasonable conjecture see Clark in Orrery, *Dramatic Works,* I, 34.

10. Morrice, f. 102. When Burlington visited his brother at Charleville in June, 1666, Orrery entertained him, after a morning's hunt, by reading to him four acts of this play. See Burlington, Diary, III.

11. SP 63. 221. 18.

12. On July 17, 1666, Orrery had written to Conway that he hoped to see this play with him the "next winter" in London. See SP 63. 321. 114.

13. Orrery MSS. (Harvard), MS. Eng. 218. 22 F.

14. See Clark in Orrery, *Dramatic Works,* II, 516.

15. *Ibid.,* I, 167.

16. John Downes, *Roscius Anglicanus* (London, 1886), 27–28.

17. Pepys, IV, 202.

18. *Ibid.,* VI, 110.

19. *Ibid.,* VIII, 58.

20. Orrery, *Dramatic Works,* I, 183.

21. *Ibid.,* 198.

22. *Ibid.,* 174.

23. *Ibid.,* 211.

24. *Ibid.,* 223.

25. Stowe MSS. 744, f. 81.

26. Pepys, IV, 236.

27. *Ibid.,* 241–242.

28. *Ibid.,* VIII, 287.

29. Orrery, *Dramatic Works,* I, 118.

30. *Ibid.,* 143.

31. *Ibid.,* 163.

32. Pepys, IV, 362.

33. Downes, 26.

34. See Allardyce Nicoll, *The Development of the Theatre* (New York, 1937), 158–161.

35. *The Diary of John Evelyn,* ed. E. S. De Beer (Oxford, 1955), III, 466.
36. Pepys, VII, 93.
37. *Ibid.,* 294.
38. Orrery, *Dramatic Works,* I, 304.
39. Pepys, VII, 147–148.
40. *Ibid.,* 157.
41. *Ibid.,* 360.
42. Orrery, *Dramatic Works,* I, 308.
43. *Ibid.,* 372.
44. *Ibid.,* 314–315.
45. See Arthur I. Dasent, *Nell Gwynne* (London, 1924), 95–97.
46. Burlington, Diary, IV.
47. Pepys, VIII, 166.
48. Cyril H. Hartmann, *The King My Brother* (London and Toronto, 1954), 227.
49. Orrery, *Dramatic Works,* I, 383.
50. *Ibid.,* 432.
51. *Ibid.,* 401.
52. *Ibid.,* 379.
53. *Ibid.,* 380.
54. *Ibid.,* 433.
55. *Ibid.,* 435.
56. *Ibid.,* II, 614.
57. *Ibid.,* 619.
58. *Ibid.,* 607.
59. *Ibid.,* 762.
60. *Ibid.,* 737.
61. *Ibid.,* 758.
62. *Ibid.,* 740.
63. *Ibid.,* 760.
64. These words are used of Abner in *Herod the Great.* See Orrery, *Dramatic Works,* II, 619.
65. *Ibid.,* 580.
66. *Ibid.,* 578–579.
67. Orrery, *Art of War,* Dedication.
68. *Ibid.,* 197.
69. *Ibid.,* 133.

70. *Ibid.,* 198.

71. *Ibid.,* Dedication.

72. See undated, unaddressed letter by Captain Henry Boyle, recording Richard Talbot's impressions of Lord Orrery, Leconfield MSS.

73. Pepys, VIII, 113–114.

74. Dalrymple, II, 19.

75. Hartmann, 233.

76. *Ibid.,* 235.

77. Dalrymple, II, 24.

78. Hartmann, 290.

79. *Ibid.,* 345.

80. Dalrymple, II, 76.

81. *Rawdon Papers,* 240.

82. Leconfield MSS.

83. Burlington, Diary, V.

84. Morrice, ff. 110–111.

85. SP 63. 327. 66.

86. Leconfield MSS.

87. Eustace Budgell, *Memoirs of the Lives and Characters of the Illustrious Family of the Boyles* (Dublin, 1755), 69.

88. Morrice, f. 112.

89. *Ibid.,* f. 125.

6

By a Person of Quality

1. Horace Walpole, *A Catalogue of the Royal and Noble Authors of England* (Strawberry Hill, 1758), II, 206.

2. Carte MSS. 70, f. 482.

3. See Clark's account of the history of the manuscript in Orrery, *Dramatic Works,* II, 827–829. *The General* was first printed by J. O. Halliwell-Phillipps in a volume of miscellaneous pieces and was attributed to James Shirley. A manuscript of the play with some variations from the text used by Halliwell-Phillipps has been preserved in the library of Worcester College, Oxford. Clark carefully collated the two texts.

4. D'Avenant, *Works,* "Poem to the Earl of Orrery," 275.

5. Walter Charleton, *Chorea Gigantum* (London, 1663), "To my Honour'd Friend, Dr Charleton," by John Dryden.

6. See Charles E. Ward, *The Life of John Dryden* (Chapel Hill, North Carolina, 1961), 36.

7. John Dryden, *The Rival Ladies* (London, 1664), Dedication.

8. Orrery, *Dramatic Works,* I, 133. See a verbal parallel in Brennoralt's boast:

> *I will deserve her, though*
> *I have her not: There's something yet in that.*

See Suckling, *Works,* 325.

9. Orrery, *Dramatic Works,* I, 123.

10. Burlington, Diary, III.

11. For a detailed account of the influence of pre-Restoration Platonic drama on Restoration drama, see the present writer's *The Social Mode of Restoration Comedy* (New York and London, 1926).

12. Edward Howard, *The Womens Conquest* (London, 1671), Preface.

13. Orrery, *Dramatic Works,* I, 174.

14. For a discussion of Orrery's sources for this play see Clark's Preface to *Mustapha* in Orrery, *Dramatic Works,* I, 225–226.

15. Orrery, *Dramatic Works,* I, 265.

16. *Ibid.,* 255.

17. *Ibid.,* 283.

18. *Ibid.,* 296. When Elizabeth Barry played the Queen of Hungary at Dorset Garden in 1673, she portrayed "majesty distressed" so feelingly that "the theatre resounded with loud applause." Charles II and the Duke and Duchess of York attended this performance. See Thomas Davies, *Dramatic Miscellanies* (London, 1784), III, 201.

19. Orrery, *Six Plays* (London, 1694), Epistle Dedicatory of *Guzman* to Lionel, Earl of Orrery, by Nahum Tate. *Mustapha* is included in Bonamy Dobrée's edition of *Five Heroic Plays* (London, 1960).

20. Orrery, *Dramatic Works,* I, 289.
21. *Ibid.,* 294.
22. *Ibid.,* 261.
23. *Ibid.,* 245.
24. *Ibid.,* 263.
25. *Ibid.,* 238.
26. *Ibid.,* 272.
27. *Ibid.,* 271.
28. *Ibid.,* 247.
29. Pepys, VII, 147.
30. Orrery, *Dramatic Works,* I, 325–326.
31. *Ibid.,* 422.
32. *Ibid.,* 431.
33. For a discussion of Orrery's limited use of these source materials see Clark's Preface to *Herod the Great* in Orrery, *Dramatic Works,* II, 585–586.
34. See Clark in Orrery, *Dramatic Works,* I, 88–89.
35. Leconfield MSS.
36. Clark in Orrery, *Dramatic Works,* I, 88.
37. Orrery, *Dramatic Works,* II, 606.
38. *Ibid.,* 641.
39. *Ibid.,* 597.
40. *Ibid.,* 628.
41. *Ibid.,* 620.
42. *Ibid.,* 611.
43. *Ibid.,* 636.
44. *Ibid.,* 637.
45. *Ibid.,* 592.
46. *Ibid.,* 610.
47. *Ibid.,* 633.
48. *Ibid.,* 629.
49. John Crowne thus paid homage to Orrery in the Preface to his tragicomedy *Juliana* (London, 1671).
50. Orrery, *Dramatic Works,* II, 614–615.
51. *Ibid.,* 621.
52. For a description of this manuscript see Clark in Orrery, *Dramatic Works,* II, 928–929.
53. Clark discusses these sources in Orrery, *Dramatic Works,* II, 643.

54. Clark notes the probable indebtedness of Orrery to Shadwell's *The Tempest* and *Psyche,* Orrery, *Dramatic Works,* II, 644.

55. See Clark in Orrery, *Dramatic Works,* II, 933.

56. Clark reprints this title page in Orrery, *Dramatic Works,* II, 700.

57. Add. MSS. 37,206, f. 54.

58. Robert Boyle, *Works,* I, xx.

59. Pepys, VIII, 279.

60. Downes, 28.

61. Walpole, II, 207.

62. Orrery, *Parthenissa, That most Fam'd Romance. The Six Volumes Compleat* (London, 1676), 713.

63. *Ibid.,* 1.

64. *Ibid.,* 714.

65. *Ibid.,* 329.

66. *Ibid.,* 628.

67. *Ibid.,* 558.

68. *Ibid.,* 651.

69. *Ibid.,* 789.

70. *Ibid.,* 798.

71. *Ibid.,* 381.

72. *Ibid.,* 371.

73. *Ibid.,* 707.

74. *Ibid.,* 347.

75. *Ibid.,* 706.

76. A manuscript note in James Bindley's copy attributes this work to "Roger Boyle." See Thomas Otway, *Works,* ed. Thomas Thornton (London, 1813), III, 325.

77. Leconfield MSS.

78. Orrery, *English Adventures* (London, 1676), 57.

79. *Ibid.,* 125.

80. *Ibid.,* 88.

81. Orrery, *Art of War,* Dedication.

82. *Ibid.,* 22.

83. *Ibid.,* 2.

84. *Ibid.,* 186.

85. C. H. Firth in *Cromwell's Army* (London, 1902) quotes extensively from Orrery's *Treatise.*

86. Peter Walsh, *A Letter* . . . prefixed to *An Answer to a Scandalous Letter* . . . *By the Right Honourable the Earl of Orrery* (Dublin, 1662).

87. Orrery, *An Answer,* 10.

88. *Ibid.,* 28.

89. *Ibid.,* 33.

90. Orrery, *The Irish Colours Displayed,* 2.

91. *Ibid.,* 3.

92. *Ibid.,* 6–7.

93. *Ibid.,* 10.

94. Walsh, *The Irish Colours Folded* (London, 1662), 15.

95. Walsh, *P. W.'s Reply to the Person of Quality's Answer* (London, 1664), 48.

96. Abraham Cowley, *Works* (London, 1688). Orrery's poem heads the commendatory verses prefixed to this edition.

97. Orrery, *Poems on Most of the Festivals of the Church* (London, 1681), Preface.

7

AT CASTLEMARTYR

1. Stowe MSS. 200, f. 255. There are only a few picturesque remains of the old castle. The modern house has been converted to a Carmelite college, where visitors are hospitably received. On the wall of the Prior's study a framed parchment testifies that Castlemartyr is no longer "an outpost of alien rule and foreign domination."

2. Stowe MSS. 200, f. 116.

3. *Ibid.,* 215, f. 6.

4. *Ibid.,* f. 27.

5. *Ibid.,* 201, f. 291.

6. *Ibid.,* 200, f. 158.

7. Orrery MSS. (Dublin), II, f. 181.

8. *Ibid.,* f. 182.

9. *Ibid.,* f. 184.

10. *Ibid.,* f. 185.

11. *Ibid.,* f. 187.

12. Stowe MSS. 201, f. 261.
13. SP 63. 333. no. 52.
14. SO 1. 8. 394.
15. Stowe MSS. 201, f. 261.
16. *Idem.*
17. Stowe MSS. 215, f. 215.
18. *Ibid.,* f. 188.
19. *Ibid.,* 204, f. 171.
20. *Ibid.,* 203, f. 267.
21. SP 29. 333. 132.
22. Stowe MSS. 203, f. 67.
23. *Ibid.,* 205, f. 29.
24. *Ibid.,* 204, f. 182.
25. *Ibid.,* 205, f. 129.
26. *Ibid.,* f. 112.
27. SO 1. 9. 120.
28. Stowe MSS. 205, f. 344.
29. Orrery MSS. (Dublin), II, f. 234.
30. Stowe MSS. 214, f. 212.
31. *Ibid.,* f. 220.
32. *Ibid.,* f. 235.
33. *Ibid.,* f. 227.
34. Dorset to Orrery, July 6, 1674, Orrery MSS. (Dublin), II, f. 231.
35. Stowe MSS. 206, f. 222.
36. *Ibid.,* f. 102.
37. *Ibid.,* 207, f. 34.
38. *Ibid.,* f. 124.
39. *Ibid.,* f. 316.
40. *Ibid.,* 208, f. 100.
41. Portland MSS., Cavendish Papers, 1661–1695, ff. 364–370.
42. It failed to do so at the autumn session of Parliament. See "A Letter from a Person of Quality, to His Friend in the Country," attributed to Shaftesbury, in *State Tracts* (London, 1689), 41–56.
43. Portland MSS., Cavendish Papers, 1661–1695, f. 366.
44. Stowe MSS. 215, f. 167.

45. *Ibid.*, f. 182.
46. *Ibid.*, f. 224.
47. Sir Arthur Forbes was created Viscount Granard in 1675.
48. See Clement E. Pike, "The Intrigue to Deprive the Earl of Essex of the Lord Lieutenancy of Ireland," in *Transactions of the Royal Historical Society,* third series, V (London, 1911), 89–103.
49. Stowe MSS. 209, f. 209.
50. Orrery MSS. (Dublin), II, f. 256.
51. Stowe MSS. 207, f. 276.
52. Orrery MSS. (Dublin), II, f. 244 a.
53. Morrice, f. 115. But Orrery contrived, in some fashion, to get in and out of boats, when the fortifying of Kinsale harbor was resumed.
54. Stowe MSS. 210, f. 49.
55. *Ibid.*, 216, f. 96.
56. *Ibid.*, f. 138.
57. *Ibid.*, f. 145.
58. *Ibid.*, 210, f. 180.
59. Leconfield MSS.
60. SO 1. 10. 99.
61. Leconfield MSS.
62. Stowe MSS. 200, f. 248.
63. *Ibid.*, f. 254.
64. Orrery MSS. (Dublin), III, f. 352.
65. Alexander Brett was the second husband of Richard Brett's sister Elizabeth. In 1673 Richard Brett was commissioned an ensign in the regiment of foot of Henry, Earl of Peterborough. See Charles Dalton, *English Army Lists and Commission Registers, 1661–1714* (London, 1892–1904), I, 135. Also in 1673 Brett was appointed a commissioner of excise for England and Wales. See Joseph Haydn, *The Book of Dignities* (London, 1890), 278.
66. For their quarterly allowances see Leconfield MSS.
67. Orrery MSS. (Dublin), III, f. 263.
68. *Ibid.*, f. 261.
69. *Ibid.*, f. 266.

70. *Ibid.,* f. 269.
71. *Ibid.,* f. 267.
72. *Ibid.,* f. 284.
73. *Ibid.,* f. 287.
74. Stowe MSS. 217, f. 143.
75. *Ibid.,* f. 176.
76. *Ibid.,* 212, f. 90.
77. *Ibid.,* f. 203.
78. *Ibid.,* 217, f. 197.
79. *Ibid.,* 212, f. 232.
80. *Ibid.,* 211, f. 204.
81. *Ibid.,* 217, f. 251.
82. *Ibid.,* f. 248.
83. *Ibid.,* 212, f. 5.
84. *Ibid.,* f. 322.
85. *Ibid.,* f. 326.
86. *Ibid.,* f. 251.
87. *Ibid.,* f. 340.
88. Ormonde MSS. 67, f. 273.
89. *Ibid.,* f. 419.
90. Bath MSS., Portland Papers, II, 1613–1772, f. 216.
91. Orrery MSS. (Dublin), III, f. 353.
92. Ormonde MSS. 72, f. 389.
93. *Ibid.,* 77, f. 173.
94. *Ibid.,* 72, f. 7.
95. *Ibid.,* 76, f. 25.
96. Leconfield MSS.
97. Carte MSS. 70, f. 476.
98. Ormonde MSS. 80, ff. 219–232.
99. *Ibid.,* f. 441.
100. *Ibid.,* 81, ff. 49–65.
101. See Ormonde to Burlington, December 21, 1678, Carte MSS. 70, f. 529.
102. *Ibid.,* f. 523.
103. *Ibid.,* f. 476.
104. Leconfield MSS.
105. Orrery MSS. (Dublin), III, f. 310.
106. *Ibid.,* f. 312.

107. Leconfield MSS.

108. Orrery MSS. (Dublin), III, f. 346.

109. Leconfield MSS.

110. Portland MSS., Cavendish Papers, 1661–1695, f. 403.

111. Add. MSS. 32,680, f. 296.

112. See Lady Broghill's letter to Lady Orrery dated only "March 21," Leconfield MSS.

113. Stowe MSS. 212, f. 351.

114. Add. MSS. 32,095, f. 186.

115. Stowe MSS. 212, f. 351.

116. *Ibid.*, f. 353.

117. *Ibid.*, f. 361.

118. Ormonde MSS. 82, f. 82.

119. *Ibid.*, f. 229.

120. *Ibid.*, f. 260.

121. *Ibid.*, 86, f. 12.

122. The account books of both Lord and Lady Orrery are preserved among the Leconfield MSS.

123. The two young grandsons were kept well supplied with suits, hats, holland shirts, dimity waistcoats, laced cravats, laced cuffs, gloves, etc.

124. Orrery MSS. (Dublin), III, ff. 352–353.

125. Ormonde MSS. 92, f. 157.

126. Michael Boyle had been appointed Archbishop of Armagh in 1678.

127. Ormonde MSS. 93, f. 197.

128. *Ibid.*, 92, f. 341.

129. John Love to Robert Boyle, in Robert Boyle, *Works,* VI, 670.

130. Ormonde MSS. 90, f. 185.

8

Epilogue

1. Ormonde MSS. 92, f. 361; and 93, f. 51.

2. Carte MSS. 146, f. 224.

3. Ormonde MSS. 93, f. 335.

4. Orrery MSS. (Dublin), III, f. 370.

5. Anglesey to Lady Orrery, February 10, 1680, Leconfield MSS.

6. Orrery MSS. (Harvard).

7. Orrery MSS. (Dublin), IV, f. 400.

8. *Ibid.,* III, f. 383.

9. Margaret Brett was baptized in Richmond on October 22, 1680.

10. HMC, *Rutland* (London, 1889) II, 58–59.

11. On May 30, 1682, Lady Ogle married Charles Seymour, sixth Duke of Somerset.

12. SP 29. 418. no. 58.

13. Lady Katherine Brett was buried in Richmond on the fifteenth of September. Richard Brett died in November, 1689. In his will (PCC 1689, 149 Ent) he bequeathed to his sister, Elizabeth Klee, "the Jewell and knott of Diamonds my deare Lady Katherine did usually weare at her brest."

14. Orrery MSS. (Dublin), IV, f. 422.

15. This entire collection was kept among the Leconfield MSS. at Petworth House until 1928, when a portion of the collection was sold and purchased by the National Library in Dublin. Recently, through the courtesy of Lord Egremont, the remainder of the collection has been placed in the National Library on indefinite loan.

16. Orrery MSS. (Dublin), IV, f. 432.

17. Orrery MSS. (Harvard).

18. Orrery MSS. (Dublin), IV, f. 444.

19. *Ibid.,* f. 443.

20. Leconfield MSS. Lady Donegal was buried on November 24, 1682, in St. Patrick's Cathedral.

21. Leconfield MSS.

22. Orrery MSS. (Dublin), V, 606.

23. Leconfield MSS.

24. *Ibid.* Lady Powerscourt was the last survivor of the children of Lord and Lady Orrery. She died on October 17 and was buried on October 20, 1709, in St. Patrick's Cathedral.

25. Leconfield MSS.

26. Orrery MSS. (Dublin), V, f. 610.

27. *Ibid.*, f. 659.

28. Leconfield MSS.

29. *Ibid.*

30. King James had taken the present Chancellor, Sir Alexander Fitton, out of gaol to preside over the Court of Chancery. See William King, *The State of the Protestants of Ireland under the Late King James's Government* (London, 1691), 58.

31. Orrery MSS. (Dublin), V, f. 707. The grasping nature of the junior Dowager Countess is indicated in a letter of November 3, 1688, from Lady Katherine Paulet to Lady Margaret Russell. Lady Katherine wrote: "My father . . . is at present fighting with Lady Orrery for rifling her mother's cabinetts when shee lay a diying and carrying away whatt hee thinks his." See HMC, *Rutland*, II, 123.

32. *The Correspondence of Henry Hyde, Earl of Clarendon and of his Brother Lawrence Hyde, Earl of Rochester . . .* ed. S. W. Singer (London, 1828), I, 208.

33. Leconfield MSS.

34. Narcissus Luttrell, *A Brief Historical Relation of State Affairs* (Oxford, 1857), I, 501.

35. See Charles Smith, *County and City of Cork,* II, 113.

36. Luttrell, I, 566.

37. Orrery MSS. (Dublin), V, f. 729.

38. Dalton, III, 24.

39. Orrery MSS. (Dublin), V, f. 731.

40. *Ibid.*, f. 735.

41. See Lady Orrery's will, PCC 1688, 85 Vere.

42. Add. MSS. 38,847, f. 274.

43. John Lodge, *The Peerage of Ireland* (London, 1789), I, 193.

44. C. B. Gibson, *The History of the County and City of Cork* (London, 1861), II, 134.

45. Dalton, III, 175.

46. Luttrell, III, 225.

47. Lismore MSS. 34, f. 31.

48. See Henry Boyle's will (1685), Shannon MSS.

49. SO 1. 12. 591.

50. Orrery MSS. (Harvard) and PCC 1699, 172 Degg.

Bibliography

MANUSCRIPTS

Althorp Park, Northampton: Spencer MSS.
Ashe Park, Nr. Basingstoke, Hants: Shannon MSS.
Bodleian Library, Oxford:
  Carte MSS. 21; 22; 23; 24; 28; 30; 43; 47; 48; 49;
    59; 63; 64; 66; 67; 68; 69; 70; 143; 146; 213; 220.
  Clarendon MSS. 23; 31; 38; 60; 61.
  MS. Firth c. 5.
  Rawlinson MSS. B. 35.
  Tanner MSS. 52; 53; 54; 56; 58; 60.
British Museum, London:
  Add. MSS. 4162; 19,832; 25,287; 28,053; 32,093; 32,-
    095; 32,680; 37,206; 37,207; 37,208; 38,847; 46,927;
    46,928; 46,930; 46,931; 46,932; 46,937; 47,017.
  Egerton MSS. 80; 2551.
  Lansdowne MSS. 822.
  Portland MSS., Cavendish Papers, 1661–1695.
  Sloane MSS. 1008; 4159.
  Stowe MSS. 200; 201; 203; 204; 205; 206; 207; 208;
    209; 210; 211; 212; 214; 215; 216; 217; 744.
Chatsworth, Bakewell, Derbyshire:
  MS. Diary of Richard Boyle, First Earl of Burlington,
    I–V, 1650–1672.
  Lismore MSS. 17; 18; 19; 20; 21; 22; 23; 26; 27; 31; 34.
Harvard University Library: Orrery MSS.

Longleat, Warminster, Wilts.: Bath MSS., Portland Papers,
II, 1613–1772.
National Library, Dublin:
MS. 473, Thomas Morrice, Memoirs of the most remark-
able passages in the Life and Death of the Right Honour-
able Roger Earl of Orrery.
Ormonde MSS. 67; 72; 76; 77; 80; 81; 82; 86; 90; 93;
MS. Letters of Elizabeth, Duchess of Ormonde, I.
Orrery MSS. I–V.
Orchard Cottage, Upperton, Petworth, Sussex: Cork MSS.
Petworth House, Petworth, Sussex: Leconfield MSS.
Public Record Office, Dublin: Lismore MSS.
Public Record Office, London:
SO 1. 4. 447, 533; 8. 37, 394; 9. 120; 10. 99; 12. 591.
SP 21. 8. 19; 24. 251; 25. 44; 26. 158, 166; 27.
SP 25. 75. 537–538, 586–588, 760; 76. 199; 99. 226.
SP 29. 54. 52; 241. 148; 263. no. 15; 271; 277. no. 69;
290. no. 2; 333. 132; 338. 65; 418. no. 58; 449. 84.
SP 63. 221. 18; 254. 52; 260. 22–27; 261. 64; 262. 63–67,
83–89; 304. 89; 307. 73, 200, 232, 264; 313. 147, 168;
316. 98; 317. 2 A, 222; 318. 87–88; 319. 116, 122, 162,
185, 203, 244, 314; 321. 58, 77, 114; 322. 3, 34, 140;
323. 42, 150; 325. 20, 27; 326. 67; 327. 38, 66; 328.
145; 329. 28; 330. no. 165; 331. no. 89, no. 114; 333.
no. 52; 347. 9, 40; 348. 54, 86.
SP 77. 31. 449–452.
SP 104. 174 A. 63.
Somerset House, London: PCC 1688, 85 Vere (Margaret,
Countess of Orrery); PCC 1689, 149 Ent (Richard
Brett); PCC 1699, 172 Degg (Lionel Boyle, third Earl
of Orrery).
Trinity College, Dublin: MS. F. 3. 11. no. 21.

PRINTED WORKS
Only works cited in the main text are included.

Abbott, Wilbur C. *The Writings and Speeches of Oliver
Cromwell*, vol. IV. Cambridge, Mass., 1947.

An Act for the better Execution of His Majesties Declaration For the Settlement of His Kingdome of Ireland, and Satisfaction of the Several Interests of Adventurers, Souldiers and other His Majesties Subjects there. Dublin, 1662.

An Act for the Explaining of some Doubts arising from an Act . . . for the better execution of His Majesties Gracious Declaration for the Settlement of His Kingdom of Ireland. Dublin, 1665.

Adams, Joseph Quincy, ed. *The Dramatic Records of Sir Henry Herbert, Master of the Revels, 1623–1673.* New Haven, London, and Oxford, 1917.

"Admiral Penn, William Penn, and their Descendants in the Co. Cork," in *Journal of the Cork Historical and Archaeological Society,* second series, vol. 14 (1908), 105–114.

Articles Exhibited to the Honourable House of Commons. London, 1647.

Baillie, Robert. *Letters and Journals,* vol. II. Edinburgh, 1775.

Bellings, Sir Richard. *Desiderata Curiosa Hibernica,* vol. II. Dublin, 1772.

Boyle, Robert. *Works.* 6 vols. London, 1772.

Budgell, E[ustace]. *Memoirs of the Lives and Characters of the Illustrious Family of the Boyles.* Dublin, 1755.

Carew, Thomas. *The Poems of Thomas Carew,* ed. Arthur Vincent. London and New York, 1899.

Carte, Thomas. *A Collection of Original Letters and Papers,* vol. II. London, 1739.

——— *The Life of James, Duke of Ormond.* 6 vols. Oxford, 1851.

Caulfield, James. *Cromwelliana.* London, 1810.

Charleton, Walter. *Chorea Gigantum.* London, 1663.

Clarendon, Edward [Hyde, first Earl of]. *The Life of Edward Clarendon . . . Written by Himself.* Oxford, 1759.

——— *The Continuation of the Life of Edward Earl of Clarendon . . . Written by Himself.* Dublin, 1760.

Clarendon, Henry Hyde, [second] Earl of. *The Correspondence of Henry Hyde, Earl of Clarendon, and of His Brother, Lawrence Hyde, Earl of Rochester,* ed. S. W. Singer. 2 vols. London, 1828.

Clark, William S., ed. *The Dramatic Works of Roger Boyle, Earl of Orrery.* 2 vols. Cambridge, Mass., 1937.

Cobbett, William. *Complete Collection of State Trials,* vol. VI. London, 1810.

Collins, Arthur. *Letters and Memorials of State.* 2 vols. London, 1746.

Coote, Sir Charles. *The Declaration of Sir Charles Coot, Lord President of Connaught and the Officers and Soldiers under his Command.* London, 1660.

Cowley, Abraham. *Works.* London, 1688.

—— *Poems.* Cambridge, 1905.

Cox, Sir Richard. *Hibernia Anglicana,* Part II. London, 1689.

Cromwell, Oliver. *The Letters and Speeches of Oliver Cromwell,* ed. S. C. Lomas, vol. I. London, 1904.

Crowne, John. *Juliana.* London, 1671.

Dalrymple, Sir John. *Memoirs of Great Britain and Ireland,* vol. II. London, 1733.

Dalton, Charles, ed. *English Army Lists and Commission Registers, 1661–1714.* 6 vols. London, 1892–1904.

Dasent, Arthur I. *Nell Gwynne.* London, 1924.

D'Avenant, Sir William. *Salmacida Spolia.* London, 1640.

—— *The Siege of Rhodes: The First and Second Part.* London, 1663.

—— *Works.* London, 1673.

Davies, Thomas. *Dramatic Miscellanies,* vol. III. London, 1784.

A Declaration of the Convention of Ireland. London, 1660.

D'Ewes, Sir Simonds. *The Journal of Sir Simonds D'Ewes,* ed. W. H. Coates. New Haven and London, 1942.

Dorian, Donald C. *The English Diodatis.* New Brunswick, New Jersey, 1950.

Downes, John. *Roscius Anglicanus.* London, 1886.

Dryden, John. *The Rival Ladies.* London, 1664.

Evelyn, John. *The Diary of John Evelyn,* ed. E. S. De Beer, vol. III. Oxford, 1955.

Fanshawe, Lady Ann. *Memoirs.* London, 1907.

Firth, Sir C[harles] H[arding]. *Cromwell's Army.* London, 1902.

—— and Godfrey Davies. *The Regimental History of Cromwell's Army.* 2 vols. Oxford, 1940.

Fitzgerald, Brian. *The Anglo-Irish.* London and New York, 1952.

Gardiner, Samuel R. *History of the Commonwealth and Protectorate, 1649–1656.* 4 vols. London, New York, and Bombay, 1903.

—— *History of England from the Accession of James I to the Outbreak of the Civil War, 1603–1642.* 10 vols. London and New York, 1894–1896.

—— *History of the Great Civil War, 1642–1649.* 4 vols. London and New York, 1894.

Gibson, C[harles] B[ernard]. *The History of the County and City of Cork.* 2 vols. London, 1861.

Gilbert, Sir John T., ed. "Aphorismical Discovery of Treasonable Faction," in *A Contemporary History of Affairs of Ireland, from 1641 to 1652,* vol. I, Part I. Dublin, 1879.

A Great and Glorious Victory Obtained by the Lord Inchiquin. London, 1647.

Guizot [François Pierre Guillaume]. *History of Richard Cromwell and the Restoration of Charles II,* tr. Andrew R. Scoble. 2 vols. London, 1856.

Hartmann, Cyril H. *The King My Brother.* London and Toronto, 1954.

Haydn, Joseph. *The Book of Dignities.* London, 1890.

His Majestie's Gracious Declaration For the Settlement of His Kingdome of Ireland, and Satisfaction of the several Interests of Adventurers, Souldiers, and other His Subjects there. London, 1660.

HMC, *Fifth Report,* Appendix. London, 1876.

—— *Eighth Report,* Appendix. London, 1881.

—— *Buccleuch,* vol. I. London, 1889.

—— *Rutland,* vol. II. London, 1889.

—— *Various Collections,* vol. VI. Dublin, 1909.

Howard, Edward. *The Womens Conquest.* London, 1671.

Inchiquin [Murrough O'Brien, first Earl of]. *A Letter from the Right Honourable the Lord Inchiquin and other the Commanders in Munster, To His Majestie.* London, 1644.

———— *Two Letters sent from the Lord Inchiquin Unto the Speaker of the Honourable House of Commons.* London, 1647.

The Journals of the House of Commons, vols. III, V, VI, VII.

King, William. *The State of the Protestants of Ireland under the Late King James's Government.* London, 1691.

Knight, William. *A Declaration of the Treacherous Proceedings of the Lord Inchiquin against the Parliament of England.* London, 1648.

Lascelles, Rowley. *Liber Munerum Publicorum Hiberniae,* Part I. London, 1824.

Lodge, John. *The Peerage of Ireland,* vol. I. London, 1789.

Ludlow, Edmund. *The Memoirs of Edmund Ludlow, 1625–1672,* ed. C. H. Firth. 2 vols. Oxford, 1894.

Luttrell, Narcissus. *A Brief Historical Relation of State Affairs from September, 1678 to April, 1714,* vol. I. Oxford, 1857.

Lynch, Kathleen M. *The Social Mode of Restoration Comedy.* New York and London, 1926.

MacLysaght, Edward, ed. *Calendar of the Orrery Papers.* Dublin, 1941.

Manchester [William Drogo Montagu, seventh], Duke of. *Court and Society from Elizabeth to Anne,* vol. I, London, 1864.

A Manifestation Directed to the Honourable Houses of Parliament in England. London, 1644.

Maseres, Francis. *Select Tracts Relating to the Civil Wars in England.* 2 vols. London, 1815.

Mercurius Publicus, no. 43 (from October 23 to October 30, 1662).

Murdock, Kenneth B. *The Sun at Noon.* New York, 1939.

Murphy, Denis. *Cromwell in Ireland.* Dublin, 1902.

Nicoll, Allardyce. *The Development of the Theatre.* New York, 1937.

Notes which Passed at Meetings of the Privy Council Between Charles II and the Earl of Clarendon, 1660–1667, ed. W. D. Macray. London, 1896.

Orrery, Roger Boyle [first] Earl of. *An Answer to a Scandalous Letter. . . .* Dublin, 1662.

——— *A Collection of the State Letters of the Right Honourable Roger Boyle*. London, 1742.

——— *A Declaration of the Lord Broghill, and the Officers of the Army of Ireland in the Province of Munster*. London, 1660.

——— *Dramatic Works*. 2 vols. London, 1739.

——— *The Dramatic Works of Roger Boyle, Earl of Orrery*, ed. William S. Clark. 2 vols. Cambridge, Mass., 1937.

——— *English Adventures*. London, 1676.

——— *How the Irish Rebels fell on Bunracy with fire and sword and were after Routed by the Lord Broghill*. London, 1646.

——— *The Irish Colours Displayed*. London, 1662.

——— *A Letter from the Lord Broghil to the Honourable William Lenthall, Esq., Speaker of the Parliament of England*. London, 1651.

——— *A Letter . . . To His Majestie*. London, 1644.

——— *A Manifestation Directed to the Honourable Houses of Parliament in England*. London, 1644.

——— *Parthenissa, A Romance. The Last Part, The Fifth Tome*. London, 1656.

——— *Parthenissa, That most Fam'd Romance. The Six Volumes Compleat*. London, 1676.

——— *Poems on Most of the Festivals of the Church*. London, 1681.

——— *Six Plays*. London, 1694.

——— *A Treatise of the Art of War*. London, 1677.

Osborne, Dorothy. *The Letters of Dorothy Osborne to William Temple*, ed. G. C. Moore Smith. Oxford, 1928.

Otway, Thomas. *Works*, ed. Thomas Thornton, vol. III. London, 1813.

Pepys, Samuel. *The Diary of Samuel Pepys*, ed. Henry B. Wheatley. 9 vols. London and New York, 1902–1909.

A Perfect Narrative of the Grounds & Reasons Moving Some Officers of the Army in Ireland To the Securing of the Castle of Dublin for the Parliament, On the 13. of December last. London, 1660.

Philips, Katherine. *Letters from Orinda to Poliarchus*. London, 1705.

——— *Poems by the most deservedly Admired Mrs Katherine Philips, The Matchless Orinda.* London, 1678.

Pike, Clement E. "The Intrigue to Deprive the Earl of Essex of the Lord Lieutenancy of Ireland," in *Transactions of the Royal Historical Society,* third series, vol. V (1911), pp. 89–103.

Prendergast, John P. *The Cromwellian Settlement of Ireland.* London, 1865.

Rawdon Papers, ed. Edward Berwick. London, 1819.

Rushworth, John. *Historical Collections,* vol. IX. London, 1721.

A Second Collection of Scarce and Valuable Tracts, ed. John Somers, Baron Somers. London, 1750.

Smith, Charles. *The Ancient and Present State of the County and City of Cork.* 2 vols. Dublin, 1774.

State Tracts. London, 1689.

Strafford [Thomas Wentworth, first] Earl of. *The Earl of Straffordes Letters and Dispatches,* ed. William Knowler. 2 vols. London, 1739.

Suckling, Sir John. *Works.* London, 1709.

Sydney Papers, ed. R. W. Blencowe. London, 1725.

Thirty-Second Annual Report of the Deputy Keeper of the Public Records, Appendix I. London, 1871.

Thurloe, John. *A Collection of the State Papers of John Thurloe, Esq.* 7 vols. London, 1742.

Townshend, Dorothea. *The Life and Letters of the Great Earl of Cork.* London, 1904.

The Treaty with the Earl of Southampton . . . The Ship Called the Sovereigne taken by Captain Moulton . . . Also how the Irish Rebells fell on Bunracy with fire and sword and were after Routed by the Lord Broghill. London, 1646.

Verney, F[rances] P[arthenope (Nightingale), Lady] and M[argaret] M., eds. *Memoirs of the Verney Family.* 2 vols. London, New York, and Bombay, 1904.

Waller, Sir Hardress. *A Letter from Sir Hardress Waller and several other Gentlemen at Dublin, To Lieutenant General Ludlowe: With His Answer to the Same.* London, 1660.

Walpole, Horace. *A Catalogue of the Royal and Noble Authors of England,* vol. II. Strawberry Hill, 1758.

W[alsh], P[eter]. *The Irish Colours Folded.* London, 1662.

———— *A Letter . . . prefixed to An Answer to a Scandalous Letter . . . By the Right Honourable the Earl of Orrery.* Dublin, 1662.

———— *P. W.'s Reply to the Person of Quality's Answer.* London, 1664.

Ward, Charles E. *The Life of John Dryden.* Chapel Hill, North Carolina, 1961.

Ware, Sir James. *The History of the Writers of Ireland,* rev. Walter Harris, Book I. Dublin, 1764.

Warwick, Mary [(Boyle) Rich, fourth] Countess of. *Autobiography,* ed. T. Crofton Croker. Percy Society Publications, vol. 76. London, 1848.

Whitelocke, Bulstrode. *Memorials of the English Affairs.* London, 1732.

Wilson, Philip. "Ireland under Charles II," in R. B. O'Brien, *Studies in Irish History.* Dublin, 1903.

Index